Perspectives on Justice, Equity, Diversity, and Inclusion in Libraries

Nandita S. Mani
University of Massachusetts, Amherst, USA

Michelle A. Cawley
University of North Carolina at Chapel Hill, USA

Emily P. Jones
University of North Carolina at Chapel Hill, USA

A volume in the Advances in Library and
Information Science (ALIS) Book Series

Published in the United States of America by
    IGI Global
    Information Science Reference (an imprint of IGI Global)
    701 E. Chocolate Avenue
    Hershey PA, USA 17033
    Tel: 717-533-8845
    Fax: 717-533-8661
    E-mail: cust@igi-global.com
    Web site: http://www.igi-global.com

Copyright © 2023 by IGI Global. All rights reserved. No part of this publication may be reproduced, stored or distributed in
any form or by any means, electronic or mechanical, including photocopying, without written permission from the publisher.
Product or company names used in this set are for identification purposes only. Inclusion of the names of the products or
companies does not indicate a claim of ownership by IGI Global of the trademark or registered trademark.
    Library of Congress Cataloging-in-Publication Data

Names: Mani, Nandita S., 1978- editor. | Cawley, Michelle, 1970- editor. |
    Jones, Emily P., 1989- editor.
Title: Perspectives on justice, equity, diversity, and inclusion in
    libraries / edited by Nandita S. Mani, Michelle A. Cawley, and Emily P.
    Jones.
Description: Hershey, PA : Information Science Reference, [2023] | Includes
    bibliographical references and index. | Summary: "Perspectives on
    Justice, Equity, Diversity, and Inclusion in Libraries examines how JEDI
    initiatives and actions have been incorporated into all aspects of
    librarianship and various types of libraries. The book serves as a
    collection of exemplary cases across all settings of librarianship to
    showcase how this work is being implemented, as well as provide
    commentary on implications and future opportunities for growth. Covering
    key topics such as community, ethics, and inclusive spaces, this premier
    reference source is ideal for administrators, policymakers,
    academicians, researchers, scholars, practitioners, librarians,
    instructors, and students"-- Provided by publisher.
Identifiers: LCCN 2022060061 (print) | LCCN 2022060062 (ebook) | ISBN
    9781668472552 (Hardcover) | ISBN 9781668472590 (Paperback) | ISBN
    9781668472569 (eBook)
Subjects: LCSH: Libraries and minorities--United States. | Minority library
    employees--United States. | Social justice--United States.
Classification: LCC Z711.8 .P465 2023 (print) | LCC Z711.8 (ebook) | DDC
    027.6/30973--dc23/eng/20230123
LC record available at https://lccn.loc.gov/2022060061
LC ebook record available at https://lccn.loc.gov/2022060062

This book is published in the IGI Global book series Advances in Library and Information Science (ALIS) (ISSN: 2326-
4136; eISSN: 2326-4144)

British Cataloguing in Publication Data
A Cataloguing in Publication record for this book is available from the British Library.
All work contributed to this book is new, previously-unpublished material. The views expressed in this book are those of the
authors, but not necessarily of the publisher.
For electronic access to this publication, please contact: eresources@igi-global.com.

Advances in Library and Information Science (ALIS) Book Series

Alfonso Ippolito
Sapienza University-Rome, Italy
Carlo Inglese
Sapienza University-Rome, Italy

ISSN:2326-4136
EISSN:2326-4144

Mission

The **Advances in Library and Information Science (ALIS) Book Series** is comprised of high quality, research-oriented publications on the continuing developments and trends affecting the public, school, and academic fields, as well as specialized libraries and librarians globally. These discussions on professional and organizational considerations in library and information resource development and management assist in showcasing the latest methodologies and tools in the field.

The **ALIS Book Series** aims to expand the body of library science literature by covering a wide range of topics affecting the profession and field at large. The series also seeks to provide readers with an essential resource for uncovering the latest research in library and information science management, development, and technologies.

Coverage

- Libraries as Community Centers
- Staffing and Salaries in the Library Field
- Web-Based Bibliographic Instruction
- Intellectual Freedom
- Discoverability of E-Content in Libraries
- Green Libraries
- Joint-Use Libraries
- Visual Literacy
- Free Online Resources
- Mobile Library Services

IGI Global is currently accepting manuscripts for publication within this series. To submit a proposal for a volume in this series, please contact our Acquisition Editors at Acquisitions@igi-global.com or visit: http://www.igi-global.com/publish/.

The Advances in Library and Information Science (ALIS) Book Series (ISSN 2326-4136) is published by IGI Global, 701 E. Chocolate Avenue, Hershey, PA 17033-1240, USA, www.igi-global.com. This series is composed of titles available for purchase individually; each title is edited to be contextually exclusive from any other title within the series. For pricing and ordering information please visit http://www.igi-global.com/book-series/advances-library-information-science/73002. Postmaster: Send all address changes to above address. Copyright © 2023 IGI Global. All rights, including translation in other languages reserved by the publisher. No part of this series may be reproduced or used in any form or by any means – graphics, electronic, or mechanical, including photocopying, recording, taping, or information and retrieval systems – without written permission from the publisher, except for non commercial, educational use, including classroom teaching purposes. The views expressed in this series are those of the authors, but not necessarily of IGI Global.

Titles in this Series

For a list of additional titles in this series, please visit: http://www.igi-global.com/book-series/advances-library-information-science/73002

Applying Positivist and Interpretivist Philosophies to Social Research Practices
C.C. Jayasundara (University of Kelaniya, Sri Lanka)
Information Science Reference • © 2023 • 300pp • H/C (ISBN: 9781668454312) • US $215.00

Handbook of Research on Technological Advances of Library and Information Science in Industry 5.0
Barbara Jane Holland (Independent Researcher, USA)
Information Science Reference • © 2023 • 549pp • H/C (ISBN: 9781668447550) • US $270.00

Global Perspectives on Sustainable Library Practices
Victoria Okojie (University of Abuja, Nigeria) and Magnus Osahon Igbinovia (Ambrose Alli University, Nigeria)
Information Science Reference • © 2023 • 376pp • H/C (ISBN: 9781668459645) • US $240.00

Cases on Establishing Effective Collaborations in Academic Libraries
Mary E. Piorun (University of Massachusetts Chan Medical School, USA) and Regina Fisher Raboin (University of Massachusetts Chan Medical School, USA)
Information Science Reference • © 2023 • 358pp • H/C (ISBN: 9781668425152) • US $215.00

Handbook of Research on Academic Libraries as Partners in Data Science Ecosystems
Nandita S. Mani (University of North Carolina at Chapel Hill, USA) and Michelle A. Cawley (University of North Carolina at Chapel Hill, USA)
Information Science Reference • © 2022 • 415pp • H/C (ISBN: 9781799897026) • US $270.00

Technological Advancements in Library Service Innovation
Manika Lamba (University of Delhi, India)
Information Science Reference • © 2022 • 300pp • H/C (ISBN: 9781799889427) • US $215.00

Handbook of Research on Emerging Trends and Technologies in Librarianship
Innocent Isa Ekoja (Benue State University, Makurdi, Nigeria) Esoswo Francisca Ogbomo (Delta State University, Nigeria) and Omorodion Okuonghae (Samuel Adegboyega University, Ogwa, Nigeria)
Information Science Reference • © 2022 • 430pp • H/C (ISBN: 9781799890942) • US $270.00

701 East Chocolate Avenue, Hershey, PA 17033, USA
Tel: 717-533-8845 x100 • Fax: 717-533-8661
E-Mail: cust@igi-global.com • www.igi-global.com

To library workers everywhere – whether on the front lines or behind the scenes – thank you for continually finding ways to make things more open, accessible, inclusive, and just. This is a journey I am happy to be taking with all of you. To my parents who taught me from the very start the importance of approaching life from an inclusive and just lens, and to Scotia, Maya, and Kailash for reminding me everyday why this work is so vital - Nandita

For those advancing justice, equity, diversity, and inclusion in all spaces, and for Alliz. - Emily

To my daughters, Grace and Ava, who are evidence that progress is possible and who aren't afraid to tell me what's what. Also to Jenny for her steady support.

Table of Contents

Preface xvi

Section 1
Professional Development

Chapter 1
Counterspace Support for BIPOC Employees Within a Holistic JEDI Library Framework 1
Isabel Espinal, University Libraries, University of Massachusetts, Amherst, USA
Anne Graham, University Libraries, University of Massachusetts, Amherst, USA
Maria Rios, University Libraries, University of Massachusetts, Amherst, USA
Katherine Freedman, University Libraries, University of Massachusetts, Amherst, USA

Chapter 2
Justice, Equity, Diversity, and Inclusion in Mentorship: The ARL Kaleidoscope Program
Framework for Change 20
DeLa Dos, Association of Research Libraries, USA
Alanna Aiko Moore, University of California, San Diego, USA

Chapter 3
Co-Creating the Beginnings of a Culture of Belonging at the Georgia Tech Library: Supervisors,
Leaders, and a Proposed Model Forward 40
John Mack Freeman, Georgia Institute of Technology, USA
Leslie N. Sharp, Georgia Institute of Technology, USA

Section 2
Information Resources and Collections

Chapter 4
Citation Power: Overcoming Marginalization One Citation at a Time 62
Jodi H. Coalter, Michigan State University, USA

Chapter 5
The Power of Collaboration in Creating and Sustaining Anti-Racism Resource Guides: A Case
Study From Binghamton University Libraries.. 78
> *Jennifer K. Embree, Binghamton University, USA*
> *Megan L. Benson, Binghamton University, USA*
> *Rachel Berman Turner, Virginia Commonwealth University, USA*
> *Sharon Bunch-Nunez, Binghamton University, USA*
> *Elise Ferer, Binghamton University, USA*
> *Amy Gay, Binghamton University, USA*
> *Neyda V. Gilman, Binghamton University, USA*
> *Laura Christine Haynes, Broome County Public Library, USA*
> *Lauren Loewen, Binghamton University, USA*
> *Rennae Robinson, Binghamton University, USA*

Chapter 6
Starting and Sustaining JEDI Acquisitions and Collections in Academic Libraries: Considerations
and Strategies for Success... 104
> *Colleen S. Mullally, Pepperdine University, USA*
> *Jeremy Whitt, University of California, Los Angeles, USA*
> *Kayla Valdivieso, Wellesley College, USA*

Section 3
Programmatic Approaches

Chapter 7
Challenging the Silences: Leading Change to Support Indigenous Representation and Priorities in
Australian Libraries 124
> *Kirsten Thorpe, University of Technology Sydney, Australia*
> *Monica Galassi, University of Technology Sydney, Australia*
> *Lauren Booker, University of Technology Sydney, Australia*
> *Tracy Barber, University of Technology Sydney, Australia*

Chapter 8
Forging Alliances for Reparative Documentation and Revitalization of Marginalized
Communities: Reclaiming the African American Heritage of Southern Illinois 146
> *Anne Marie Hamilton-Brehm, Southern Illinois University, Carbondale, USA*
> *Pam Hackbart-Dean, University of Illinois, Chicago, USA*
> *Walter Ray, Southern Illinois University, Carbondale, USA*
> *Aaron M. Lisec, Southern Illinois University, Carbondale, USA*
> *Melvin "Pepper" Holder, Southern Illinois University, Carbondale, USA*

Chapter 9
The Foundation of and Future Directions for JEDI @ University of Massachusetts Amherst
Libraries 166
    Michael W. Mercurio, University of Massachusetts, Amherst, USA
    Adam Holmes, University of Massachusetts, Amherst, USA
    Carole Connare, University of Massachusetts, Amherst, USA
    Nandita S. Mani, University of Massachusetts, Amherst, USA
    Jennifer Friedman, University of Massachusetts, Amherst, USA

Chapter 10
Assessment of Justice, Equity, Diversity, and Inclusion (JEDI) Initiatives in Public Libraries:
Perspectives From a Public Library in a Developing Country 187
    Ismail Olatunji Adeyemi, Kwara State University, Nigeria

Chapter 11
Thriving in the Community: The Creation and Sustainment of a Community-Driven Literacy
Center 198
    Nicole R. Peritore, Augusta University, USA
    Elizabeth A. VanDeusen, Augusta University, USA
    Kim Barker, Augusta University, USA
    Juan Walker, Augusta University, USA
    Jessica Simpson, Augusta University, USA

Chapter 12
Addressing the History of Discrimination and Bias in Past and Current Library Systems 219
    Kayla Reed, Grinnell College, USA

Chapter 13
Advancing Justice Through Strategic Partnerships: Academic Libraries and Student Affairs 243
    DeLa Dos, Association of Research Libraries, USA
    Saira Raza, Emory Libraries, USA

Chapter 14
Creating Inclusive Spaces in Different Types of Libraries 260
    Grace Turney, University of Missouri, USA

Compilation of References 276

About the Contributors 309

Index 317

Detailed Table of Contents

Preface xvi

Section 1
Professional Development

Chapter 1

Counterspace Support for BIPOC Employees Within a Holistic JEDI Library Framework 1
Isabel Espinal, University Libraries, University of Massachusetts, Amherst, USA
Anne Graham, University Libraries, University of Massachusetts, Amherst, USA
Maria Rios, University Libraries, University of Massachusetts, Amherst, USA
Katherine Freedman, University Libraries, University of Massachusetts, Amherst, USA

This chapter presents a case study of how an academic library supports Black, Indigenous, and People of Color (BIPOC) employees with funding so these workers can find counterspaces (spaces where they can feel safe in community with other BIPOC who are navigating similar struggles while working in a predominantly white institution). Through its Inclusion, Diversity, Anti-Racism and Equity (IDARE) Committee, the University of Massachusetts (UMass) Amherst Libraries worked to establish a fund for meeting some of the cultural and racial equity needs of library employees who are BIPOC. With a new Woman of Color Dean, the fund transformed into a funding priority and criterion that puts the needs of BIPOC employees at the center, while asking everyone in the library to undertake JEDI work and view all of their work through a JEDI lens. This chapter discusses the "Why" and the "How" of this JEDI initiative, placing it in the context of a larger holistic vision for inclusive librarianship outlined by current and former BIPOC employees and the JEDI vision of the Dean and her leadership team.

Chapter 2

Justice, Equity, Diversity, and Inclusion in Mentorship: The ARL Kaleidoscope Program
Framework for Change 20
DeLa Dos, Association of Research Libraries, USA
Alanna Aiko Moore, University of California, San Diego, USA

Mentoring programs are a common and extremely beneficial offering in numerous settings, including academic libraries. Given their almost ubiquitous nature, these programs can occasionally become unintentionally outdated while still being successful at serving their core functions. The Association of Research Libraries (ARL) Kaleidoscope Program, in which mentoring is a core component, underwent a full review process of all aspects of its program. This chapter presents this review as a case study that demonstrates a series of approaches that resulted in providing revitalization to the program while building on and respecting the program's more than two decades of history and successes. Using mentoring as a lens, the authors outline the broader review process that included numerous administrative updates and changes to the implementation of program components. This context is critical as a key lesson learned focuses on the importance of systemic change.

Chapter 3
Co-Creating the Beginnings of a Culture of Belonging at the Georgia Tech Library: Supervisors, Leaders, and a Proposed Model Forward... 40
> *John Mack Freeman, Georgia Institute of Technology, USA*
> *Leslie N. Sharp, Georgia Institute of Technology, USA*

In 2019, the Georgia Tech Library was coming out of a painful period of transition where lofty change initiatives had created significant toxicity in the culture. New leadership was brought in to rectify the situation. Through a series of efforts that translated institutional efforts, departmental actions, and team-based support, the Georgia Tech Library turned a corner and started working towards creating a culture of belonging. In this participatory case study, the authors proposed a nested model of cultural support in which the underpinnings of individual support flow from the team, the department, and the institution. Each part has a role to play in working to create a culture of belonging, understanding that the work is never complete, and that while the example of the Georgia Tech Library has made progress, there is still much work to be done.

Section 2
Information Resources and Collections

Chapter 4
Citation Power: Overcoming Marginalization One Citation at a Time 62
> *Jodi H. Coalter, Michigan State University, USA*

Emerging from research dating back to the 1980's, citation justice is the practice of citing research based on both content and an author's identity. Due to citation gaps that exist across disciplines, citation practice is changing to cite authors of more diverse genders, races, and other marginalized identities. Librarians are uniquely situated in academic institutions to teach and encourage students and faculty to adjust their citation practice to close these gaps. This chapter describes citation justice in detail and describes the evidence for the need adjust citation practice to include identity. In addition, this chapter explores why librarians can effect the most change, and how this change needs to begin with students, before discussing the various ways librarian instruction can incorporate citation justice into their work.

Chapter 5
The Power of Collaboration in Creating and Sustaining Anti-Racism Resource Guides: A Case
Study From Binghamton University Libraries... 78
> *Jennifer K. Embree, Binghamton University, USA*
> *Megan L. Benson, Binghamton University, USA*
> *Rachel Berman Turner, Virginia Commonwealth University, USA*
> *Sharon Bunch-Nunez, Binghamton University, USA*
> *Elise Ferer, Binghamton University, USA*
> *Amy Gay, Binghamton University, USA*
> *Neyda V. Gilman, Binghamton University, USA*
> *Laura Christine Haynes, Broome County Public Library, USA*
> *Lauren Loewen, Binghamton University, USA*
> *Rennae Robinson, Binghamton University, USA*

In this book chapter and case study, the authors tell the story of how they created and sustained the
Binghamton University Libraries' Anti-Racism and Resource Guide. They discuss how they first came
together on this project to develop their vision of the guide and how they were able to evolve and adapt the
project over time so that it remains updated, relevant, and sustainable. They also highlight the extremely
collaborative nature of their work in this guide, and reflect on how bringing together their varied voices
to collectively develop a resource on the topic of anti-racism led to the creation of an extremely unique
and dynamic guide.

Chapter 6
Starting and Sustaining JEDI Acquisitions and Collections in Academic Libraries: Considerations
and Strategies for Success.. 104
> *Colleen S. Mullally, Pepperdine University, USA*
> *Jeremy Whitt, University of California, Los Angeles, USA*
> *Kayla Valdivieso, Wellesley College, USA*

Academic libraries are increasingly seeking to incorporate Justice, Equity, Diversity, and Inclusion
(JEDI) initiatives at their institutions. While many librarians recognize these as important values, the
process of implementing them into daily workflows proves to be more challenging. In this chapter, the
authors provide recommendations intended for those at all levels within an academic library to initiate
and enact JEDI initiatives within library collections and acquisitions. These steps include creating an
action plan, communicating with fellow constituents, and considering different vendor selection criteria
in acquisitions. The authors also address how to navigate challenges that may arise while conducting
this work such as budget constraints, staffing shortages, and the limited diversity within the library and
publishing fields.

Section 3
Programmatic Approaches

Chapter 7
Challenging the Silences: Leading Change to Support Indigenous Representation and Priorities in
Australian Libraries 124
    Kirsten Thorpe, University of Technology Sydney, Australia
    Monica Galassi, University of Technology Sydney, Australia
    Lauren Booker, University of Technology Sydney, Australia
    Tracy Barber, University of Technology Sydney, Australia

The complex history of Indigenous and colonizer relations in Australia has significantly impacted the terms of engagement between Indigenous peoples with libraries and archives. The library and archive sectors are now being challenged to be responsive to Indigenous calls for action for better representation and engagement with institutions and within collections. This chapter discusses developing and evaluating an Indigenous-led staff capability program designed to increase Indigenous representation and priorities in Australian libraries. By responding to the historical gaps of Indigenous perspectives and worldviews in library, archive, and information studies curriculum, the program provides learning opportunities for participants to activate support for Indigenous self-determination and sovereignty in libraries. The program aims to increase support for implementing protocols and practices that engage appropriately with racist and offensive legacy materials in library collections.

Chapter 8
Forging Alliances for Reparative Documentation and Revitalization of Marginalized
Communities: Reclaiming the African American Heritage of Southern Illinois 146
    Anne Marie Hamilton-Brehm, Southern Illinois University, Carbondale, USA
    Pam Hackbart-Dean, University of Illinois, Chicago, USA
    Walter Ray, Southern Illinois University, Carbondale, USA
    Aaron M. Lisec, Southern Illinois University, Carbondale, USA
    Melvin "Pepper" Holder, Southern Illinois University, Carbondale, USA

Describing efforts to uncover the largely undocumented history of African Americans in southern Illinois, this case study demonstrates how universities and activists can empower local communities to preserve and share their heritage. The Special Collections Research Center (SCRC) of Southern Illinois University's Morris Library, SIU faculty, and community partners have substantially increased knowledge about many extraordinary individuals and communities by actively pursuing digitization of correspondence and images collected by families and organizations and conducting oral histories and preservation workshops. New plans for a coordinating center aim to radically expand revitalization efforts.

Chapter 9
The Foundation of and Future Directions for JEDI @ University of Massachusetts Amherst
Libraries 166
 Michael W. Mercurio, University of Massachusetts, Amherst, USA
 Adam Holmes, University of Massachusetts, Amherst, USA
 Carole Connare, University of Massachusetts, Amherst, USA
 Nandita S. Mani, University of Massachusetts, Amherst, USA
 Jennifer Friedman, University of Massachusetts, Amherst, USA

This chapter per the authors provides an in-depth overview of how the University of Massachusetts Amherst Libraries has leveraged historical connections and special collections to provide a robust foundation for justice, equity, diversity, and inclusion programming and initiatives on campus, in the community, and worldwide. Readers will be provided with examples that will inform conversations about JEDI efforts at their own libraries and on their own campuses, as well as insights gleaned during the process of doing this work at University of Massachusetts Amherst Libraries.

Chapter 10
Assessment of Justice, Equity, Diversity, and Inclusion (JEDI) Initiatives in Public Libraries:
Perspectives From a Public Library in a Developing Country 187
 Ismail Olatunji Adeyemi, Kwara State University, Nigeria

This chapter focuses on the assessment of justice, equity, diversity, and inclusion (JEDI) initiatives in a public library in a developing country; a focus on Kwara State Library Board (KSLB) in Ilorin, Nigeria. This study is case-study research designed, adopting a qualitative research approach. The findings of the study showed that there is no form of diversity in the staffing at Kwara State Library Board, which will hinder its globalization. It was revealed in the study that there is no JEDI initiative in the workforce of the library. Moreover, it was found that there is no form of book censorship in Kwara State Library Board and there is diversity in the provision of information resources for the visually impaired users. It was, however, shown that there is no form of JEDI initiative as to the information services provided at Kwara State Library Board. It was concluded that Kwara State Library Board has JEDI initiatives in information resources available in the library, but it is lacking in JEDI initiatives for information services and workforce.

Chapter 11
Thriving in the Community: The Creation and Sustainment of a Community-Driven Literacy
Center 198
 Nicole R. Peritore, Augusta University, USA
 Elizabeth A. VanDeusen, Augusta University, USA
 Kim Barker, Augusta University, USA
 Juan Walker, Augusta University, USA
 Jessica Simpson, Augusta University, USA

Cross-sector, interprofessional partnerships and community collaborations offer promise for identifying and addressing the web-like factors that entangle both literacy achievement and negative public health outcomes for vulnerable populations. Literacy centers can be a conduit to promote justice, equity, diversity, and inclusion as they exist to serve all community members. This is especially impactful when partnered with minority and disadvantaged populations. This university-based literacy center (LC) utilizes a community-driven design to attain and sustain their work. This chapter will illustrate the effort made by the LC to establish access, coordinated services, education of stakeholders, and support for students of all ages, and cultural engagement which are foundational to the work being done. Lastly, the chapter will describe the past, present, and future plans for improving community engagement.

Chapter 12
Addressing the History of Discrimination and Bias in Past and Current Library Systems 219
Kayla Reed, Grinnell College, USA

Reviewing the history of Academic and public libraries in the United States reveals the origins and progress of inclusivity within library spaces. Although libraries take pride in being active in inclusion events and ideas, there is still a long way to go. Libraries are still prone to white bias and with that comes discrimination and exclusion of non-white, striaght, able-bodied individuals. In addition, Library Science as a field has a diversity problem and needs to improve training methods based around discrimination and biases. For libraries to move forward, library professionals must acknowledge the past and work towards reconciliation versus repentance. Past mistakes cannot be made up, actions cannot be undone. But the prevention of future instances of bias and discrimination can be achieved.

Chapter 13
Advancing Justice Through Strategic Partnerships: Academic Libraries and Student Affairs 243
DeLa Dos, Association of Research Libraries, USA
Saira Raza, Emory Libraries, USA

As academic libraries continue to investigate and invest in justice, equity, diversity, and inclusion (JEDI) efforts, there are numerous opportunities to enhance the impact of these efforts through intentional, sustainable collaborations with other administrative units of the institution—particularly student affairs. This chapter will explore the benefits and challenges of collaborating with student affairs departments for academic libraries interested in creating, maintaining, and advancing inclusive and just learning and research communities. Using a case study, the chapter highlights specific collaborative efforts to demonstrate the value of cultivating relationships across campus divisions; additionally, it offers insights into identifying opportunities to share resources and enhance the experiences of the libraries' stakeholders. While framed by the context of the situation, the chapter presents recommendations that may be effectively implemented within academic libraries at many types of institutions.

Chapter 14
Creating Inclusive Spaces in Different Types of Libraries 260
Grace Turney, University of Missouri, USA

This chapter explores five key components of building an inclusive library space: community, collection, environment/promotions, programming, and policies/staff. These components can be implemented in every type of library, including public, school, academic, special, and more. The "Community" section explains how to identify and connect with the library's community. The "Collection" portion explores building a diverse and inclusive collection of resources. The "Environments/Promotions" section discusses the library atmosphere, including signage, displays, and digital spaces. "Programming" explains how library programs can be designed and implemented to support justice, equity, and diversity. And "Staff and Policies" explores the rules and guidelines of the library for staff and patrons, as well as hiring and training staff for inclusivity and diversity.

Compilation of References 276

About the Contributors 309

Index 317

Preface

The vision for this book was sparked by a research project conducted by the authors to evaluate the current state of library and information science (LIS) scholarship pertaining to anti-racism, equity, inclusion, and social justice initiatives. That project identified nearly 700 articles and while a broad array of topics and populations were covered by the database most articles addressed access to information and multiculturalism. From our work on this project and engagement in related initiatives at our institutions, we became aware of other compelling projects that would benefit the LIS community's shared goal of advancing justice, equity, diversity, and inclusion (JEDI).

From our experience most, if not all, LIS-based professional organizations are engaged in JEDI work including offering professional development opportunities for members. The Association of Research Libraries (ARL) Kaleidoscope Program is a great example and a chapter in section 1 details the recent review and update to this program.

JEDI-focused professional development and support at the institutional level is also becoming more prevalent. Authors from the University of Massachusetts Amherst share a case study on a funding initiative designed to support Black, Indigenous, and People of Color (BIPOC) employees and librarians at the Georgia Institute of Technology describe a nested model to imbue a culture of belonging at their institution.

There are also several chapters related to information resources and collections. The practice of 'citation justice' is explored as a means to close the gap that has existed historically with respect to underrepresentation of citations by marginalized identities. Libraries engage most often with patrons through online resources including websites and library guides. A team from Binghamton University Libraries have created and maintained an outstanding Anti-Racism and Resource library guide. They describe the vision for the project and how they have brought together a variety of viewpoints to inform the content in a highly collaborative process. This section also includes a chapter with practical recommendations for academic libraries seeking to apply JEDI principles to library collections and acquisitions.

A wide range of programmatic initiatives are also explored in multiple chapters including a program to support decolonial and anti-racist initiatives in Australian libraries and archives. The program aims to establish protocols and practices to address racist and offensive legacy materials in library collections. Readers are likely to find that ideas put forth by the authors are applicable to a variety of audiences and populations.

Authors from Southern Illinois University share a case study of how they have partnered with faculty and community partners to shed light on the largely undocumented history of African Americans in Southern Illinois. A team at University of Massachusetts Amherst Libraries detail their success in

Preface

creating programming rooted in justice, equity, diversity, and inclusion on campus, in the local community, and globally.

Voices from libraries and centers serving local communities are also included in this section including a chapter evaluating the JEDI initiatives at the Kwara State Library Board and a chapter contending that literacy centers are an important avenue to promote justice, equity, diversity, and inclusion in the community.

Academic and public libraries are actively engaged in JEDI work but must also reckon with a history of discrimination and bias. Exclusion of marginalized groups in the field is an ongoing issue and the profession must guard against 'vocational awe'. The author of this chapter argues that acknowledging past mistakes is an important step in moving towards reconciliation.

Libraries are typically ready and willing partners and one case study reports how a strategic partnership between the library and student affairs can help to create inclusive and just learning and research communities.

The final chapter in section 3 details five key components of building an inclusive library space including how to identify and connect with the library's community, how to establish diverse and inclusive resources, why library atmosphere, including signage, displays, and digital spaces matter, how to design and implement programming to advance justice, equity, and diversity, and the role of rules and guidelines for staff and patrons.

Throughout this book, readers will hear and learn from a wide variety of information professionals who are tackling how to bring a JEDI-lens to all aspects of library work from professional support and development to collections and acquisitions to large-scale programmatic approaches. Ultimately, our wish is for this book to inspire and inform initiatives, programming, approaches, and conversations designed to increase belonging and advance justice, equity, diversity, and inclusion for individuals, teams, departments, and institutions.

ORGANIZATION OF THE BOOK

This book is organized into three sections with 14 chapters. A brief description of the sections and chapters follows:

Section 1: Professional Development

Chapter 1 provides a case study describing how the University of Massachusetts (UMass) Amherst Libraries provides support through a funding initiative that connects Black, Indigenous, and People of Color (BIPOC) employees with safe spaces to connect with other BIPOC employees at the institution. This approach was initiated by the UMass Libraries' Inclusion, Diversity, Anti-Racism, and Equity (IDARE) Committee to address equity and inclusion needs of employees.

Chapter 2 shares how the Association of Research Libraries (ARL) Kaleidoscope Program underwent a thorough review and highlights methods of revitalizing the program while respecting its history. This chapter details how the program uses mentoring to guide the review process and administrative changes.

Chapter 3 describes a model of cultural support by authors from Georgia Institute of Technology. They describe a nested model of cultural support where individuals are supported at the team, department, and institutional levels.

xvii

Section 2: Information Resources and Collections

Chapter 4 describes the concept of citation justice which entails citing research on both the content but also the identity of its author. This chapter provides a comprehensive overview of citation justice, examines the evidence supporting the need to adjust citation practices to consider identity, and explains how librarians can be the catalyst for change.

Chapter 5 details the creation and upkeep of an Anti-Racism Research & Resource Guide by the Binghamton University Libraries. The authors describe the vision and implementation of the project, as well as their collaborative approach to using diverse perspectives and voices in the resource.

Chapter 6 focuses on justice, equity, diversity, and inclusion initiatives specifically in library collections and acquisitions. The authors provide practical insight into many areas of collection development including creating an action plan, communicating with stakeholders, vendor selection criteria, budget considerations, and more.

Section 3: Programmatic Approaches

Chapter 7 provides a case study in designing and delivering a program to support decolonial and anti-racist initiatives in libraries. The authors provide a detailed description of the program's content, support, and guidance for implementing similar initiatives in other spaces. This chapter highlights Indigenous voices and programming in libraries as well as describes gaps in knowledge and advises on how to intentionally incorporate Indigenous voices and perspectives into libraries.

Chapter 8 describes a project initiated by staff at Southern Illinois University Carbondale titled *Reclaiming the African American Heritage of Southern Illinois (RAAHSI)*. A description of this program, created to acknowledge and share Black people's contributions to the history and culture of southern Illinois, is included. Readers will gain valuable insights and examples to guide their own efforts at their respective libraries and campuses, while also learning from the experiences of the authors.

Chapter 9 offers a comprehensive overview of how the University of Massachusetts Amherst Libraries created programs focused on justice, equity, diversity, and inclusion by using strategic partners and special collections.

Chapter 10 provides an overview of justice, equity, diversity, and inclusion initiatives in public libraries and highlights specific initiatives at the Kwara State Library Board in Nigeria. Specific initiatives discussed include staffing, information resources, and services.

Chapter 11 details work undertaken at the Augusta University Literacy Center as they implement a community-driven literacy model. The authors use this case study to describe how literacy centers can be used to advance justice, equity, diversity, and inclusion work.

Chapter 12 provides an overview of how discrimination and bias have occurred in past and current library systems. A detailed history of exclusion and oppression, across many marginalized groups and issues, is presented in public, academic, and the larger field of library and information science.

Chapter 13 presents a case study of partnering with an office of student affairs to advance the diversity, equity, and inclusion priorities of both. Impact of this partnership, along with benefits and challenges associated with these types of collaborations are reported.

Chapter 14 describes how to create inclusive library spaces across five areas: community, collections, environment/promotions, programming, and policies/staff. This chapter offers practical insight into ways to thread justice, equity, diversity, and inclusion work across common domains of librarianship.

Preface

Nandita S. Mani
University of Massachusetts Amherst, USA

Michelle A. Cawley
University of North Carolina at Chapel Hill, USA

Emily P. Jones
University of North Carolina at Chapel Hill, USA

Section 1
Professional Development

Chapter 1
Counterspace Support for BIPOC Employees Within a Holistic JEDI Library Framework

Isabel Espinal
https://orcid.org/0000-0003-4874-5290
University Libraries, University of Massachusetts, Amherst, USA

Anne Graham
https://orcid.org/0000-0003-1180-6352
University Libraries, University of Massachusetts, Amherst, USA

Maria Rios
https://orcid.org/0009-0007-3406-1687
University Libraries, University of Massachusetts, Amherst, USA

Katherine Freedman
https://orcid.org/0000-0002-7516-9332
University Libraries, University of Massachusetts, Amherst, USA

ABSTRACT

This chapter presents a case study of how an academic library supports Black, Indigenous, and People of Color (BIPOC) employees with funding so these workers can find counterspaces (spaces where they can feel safe in community with other BIPOC who are navigating similar struggles while working in a predominantly white institution). Through its Inclusion, Diversity, Anti-Racism and Equity (IDARE) Committee, the University of Massachusetts (UMass) Amherst Libraries worked to establish a fund for meeting some of the cultural and racial equity needs of library employees who are BIPOC. With a new Woman of Color Dean, the fund transformed into a funding priority and criterion that puts the needs of BIPOC employees at the center, while asking everyone in the library to undertake JEDI work and view all of their work through a JEDI lens. This chapter discusses the "Why" and the "How" of this JEDI initiative, placing it in the context of a larger holistic vision for inclusive librarianship outlined by current and former BIPOC employees and the JEDI vision of the Dean and her leadership team.

DOI: 10.4018/978-1-6684-7255-2.ch001

This chapter published as an Open Access Chapter distributed under the terms of the Creative Commons Attribution License (http://creativecommons.org/licenses/by/4.0/) which permits unrestricted use, distribution, and production in any medium, provided the author of the original work and original publication source are properly credited.

INTRODUCTION

In this chapter we present a case study of how an academic library supports Black, Indigenous, and people of color (BIPOC) employees with funding so that these workers can find counterspaces (spaces where they can feel safe in community with other BIPOC who are navigating similar struggles while working in a predominantly white institution). Through its Inclusion, Diversity, Anti-Racism, and Equity (IDARE) Committee, the University of Massachusetts (UMass) Amherst Libraries worked to establish a fund for meeting some of the cultural and racial equity needs of library employees who are BIPOC. With a new woman of color dean, the fund transformed into a funding priority and criterion that put the needs of BIPOC employees at the center, while asking everyone in the library to undertake justice, equity, diversity, and inclusion (JEDI) work and view all of their work through a JEDI lens. We discuss the why and the how of this JEDI initiative, placing it in the context of a larger holistic vision for inclusive librarianship outlined by current and former BIPOC employees and the JEDI vision of the dean and her leadership team.

THE WHAT

Libraries can heed the call for racial healing by making funding clearly and easily available to racially marginalized and underrepresented workers to find counterspaces: community where they would not feel so culturally and racially isolated. Here we outline why and how we did this at our university library.

THE WHY

Racial Inequities Experienced by BIPOC Who Work in Academic Libraries

Academic libraries in the United States are strikingly white enterprises. Black, Indigenous, and people of color (BIPOC) employees who work in spaces dominated by white people are exposed to a generalized culture that doesn't see or understand their lived experiences. "Diversity" is valued in documents, but often not in practice. The very term BIPOC encompasses a wide range of identities, histories, perspectives and everyday experiences, but in the context of most library workplaces, they all become "the other" against which the unspoken invisible norms of whiteness are always pressing. White supremacist culture encourages assimilation and conformity. Although these terms often seem abstract and analytical, they affect everyone who works in libraries. White people in this culture have trouble observing, understanding, and absorbing the experiences of BIPOC. In academic libraries, BIPOC are not encouraged to talk about and share their experiences when they make white people uncomfortable. The Library and Information Studies (LIS) literature includes many examples of BIPOC library workers speaking to the deleterious effects of working in a predominantly white space and their need to find BIPOC professional community (Blas et al., 2019, 2021; Brown et al., 2018; Echavarria & Wertheimer, 1997; Fiedler & Sterling, 2021; Garnar, 2021; Hodge & Williams, 2021; Oates, 2022; Shearer & Chiewphasa, 2021; Swanson et al., 2018). In her chapter in the book, *Dismantling Constructs of Whiteness in Higher Education*, librarian Evangela Q. Oates stated, "As part of the higher educational enterprise, Black administrators, faculty, and staff may spend one-third or more of their days in spaces that are foundationally oppositional to their worldviews, epistemologies, status as free people, and authority" (Oates, 2022, p. 173).

While some white people in academic libraries are recognizing their whiteness and are trying to figure out how to change the racial demographics of the people who work in libraries, efforts and policies that *effectively* create change too often continue to be largely the work of the very few BIPOC who currently work in libraries. Unfortunately, this work is done within systems of oppression in which *institutional* diversity, equity, and inclusion programs often do more harm than good to BIPOC in the field (Gabiola, 2018). Susan VanDeventer Iverson concluded 16 years ago that "diversity policies reproduce whiteness by centering dominant discourses while simultaneously failing to name whiteness as a barrier to inclusion ... positioning white people as the primary beneficiaries of diversity initiatives that purportedly support marginalized staff" (Brown et al., 2021, pp. 98–99). When diversity initiatives and values are stated as being good for the organization, or "good for business," but not necessarily good for BIPOC, these diversity efforts backfire and have detrimental effects for BIPOC people's sense of belonging and even their interest in joining these organizations (Georgeac & Rattan, 2023). Brown, et al. (2021) argued that "diversity work can mask discriminatory practices and even become discriminatory itself, especially considering the absence of CRT strategies ..., such as creating counterspaces for BIPOC and fostering community building" (p. 101).

These outcomes create burnout in people who are already isolated. Oates (2022) asked, "How does one teach, advise, motivate, write, conduct research and serve on committees when their daily realities are not represented in the spaces, curriculum, leadership, pedagogical approaches, and values at their institutions?" (p. 175). To achieve equity, there is a necessity for institutions to pay attention to the needs of BIPOC workers and to allocate appropriate resources to meeting those needs. Jones et al. (2022) stated,

After hundreds of years of prioritizing white voices and interests in collections and programming decisions, it is only natural that library funding be specifically devoted to expanding and facilitating work toward closing the equity gap and dismantling racist systems and structures (p. 96).

The Racial Climate at University of Massachusetts Amherst

The racial climate at the institution where we work, the University of Massachusetts, Amherst (UMass Amherst), is fraught with well-intentioned statements of solidarity, pervasive anti-Black bias, and persistent discrimination against marginalized (i.e., nondominant/majority groups [any group that does not identify as white and/or cisgender and/or able bodied]). The aspirational anti-racist action plans and commitments that the university espouses often fail to truly protect, uphold the dignity of, and preserve the authentic self of BIPOC students, faculty, and staff.

The UMass Amherst Campus Climate Survey results, pooled from respondents in November 2021, featured a 41.6% response rate and illustrated the tense racial campus climate landscape. The four main categories of the Campus Climate Survey were Classroom Climate for Students and Instructors, Perceptions of the Campus Climate, Feelings of Connection and Friendship, and Sense of Belonging (Office of Academic Planning and Assessment, 2022). Communities were formed, solidified, and sustained through a felt sense of belonging; so that is the metric we will share.

Among BIPOC undergraduate students, graduate students, faculty, and staff there was a high percentage of No Sense of Belonging reported (Office of Academic Planning and Assessment, 2022). To break down the statistics further, 26% of Black undergraduates, 18% of Black graduate students, 14%

of Black staff, and 14% of Black faculty felt they have No Sense of Belonging. The numbers were similar for Latinx/Latiné undergraduate students at 17%, while 27% of graduate students, 18% of staff, and 15% of faculty report feeling No Sense of Belonging. The results look bleak, but in our experience, the emotional reality of life for BIPOC community members on our campus is even bleaker than these results show because the blandness of these numbers cannot accurately capture the trauma, grief, and pain of ongoing racial injustices.

Need to Support Counterpaces in Library Institutions

Libraries as institutions must persist in prioritizing tangible, creative, and innovative ways to bring vitality to statements of solidarity, aspirational action plans, and anti-racist commitments. One way is by providing the financial means for BIPOC to find counterspaces in this very white field. The concept of counterspaces has been prevalent in the field of education, sociology, and psychology for some time, but is not much discussed in the library and information studies field. Keels (2019) defined counterspaces as "safe spaces that simultaneously validate and critique one's interconnected self and group identity" (p.2) and as "critical spaces where marginalized students challenge each other to push beyond stereotypical narratives, develop counterstories, and learn adapting strategies from others who are navigating similar struggles" (p. 161). Keels cautioned against a "college for all" narrative that brings BIPOC students onto campus, but does not attend to the specific needs and experiences of BIPOC students (pp. 1-2).

Counterspaces for BIPOC library workers are spaces where these workers can find some relief and build community with other BIPOC, a space where there is a sense of belonging from having a shared racial and cultural experience. Librarians Jennifer Brown and her colleagues discussed the need for BIPOC counterspace in LIS as the reason that they formed the group *We Here* in 2016: "Counterspaces are invaluable peer mentorship resources because so many of the issues we face are dangerous to express in predominantly white spaces. Fear of discrimination, being further marginalized, or being passed over for promotions silences those at the margins" (Brown et al., 2018, p. 176). They also referred to the following quote from April Hathcock, who wrote,

…. *We need exclusive spaces where we can curse our lot, speak our minds, and then dry our faces and take back up our fighting stances. We need places where we can be weak and vulnerable without being in danger or exposed (Brown et al., 2018, p. 176).*

The Rationale: What Motivated Us to Make a Counterspace Funding Proposal

Motivated by Our Positionalities

Education researcher H. Richard Milner (2007) cautioned that "when researchers are not mindful of the enormous role of their own and others' racialized positionality and cultural ways of knowing, the results can be dangerous to communities and individuals of color" (p. 388). Those of us who advocated and succeeded in securing library administrative commitment for BIPOC counterspace support came to this work with different racial, gender, cultural, and class experiences, knowledge, and motivations. This was neither a BIPOC-only effort, nor a paternalistic effort on the part of white staff or administrators.

Isabel Espinal

I am a light-skinned Latina, a Dominican American librarian. I am not only a first-generation college graduate but also a first-generation high school graduate. I started in this field in public libraries in 1991 and have been in the same academic library since 1998. Black, Indigenous, People of Color spaces in librarianship have been important to me from day one—actually since before I became a librarian—because I learned about REFORMA (The National Association to Promote Library and Information Services to Latinos and the Spanish Speaking) and the Black Caucus of ALA while researching library schools and libraries as a career choice. I might not have become a librarian had it not been for these organizations. I was lucky to have lived in places (the California Bay Area and the New York Metro area) while in library school and after becoming a librarian where I could attend local REFORMA meetings. The REFORMA meetings were spaces where I felt not just included, but also respected, celebrated, and treasured. I felt like I was part of a bigger mission and movement of people who were often very different from each other in many ways, but who had an expansive and inclusive vision of library and information services that included my communities. It was a space that was both comfortable and cutting edge, generative and restorative; a place where people valued me and where I felt I could be myself.

After arriving at the University of Massachusetts Amherst, I was lucky to have professional development funds and grants that I could apply for to attend national meetings of these groups and to attend the Joint Conference of Librarians of Color. But every time I did so, I felt that I had to sacrifice going to mainstream conferences, such as ACRL (Association of College and Research Libraries) or going to conferences in my subject or collecting areas, such as the Seminar for the Acquisition of Latin American Materials or the Latin American Studies Association or the Association for the Study of African American Life and History. To this day I have yet to attend an ACRL conference. Given the choice of BIPOC spaces or a mainstream conference space, I would choose the BIPOC space because I hunger for the community of other librarians of color. I felt starved at my place of work in regard to this community. In thinking and writing about the pervasiveness of whiteness in our profession, the inequity of this situation hit me hard. So I decided to speak to it by making this proposal in the article I cowrote with Tonia Sutherland and Charlotte Roh (Espinal et al., 2018), and to go further and actually propose this at my library.

Anne Graham

I came to libraries from a science, technology, engineering, and mathematics (STEM) field and identify as a white, cisgender woman. My college major was geology. My first job after college had the title mud logger. It involved creating a log of the geologic units being drilled through by oil company drilling rigs. To do this work, I needed reports on the geology of the areas I was covering in the western region of the United States. I found these reports in university libraries, with the help of librarians who knew about the information I needed and led me to it. Later, I lived in Virginia and worked for a consulting engineering firm. Again, I needed geologic information in the form of United States Geological Survey reports on the areas where I was working. I found them in the Geology Library at Virginia Tech. The librarian there knew what I was looking for and let me explore the collection. She was fielding questions from other people, leading them to information. That was where I started to think about becoming a librarian.

I am now a STEM librarian at a large university. I came to libraries as a white person and discovered that I was in the dominant racial group, the dominant gender group, and the dominant physical ability group. I was drawn into attempting to change the detrimental effects of my positionality while realizing that I grew up in a culture that had always nurtured me, but not people of color, not people with different abilities. Breonna Taylor's and George Floyd's murders brought me out of that position of comfort to the reality that everything I had been taught was coming from a culture of white supremacy. At a protest on our town common when a senior in high school spoke about her experience as a young Black woman, she asked the people gathered around her to change the curriculum. I want to do that and to change the culture we live in.

Maria Rios

I was born and raised in the southeastern United States and identify as a Black/Puerto Rican, queer, nonbinary woman with higher education (master's degree) privilege.

Libraries, as physical space, have always *personally* invoked a sense of joy, freedom, and community.

At the start of my sophomore year in college, I was a full-time student while also working at my local public library. One day a patron asked me for book recommendations, and unbeknownst to me, I did my first reader's advisory. The experience resonated with me so much that I shifted my entire undergraduate career toward librarianship. I sought out and secured an unpaid internship at my university library; this position blossomed into a student peer research assistant position the next semester and served as source material for both my honor's project and final project. Eager to join the field, I immediately went to graduate school following my graduation in December 2015.

During graduate school, I maintained a full-time courseload and two part-time positions at the same time—library specialist at a small technical college and graduate assistantship within my Master's in Library Science (MLIS) program's department. A newly minted MLIS holder in December 2017, I immediately began seeking full-time employment. My search ended in 2018 when I secured a position at a large land grant university in the northeastern United States.

The student community is diverse, but unfortunately, I find myself as the sole Black librarian within my department. For scope and scale purposes, my library employs between 150 and 160 full-time library workers at any point in time—and I am one of potentially five self-identified Black staff. Imagine my surprise when I found that working as a professional librarian was especially isolating as a Black/Puerto Rican individual. My journey to professional librarianship has been resourced largely through scholarships, grants, and programs aimed at supporting librarians from marginalized populations. I am incredibly grateful that now, as a professional librarian, I have access to institutional resources like professional development funds. These resources are essential for me to maintain community within Black, Indigenous, POC library spaces.

Kate Freedman

I am queer, nonbinary, and white. I come from a lower-middle-class background and was also the only person in my immediate family to earn a college degree or go to graduate school. I earned both my master's degree in library and information studies (2007) and my doctorate in history (2018). The aspects of my identity that are marginalized within the higher education sphere have increased my sensitivity to the engines of inequality and oppression within American society. They also drew me to researching the history of white supremacy in my graduate studies in history. My doctoral research illuminated the ways that a social-justice-oriented white-majority religious group, the Quakers, went against the seemingly egalitarian spirit of their religious doctrines to profit from the institution of slavery in the 17th and 18th centuries; my research also showed me how right thought alone does not translate into right action, especially within the profit driven economic system in which we still exist (Freedman, 2018). I am now a history librarian at a large public research university. I joined my current library in 2013, and my extensive research on the history of the economic and cultural systems that have enabled white supremacy led me early in my career to join informally with BIPOC and white-ally colleagues to discuss ways that we could improve justice, equity, diversity, and inclusion within the libraries. In 2017, I was a founding member of the Libraries' Inclusion, Diversity, Anti-Racism, and Equity (IDARE) Committee, and I have worked with members of this committee on a number of projects and proposals that will be discussed further on in this article.

Motivated by a Documented Need for BIPOC Library Counterspaces

Our library is not unique, and neither are libraries, as a professional space in which whiteness and white supremacy cultural norms dominate. Numerous studies indicate that BIPOC in predominantly white workplaces have to perform many hidden and often unconscious maneuvers in order to maintain or succeed in these environments, what Wingfield and Alston (2014) term "racial tasks": modifying their self-presentation, conducting emotion work, and smoothing interactions with white peers. Additionally, "workers of color are assigned positions and tasks which reinforce that racial status quo" (Wingfield & Alston, 2014, p. 274). Okun's (n.d.) widely circulated list of characteristics of white supremacy culture that show up in organizations has resonated with BIPOC in many fields, including nonprofit institutions dedicated to social justice. Many organizational leaders say they "want to be multicultural," but "actually only allow other people and cultures to come in if they adapt or conform to already existing cultural norms" (Okun, n.d.). In her book *Community as Rebellion: A Syllabus for Surviving Academia as a Woman of Color*, Latinx Studies scholar Lorgia García-Peña discussed the phenomenon of tokenism within traditional organizational diversity and inclusion frameworks (García Peña, 2022). Using the term "The One," García-Peña (2022) pointed out its pervasiveness not only in academia, but across many professions and industries, resulting in BIPOC employees feeling at odds with their coworkers on a daily basis often for the most basic cultural practices. She told the story of a white male colleague's response to her expressiveness and comfort in greeting another woman of color in the workplace:

He was clearly made uncomfortable by our expressions of affection. I am by nature a warm person. I express care to people. The comment took me by surprise, as it made me realize how much of who I am and how I move in the world is unacceptable within these spaces of whiteness (García Peña, 2022, p. 16).

García-Peña urges women of color in academia and beyond to make community with each other to not only survive but to thrive.

Using similar language, BIPOC librarians have also written about this experience of isolation and need for community with other BIPOC. For example, Fiedler and Sterling (2021) wrote that "sometimes it feels like we exist in a different professional world from our counterparts" (p. 82). Jennifer Brown, Jennifer A. Ferretti, Sofia Leung, and Marisa Méndez-Brady testified about their experiences in library workplaces and mainstream library conferences, such as ALA: "We feel isolated and lonely when we realize we are the 'only' person of color in all of the rooms that comprise these events, no matter how big those rooms are" (p. 169). Teresa Neely (2018) reported that after nearly 25 years in academic libraries, she had "never worked at an institution where there was another credentialed Black librarian, female or otherwise, on the faculty." Neely (2018) added the following comment:

Most days, it is a real struggle to just get out of bed in the morning, knowing that a hostile workplace is waiting for you to arrive. A workplace that is hostile because you are the only Black faculty librarian who ever worked here, and your colleagues have no idea what it is like to be you.

An anonymous respondent in a study of "the lived experience of academic librarians of color" reported: "I feel more disconnected from my cultural heritage because of the homogenous community and lack of diversity in my institution and profession. I have debated leaving the profession because of how isolated [I feel] from other minority members" (Swanson et al., 2018, p. 884). Janis J. Shearer and Ben B. Chiewphasa (2021) stated that "being on the defensive role has been exhausting, and being in an environment where pushback is welcome is liberating: We've been excluded for decades." also asked, "Can we have something for ourselves for once?" They wrote of their yearning for:

a space where BIPOC librarians learn from one another, which is not possible, when 'you're the only one.' Library workers in academia oftentimes embrace collective knowledge organization and building to navigate around new and accurate information. For BIPOC librarians, collective knowledge mechanisms also provide invaluable spaces that help negate or challenge epistemic supremacy.

Similarly, Fiedler and Sterling (2021) extolled the virtues of the Joint Conference of Librarians of Color (JCLC) for building community:

Although these conferences are open to all races and ethnicities, our experience at JCLC was that the majority of attendees were librarians of color. In a field that is 88% white, it is a rare opportunity to not be a minority in a professional space" (p. 83)

Fiedler and Sterling (2021) also analyzed the offerings of the Association of College and Research Libraries (ACRL) national conference vis-a-vis JCLC and found that JCLC was more attuned to the holistic needs of BIPOC library workers: Among their findings, they noted that "the JCLC conferences cultivated the entire career path of librarians of color while ACRL focused mostly on recruitment of those same librarians" (p. 83).

This clearly is a justice and equity issue because BIPOC library workers aren't getting something that is routine for white library workers. Fiedler and Sterling (2021), to this point, noted that "attending a conference like JCLC, the People of Color in Library and Information Science Summit, or any national or regional event hosted by an ALA ethnic caucus is an opportunity for librarians of color to experience what white librarians experience every day: what it's like to be a part of the majority" (p. 89). Fiedler and Sterling (2021) further suggested that if "libraries want to recruit, retain, and support librarians of color, they should also provide financial opportunities for them to attend conferences where they will not be in the minority" (p. 88).

In a talk to the UMass Community, Dr. Micere Keels, Associate Professor in Comparative Human Development at the University of Chicago, promoted asking our institutions to move beyond tolerance and toward full inclusion. She talked about the creation of counterspaces, where people of color can feel safe in community with each other on a historically white campus. She stated in her book, *Campus Counterspaces: Black and Latinx Students' Search for Community at Historically White Universities,* "Institutions that recognize that historical marginalization is often sustained by present-day disenfranchisement, discrimination, and stereotyping would more likely provide resources and opportunities to

Counterspace Support of BIPOC Employees in a JEDI Library Framework

create and normalize formal and informal counterspaces" (Keels, 2019, p.152). These ideas fueled the existing desire to build structural identity-conscious support for our BIPOC coworkers in the form of a fund to enable access to counterspaces in a primarily white workspace. The provision of professional development funding was an effort to support BIPOC library employees with the financial means to seek BIPOC spaces within the national and international libraries community. The shared language of counterspaces on our campus that we gained from Dr. Keels' visit helped us make the case to our library colleagues and administration at the time.

THE HOW

Building a Proposal and Seeking Buy-In From a Predominantly White Staff and Administration

Getting a commitment from the library administration for funding BIPOC counterspace and conference support took many conversations, explanations, and presentations over a period of years with significant administrator turnover (2018–2021). From seeding the idea with the Libraries' Diversity and Inclusion committee in 2018, (which later became the Inclusion, Diversity, Anti-Racism and Equity (IDARE) committee), to sharing it in a library-wide sociocracy training session (Rau & Koch-Gonzalez, 2018; Sociocracy for All, 2023), to facilitating conversations with the Librarians Council (a standing committee of approximately 40 library workers who are members in the faculty/librarian union on campus), with the Libraries' Staff Council (a standing council of non-librarian library workers) and with individual BIPOC library workers, to discussions with administrators, to bringing a proposal forward to the library administration, the path to this initiative was long and winding.

An important component was the formation of an anti-racism "helping circle" of four people within the Librarians Council who urged the library administration at the time to create an action plan that would back up the Libraries' anti-racism statement made in summer 2020, a time when libraries joined many organizations and corporations across the United States that made public anti-racism statements (Gibson et al., 2021; Mehra, 2021). A BIPOC support fund thus was presented as one part of a greater anti-racism plan for the libraries. The Librarians Council's anti-racism helping circle decided to work on moving the idea forward by proposing the creation of a task force within the council to work on implementing this particular anti-racism effort. The Librarians Council endorsed the task force with the charge to research vital steps in the creation of a BIPOC professional racial support fund for current BIPOC employees and those we hope to welcome to our Libraries community in the future. After several meetings and discussions with various coworkers in the libraries, the task force reported the following findings and implementation recommendations to the Librarians Council:

- Form a BIPOC support working group within IDARE, the committee that is open to all library workers.
- Write a proposal to the interim dean of libraries.
- Work with the dean of libraries to find funding from our current funds (or find other possible funding partners) to determine how to create a perpetual fund within the UMass Amherst Libraries
- Determine who will vet requests for funding, streamlining the process as much as possible.
- Recommend how to move finances in and out of the fund.

The Librarians Council endorsed these recommendations, and the IDARE committee took up work and endorsed them. IDARE asserted that this would be a good recruitment and retention tool for employees at all levels. It would show future BIPOC employees that there is a support mechanism for those seeking counterspaces in their library work.

In addition, current BIPOC employees volunteered feedback that they welcomed funding support. They suggested that any fund not be made difficult for BIPOC employees to utilize, that the process be streamlined, and that BIPOC could request funds in a timely manner, and that student workers be included.

The final proposal to the dean of libraries included these subjects:

- The purpose of BIPOC support funding and why it is necessary across the entire library organization.
- Support is for library BIPOC employees across the entire organization.
- Proposed budgeted amount of $10,000 to be provided.
- Eligibility and application procedure
- Description of what funding would be used for
- Who could oversee the fund?

Through discussions in IDARE, the BIPOC support working group was able to meet with and gain valuable procedural knowledge from a group of coworkers who oversee a separate endowed fund to support professional development for nonlibrarian workers. These two groups met to learn how to create a working model for the implementation of the proposed funding. This meeting assisted in the generation of an application form and other elements that would be necessary to include such as:

- Guidelines for our colleagues to consider and to communicate the idea of professional development funding for counterspaces
- Content to share the idea on a public-facing web page was created to communicate with future employees the nature of our commitment to supporting their needs.
- A rubric for determining how to distribute professional development funding in a just, equitable way.
- An application form was created as part of the method for easily vetting applications while informing supervisors.
- A subgroup of employees from the IDARE group was solicited to oversee this process, and the Director of Diversity, Inclusion, and Human Resources was asked to be on this subgroup.

The Importance of Messaging and One-on-One BIPOC Outreach and Conversations

Although many BIPOC library workers, especially BIPOC librarians, are familiar with spaces such as JCLC and the People of Color in Library & Information Science (POCinLIS) Summit, many are not, as has been the case at UMass Amherst. Additionally, it was apparent that more communication would be needed to ensure people were aware of opportunities such as JCLC and that when opportunities arise, clear descriptions and easy access to registration links and associated forms would be needed. Supervisors encouraging one-on-one conversations and email exchanges with BIPOC employees encouraging them to make use of funding would be necessary. Going into the future, our expectation is that all people in the library would continue to communicate similar opportunities, such as the REFORMA National conference, the National Conference of African American Librarians, Racial Equity Institute, and the POC in LIS Summit, amongst others.

From a "Fund" to a Funding Priority and Criterion for Engagement

In the summer of 2022, the University hired a new dean, Nandita Mani, whose commitment to justice, equity, diversity, and inclusion) is front and center. The dean will continue to support funding for BIPOC library workers and has instituted a library-wide funding request process in support of JEDI initiatives. Under Dean Mani, JEDI at UMass Amherst Libraries will take a holistic approach that will encourage all Libraries employees to pursue professional development, engage in JEDI project work, cultivate JEDI engagement activities, support JEDI collections, and encourage BIPOC employees to apply for funding that will support their need for counterspaces outside of the libraries, where they are currently unavailable.

WHAT THIS APPROACH IS AND ISN'T

Not Asking BIPOC to Do the Work of JEDI

A common misunderstanding in JEDI initiatives that focus on BIPOC workers is that the initiative is asking BIPOC to do the work of JEDI (Brown et al., 2018, 2021). For example, many library diversity residents are hired to add diversity to a library, but an assumption is made that they will also be on diversity or JEDI or diversity, equity, and inclusion (DEI) committees and that they will do de facto outreach to communities of color, regardless of their job title and duties. When we proposed the BIPOC support fund, we encountered a similar misunderstanding among some library employees and administrators. A BIPOC support fund would be the opposite of asking BIPOC to do the work of JEDI; rather, it is asking the institution to support BIPOC by funding their ability to tap into BIPOC library worker counterspaces.

Part of a Holistic Approach, Not a "One and Done"

Keels (2019) cautioned that "counterpaces are not a panacea" for Black and Latinx students' sense of belonging and academic success, and noted that substantial financial assistance to attain a higher education degree is key for many of these students (p. 164). The BIPOC support fund is also not enough on its own to do all the anti-racism work of the library; it is not a "one and done." It is but one very important piece of a greater holistic vision that Isabel Espinal, Tonia Sutherland, and Charlotte Roh (2018) proposed, some of which the UMass IDARE Committee embraced in their strategic planning and has been building on.

Suggestions in *"A Holistic Approach to Inclusive Librarianship"*

Espinal, Sutherland and Roh's (2018) comprehensive holistic approach includes these elements:

- Creating positions that do not require the MLS and that would pay BIPOC employees to obtain the MLS on the job, thus increasing the numbers of BIPOC with MLS degrees.

- Allocating funding for librarians of color to attend conferences of librarians of color.
- Launching an education program for all levels of library employees and managers that would include promoting and advancing the understanding of whiteness in society generally and librarianship specifically.
- Implementing programs for the BIPOC veterans of the racial battles of whiteness in libraries, who have endured years of microaggressions.
- Combining technological and "cutting-edge" librarianship with diversity librarianship, such as open access projects and digital/data curation roles and media/digital literacy efforts
- Infusing more flexibility, agility, risk-taking, and commitment to BIPOC representation and leadership in library hiring practices
- Moving from microaggressions to microaffections in interpersonal library relationships

Since Espinal et al.'s (2018) work was published, Espinal initiated the task of fleshing out some of these ideas and trying to actually put them into practice at her library. She took the first idea to the UMass Amherst Diversity group before it had formed into a committee, and with coworkers Laura Quilter, Pete Smith, Sarah Hutton, and Kate Freedman, developed a proposal for establishing a post-baccalaureate fellowship program to bring BIPOC into librarianship. With Maria Rios and April Hatchcock, this proposal was explained within a Critical Race Theory framework as a way to address the racial wealth gap (Espinal et al., 2021). Her supervisor, Jennifer Friedman, joined the effort in researching and writing grants to help fund this initiative. Espinal also has fleshed out the last suggestion on the list, with presentations and a book chapter on microaffections and microaffirmations as forms of "micro affirmative actions."

Other Recommendations by UMass Woman of Color Librarian within a Holistic Approach

Espinal also proposed some specific recommendations for UMass Amherst that had not been outlined in her 2018 article, but that are part of a holistic approach. In the libraries' strategic initiatives proposal process, Espinal proposed that the diversity residency be made a permanent ongoing program with a guaranteed cohort of residents. She also proposed the creation of two new positions in the then-called Research Services department: a Native American and Indigenous Studies Community Librarian and an Afro American, Black Diaspora, and African Studies Community Librarian. For equitable library service, the fields that study racialized and oppressed groups require more librarian hours than we have structurally been allocating. Collecting materials requires more time, outreach requires more time, and individual consultations require more time. The job also often extends beyond the normal librarian official duties. Just as faculty of color often have to step in as informal advisors to students and other faculty of color, so too do librarians who serve racialized constituents and knowledge traditions have to do much work outside of the standard job description.

Strategic Holistic Suggestions of the UMass Amherst IDARE Committee

When the Libraries' Diversity and Inclusion (now IDARE) Committee was formed in 2017, the group worked to move forward on the recommendations outlined in Espinal et al. (2018), which was drafted in the year before the formation of the committee. The committee formed working groups to begin implementing parts of the vision proposed in Espinal et al. (2018). In addition to the projects listed in the sections above, working groups within the committee also completed these tasks:

- Coordinated a monthly anti-racism and white supremacy learning group open to all libraries' staff to raise awareness of the experiences of BIPOC staff and patrons and begin to change the libraries' culture toward one that was more inclusive
- Built an extensive curated bibliography (LibGuide) of readings, podcasts, and videos about JEDI issues. Although this guide was created and maintained with the intention of using it as an educational resource for the staff of the libraries, it was also shared and used widely throughout the university and beyond in 2020, following the nationwide protests after the murder of George Floyd.
- Worked with the libraries' administration to begin the process of reviewing and implementing HR practices that improved BIPOC recruitment and better supported BIPOC staff members who came to work at our majority white institution. The initiative to establish the BIPOC support fund is one piece of this effort.
- Developed a proposal to create an associate dean of the Libraries for Diversity and Inclusion, or a similarly high-ranking position, to coordinate a holistic approach to JEDI work within the libraries

In addition to these working groups, the committee also identified a number of additional areas to move forward on when time and staffing resources allowed. These further ideas included:

- Reviewing all current library policies and making recommendations to include diversity, inclusion, equity, access, and social justice
- Reviewing our collections to establish a baseline of how representative they are of diverse publishers, languages, cultures and perspectives

Members of the IDARE committee and others in the UMass Amherst Libraries also sought to leverage the UMass Amherst Libraries' consortial partnership with Amherst, Hampshire, Mount Holyoke, and Smith Colleges (the Five College Consortium) to learn from and creatively move forward on various JEDI initiatives. This included:

- Participating in meetings of the informally organized Five College Critical Librarianship Group, which has served as a forum to discuss, learn about, and brainstorm JEDI initiatives on our various campuses
- Participating in talks between nonadministrative staff at the Five College Libraries to create a consortium-wide version of post-baccalaureate program for BIPOC librarians, as a way to leverage Five College budgetary resources and to propose creating a multicampus post-baccalaureate cohort that would serve as more robust counterspace for the post-baccalaureate program participants than a cohort that could be created at UMass Amherst alone; this would not be a substitute for the creation of cohorts at each campus.
- Participating in and promoting JEDI events through the preexisting Five College Libraries' committee structure. For example, a Five College learning circle that engaged the book *Research as Ceremony*, which delved into Indigenous ways of knowing and researching.

Holistic Vision of New Dean of Libraries

Of course, even this is not an exhaustive list! Our new dean of libraries has a vision for creating a holistic framework including work that complements work previously done. How we approach these ideas and strategies is a work in progress.

A Holistic Approach to JEDI Supports BIPOC Employees—If It Doesn't Forget Them

We advocate that libraries simultaneously support BIPOC with funding and other resources for accessing counterspaces while also building a strong holistic racial equity program that includes the elements above–and more. A holistic approach is good and necessary for BIPOC individuals in many ways. For example, it is imperative to recruit more BIPOC individuals for the sake of current BIPOC individuals, to help bring more BIPOC community into the library. And recruiting more BIPOC is also not enough. Many libraries need to work on becoming less hostile and more welcoming and warm environments. Training and awareness building for white employees is also necessary to ensure they know how to be supportive and honestly not continue to perpetuate racism. In many instances, it is additionally important to not just support BIPOC as a category, but to be more specific about the communities that BIPOC encompasses and direct support in more targeted ways (Paradkar, 2021; Garcia, 2020). For example, to direct support to Black library employees, to Asian library employees, to Indigenous library employees, to Latinx library employees, acknowledging that many of these broad racial or cultural categories include subcategories as well. And libraries need to tend to intersectionality, to deal with all the other components of diversity and equity that are not only about race or racialized ethnicity because BIPOC are multidimensional with many intersecting identities. Libraries need to address neurodiversity in employees, LGBTQIA+ issues, gender equity, disability, classism, and more. But the focus and need for BIPOC support should never be left unsaid or unaddressed.

In Other Contexts

There are many challenges to creating this kind of funding for racial equity. Even when the executive leader is a champion of JEDI, the larger sociopolitical forces may limit perceived options. In our case, we had originally proposed a separate fund called the BIPOC support fund, but had to change that approach even though we received a strong commitment from the dean to fund specific requests; it became a funding priority rather than a named program. In other contexts, the dean or director might not be as supportive. In our own case, when we started to work on this, we did not take for granted that the dean would be onboard. Before we took it to the dean and library leadership, in our discussions, librarians suggested that the funding could be crowdsourced from all the librarians. Another option is for funding to come from a union. Professional associations might be tapped as well. Without diminishing the call for action and ownership at these executive and institutional levels of the libraries, white allies and accomplices can find alternate ways to step in to support their BIPOC colleagues.

CONCLUSION

Regardless of what libraries and institutions or white allies do to be supportive, librarians of color will seek community as a matter of survival and more. BIPOC within the field of librarianship have already produced their own spaces and are not waiting for white-dominated institutions to do that. This is the history of organizations such as the Black Caucus of ALA, REFORMA, AILA, APALA, CALA, the POC in LIS Summit, *We Here*, and others. What our approach does is direct libraries to acknowledge the need for and existence of these spaces and ask institutions to make it easier for BIPOC to take advantage of these affirming spaces by providing funding.

The new library dean is the first library leader at our university in many years who has made JEDI a centerpiece of her vision and expectation for the library and for all library employees, consistently asking us to see our work through a JEDI lens, and in that process making clear that support for BIPOC is paramount. In asking everyone in a library to take on JEDI work, it will be a continuing challenge to keep centering the voices, experiences, and needs of the traditionally marginalized so that they do not continue to be at the margins—in this case the experiences of BIPOC employees of the library. But it is a challenge that our library is committed to engaging in.

In explaining how organizations have transitioned "from DEI to JEDI," Martinez and Truong (2021) stated that "leading with Justice and Equity is a significantly different framework" from traditional diversity and inclusion or even EDI frameworks "because it prompts us to think about the systemic barriers to access, engagement, and success at the forefront of our work and how we can transform an organization to try to eliminate these barriers" (p.).

Taking the elements that make up JEDI, we can see that financially supporting BIPOC employees to find counterspaces furthers all these elements: justice, equity, diversity and inclusion. It fosters justice because it helps provide something in the library workspace for BIPOC that they do not normally receive, but that white workers routinely receive. It fosters equity because it provides a concrete way to level the injustice and imbalance for BIPOC through funding. It fosters diversity because it supports employees who are racially different from the traditional library demographic, helping with retention of current diversity and can even act as a recruitment incentive to bring more BIPOC into a library workplace. It fosters inclusion because it takes the needs and proposals of BIPOC seriously when making budgeting decisions in the library because this is an idea that originated with BIPOC at our library and is supported by the vast literature of BIPOC in LIS.

Ultimately, we want to center the needs of BIPOC because injustices have been done to them in library workspaces that do not reflect or celebrate or let alone love their life experience and ways of being. Ultimately our aim is to promote racial healing for BIPOC library workers. We want BIPOC employees to hear the eloquent message of Fiedler & Sterling (2022):

If you have grown weary of speaking up for what is right, representing the dissenting opinion for the benefit of the collective, knowing eyes will roll in the faculty meeting when you open your mouth, or any other scenario which has rewarded your unveiling with contempt, I want you to be recognized and validated here. I see you. I hear you. You are valid. You are necessary. You are loved HERE (p).

Those of us who are BIPOC and have been in BIPOC library counterspaces have heard or felt some version of this when participating in BIPOC spaces, as in this example from a participant of the POC in LIS Summit (Blas et al., 2019, p. 273):

I have never in my professional career been in a room full of beautifully diverse information professionals. I am part of a greater movement and our voices are powerful. That due to our determination, this profession is changing. Thank you for holding up a mirror to allow me to see dignity, grace, and strength within myself.

This is an affirmation we want for everyone in the library workplace.

REFERENCES

Blas, N., Conner-Gaten, A., Deras, R., & Young, J. (2019). Empowering collaborations and creating brave spaces: People of Color in Library and Information Science Summit. *College & Research Libraries News, 80*(5), 270–273. doi:10.5860/crln.80.5.270

Blas, N., Conner-Gaten, A., Masunaga, J., & Young, J. (2021). POC in LIS summit 2021 impact report. *LMU Librarian Publications & Presentations, 131*, 164–171. https://digitalcommons.lmu.edu/librarian_pubs/131

Brown, J., Cline, N., & Méndez-Brady, M. (2021). Leaning on our labor: Whiteness and hierarchies of power in LIS work. In S. Y. Leung & J. R. López-McKnight (Eds.), *Knowledge justice: Disrupting library and information studies through critical race theory* (pp. 95–110). The MIT Press. https://direct.mit.edu/books/oa-edited-volume/5114/chapter/3075317/Leaning-on-Our-Labor-Whiteness-and-Hierarchies-of doi:10.7551/mitpress/11969.003.0007

Brown, J., Ferretti, J. A., Leung, S., & Méndez-Brady, M. (2018). We here: Speaking our truth. *Library Trends, 67*(1), 163–181. doi:10.1353/lib.2018.0031

Echavarria, T., & Wertheimer, A. B. (1997). Surveying the role of ethnic-American library associations. *Library Trends, 46*(2), 373–391.

Espinal, I. (2022). Microaffections and microaffirmations: Refusing to reproduce whiteness via microaffirmative actions. In T. Y. Neely & M. Montañez (Eds.), *Dismantling constructs of whiteness in higher education: Narratives of resistance from the academy* (pp. 65–76). Routledge. doi:10.4324/9781003029564-7

Espinal, I., Hathcock, A., & Rios, M. (2021). Dewhitening librarianship: A policy proposal for libraries. In S. Y. Leung & J. R. López-McKnight (Eds.), *Knowledge justice: Disrupting library and information studies through critical race theory* (pp. 223–240). The MIT Press., doi:10.7551/mitpress/11969.003.0017

Espinal, I., Sutherland, T., & Roh, C. (2018). A holistic approach for inclusive librarianship: Decentering whiteness in our profession. *Library Trends, 67*(1), 147–162. doi:10.1353/lib.2018.0030

Espinal, I. R. (2020). *Microaffections & microaffirmations in library learning.* Five Colleges Innovative Learning Symposium. https://works.bepress.com/isabel_espinal/11/

Fiedler, B. P., & Sterling, B. (2021). Conference critique: An analysis of equity, diversity, and inclusion programming. In: *Ascending into an Open Future: Proceedings from ACRL 2021 Virtual Conference*, (pp. 82–91). ACRL. https://digitalscholarship.unlv.edu/libfacpresentation/209

Freedman, K. K. (2018). *A tangled web: Quakers and the Atlantic slave system 1625–1770* [Doctoral dissertation, University of Massachusetts, Amherst]. doi:10.7275/12597546

Gabiola, J. (2018, July 13). *"Mesearching" the network of whitenessharmdiversity* [Paper presentation]. People of Color in Library & Information Science (POCinLIS) Summit, Loyola Marymount University, Los Angeles, CA, United States. https://digitalcommons.lmu.edu/pocinlis/2018/schedule/6

Garcia, S. E. (2020, June 17). Where did BIPOC come from? *The New York Times.* https://www.nytimes.com/article/what-is-bipoc.html

García Peña, L. (2022). *Community as rebellion: A syllabus for surviving academia as a woman of color.* Haymarket Books.

Garnar, M. L. (2021). *Understanding the experiences of academic librarians of color* [Doctoral dissertation, University of Colorado, Colorado Springs]. ProQuest Dissertations and Theses database. https://www.proquest.com/docview/2618560641/abstract/59B5D3A66C8643F4PQ/1

Georgeac, O. A. M., & Rattan, A. (2023). The business case for diversity backfires: Detrimental effects of organizations' instrumental diversity rhetoric for underrepresented group members' sense of belonging. *Journal of Personality and Social Psychology, 124*(1), 69–108. doi:10.1037/pspi0000394 PMID:35679195

Gibson, A. N., Chancellor, R. L., Cooke, N. A., Dahlen, S. P., Patin, B., & Shorish, Y. L. (2021). Struggling to breathe: COVID-19, protest and the LIS response. *Equality, Diversity and Inclusion, 40*(1), 74–82. doi:10.1108/EDI-07-2020-0178

Hodge, T., & Williams, J. (2021). Call to action: Envisioning a future that centers BIPOC voices. *American Libraries, 52*(1/2), 54–54. https://americanlibrariesmagazine.org/magazine/issues/january-february-2021/

Jones, E. P., Mani, N. S., Carlson, R. B., Welker, C. G., Cawley, M., & Yu, F. (2022). Analysis of antiracism, equity, inclusion and social justice initiatives in library and information science literature. *RSR. Reference Services Review, 50*(1), 81–101. doi:10.1108/RSR-07-2021-0032

Keels, M. (2019). *Campus counterspaces: Black and Latinx students' search for community at historically white universities.* Cornell University Press. https://www.jstor.org/stable/10.7591/j.ctvq2w2c6

Martinez, K., & Truong, K. A. (2021, April 9). From DEI to JEDI. *Diverse: Issues in Higher Education.* https://www.diverseeducation.com/opinion/article/15109001/from-dei-to-jedi

Mehra, B. (2021). Enough crocodile tears! Libraries moving beyond performative antiracist politics. *The Library Quarterly, 91*(2), 137–149. doi:10.1086/713046

Milner, H. R. IV. (2007). Race, culture, and researcher positionality: Working through dangers seen, unseen, and unforeseen. *Educational Researcher, 36*(7), 388–400. doi:10.3102/0013189X07309471

Neely, T. Y. (2018). I AM My Hair, and My Hair is Me: #BlackGirlMagic in LIS. In R. L. Chou & A. Pho (Eds.), *Pushing the Margins: Women of Color and Intersectionality in LIS* (pp. 121–146). Library Juice Press. https://digitalrepository.unm.edu/ulls_fsp/122

Oates, E. Q. (2022). They took my hair—Racial battle fatigue in academe: Accounts from the plantation. In *Dismantling constructs of whiteness in higher education* (pp. 171–186). Routledge. doi:10.4324/9781003029564-17

Office of Academic Planning and Assessment. (2022). *UMass Amherst campus climate survey 2021: Sense of belonging matters in important ways*. Office of Equity and Inclusion. https://www.umass.edu/diversity/campus-climate-2021-belonging

Okun, T. (n.d.). *White supremacy culture*. Dismantling Racism. https://www.whitesupremacyculture.info/uploads/4/3/5/7/43579015/okun_-_white_sup_culture_2020.pdf

Paradkar, S. (2021, December 11). Why I'm saying bye-bye to 'BIPOC' this year. *Toronto Star*. https://www.thestar.com/opinion/star-columnists/2021/12/11/why-im-saying-bye-bye-to-bipoc-this-year.html

Rau, T. J., & Koch-Gonzalez, J. (2018). *Many voices one song: Shared power with sociocracy*. Institute for Peaceable Communities, Inc.

Shearer, J. J., & Chiewphasa, B. B. (2021). Radical re-imagination: Centering a BIPOC library workforce in an asset-based autoethnography. *RSR. Reference Services Review*, *50*(1), 113–126. doi:10.1108/RSR-07-2021-0029

Sociocracy For All. (2023). *Learn and Share Sociocracy with the World*. Sociocracy For All. https://www.sociocracyforall.org/

Sterling, B. (2022). Can't we all just cathect along? *Up//Root*. https://www.uproot.space/features/bell-series-sterling

Swanson, J., Tanaka, A., & Gonzalez-Smith, I. (2018). Lived experience of academic librarians of color. *College & Research Libraries*, *79*(7), 876–894. doi:10.5860/crl.79.7.876

Wingfield, A. H., & Alston, R. S. (2014). Maintaining hierarchies in predominantly white organizations: A theory of racial tasks. *The American Behavioral Scientist*, *58*(2), 274–287. doi:10.1177/0002764213503329

ADDITIONAL READING

Chou, R. L., & Pho, A. (Eds.). (2018). *Pushing the margins: Women of color and intersectionality in LIS*. Library Juice Press.

Hankins, R., & Juárez, M. (Eds.). (2015). *Where are all the librarians of color?: The experiences of people of color in academia*. Library Juice Press.

Hartlep, N. D., & Ball, D. (Eds.). (2019). *Racial battle fatigue in faculty: Perspectives and lessons from higher education*. Routledge. doi:10.4324/9780429054013

Hernandez Rivera, S. (2020). A space of our own: Examining a womxn of color retreat as a counterspace. *Journal of Women and Gender in Higher Education*, *13*(3), 327–347. doi:10.1080/26379112.2020.1844220

Margherio, C., Horner-Devine, M. C., Mizumori, S. J. Y., & Yen, J. W. (2020). Connecting counterspaces and community cultural wealth in a professional development program. *Race, Ethnicity and Education*, 1–21. doi:10.1080/13613324.2020.1798378

Martínez-Carrillo, N. I. (2019). "Counterspaces" and mentorship as resources for immigrant faculty of color facing racial battle fatigue. In N. D. Hartlep & D. Ball (Eds.), *Racial battle fatigue in faculty: Perspectives and lessons from higher education* (pp. 115–127). Routledge. doi:10.4324/9780429054013-9

Masunaga, J., Conner-Gaten, A., Blas, N., & Young, J. (2022). Community-building, empowering voices, and brave spaces through LIS professional conferences. In *Practicing social justice in libraries* (1st ed., pp. 14–27). Routledge. doi:10.4324/9781003167174-3

Neely, T. Y., & López-McKnight, J. R. (Eds.). (2018). *In our own voices, redux: The faces of librarianship today*. Rowman & Littlefield.

Neely, T. Y., & Montañez, M. (Eds.). (2023). *Dismantling constructs of whiteness in higher education: Narratives of resistance from the academy*. Routledge.

West, N. M. (2019). By Us, For Us: The impact of a professional counterspace on African American women in student affairs. *The Journal of Negro Education*, 88(2), 159–180. doi:10.7709/jnegroeducation.88.2.0159

Chapter 2

Justice, Equity, Diversity, and Inclusion in Mentorship:
The ARL Kaleidoscope Program Framework for Change

DeLa Dos
Association of Research Libraries, USA

Alanna Aiko Moore
University of California, San Diego, USA

ABSTRACT

Mentoring programs are a common and extremely beneficial offering in numerous settings, including academic libraries. Given their almost ubiquitous nature, these programs can occasionally become unintentionally outdated while still being successful at serving their core functions. The Association of Research Libraries (ARL) Kaleidoscope Program, in which mentoring is a core component, underwent a full review process of all aspects of its program. This chapter presents this review as a case study that demonstrates a series of approaches that resulted in providing revitalization to the program while building on and respecting the program's more than two decades of history and successes. Using mentoring as a lens, the authors outline the broader review process that included numerous administrative updates and changes to the implementation of program components. This context is critical as a key lesson learned focuses on the importance of systemic change.

INTRODUCTION

People often have complex relationships with the concept of change. It can surge from seemingly nowhere and emerge at wholly inopportune moments, and it can be an elusive wish that appears to disregard all pleas for its arrival. It can be a source of tremendous anxiety and strife, and it can open pathways to liberation and relief. It can be all these things and more at the same time. Change offers few constants beyond its existence. Still, when working to advance justice, equity, diversity, and inclusion (JEDI),

DOI: 10.4018/978-1-6684-7255-2.ch002

Copyright © 2023, IGI Global. Copying or distributing in print or electronic forms without written permission of IGI Global is prohibited.

Justice, Equity, Diversity, and Inclusion in Mentorship

it is almost always a required consideration as current systems, structures, policies, and practices are often in need of adjustments—or complete overhauls. This chapter presents a case study that explores a series of changes designed to deepen the integration of JEDI into the Association of Research Libraries (ARL) Kaleidoscope Program, which is a two-year learning and professional development program for BIPOC masters students.

Mentoring programs have a long-standing tradition of supporting and helping new librarians to succeed in the profession. The focus is often on the needs and career goals of the mentee—centering on career progress, professional development, and building an understanding of the culture of librarianship (Neyer & Yelenick, 2011, p. 215). These programs rarely address the underlying systems of white supremacy culture that permeate organizations and affect the career trajectory and well-being of BIPOC library workers. Best practices often focus on how to build a relationship between mentor and mentee but frequently fail to meaningfully acknowledge and value the culturally distinct ways of engaging with others that BIPOC mentees may utilize. New librarians of color are often in the impossible position of attempting to demystify and decipher an institutional culture with which they may have had little to no exposure prior to their first professional experience (Hansman, 2002). Additionally, BIPOC mentees can be better supported through an intentional acknowledgement of and informed response to the power and privilege that are inherent in all interactions.

The Kaleidoscope Program is grounded in the principles of social justice, inclusivity, and creating a sense of belonging in librarianship. It includes numerous components including educational and capacity development sessions, financial support, and mentoring. The mentorship component of the Kaleidoscope Program matches participants, referred to as Scholars, with exceptional individuals working in libraries, archives, associations, and other related areas for a formal two-year mentoring relationship. Recent U.S. Census (2019) statistics show that 81.4% of librarians are white. Many BIPOC entering the workforce are harmed by white supremacy culture and the deep-rooted racism of the profession. A strong relationship with a mentor that possesses shared culture or identities can disrupt these impacts and provide Scholars with tools, solidarity, and a strong foundation in anti-racist principles to help them succeed in primarily white workplaces.

ARL undertook a multifaceted process to update the Kaleidoscope Program, which included changes to the program design, governance, and administration. These changes also encompass significant adjustments to the program's components, which includes the mentoring relationships. These changes also demonstrate the importance of systemic approaches and strategies when seeking sustainable transformation; while individual positive decisions and changes are incredibly valuable, their value can increase exponentially when they are part of a larger, intentional process that recognizes the interconnectedness of each decision and maintains a commitment to its overall goals. Additionally, this chapter explores how aspects of this process can be applied to other institutional and organizational settings. This case study provides an example of how intentional, systemic, sustainable change can honor and build upon the history and legacy of established programs while adapting to contemporary needs. Such transformation is a powerful tool that can be used to dismantle systems of oppression and white supremacy culture in academic libraries.

MENTORING

While there are many definitions of mentoring, there are common threads that underlie most definitions of the term. In traditional mentoring, a skilled or experienced professional–the mentor–partners with a newer person wanting to gain skills for the purpose of promoting the latter's professional development and career goals (Neyer & Yelenick, 2011, p. 215). This partnership allows individuals to share professional and personal knowledge, skills, and experiences to promote a mentee's critical professional, personal, and career development. Mentors can provide a wide range of guidance, share life experiences, help with decision-making, identify professional development needs, and assist the mentee in determining the risk and benefits when considering employment options. The use of terminology used when describing mentors and those they mentor involved conscious decisions. While some use the term protégé–ARL uses the term mentee within the Kaleidoscope Program. The Cambridge English Dictionary states that protégés are young individuals taught and helped by an older individual, as well as one who is "helped, taught, or protected by an important or more experienced person" while Oxford uses descriptors like "guided and supported" by an "older" and more "influential" person. The unequal power dynamic and the expectation that the protégé is an inexperienced, empty vessel to be filled is not in alignment with the ARL model for mentoring relationships, which is reciprocal and enriching.

The benefits of a mentoring relationship for a mentee are vast. They include improved clarity on career choices and goals, opportunities to develop new networks and contacts, increased skill development, and greater career satisfaction. Their awareness of leadership styles, organizational culture, the tenure and promotion process, association and service work, and research and publishing venues can be invaluable. Mentors can help mentees to explore their vision, encourage self-reflection, and model self-care practices and work-life balance creating a passionate and continuous circle of support (Golian-Lui 2003). Mentoring is more than a "top-down" relationship; it is an empowering learning partnership for all parties—dynamic, and reciprocal (Allen & Eby 2007). It is built on a foundation of mutual respect and trust. A mentoring relationship is a living thing that changes and evolves over time. It is a voluntary engagement that requires hard work, dedication, and passion from both the mentor and the mentee, who are equally responsible for the effectiveness of the relationship.

Types of Mentoring Relationships

The two most common types of mentoring are informal and formal. Informal mentoring relationships are common and occur naturally, are typically unstructured, and participants determine the duration and context of the relationship. Mentees may ask someone they admire or want to work with to mentor them (Golian-Lui 2003). Mentors may take a newer colleague under their wing. Informal mentoring can be fraught, as mentors often tend to choose people to mentor who are similar in race or ethnicity. In a profession that is predominantly white, this normative approach to mentorship means most white mentors will choose a mentee who looks like them; this exclusivity leaves many BIPOC out in the cold.

In formal mentoring programs, mentors and mentees are assigned to each other through a program, organization, or institution for a set amount of time. The relationship is structured, with regular meetings, discussions, goals, and outcomes. Qualities and characteristics most valued by mentees in formal mentor matches include knowledge, experience, and goal setting (James, Raynor and Bruno 2015, p.535). In Hussey and Campbell-Meier's (2017), study of mentoring in the library and information science profession, over 38% of respondents had participated in a formal, structured mentoring program (p. 507).

Mentoring Programs in Academic Libraries

Many academic libraries engage in formal mentoring through programs that aim to support newer professionals, as shared location can provide better quality mentoring and more opportunities for interaction (Desimone et al. 2014, p. 89) Mentors can provide guidance as mentees start their careers, assist during times of transition, and provide ongoing support with career development and professional challenges (Bosch, Ramachandran, & Wakiji, 2010, p. 58). Mentoring can play a role in succession planning providing a "mechanism for knowledge transfer" (Robbeloth, Eng & Weise, 2013, p. 4) and bolstering the leadership and/or management skills of an employee, which can help them to advance within the organization (Springs 2014). It can also be deployed as a retention strategy, increasing employee confidence (Lee 2009, p 35) and offering support and guidance in fulfilling the tenure and promotion requirements like research, service to professional associations, and original research (Wilson, Gaunt, & Tehrani, 2009).

Springs (2014) explored mentoring practices at ARL institutions, finding that 22 institutions had standing programs. Their findings indicate that most of the programs focused on support for orientation and promotion, with less attention paid to leadership development or advancement in career (Spring 2014, p. 47). Farmer, Stockham, and Trusell (2009) found that programs cannot remain static and must be revitalized, assessed, and regularly adjusted to meet changing mentee needs. Approximately 46% of libraries contacted for a 2013 study had formal mentoring programs that lasted one or more years for newly hired and non tenured librarians. A little under half of the library associations had formal mentoring programs spanning 1-2 years (Robbeloth, Eng & Weise, 2013, p. 10-11). The American Library Association (n.d.) lists ten mentoring programs in its divisions, sections and roundtables—three in discussion groups and seven in affiliate organizations.

Shifting Needs of the Field

The climate of higher education has changed in the past few years, with an increased reckoning of race and racism within institutions and calls for systemic change. Following the murder of George Floyd, statements were made by college leaders, which often focused more on words and less on action (Chamberlain, Dunlap, Russell 2021); 84% of university and college presidents in the United States said issues of race and ethnicity have become more important for their institutions (Jaschik and Lederman, 2021). BIPOC faculty continue to be underrepresented and move through the ranks slower than their white counterparts. These trends are replicated within academic libraries, which are situated within their respective campus environments. A 2019 *Ithaka S+R U.S. Library Survey* found that few library directors believe they have "well-developed strategies related to equity, diversity, inclusion, and access" (Frederick and Wolff-Eisenberg 2020, p.5); additional data shows that libraries will become increasingly involved in ongoing efforts toward social justice (American Library Association, 2021). The number of BIPOC librarians in academic libraries remains low and retention remains an issue. Due to the scarcity of BIPOC librarians, the pool from which to pull mentors for BIPOC mentees is limited.

BIPOC Needs, Challenges, and Communities

Mentoring relationships can be especially important to BIPOC who often lack access to informal networks and the information required to be successful in a professional environment and library. That lack of access is recognized by ARL which is why the mentorship component of the Kaleidoscope Program is given so much attention. In formal mentoring programs, BIPOC mentees are often paired with mentors who can provide expertise and support the career development of the mentee. In theory, this is positive; however, this does not always mesh with what the mentees would find most desirable (Hussey & Campbell-Meier 2017, p. 504, Ragins & Cotton, 1999) and may lead to "mismatches in expectations, goals, and overall commitment" (Hussey & Campbell-Meier 2017, 504). For BIPOC mentees, having a mentor who shares their racial or ethnic identity may actually be the most important characteristic and outweigh other qualifications. Having a mentoring match like this can be incredibly difficult in the library and information science profession, which is overwhelmingly white. Indeed, the U.S. Census (2019) numbers show that 81.4% of librarians are white, 6.8% of librarians are Hispanic or Latino, 6.0% of librarians are Black or African American, 3.7% of librarians are Asian, 1.8% of librarians are Unknown, and 0.3% of librarians are American Indian and Alaska Native. Despite statistics from the U.S. Census Bureau showing that the nation is increasingly diverse and "less white," the numbers in LIS have remained stagnant and unmoving for over a decade.

Many BIPOC find community within the National Associations of Librarians of Color (i.e., the American Indian Library Association [AILA], the Asian/Pacific American Librarians Association [APALA], the Black Caucus of the American Library Association [BCALA], the Chinese American Library Association [CALA], REFORMA [The National Association to Promote Library and Information Services to Latinos and the Spanish-Speaking], and the Joint Council of Librarians of Color [JCLC]). These associations aim to grow their own leadership; AILA, APALA, BCALA, CALA and REFORMA all have their own internal mentoring programs where long standing members mentor those newer to the profession or to their association.

In addition to race and ethnicity, many mentoring approaches do not examine the inherent position of power that the mentor occupies or work to disrupt the hierarchical nature of the relationship. An inclusive and equitable approach to mentorship must reimagine the power dynamic of those two roles, which the model of "reverse mentoring" aims to address (Gandhi 2019). Reverse mentoring sees the relationship as mutually enriching, positive and reciprocal and acknowledges that the mentee also has much to offer the mentor. Reverse mentoring can strengthen a sense of belonging and "break down traditional barriers that impeded the advancement of racial minorities in the workplace" (Gandhi 2019). This approach interrogates what it means to be an "expert" and what competencies are valued not only in the relationship, but in the profession. Does expertise only come in the form of professional experience, number of years in the workforce, completion of higher education, and title (Lee 2020), or—as diversity expert Yejin Lee (2020) posits—can expertise be reframed and competencies like "technological fluency, experience in conflict mediation, high levels of emotional intelligence, ability to link everyday work with social justice" be given higher value?

CASE STUDY

The case study presented includes a wide range of changes that impact virtually every aspect of the ARL Kaleidoscope Program. While these changes happened in a relatively short period of time (approximately 18 months), there were multiple factors that contributed to the creation of conditions that allowed for the events to unfold as they did. Three of the key considerations were the longstanding commitment of ARL to the program, responding to COVID-19, and staff changes. The Kaleidoscope Program has existed for multiple decades. As time progressed, ARL continued to deepen its support for the program

Justice, Equity, Diversity, and Inclusion in Mentorship

by expanding the program's capacity to increase the number of Scholars accepted into the program as well as shifting it to be funded directly from the dues of its Member Institutions. The commitment to the purpose and sustainability of the program created an environment that was welcoming to strategic and informed change.

Additionally, ARL made numerous adjustments to the program implementation in response to CO-VID-19. These included offering more opportunities for virtual connection, which led to more frequent points of contact with the Scholars. This provided direct lines of communication with the program participants that allowed for their needs to be more readily shared and explored. Finally, ARL experienced a number of staff transitions. Prior to these changes, a new executive director adjusted the larger governance structures of the Association, which impacted how the program was managed. ARL also hired a new senior director of diversity, equity, and inclusion, who was responsible for the Kaleidoscope Program. As previous program directors had established a strong and successful core for the program, the new director was well-positioned for success. They also joined the ARL staff from outside of the research library and archive community. As such, they were able to provide fresh perspectives and offer constructive critique while building on the excellent foundation of the program. In partnership with a newly charged program task force, the ARL staff were prepared to make changes that would enhance the experience of multiple program stakeholders.

Program Overview

The ARL Kaleidoscope Program was established in 2000 as the ARL Initiative to Recruit a Diverse Workforce (IRDW) with the goal of attracting master of library and information science students from historically underrepresented racial and ethnic groups to careers in research libraries and archives. It was originally funded by voluntary contributions from ARL member institutions; this required active fundraising and advocacy efforts and led to unpredictability in the capacity and sustainability of the program. To address these concerns, the ARL membership eventually agreed to fund it directly from membership dues; this allowed ARL staff to be able to redirect attention to strategic planning and program enhancements. In 2019, IRDW was renamed to the Kaleidoscope Program. In part, this change reflects the importance of shifting and changing as the library and archives profession evolves over time.

Program Updates

While the Kaleidoscope Program name had been updated, the program's operations remained largely unchanged. To ensure that the new name came with meaningful impact, additional changes were needed at various places in the program's management and implementation. These changes included larger structural changes related to ARL's governance and staffing models as well as shifts within the program's policies, procedures, and curriculum. It was within this larger setting of transformation that the mentoring component of the Kaleidoscope Program was also revised; the impact of these individual changes was magnified due to the collective impact of their interconnected implications. As such, through this systemic approach, the revisions to the mentoring aspects of the program were more profound and able to be sustained.

Governance and Staffing

As part of a larger realignment process, ARL replaced a general DEI program advisory group with program specific Task Forces. This meant that the Kaleidoscope Program had a dedicated group of people who were committed to reviewing and advising the program. The Task Force is charged by the ARL Diversity, Equity, and Inclusion Committee, which is one of ARL's association committees responsible for advancing the Association's action plan. The new Task Force structure acknowledged the importance of the Kaleidoscope Program to the Association as well as demonstrated ARL's continued commitment to supporting the program. The Task Force membership includes representation from multiple ARL stakeholder communities, particularly alums of the Kaleidoscope Program.

In addition to these governance changes, ARL made changes to its staffing model. Within the updated staffing model, the full suite of ARL's learning programs, which includes the Kaleidoscope Program, gained additional support through increased staff capacity. Additionally, ARL recognized the value of integrating perspectives and experiences from beyond the research library and archive community. In recruiting staff from adjacent professional fields, ARL was able to access a richer breadth of knowledge; this shift complimented, and was enabled by, the creation Task Force as it ensured that the content expertise related to research libraries and archives remained embedded in the program operations.

It is important to note that these changes to governance and staffing were not exclusively focused on improving the Kaleidoscope Program. While such improvement was a desired outcome of these updates, it was one of many factors that led to the changes. Still, without these structural shifts, the subsequent changes would not have been possible—or at least not as readily identified and supported. These structural changes not only facilitated updates in other areas of the program but also ensured that the updates would be maintained, assessed, and advanced through iterative implementation that remained focused on the program's purpose.

Policies & Procedures

With expanded structural support in place, the newly formed Task Force and ARL staff undertook the process of reviewing all aspects of the program. This process was not motivated by specific, identified deficits in the program; rather, the intention was to build on the decades of meaningful impact by determining where opportunities to increase inclusion and efficacy existed as well as what aspects of the program should remain unchanged. As the majority of Task Force members were program alums, the process was well informed by the experiences of past Scholars. Additionally, feedback from previous and current Scholars was included throughout decision making processes. ARL staff intentionally sought to create spaces that encouraged team building and openness, as the specific structures and membership of the Task Force were all new.

Positional leadership for the Task Force existed through a chair position as well as staff lead. Working together, the leadership team sought to create a person-centered process that honored and valued the humanity as well as the contributions of the Task Force members while remaining effective and productive. The groups agendas were consistently full of tasks and included a rolling list of parking lot items; still, the chair and staff lead made a concerted effort to ensure that the group was able to develop the rapport and trust necessary to engage in the work that was required by the group. This meant that dissent was invited throughout processes—particularly at key decision points—and disagreements were treated as an opportunity to learn. The Task Force cultivated a culture that welcomed and encouraged

Justice, Equity, Diversity, and Inclusion in Mentorship

dialogue and debate within its deliberations. It was within this context that the group identified numerous opportunities to refine policies and procedures within the Kaleidoscope Program, which included the application and selection process, access to scholarship funds, and interrogating assumptions within program practices.

Application and Selection Process

The application and selection process for the Kaleidoscope program comprised many elements that are also required by similar programs. Applicants were requested to provide an essay describing their interests and goals, a resume or curriculum vitae, transcripts, and letters of recommendation. These materials were then provided to a working group charged with building a cohort roster. While this structure produced the desired result—Scholars selected for the program—the Task Force decided to reenvision these processes by centering the applicant in the overall experience. Any changes would still need to result in a cohort being selected through a process with high rigor and integrity; additionally, the Task Force was mindful of the implications of changes on the experiences of other parties involved in the application and selection process: the Task Force, the working group, and ARL staff.

Application Process Updates

The update process started with the Task Force examining the foundational purpose of the application. The purpose seemed simple: the application was the mechanism by which individuals interested in the Kaleidoscope Program would submit materials to be assessed in order to determine if they would be invited to become a Scholar. When distilled to this core function, the Task Force recognized that it was not the purpose that needed additional interrogation—it was the design. With this clarity on the area in need of attention within the application process, the Task Force continued with a "zero-base" exploration of each aspect of the application. The group explicitly assessed the value that each of the requested application materials could provide to the selection working group. Additionally, they considered the implications of removing each item and the experience of applicants when each item is requested. Finally, they brainstormed alternatives for each item that was currently requested while also seeking to identify gaps in the information that would ultimately be provided to the working group to make their decisions.

In reexamining the design of the process, the Task Force explicitly pondered one specific question: should the application process mirror potential future application processes that Scholars might encounter later in their careers or should the Kaleidoscope Program take a different approach. The Task Force acknowledged that it would be doing a disservice to Scholars if the program failed to provide opportunities for the cohort to learn about and prepare for future career advancement experiences. As such, the program should not pretend that there are not rigorous, challenging, and even problematic application processes that are required for other opportunities; however, the Task Force also recognized that the program could provide education and support to the Scholars related to navigating those systems without using the same approaches in the Kaleidoscope Program's application process. This was another reminder of the importance of and need for systemic change that goes beyond singular decisions made in isolation from one another.

After the Task Force completed their review, ARL made the following changes to the application process of the Kaleidoscope Program:

- the essay was replaced with a series of reflection prompts;

- the transcripts could be official or unofficial versions;
- one of the letters of recommendation could come from any person chosen by the applicant; and
- an expanded yet streamlined online form was created to collect information from applicants.

These changes to the application materials were one part of the overall updates to the application process. The Task Force also updated many of the practices in an effort to provide more support to applicants. These were all done based on a key shift in mentality—the Kaleidoscope Program application process should allow applicants to succeed in presenting themselves with authenticity, confidence, and integrity rather than create undue burden and unnecessary challenges that can intimidate and discourage engagement. To this end, ARL initiated procedural updates to the application process that provided additional support to the applicants. These efforts were guided by three foundational principles: increase transparency, decrease barriers, increase access.

One of the key recommendations to increasing transparency was to provide more information to applicants about the application and selection processes. The group recognized that there is a power disparity inherent in any application process; while this disparity would never be eliminated, this awareness could inform decisions that would help empower and support applicants. As such, ARL decided that it would publicly share the criteria that would be used on the rubric for assessing application materials. Additionally, the ARL website provided more direct recommendations about the content of the letters of recommendation, which directly corresponded to selected criteria from the rubric.

Building on these actions to increase transparency, ARL also hosted a virtual informational session for potential applicants to attend and learn more about the application process and ask questions directly to ARL staff. A separate recorded version of the information session was posted on the website for audiences to review asynchronously. In addition to providing more information to applicants, these efforts were aimed at removing barriers from the application process. Applicants could learn about the process and requirements through different modalities on their own schedules without relying solely on their interpretation of the static information on the website or being required to communicate with ARL staff via email. Moreover, during both the live and recorded versions of the informational session, ARL staff emphasized the intentionality behind the design of the application process. Aligned with the pursuit of increased transparency, this emphasis was also meant to highlight the person-centered approach being taken in this process, especially as it may be less familiar to some applicants when compared to other application designs.

Lastly, the updated Kaleidoscope Program application design made a concerted effort to invite applicants to share their questions and communicate their needs throughout the process. ARL intentionally included and repeated instructions regarding submitting requests for accommodations by applicants. Alone, such action is merely a minimum of what should be expected behavior. ARL attempted to build on this by inviting applicants to go beyond a limited perception of accommodation. ARL was less interested in having people provide proof of their need for accommodations; instead, ARL prioritized opportunities that would enable applicants to present themselves in the most favorable light while still enabling the selection working group to be able to fulfill their responsibilities. This manifested through ARL inviting open communication about applicants' questions, needs, and challenges. This allowed ARL staff to explore tailored, creative solutions based on the individualized circumstances of applicants. Examples of accommodations included adjusting timelines, providing support for applicants interested in clarifying or updating submitted materials, and allowing applications to be fully considered without all application materials. Communication between applicants and ARL was at the core of this process. ARL sought to

Justice, Equity, Diversity, and Inclusion in Mentorship

create multiple avenues for engagement and a consistent message inviting communication that aligned with its commitment to conducting an inclusive process. This required that the changes not only apply to the application but to the selection as well.

Selection Process Updates

The Kaleidoscope Program selection process also underwent numerous changes. The composition of the selection working group already included representation from multiple stakeholder groups, including program alums. The Task Force did not identify a reason to change this aspect of the structure; however, they did seek to improve the experience of the selection working group members. The person-centered approach that informed the changes to the application process was still used to update the selection process; however, at this point, the members of the selection working group were taken into deeper consideration. While it can be challenging to accurately estimate the number of applications that will be received in a program year, service on the selection working group is a significant commitment of time and effort. The Task Force sought to decrease the amount of work required of working group members while still ensuring a productive selection process that valued and respected the efforts of applicants.

The first part of this process was to update the rubric provided to the Task Force. While the ARL website shared the criteria with general descriptions with the call for applications, ARL provided more detailed information to the working group. Informed by feedback from members of previous years' working groups, the updated rubric provided more clarity about how to review and rate applications. To ensure the members of the working group felt prepared for their responsibilities, ARL held an orientation session for the group where they learned about the updates to the application design and reviewed the group's expectations, the rubric, and the overall process. Finally, ARL updated the manner in which working group members were able to access application materials and submit their ratings so that it was much less labor intensive.

In addition to the rubrics detail and clarity, the Task Force and ARL also decided to adjust the overarching, conceptual approach of how application materials were evaluated. In previous years, each application material was given a score. An applicant's final rating was based on the separate scores given to their essay, resume, transcripts, and letters of recommendation. This approach meant that a less than stellar application material could heavily impact the overall rating. As the applicants have little agency related to the letters of recommendation, an unintended consequence of this rating structure was that the work, interest, skills and capacity of individuals other than the applicants (i.e., the recommenders) played a significant role in the ultimate outcome. The by-material approach to ratings also contributed to the limitations of the previous versions of the selection rubric, which lacked clarity about how to operationalize the assessment of applicants' resumes and curricula vitae in a consistent manner.

The updated approach utilized a criteria based rating process. The Task Force identified four criteria that they believed should be the basis for determining which applicants should be invited to participate in the Kaleidoscope Program. These criteria served as the lens through which all application ratings were conducted. Evidence for each criterion could be found in any of the application materials. This structure ensured that letters of recommendation could not solely skew an applicant's rating; additionally, it was the mechanism that allowed ARL to provide more flexible accommodations. If an applicant was unable to provide one item from the list of requested application materials, the selection working group could still review the other materials using the same criteria. This criteria approach also enabled

Justice, Equity, Diversity, and Inclusion in Mentorship

a more efficient review process that lessened the time commitment required from the working group while providing a consistent, evidence-based process.

With the experience of the selection group members addressed, the Task Force also sought to ensure the review and rating process was conducted with fairness and integrity. To this end, ARL decided to redact application materials, including the resumes, curricula vitae, and letters of recommendation, so none of the applicants' personally identifiable information was shared with the working group. While this was a labor intensive process for ARL staff, it allowed the working group members to remain focused on the content of the application materials and decreased the opportunities for bias to impact their ratings. The members of the selection working group shared that receiving redacting information was beneficial for them through the evaluation tools used after the selection process concluded. The evaluation results also confirmed that the rubric used was very helpful in enabling them to carry out their responsibilities in an efficient and effective manner. These changes to the application and selection process provided the foundation and frame for the Scholars experience. Additional policy and procedure changes were also implemented to support the Scholars as they progressed through the two-year program. These changes provided reinforcement to the efforts to increase inclusion and deepen the impact of the Kaleidoscope Program, including its mentoring component.

Scholarship Funds

One additional area of change is the financial support provided through the Kaleidoscope Program. As a scholarship program, there is no financial cost to participate. Scholars are eligible to receive tuition support, funding for professional development opportunities, and full coverage of expenses to participate in a combination of in-person and virtual experiences. While the Task Force was reviewing all aspects of the program, there were no additional funds available to invest into the program. This meant that program costs—and by extension, financial support provided to Scholars—could not be increased. Still, the Task Force identified multiple opportunities to improve the experience of Scholars with the same amount of funding.

The first change that ARL made was to simplify the way the funds were described and categorized. No changes were made to the tuition support; however, there were changes made to the professional development funds. The previous structure of the professional development funds included specific subcategories and amounts that restricted how the funds could be used by Scholars. This resulted in many Scholars not accessing the funds available to them because the limited use did not align with the Scholars' interests, goals, needs, or timing. Instead of keeping these distinct categories, ARL combined all the professional development funds into a single amount per Scholar; each Scholar was empowered to use the funds in whatever manner they wished provided it aligned with the professional development funding guidelines of the program. As these guidelines were now the first line of limitation on the Scholars access to funds, they became the Task Force's next topic for review.

The professional development funding guidelines are meant to ensure that funds are distributed in fiscally responsible manners that align with the purpose of the Kaleidoscope Program as well as the vision and mission of ARL. In pursuing this goal, the guidelines appeared to have a chilling effect on some Scholars' decisions to request funding, particularly if it was not neatly aligned with the opportunities listed as examples. In response, the Task Force again asked the foundational question about the purpose of the funding in the overall program. This discussion resulted in a recognition that the guidelines did not meet their purpose due to them being more restrictive than necessary. Based on the group's recom-

Justice, Equity, Diversity, and Inclusion in Mentorship

mendations, ARL updated the guidelines while still ensuring that the program was operated with solid fiscal stewardship. A broader list of opportunities was written into the document. Additionally, aligned with the emphasis on communication integrated into the application process, ARL actively invited Scholars to articulate their interests, needs, and concerns related to requesting professional development funding. A core metric used in reviewing requests was the question of whether not having the funding would serve as a barrier to participation for the Scholar.

In addition to this shift, ARL implemented another critical update to the process of distributing funds. Rather than require that Scholars pay with their personal funds and wait for reimbursements, ARL began working with Scholars to project expenses and provide funds in advance. This removed numerous financial burdens for the Scholars and enabled them to more actively participate in professional development opportunities. This practice was also expanded to covering expenses for the program's in person events. Travel day expenses related to ground transportation, meals, and incidentals were covered in advance allowing Scholars to focus on the other aspects of traveling, which can be complicated and stressful as a binational program. These changes represent the final theme of program updates as it relates to the assumptions that are embedded in different aspects of its administration and implementation, which directly impact Scholars' experiences.

Interrogating Assumptions

Kaleidoscope Program Scholars must be enrolled in an ALA accredited master's program at the start of their two-year program cycle; they can be at any point in the program—from just starting to their last term. Whether by design or coincidence, many Scholars would lose touch with ARL and the program upon the completion of their degree. With the encouragement of the new program director, the task force began to reconsider aspects of the program that could shift how the program functioned and the impact it could have on participants. As noted earlier, the group reconsidered the program at multiple levels. They confirmed—and updated—the program's purpose to better reflect the contemporary needs, challenges, and opportunities for BIPOC graduate students in the field. Shifting away from the transactional language used to describe the IRDW, the Kaleidoscope Program is now described as a two-year commitment that aims to prepare BIPOC graduate students for purposeful and consequential careers in research libraries and archives through enriched leadership development and community building opportunities. The Task Force also revised many policies and procedures. They established clearer recommendations for the program components and content. All of this was based on the recognition that a successful program could still have opportunities for improvement.

While the Kaleidoscope Program was working well, the group was committed to exploring its unactualized potential. Many of the relatively small changes in the application, selection, and funding aspects of the program had a significant impact on the experiences of the program stakeholders. One Scholar who applied for the program twice before being accepted noted how the updated application process was much easier to understand and navigate than that of the previous year. Numerous Scholars have described positive experiences from participation at professional development opportunities that were previously ineligible for funding. The travel stipends provided to Scholars in advance of events and travel—rather than requiring receipts to be processed for reimbursement—has provided increased access and support for Scholars. One note is that under this new practice of providing funds in advance, current Scholars do not know that the practice is new. Instead, they simply experience the program without a barrier that previously existed. This is an example of how JEDI efforts are often less about the explicit recognition of a job well done or problem solved and more about the creation of systems and environments that meet the needs of its communities. It is also a reminder that the achievement of a goal (e.g., Scholars attending an in-person event) does not mean that there are no problems or opportunities for improvement (e.g., removing barriers and burdens through the disbursement of funds in advance).

Program Components

Over the 20+ years of the Kaleidoscope Program's existence, several offerings, events, and traditions have become signature parts of the program experience. The funding, mentoring, and development of a broad community of support have been present since the beginning of the program in 2000. Other components, such as the ARL Leadership Symposium as well as the research library site visit, would quickly become cornerstones of the Kaleidoscope Program. Still, these components were subjected to the same review as the other parts of the program—and resulted in additional enhancements for the program stakeholders.

Education and Development

Prior to this series of changes, there were limited opportunities for cohorts to connect with one another during their program participation. The signature events offered the key opportunities for these connections; still, as noted earlier, graduation and other factors would often impact Scholars' ability and willingness to participate in these events. The task force responded to this by examining ways to both increase the attractiveness of these offerings while clarifying the expectations of program participation. The group wanted Scholars to access the benefits of the program components; as such, they recommended a series of changes, starting with adding language about the program being a two-year commitment to the ARL website. This was an indication of the intentional design that went into ensuring that the program would be of value to Scholars regardless of where they were in their academic program. Scholars maintained access to their tuition stipends when enrolled in classes; however, even after graduation, Scholars would still have access to the other program benefits including an updated structure of educational and developmental opportunities.

Many of the changes in this area were informed by COVID-19. As in-person events were canceled for multiple years, ARL reconsidered the why and the how of the Kaleidoscope Program's two signature events: the Leadership Symposium and the site visit. The group determined that the in-person aspects were important, but there were opportunities to update how they would occur. ARL member institutions were invited to serve as hosts for the Leadership Symposium, shifting away from the practice of holding the event in conjunction with a larger conference. This provided more opportunities for tailored experiences and other areas of increased flexibility while decreasing operational costs. Additionally, the in-person events were identified as key moments for the development of connections and community within cohorts.

With the establishment of structured opportunities for intra-cohort connections, the task force then considered opportunities for inter-cohort connections. Again, lessons learned during COVID-19 would prove to be useful. One of the adjustments to the program implementation in 2020 was to offer regular (e.g., monthly) virtual calls for Scholars. This provided opportunities for the program participants to connect during a time when many other opportunities for community and connection were not available. Eventually, however, the virtual calls became challenging for many Scholars. While the benefit of con-

Justice, Equity, Diversity, and Inclusion in Mentorship

necting was still present, many Scholars were experiencing fatigue from being called into so many virtual spaces. Additionally, the Scholars had some combination of school, work, family, and other commitments. The Kaleidoscope Program was at risk of becoming a burden to the population it was intended to serve.

The task force decided to reduce the frequency of the meetings while increasing the predictability and structure of the spaces. The group identified eight topics that would be offered on a two-year rotation with two sessions happening every fall and two sessions happening every spring. This meant that over the two years of a cohort's participation in the program, they would be able to experience all eight sessions. The task force also recommended that the sessions be open to both cohorts of active Scholars. This provided opportunities for wider community building while creating more efficient program implementation and operations. Through these informed changes, Scholars have been able to broaden their network of BIPOC colleagues in the field while still having meaningful, in-person connections with the members of their cohort.

Mentoring

Results from a survey of Scholars indicated that most desired mentors who shared social identities around race, ethnicity, and sexual orientation. The benefits of matching BIPOC mentors with BIPOC mentees are numerous. Farrell et al. (2017) posited that early-career BIPOC librarians often face psychological and social challenges that affect career satisfaction. A reciprocal, authentic, and reverse mentoring approach can address real issues that librarians of color face—such as racial microaggressions, impostor phenomenon, tokenism, and burnout.

Mentor Selection Process and Matching

One significant shift made to the mentoring program was the hiring of a consultant to conduct the mentor selection and matching process; in previous years, this was included in the responsibilities of a DEI Visiting Program Officer. The main challenge with this was the high workload that the task required without resulting in a tangible product that could demonstrate the expertise, skills, and contributions of the VPO to other entities—such as the VPO's home institution. By engaging a consultant, ARL was recognizing the value and labor involved in this important process, which had usually been undertaken by women of color. A few months prior to the announcement of the Kaleidoscope Scholars, the consultant reviewed the evaluations from the previous years Scholars and mentors, identified themes, and incorporated relevant feedback into the mentor selection process. After Scholars were accepted into the program, they were asked to fill out a six question "mentor preferences" survey. Survey questions included:

1. Do you have a preference for the current career level of your mentor?
2. Describe what you would most like to get out of the mentor/protégé relationship.
3. What are your professional areas of interest?
4. What skills are you interested in learning or developing?
5. Describe your preferences related to the identities or life experiences of your mentor.
6. Do you have any specific requests for a mentor?

The consultant carefully reviewed the survey responses as Scholars often had specific requests (e.g., a mentor who is Black, non-binary, and with archival and digital humanities experience). The consultant then contacted each Scholar individually; the consultant reviewed their survey responses and Scholars were invited to make additional comments and changes as needed to the data.

Over the next month, the consultant developed a spreadsheet of possible mentors. This was developed from personal knowledge of BIPOC in the profession, lists of past mentors from ARL programs, postings on the listservs for the National Associations of Librarians of Color, and recommendations from past mentors. This list was reviewed for possible matches with Scholars around career goals, skill acquisition, mutual interests, and social identities. When a possible match was identified, the consultant emailed an invitation to serve as a mentor with detailed information on the Kaleidoscope Program, the mentoring component, timeline, and expectations of the mentor. ARL engaged in follow up conversations with mentors, answering additional questions before mentors decided to sign the mentoring agreement. Approximately 25% of invited mentors end up declining due to lack of time to devote to a mentee and the length of the two-year commitment. When this occurred, the consultant went back to the spreadsheet and identified a second (or sometimes third) mentor who would be a strong match with the specific Scholar. After a mentor agreed to serve, ARL facilitated introductions between the mentor and the Scholar, and shared short biographies with each person. Over the course of the two year mentorship program, mentors were expected to meet at least once a month with their Scholar, for approximately one hour via telephone, video conference, or other real-time communication, and to engage in email communication or other forms of asynchronous communication in between meetings.

Mentor Selection Process Updates

ARL made many changes to how Scholars were matched with mentors as part of the Kaleidoscope Program. In the past, geographic location as a criteria had held more relevance in the matching process, as Scholars and mentors were encouraged to meet in person as often as possible. Over the course of the pandemic, geographic location was less important, as both parties became more comfortable with virtual meetings and travel had decreased. Additionally, ARL moved away from recruiting primarily from ARL libraries; this enabled individuals with stellar experience from other academic libraries to be invited to serve as mentors in the program. Furthermore, years of experience and position were given less prioritization. ARL affirmed that stronger mentor matches would be made possible by prioritizing social identities, skills, willingness, and time to engage; additionally, having fewer years in the profession was recognized as a beneficial characteristic, as a mentor 5-7 years out of graduate school can often more easily relate to and offer advice around issues faced my newer professionals. Finally, while tremendous energy was invested into attempts to match a Scholar to a mentor with the social identities as well as the professional area of interest that they requested, it was not alway possible. In these occasions, social identities were given more weight, as a strong mentor can share their network with the Scholar and introduce them to other library professionals who have the skills the Scholar desires to learn.

Mentor Curriculum and Experience

ARL enhanced the support provided to the mentors by hosting quarterly, virtual meetings for mentors throughout both years of their service in the program. While the meeting is scheduled and moderated by ARL, the space is designed to provide a space for the mentors to build community, ask for advice, share their experiences, and create a cohort experience of their own. In these meetings, mentors discuss recent successes and challenges of working with their Scholar. Success stories could include assisting with job search processes and interview preparation after graduation, facilitating introductions to other academic

Justice, Equity, Diversity, and Inclusion in Mentorship

librarians, and advising on how to start a research project. Mentors also used this time to share resources with each other and activities that they did with their Scholar, such as reading and discussing an article, working on a poster presentation, demystifying library associations, conducting mock interviews, and creating a mind map for goal setting.

Mentors regularly expressed their appreciation for the opportunity to be in a space with other BIPOC mentors. In these meetings, the mentors were able to discuss important topics, like navigating primarily white workspaces and dealing with microaggressions, and strategize how to share these lived experiences with Scholars while supporting their own individual journey. Mentors also shared the joy and inspiration they felt working with their Scholar, especially around shared identity. Mentors noted the very real disruptions that the pandemic caused to both themselves and their Scholars. For Scholars, school was disrupted by closures and shifts to online teaching; for mentors, there were many unfilled vacancies at their institutions, causing overwork and burnout. In addition to the quarterly meet-ups, mentors also have the opportunity to engage via email in a group coordinated by ARL; through this channel, they often share scholarship and professional development opportunities and ask for assistance in identifying other professionals with specific skill sets to introduce to their Scholars.

APPLICATION AND CONCLUSION

There are numerous opportunities to apply ideas and strategies detailed in this case study to other environments—both within and outside of formal mentoring programs. Mentoring programs can be well served through a systemic evaluation of the different experiences and processes that are impacting the program's operation as well as the experiences of the different stakeholders. This will often require examining items that are outside the explicit structure of the mentoring program itself. By taking such an approach, individuals responsible for the programs are able to gain a better understanding of the interconnected nature of items that may be assumed to be unrelated. This can be everything from the institutional culture of the organization that hosts the program to the operational procedures and implementation practices of the program and its components.

Another opportunity is to ensure that the program is informed by a team of individuals with different connections to the work. This allows a balance of perspectives and priorities to be considered when making decisions. There is additional potential value in involving individuals that have been previously disconnected from the work or work in a different discipline. When leveraged intentionally, fresh perspectives can prompt critical thinking and challenge assumptions in manners that unlock untapped potential.

Finally, while mentoring programs are often well attuned to the needs and interests of the mentees, increasing attention on the experiences of the mentors can have tremendous benefits for the overall program. Not only are mentors who are well supported better positioned to support their mentees, a positive mentor experience contributes to the sustainability of a mentoring program. By creating an environment where mentors benefit from the experiences they share with the mentees (i.e., reverse mentoring) as well as a separate experience intentionally designed for them, mentors are more likely to continue serving and support the recruitment of others into the program. These environments also help counteract burnout that can come from professional volunteer service. Through these structural approaches, mentoring programs can have broadened, deepened, and sustained impact on multiple communities.

Additionally, these strategies are readily translated to settings outside of mentoring programs. A healthy, critical review of long-standing systems, structures, policies, and practices can often identify opportunities to integrate and advance JEDI in various settings. Frequently, the longer these items have been in place, the less likely they are to have been created with an intentional JEDI orientation. By using processes that seek to redefine structures and center the margins, leaders can effect meaningful, positive change. Again, a community engaged approach will often produce positive outcomes when it is paired with authenticity and vulnerability. Organizations and leaders must be willing to acknowledge areas of tension and limitations when inviting input from stakeholders; at the same time, they should remain open to pursuing paths that may not always be the easiest or most familiar. By balancing the realities of contextual constraints with the commitment to translating JEDI values into action, institutions can build trust with their stakeholders and increase momentum to push towards their aspirational goals.

The second opportunity for general application builds on this idea by lifting up the importance of identifying connections between different components of programs, processes, and experiences. Just as the trust built with community members is directly connected to the efficacy of a JEDI strategic plan, there are many obvious and hidden dependencies when working to create systemic change. Having a great idea is often only as useful as the buy-in and support the idea has with the relevant stakeholders; conversely, having the support of communities will be less helpful without an informed, strategic, and intentional vision for success. This speaks to the important balance of linear leadership and radial leadership. A linear approach focuses on making progress towards a goal or series of goals; a radial approach focuses on ensuring that communities are supported, engaged, and invested in the process. By pairing these approaches, systemic change becomes more accessible and achievable.

Finally, general efforts to advance JEDI can be aided by reviewing the collective impact and implications of individual decisions. This is particularly important when changes are happening or desired across multiple areas. An well-meaning decision made in one area may have unintended consequences when considered with a completely separate, though still well-meaning, decision in another area. Hypothetically, increasing access to a resource for patrons may be a welcomed change; however, this decision could have complicated interactions with a separate decision to increase the flexibility of working schedules and environments for team members. Both decisions could have the support from multiple communities; employees may advocate for increasing access for patrons while patrons are in favor of improving working conditions for employees. Still, if these decisions are made in separate spaces by separate groups, the collective impact may not have been fully considered. Frequently, the interplay of individual decisions may not be as clearly identified as this hypothetical. This could be due to the impact landing on a small number of people or a group that has limited opportunities to have their voices and experiences heard by decision makers. It could be because the organizational culture is one that accepts certain problems as the norm or unfixable. Whatever the cause, committing resources to a proactive review process can result in many positive outcomes.

There are still many areas within the ARL Kaleidoscope Program that need to be addressed. These include further developing the mentor curriculum and experience, building more space in timelines to allow more flexibility in program implementation, and examining opportunities to expand the program benefits to more individuals. As the majority of the events described in the case study occurred in a time frame of less than two years, ARL staff and the program Task Force will continue the process of strengthening the program in the future. ARL is committed to continuing to resource the program in manners that allow for the successful and storied history of the program to be honored while ensuring that the program remains relevant and responsive to the needs of the Scholars it serves. Similarly, while efforts to advance justice, equity, diversity, and inclusion are frequently met with a myriad of challenges, library leaders and organizations have many tools and opportunities to enable systematized examination

Justice, Equity, Diversity, and Inclusion in Mentorship

of structures, policies, and practices to ensure that values and statements are translated into action and impact.

REFERENCES

Allen, T., & Ebay, L. T. (2007). *The Blackwell Handbook of Mentoring: A multiple Perspectives Approach*. Blackwell Publishing., doi:10.1111/b.9781405133739.2007.x

American Indian Library Association. (n.d.). *Membership Committee*. ALA. https://ailanet.org/about/committees/

American Library Association. (2021). *National Survey Finds Libraries Play Expanded Role In Digital Equity, Bridging Gaps In Access To Technology*. ALA. https://www.ala.org/news/press-releases/2021/08/national-survey-finds-libraries-play-expanded-role-digital-equity-bridgi
ng

American Library Association. (n.d.) *Mentoring opportunities*. ALA. https://www.ala.org/educationcareers/mentoring-opportunities

Asian Pacific American Librarians Association. (n.d.). *Mentoring program*. APALA. https://www.apalaweb.org/about/committees/standing-committees/mentoring-committee/mentoring-program/

Black Caucus American Library Association. (2021, November 10). *Professional Development Committee*. BCALA. https://www.bcala.org/committees

Bosch, E. K., Ramachandran, H., Luévano, S., & Wakiji, E. (2010). The Resource Team Model: An Innovative Mentoring Program for Academic Librarians. *New Review of Academic Librarianship*, *16*(1), 57–74. doi:10.1080/13614530903584305

Chamberlain, A. W., Dunlap, J., & Russell, P. G. (2021, July). *Moving from words to action: The Influence Of Racial Justice Statements On Campus Equity Efforts*. National Association of Student Personnel Administrators (NASPA): Student Affair Administrators in Higher Education. https://www.naspa.org/report/moving-from-words-to-action-the-influence-of-racial-justice-statements-on-campus-equity-eff
orts

Deards, K. D., & Springs, G. R. (Eds.). (2014). *Succession Planning and Implementation in Libraries: Practices and Resources*. IGI Global. doi:10.4018/978-1-4666-5812-7

Desimone, L. M., Hochberg, E. D., Porter, A. C., Polikoff, M. S., Schwartz, R., & Johnson, L. J. (2014). Formal and informal mentoring: Complementary, compensatory, or consistent? *Journal of Teacher Education*, *65*(2), 88–110. doi:10.1177/0022487113511643

Farmer, D., Stockham, M., & Trussell, A. (2009). Revitalizing a Mentoring Program for Academic Librarians. *College & Research Libraries*, *70*(1), 8–25. doi:10.5860/0700008

Farrell, B., Alabi, J., Whaley, P., & Jenda, C. (2017). Addressing Psychosocial Factors with Library Mentoring. *portal. Portal (Baltimore, Md.)*, *17*(1), 51–69. doi:10.1353/pla.2017.0004

Frederick, J. K., & Wolff-Eisenberg, C. (2020). Ithaka S+R U.S. Library Survey 2019. *Ithaka SR*. https://sr.ithaka.org/publications/ithaka-sr-us-library-survey-2019/

Frederick, J. K., & Wolff-Eisenberg, C. (2021, March 17). National Movements for Racial Justice and Academic Library Leadership: Results from the Ithaka S+R US Library Survey 2020. *Ithaka SR*. doi:10.18665/sr.314931

Gandhi, S. (2019). How Reverse Mentoring Can Lead to More Equitable Workplaces. *Stanford Social Innovation Review*. doi:10.48558/NQJ8-H958

Golian-Lui, L. M. (2003). Fostering Librarian Leadership Through Mentoring. *Adult Learning*, *14*(1), 26–28. doi:10.1177/104515950301400107

Hansman, C. A. (2002). Diversity and Power in Mentoring Relationships. In C. A. Hansman (Ed.), *Critical Perspectives on Mentoring: Trends and Issues* (pp. 39–48). Center on Education and Training for Employment, Center Publications.

Hussey, L. K., & Campbell-Meier, J. (2017). Is There a Mentoring Culture Within the LIS Profession? *Journal of Library Administration*, *57*(5), 500–516. doi:10.1080/01930826.2017.1326723

James, J. M., Rayner, A., & Bruno, J. (2015). Are You My Mentor? New Perspectives and Research on Informal Mentorship. *Journal of Academic Librarianship*, *41*(5), 532–539. https://doi.org/10.1016/j.acalib.2015.07.009. doi:10.1016/j.acalib.2015.07.009

Jaschik, S., & Lederman, D. (2021). *Survey of College and University Presidents*. Inside Higher Education.

Lee, M. (2009). Growing librarians: Mentorship In An Academic Library. *Library Leadership & Management*, *23*(1), 31–37.

Lee, Y. (2020, January 6). Mentorship as a tool for growth, inclusion, and equity. *Idealist*. https://www.idealist.org/en/careers/mentorship-diversity-inclusion

Malecki, A. L., & Bonanni, M. (2020). Mentorship programs in academic libraries. *Public Services Quarterly*, *16*(1), 35–40. doi:10.1080/15228959.2019.1701613

Neyer, L., & Yelinek, K. (2011). Beyond Boomer meets NextGen: Examining mentoring practices among Pennsylvania academic librarians. *Journal of Academic Librarianship*, *37*(3), 215–221. doi:10.1016/j.acalib.2011.02.013

CALA. (n.d.) *CALA Committees*. CALA. https://cala-web.org/about/committee/2022-2023

REFORMA. (n.d.). *Mentoring Program*. Reforma. https://www.reforma.org/content.asp?contentid=34

Robbeloth, H., Eng, A., & Weise, S. (2013). Disconnect between literature and libraries: The availability of mentoring programs for academic librarians. *Endnotes*, *4*(1), 1–19.

Schonfeld, R. C., & Sweeney, L. (2017, August 30). Inclusion, Diversity, and Equity: Members of the Association of Research Libraries: Employee Demographics and Director Perspectives. *Ithaka S+R.* doi:10.18665/sr.304524

Springs, G. R. (2014). Mentoring for Retention, Promotion, and Advancement: An Examination of Mentoring Programs at ARL Institutions. In K. Deards & G. Springs (Eds.), *Succession Planning and Implementation in Libraries: Practices and Resources* (pp. 45–63). IGI Global., doi:10.4018/978-1-4666-5812-7.ch003

Wilson, M. C., Gaunt, M. I., & Tehrani, F. (2009). Mentoring Programs In U.S. Academic Libraries – A Literature Review. In V. Jana, L. Liz, & W. Graham (Eds.), *Strategies for Regenerating the Library and Information Profession* (pp. 84-95). K. G. Saur. https://doi.org/doi:10.1515/9783598441776.2. 84

Chapter 3
Co-Creating the Beginnings of a Culture of Belonging at the Georgia Tech Library:
Supervisors, Leaders, and a Proposed Model Forward

John Mack Freeman
https://orcid.org/0000-0001-9439-9128
Georgia Institute of Technology, USA

Leslie N. Sharp
https://orcid.org/0000-0003-1866-4027
Georgia Institute of Technology, USA

ABSTRACT

In 2019, the Georgia Tech Library was coming out of a painful period of transition where lofty change initiatives had created significant toxicity in the culture. New leadership was brought in to rectify the situation. Through a series of efforts that translated institutional efforts, departmental actions, and team-based support, the Georgia Tech Library turned a corner and started working towards creating a culture of belonging. In this participatory case study, the authors proposed a nested model of cultural support in which the underpinnings of individual support flow from the team, the department, and the institution. Each part has a role to play in working to create a culture of belonging, understanding that the work is never complete, and that while the example of the Georgia Tech Library has made progress, there is still much work to be done.

DOI: 10.4018/978-1-6684-7255-2.ch003

Copyright © 2023, IGI Global. Copying or distributing in print or electronic forms without written permission of IGI Global is prohibited.

Co-Creating the Start of a Culture of Belonging at the Georgia Tech Library

INTRODUCTION

A culture of belonging is one in which people are appreciated for what they bring to a group, genuine relationships are made, and the differences between people are acknowledged and celebrated as strengths (Efron, 2022). Culture does not occur in a vacuum; instead, it is discursively created through the interactions of people inside of an institution (Driskill & Brenton, 2019). As such, efforts to create a culture that centers belonging as a key aspect must inherently cope with the extant circumstances that an organization finds itself in. It must be able to assess where it is, build a framework for future action, and then put that action of care into practice.

In 2020 under the leadership of President Ángel Cabrera, The Georgia Institute of Technology(Georgia Tech or Tech) completed its ten-year strategic plan (Georgia Institute of Technology, 2020).[1] Building a culture of belonging in the Library is nested within Georgia Tech's mission, vision, values, and focus areas as the Library collectively repairs fissures in its communities, cares for its people, and prepares for interconnected futures. These priorities are framed by the Institute's strategic plan and the focus areas of expanding access, cultivating well-being, and leading by example and underscored with the values of excellence, diversity, collaboration, and nurturing. Leadership teams at the Institute and Library levels demonstrate how a focused, mission-driven, inclusive commitment to diversity can co-create a culture of belonging. On the library leader level, work can be done on a structural basis to change the overall direction of the library. Actions like Institute strategic plan alignments and initiatives, support of DEI-oriented councils, unit-wide policies, and promotion of institution goals are all actions that must be taken to move the organization. As important as these efforts are, their wide-ranging, Library-wide natures makes them resource-intensive to develop and implement, and they often occur over timelines that last months or years. This work began at the GT Library in 2019 when Leslie Sharp became the interim CEO (and subsequently Dean of Libraries in 2020), boosted by Tech's new leadership and strategic plan implementation, and continues with the hiring of a new leadership team that includes associate deans, heads of departments, and other people dedicated to redressing the past and transforming the culture. Sharp and the rest of the Library leadership work to ensure that all their work is driven by the Institute's mission, vision, and values.

This work is encapsulated in a nesting model (modified from Kennedy's [2021] model) for a culture of belonging in which the work of the supervisor for a team is situated within the work of the departmental leader which is itself situated within the work of the institution. At each level of this work, each group has different activities that they are best suited to achieve. The working theory of our approach to creating a culture of belonging is that it is embodied in leadership at all levels of an organization. As such, within academic library structures, the responsibility for developing this culture and transformation exists at the institution, library, and individual team levels or to quote Kennedy and Jain-Link, "all hands on deck: senior leaders, managers, and employees at every level of the company"(Kennedy & Jain-Link, 2021). Further, moments of change—both within and external to an organization —provide an in-built time for transition that can be leveraged to seek cultural change for the good of individuals and the library more broadly.

This case study provides a sample of this framework in action and will potentially offer others in similar situations a toolkit for emboldening their own cultures of belonging. Because of the context of this framework, the ability of frontline and non-supervisory workers (while important) is not considered within this chapter.

Related Literature

Belonging as a term is often wrapped up with related concepts of inclusion and authenticity (Jansen et al., 2014; Mor Barak, 2019; Shore et al., 2011). Belonging, in the sense of this chapter, refers to a state in which people co-create the environment based on a combination of their individual needs, their unique contributions to the group, and their genuine connections with others in the organization. It presupposes that traditional, top-down structures will inherently not work for everyone. According to self-determination theory, belonging (along with competence, autonomy, and purpose) are core parts of individual motivation that are inherent to the success of human beings (Deci & Ryan, 2012).

Culture affects both individuals and groups, but the culture of an organization can sublimate the expression of individuals through cultural pressure (Whorton & Worthley, 1981). As such, a focus on cultures of belonging can be seen as a response to the overwhelming power that culture can have on individuals to hide their differences for the sake of conformity. The psychology of belonging allows for differences to not be hidden; instead, differences can be used as a way of creating something more (Witwer, 2021). Cohesion has previously been the goal of "belonging"-style efforts by seeking to minimize the differences between individuals; this instead leads to cultural sublimation of vital aspects of people's lives, alienating them from the broader working group (Burrell & Rahim, 2018). The paradox of belonging, though, is that it is easiest to do among people who are alike; most workplaces, though, are filled with people who are different from one another. Thus, the main issue of workplace belonging is ensuring that those from a marginalized background (within the context of an organization) can still be made to feel that they belong (Kennedy & Jain-Link, 2021).

This feeling of belonging can have both positive personal effects and effects on group performance, providing a multifaceted reasoning for pursuing this work (Ferdman et al., 2010). Elaina Norlin in *The Six-Step Guide to Library Worker Engagement* explains,

Engaged employees feel that their unique talents, skills, and abilities are valued and respected within the organization and that their work makes a difference. An engaged workforce propels creativity, innovation, and a healthier work culture. Organizations that cultivate employee engagement not only perform well, but in many cases outperform their competitors (Norlin, 2021, p. viii).

The work of creating a culture of belonging is not something that can be left until all the other work has been accomplished; it is a key part of employee engagement and can be a driver of organizational growth and durability. On the flip side, toxic work environments can drive much higher turnover for organizations resulting in increased workplace turmoil, decreased service delivery capabilities, loss of firm-specific knowledge, destabilization of internal networks, separation costs, severance pay, replacement costs, and related costs of hiring, screening, and training new employees (An, 2019, pp. 448-449; Pitts et al., 2011, p. 751). Years of ongoing changes have increased employee cynicism and decreased workplace satisfaction, causing increased turnover intent due to the perception that the psychological contract between the employee and the organization has been breached (Boon et al., 2021; Stanley et al., 2005). This effect however can be moderated by employee perception of change: if the change for the organization is perceived to be a positive one, this can have a negative effect on an employee's turnover intent (Boon et al., 2021). Turnover may increase during periods of leadership transition that creates an ideological mismatch between career employees and temporal political leadership. This is particularly true during the early days of the new leadership or if the new leadership is particularly ideological opposed

Co-Creating the Start of a Culture of Belonging at the Georgia Tech Library

to the current working practice of the agency (Bolton et al., 2021). While mitigating turnover is not the only reason to seek a culture of belonging, it is one aspect that provides a direct business case towards pursuing this important work. In summary, belonging supports engagement which creates a sense of psychological safety among employees that reduces attrition and fosters innovation (Edmondson, 2019, pp. 41–42).Although culture is a deeply rooted part of organizations, it is not static; it can be changed through iterative practice that introduces new standards of what is normal in a place (Ayala et al., 2021). Leaders have a strong role to play in the changing of organizations and the creation of cultures of belonging due to their organizational influence and power (Ashikali et al., 2021; Kennedy, 2020; Kennedy & Jain-Link, 2021; Schein, 2017; Witwer, 2021). The role of leaders can mediate conflict, create norms of behavior, and provide guidelines of appropriate conduct; this can further be reflected through the work of direct supervisors. Conversely, toxic leadership can destroy trust and morale, negatively impact employee's physical and psychological health, destroy interpersonal relationships, and create cultures of fear (Ortega, 2017). These poor leadership practices create cultures of disconnection between colleagues and between individuals and the work they are doing; as such, it is an easy leap to see how toxic leadership can destroy a culture of belonging.

Previous research has provided different models for approaching cultures of belonging. Kennedy (2020) proposes a model that has a role for the organization, leader, manager, and peers in co-creating a culture of belonging, particularly through the context of interpersonal praise, transparency about values, credit giving, communication, and gratitude. Witwer (2021) posits that belonging is the intersection of diversity, inclusion, and equity but not necessarily an endpoint to the concerns of the related veins. BetterUp (2021) creates a model of belonging focused on empowerment, mentoring, learning multiple perspectives, and encouraging people to become allies. Still others place inclusion/belonging at the intersection of values-driven culture, systems, individual cultural competence, and emotional intelligence (Winters, 2013). There is also a push for more proactive rather than reactive approaches to DEIB (Mor Barak, 2019). Through these models, common communication themes and involvement of those with formal authority consistently arise. People cannot create a culture of belonging by themselves; instead, those with the power over aspects of the culture must create the environment in which people can thrive; as such the authors used Kennedy's (2020) model as the basis for their own adapted nesting model of creating cultures of belonging in academic libraries.

BACKGROUND

In March 2019, the Provost at Georgia Tech asked Leslie Sharp, the then associate vice provost for graduate education and faculty development, to step into the role of interim chief executive officer of the Tech Library. This change allowed the previous dean to retire and the Institute to address some longstanding issues within the Library. Sharp was directed to get the Library ready for the next dean and to be present (in both the sense of being engaged and physically onsite) and available. In her first meeting with the Library employees, Sharp said:

"My personal goal is for the Library to be the heart of Georgia Tech's scholarly community; however, to achieve this the library must be a place that fosters community and where people want to come. This includes the people who work at the library" (Georgia Tech Library All Staff Meeting, meeting notes, March 6, 2019)

Co-Creating the Start of a Culture of Belonging at the Georgia Tech Library

It was at that meeting that someone asked her if she "liked" staff[2]. Thus began a process of discovery into the Library's culture and work environment. The results of this inquiry would begin a process for how together the staff, faculty, management, and administration could build a culture where people feel not only that they are "liked," but also that they are valued, welcomed, and encouraged to behave authentically.

The tension felt by staff and faculty was evident from this first meeting. Both faculty and staff spoke about the perceived hierarchy with staff expressing an overall sentiment of feeling left out of conversations around the numerous changes that had occurred in the Library over the preceding years. Leadership was broadly seen as being out of touch, with Library leaders not knowing the names of Library employees and front-line employees rarely seeing or interacting with Library leadership. A reorganization of the Library that eliminated and consolidated staff-heavy departments underscored this isolation. The previous administration had terminated people who had worked in Interlibrary Loan (ILL), reserves, technical services, and cataloging and told them to reapply for positions with new titles and lower pay grades in a new department. The mistaken premise behind this was that the work they did was all similar and unspecialized. In addition, this group was moved off campus to the Library Records Center (LRC) several miles away. The new department housed there was told that the newly renovated buildings would not have room for them and that the LRC was to be their new permanent home. Their labor was devalued, and as such, the people in the department either left or carried deep wounds from their forced exile and demotion in the Library.

Back on campus, the reference and access services units were combined into a single "Public Services" department, and their titles were changed to Information Associate I or II. Their duties were then standardized with a focus on roving reference (constantly walking around the buildings seeking people who needed help). They were further barred from participating in any processing or fulfilment work as that was no longer part of the mandate of their department. That work was transferred to a new subdepartment of Facilities called Logistics.

During this period, the vast bulk of the racial diversity of the Tech Library was in staff departments. As such, the devaluing of staff labor was ipso facto a devaluing of the labor of marginalized people. A month after Sharp joined the Library as CEO, the only African American librarian retired. Sharp was shocked to learn how abysmal the faculty diversity was within the Library; this was especially jarring given that the Library is located in Atlanta, one of the most diverse cities in the country and a center of Black history and culture. While improved, diversity was and remains an ongoing concern for the Library faculty, but in the short-term, the staff had issues that needed to be addressed including lack of equity in salaries and treatment, unclear career paths, and few opportunities to engage with Library administration.

Also leading up to Sharp's appointment, the overall size of the Library's employee numbers declined dramatically during a period when Georgia Tech's enrollment was rapidly increasing at both the graduate and undergraduate levels. This decline was further exacerbated from employees leaving due to dissatisfaction and opposition to the ongoing changes in personnel and organization of the Library, elimination of longtime employee security in favor of contract security, hiring freezes, and a strategic choice to increase pay for faculty at the expense of adding new positions. These changes to operations were traumatic for many.

Coupled with a major renovation of the llibrarybuildings, these changes were a transformation initiative known as "LibraryNext[3]." While the vision of a LibraryNext was a positive, forward-looking research library of the future, the impact was bumpy and poorly received by most members of the Library and Tech community. In particular, the removal of the physical collection to the Library Service Center—an off-campus, high-density storage facility shared with Emory University—coupled with the $80 million dollar renovation of the two main library buildings displaced people and services for several years (Figure 1). This constant maelstrom of change, disregard for continuity, and continuous reimagining of core functions of a library created stress and uncertainty which undermined employee engagement and satisfaction. Leadership at that time mistook the silence and fear of the Library's employees for quiet approval of the Library's direction in what would prove to be a costly cultural mistake (Murray-Rust, 2021).

Figure 1. Crosland Tower at the Georgia Tech Library. Part of the two building, 250,000 square foot renovation concluding in Summer 2020 as part of LibraryNext. Photo courtesy of Georgia Tech.

To summarize, the library needed to replace key leadership positions, increase the diversity of management and faculty, and improve the overall culture of the Library so that it was a place where everyone felt valued, welcomed, and had the opportunity to thrive. Many extant employees had wounds from previous poor treatment, so changing the culture would have to begin by creating a better structure for everyone to exist within. As it stood in 2019, the Georgia Tech Library had a culture that few would say they belonged in and even fewer would say that they wanted to belong to.

Co-Creating a Culture of Belonging

Library Administration

The first step in reforming the culture of the library came from the Library administration. There was an initial focus on communications, devolving power, and creating more equitable and transparent structures for internal Library practices.

Sharp approached her new role by getting to know the people. Communication was key. Sharp created an anonymous survey where people could give feedback, raise issues, provide ideas, or positively recognize their colleagues with a hats off. This information was taken under regular consideration while also serving as a pressure release valve for frustrated employees. Sharp implemented weekly conversations for people to drop by and chat without an agenda. This provided an opportunity for Sharp as a new leader to meet the employees while allowing them an informal way to get to know her. Leadership also attempted to speak with one voice, holding all-employee meetings on ethical culture and encouraging transparency and psychological safety in meetings. Further, the Library arranged training in suicide prevention, active shooter, defensive driving, Safe Space (LGBTQIA+), and more to bring people together to develop as a unit.

Overhauling leadership was also a priority in addressing the ongoing cultural issues at the Library. Sharp initiated 360-degree administrative review process on the two long-term associate deans; one associate dean chose to retire instead. The Library also hosted skip-level meetings and a separate meeting for first-level managers without members of the leadership present so that everyone had a chance to discuss issues without fear of retaliation. Previous leadership had also taken too large a role in the overall control of the Library and tried to limit interactions, so authority for some matters was devolved back to the teams and employee base in general.

Some items were more systemic in nature. Sharp and the new leadership worked to increase the budget for travel, training, and professional development for both faculty and staff. For the first time, staff would have dedicated funding for professional development. Unit-level managers were empowered to approve financial decisions, to have more decision-making authority, and to grow professionally. While maintaining clear communication, the expectation became that those with expertise would be the ones driving decision making within their area of expertise. The vitality of staff in the Library was further demonstrated by a new policy that all search committees and all portfolio projects[4] must include both staff and faculty (Spring 2019) and that all faculty leadership positions would be filled utilizing competitive search processes.[5]

These actions were a good first step. However, the past perceptions of favoritism, disrespect, poor treatment of staff, misogyny, discrimination, the abundance of seemingly senseless rules, mistrust of senior leadership, poor communication of decisions (and lack of decision making), no succession planning, and a feeling that the leadership did not care were common themes that people continued to refer-

Co-Creating the Start of a Culture of Belonging at the Georgia Tech Library

ence. It was apparent that no single person, action, or change had poisoned the well; as such, no single solution was likely to solve all of the issues either.

The past must be reckoned with. As James Joyce aptly put, "History is a nightmare from which I'm trying to awake" (1922, p. 22). However, the past will always have its toxicity unless healing is allowed to occur. Because of this, the Library created a portfolio project to analyze the Library Records Center and the people and work who had been moved off campus to determine a course of action. The project team made recommendations that included bringing the department back to campus, reevaluating their positions and job titles, and reorganizing their department so that they reported through a librarian associate dean rather than facilities. The dean followed the recommendations. Library leadership worked with human resources to realign salaries and titles based on skills and experience while simultaneously creating higher level job categories with clearly defined paths for promotion and growth that reflected the actual work of the people doing those jobs. This reevaluation was successful, and a similar reclassification of the Public Services ddepartment followed shortly thereafter.

To begin to address the DEI-related concerns, Sharp re-hired Estella Richardson as Librarian Emerita to lead a diversity, equity, and inclusion (DEI) working group and serve as the Diversity Advocate. The DEI group began their work in January 2020 and submitted a report that included recommendations, including creating a DEI Council with elected members, revising search and hiring processes to reflect best practices, analyzing collections for inclusivity and deficiencies in representation, and developing a Librarian Residency program through the Association of College and Research Libraries (which had its first cohort in 2023).

The above actions moved the Library forward; however, there were still past grievances that needed to be addressed, key positions to be filled, and a continued focus on creating a positive culture while fulfilling the promise of the LibraryNext. In the midst of addressing the issues within the Library, finishing the second building renovation, and searching for a new dean, the COVID-19 global pandemic hit. Like the rest of the world, the Georgia Tech Library went home to work

The transition as a library to remote was relatively seamless as 96% of circulation pre-pandemic had been electronic; however, the employees were now separated. At the beginning of the pandemic, the manager group met three times a week and all employees met twice a week. This meeting schedule decreased over time as things settled. The Library currently has a set time for the all-employee meeting once a week, department heads bi-weekly, and senior leadership weekly. Sharp also shifted her once a week in-person open meetings to virtual. This practice continued even after work resumed on-campus. This meeting cadence provides opportunities for employees to engage with colleagues, stay informed, and bring up issues. The all-hands meetings are virtual and recorded. The attendance has decreased over time, but generally over half of the employees attend any given meeting, and others can view the recording later.

With new and diverse people in key leadership positions, the Tech Library continues to have open and frank conversations about finances, decision-making, and its culture. Communication from leadership is only part of the remediation journey. To build cultures of belonging, the talk must be supported by actions at all levels that directly impact individuals' daily lives.

Direct Supervisors

In addition to the work on creating a culture of belonging conducted by library heads, direct managers and supervisors have a key role to play in creating a culture of belonging. For the direct manager, their role in the development of a culture of belonging exists more in daily work and interpersonal interactions. As the Google Re:Work project defines them, a team is "highly interdependent" in that they require each other to accomplish work (Google Re:work Project, 2018). Their effectiveness is thus determined by a combination of psychological safety, dependability, structure, and clarity, meaning, and impact (Google Re:work Project, 2018). While these traits are important at the level of the entire Library, they generally cannot be embodied at the organizational level. Rather, they are the creation of the daily experience and interactions that happen between a team. For this example, the researchers look at the Public Services department at the Georgia Tech Library as a prototype of how a team can use the scaffolding created by the wider institution as a platform for building a team-based culture of belonging.

The Public Services department of the Tech Library is a 21 person department responsible for all aspects of access services and equipment lending at the Tech Library on a 24/7 basis. All members of the department report directly to the Head of Public Services Librarian. In the mid-2010s, the entire Library had undergone a large amount of change, resulting in the Public Services department experiencing major workflow shifts. Among these changes included the removal of the circulation desk, the elimination of certain processing functions to a new Logistics department, the transfer of course reserves to Technical Services, the closing of the Architecture Library and reassignment of former staff at that location to the department, and the introduction of a In addition, the department was without a manager from June 2019 to July 2021 due to a hiring freeze after the departure of the previous manager.

During that interim period, supervisory responsibility was formally held by the associate dean over the department and informally boosted by long-time staff members in the department who others turned to for guidance. This period without a department head coincided with a period defined by upheaval: COVID restrictions and closures, the removal of the roving model, the reintroduction of the information desk, a complete turnover of Library leadership, and many related process, procedure, and policy changes. Through all of this, the department performed admirably with numerous staff members winning awards for their contributions to services during the pandemic.

This is the context in which Head of Public Services Librarian John Mack Freeman entered the department in July 2021. The team had numerous assets going for it that contributed to the overall effectiveness of the team: the team had long tenured members and virtually no turnover, employees were generally well-compensated for their labor in comparison to the geographic market, and the department was well-regarded by both leadership and their colleagues. Further, as previously mentioned, the Library had undertaken numerous mindful and deliberate structural actions to address workplace culture issues. However, the team did have genuine issues that stood in the way of creating a true team with a culture of belonging. The 24/7 nature of services meant that the team rarely came together as a full group; further, the varied schedules presented a communications challenge. A long legacy of change had left some jaded and defensive, and there was a lack of clarity about what the future held for the department and the Library. (Figure 2).

Figure 2. A typical mid-afternoon in one of the Georgia Tech Library reading rooms (Georgia Institute of Technology)

Student enrollment has more than doubled (from 21,472 to 45,293) in ten years.

Positive supervisor interactions, characterized by perceived professional respect, support, and loyalty, can have a minimizing effect on turnover intent and increasing the overall quality of the workplace environment (Harris et al., 2008). Conversely, supervisor incivility is directly correlated with higher turnover intention and the cultural disruption that goes with that (Ghosh et al., 2013). Freeman approached the issue creating a culture of belonging on the team-level by creating a leadership model predicated on "giving a damn:" showing up, speaking up, promoting information transparency, recruiting broadly, acting authentically, and encouraging team members to be who they are. While these are values that can be simply and quickly espoused, creating an environment in which they are embodied is part of the day-to-day ongoing work of the group to build the culture that they want to work in.

Showing Up

A primary way to demonstrate that people matter and to create a culture of belonging is to show up for them. Making the team members a priority is a straightforward way to demonstrate that people are appreciated for that they can bring to the group and that the supervisor has an interest in building genuine relationships. A culture of belonging is not something that can be implemented; it is something that grows over time. One of the primary ways of feeding it is by literally showing up: putting in the time with the team and individuals to ensure that they are both actually heard and that they feel heard.

As a standard practice, Freeman holds one-on-one meetings with all 21 team members monthly. Because the team is 24/7, though, every member does not have hours that intersect with a standard workday. Due to this, Freeman shifts his schedule throughout the month in order to be able to meet face-to-face with all employees. For some of them, this is one of the few times during the month when they have direct interactions with their supervisor. Do these meetings have to occur in-person? Of course not. In a post-COVID world, teleconferencing would easily allow for these meetings to happen online. But there is something about physical presence and an acknowledgment that seeing someone in-person is worth the effort that aids in creating a feeling of value in the relationship.

This accessibility even extends to further leadership levels. Leaders, including Freeman and Sharp, stop by the desk, inquire after people, and are knowledgeable about the work of individual staffers. This is the step beyond an open-door policy that still leaves the onus of contact and relationship building on the employee. Instead of being walled off, supervisors and those in authority are not only accessible; they want people to actually use that access. When power is not correlated with access, it gives everyone the opportunity for them to have their opinions acknowledged and respected.

Speaking Up

Speaking up contributes to a culture of belonging as it shows individuals that they are regarded as individuals. Sometimes this takes this form of promoting the team and its interests: speaking up in meetings, advocating for needs, and promoting the successes of the department. But sometimes speaking up happens on the level of the individual team member. Direct supervisors can sponsor individuals for opportunities and provide chances for growth while simultaneously shining a light on achievements and labor that may traditionally go unacknowledged. Supervisors can also leverage their power and political acumen to help employees cut through red tape to solve individual problems.

For example, a member of the Public Services team was pursuing an advanced degree and discovered that they would need to take two months off one summer to pursue an internship that was standard for their field. They mentioned the issue, and Freeman took the concern to leaders in the Library and Human Resources to ascertain if this sort of leave were possible (it was) and how it would function for everyone involved. Speaking up is a fundamental tool to help people navigate the bureaucracy of large institutions. Furthermore, the supervisor is seen as a cheerleader and member of the team; thus, the team is stronger and more unified. These efforts can also be partnered with more formalized efforts to encourage culture of open communication around issues that can work to bring to light issues of bias and exclusion (Knapp et al., 2012).

Promoting Information Transparency

One important way that Freeman worked to create a culture of belonging was to ensure an equal information footing for all members of the department. On a 24/7 team, those on day shift were more likely to be aware about what was going on more broadly because of their increased exposure to their supervisor, colleagues, and leadership. Freeman instituted a practice of documenting notes in every team and departmental meeting he attended and sending them to Public Services as soon as the meeting was over (eventually archiving them in a shared drive). This allowed for all team members to have real-time access to information that affected them. While this may seem like a small standard practice, this was the single most important thing that Freeman did in the first year of his tenure, and he continued to receive positive comments about this activity for months after it was instituted.

In addition to pushing information out, Freeman adopted an attitude of transparency around inquiries. If a situation was not privileged in some way (specifically notated as private or protected under law [e.g., personnel or health matters]), Freeman readily shared information with the team. These answers would typically be shared with the team under the assumption that if one person asked about it, multiple people were probably curious. Oftentimes these inquiries centered on the reasons behind why certain actions were undertaken; the added piece of knowing the purpose made the decisions more real while also demonstrating that the team was valued enough to be included in the reasoning. In the context of the public university, there are few true secrets; any document could be the subject to a Georgia Open Records request. As such, it does not make any sense to keep team members in the dark by limiting their access to information, which creates anxiety and undermines their autonomy and competence.

Recruiting Broadly

A culture of belonging is not served well by a hegemonic culture. Ironically, when trying to create a culture where everyone feels like they have a place, the more diverse the team is, the better the future outcomes can be. It proves the point to people that they do not have to look like or be any one way to fit in. It is a source of pride and strength when teams bring a diversity of backgrounds, experiences, and viewpoints to the table. But the building of that diversity happens from the beginning: recruiting and hiring people. The Georgia Tech Library is actively working on ways to ensure that hiring is equitable and that people from a variety of backgrounds are considered. Whether it is alternative degrees or non-library experience, the pool of what is considered relevant to a job can have a broad application. In the case of Public Services, library skills are good to have out of the gate; alternatively, strong experience working in customer service or education may serve someone just as well.

But recruitment should not only happen external to an organization. As new positions open within the Library, library supervisors should work with interested employees to prepare them for pursuing the next step. Belonging over time means people will need to feel acknowledged for their labor and growth as professionals. At the Tech Library, Public Services has been running a training opportunity called Public Services Partners where other departments partner with a Public Services Associate who wants to learn about their department. This successful program collaborates with at least ten different areas of the Library, creating a high level of support for the associates while also serving as an ongoing real-time documentation of their value to the organization. Through this, people have sharpened their professional skills and pursued specialized certifications, making them contributors to the success of the Library in a broad way while simultaneously building their personal portfolio for future opportunities. Belonging is not static, so caring about what people can do today as well as what they can do tomorrow is a key piece in creating an environment where people feel like there is a place for them and they belong. When a supervisor can align the passion of an individual with what they are good at and what the organization needs, a sweet spot is created that leads to both employee engagement and institutional effectiveness (Figure 3).

Figure 3. Benefits of employee cross-training for different parts of the library

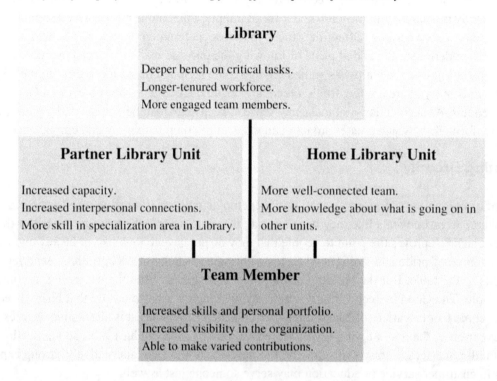

This figure shows the numerous benefits that the library, home unit, partner unit, and team member can experience from formalized cross-training experiences, contributing to an overall positive environment of growth.

Acting Authentically

As RuPaul wisely said, "Know who you are and deliver it at all times" (RuPaul [@rupaul], 2014). In the team context of creating a culture of belonging, the supervisor must know what they are bringing to the table and the goals they are striving for. If the goal is truly to build meaningful relationships and appreciation for the differences that people have, a supervisor cannot wall off who they are as a person. They, instead, must be the real person that they are. And that means electing to make appropriate disclosures about their personal life, identity, and differences. When someone reveals something about themselves first, it humanizes them, but it also demonstrates to others that they are willing to take the first step in building a relationship about something beyond water cooler conversation.

When Freeman began working with Public Services, he became a somewhat open book about liking to bake and hating to camp, about not caring about sports, and having strong opinions about horror films. But also, he revealed his age, his identity as a queer married man, and his atheistic beliefs. He also revealed industry-specific details about his past including never having held a job for longer than four years due to moving for new opportunities, ambivalent feelings about certain professional organizations, and ongoing struggles with pursuing his doctoral degree. Some of these revelations are minor; some go to the core of who a person is. But if the team is meant to feel comfortable disclosing things about themselves, the leader should go first.

Co-Creating the Start of a Culture of Belonging at the Georgia Tech Library

These revelations also have the added benefit of reducing the need for code switching in the supervisor. If everyone knows who they are and where they stand, the supervisor can be the same person in almost all situations. Knowing that the leader is consistent in their workplace presentation allows others to be consistent. It also gives the supervisor a chance to acknowledge real emotions of anger, sadness, confusion, and stress that may get revealed as people feel comfortable revealing more of themselves in the workplace. This specific approach may not work for all supervisors or for all teams, but in fostering inclusion and belonging it is critical to open the door for all to come in and to feel welcomed and valued for what they bring.

Encouraging Authenticity in Others

Getting others to behave in an authentic manner is not something that a supervisor can "do;" that choice lies with each person. But there are a few things that supervisors can do to help encourage this relationship building. First, supervisors can literally (internally) check their privilege. What advantages does the supervisor have that those they are leading might not have? Supervisors are generally better paid and have more organizational power than their team members. But also, people come into the workplace with societal privilege. White people, men, straight, cisgender, non-disabled, non-immigrant, and native English speakers have less systemic bias to deal with than those from more marginalized backgrounds. Further, just because a leader is from one marginalized background (as Freeman is as a queer person) does not mean that they do not also experience privilege from other backgrounds (as Freeman does as a cis-White man). Those facing greater levels of systemic bias have traditionally experienced a greater cost for being authentic in the workplace; as such, they may be reticent to risk doing so in the future. To build cultures of belonging in an authentic way, this must be okay. All leaders can do is open the door and make sure that the table is set appropriately; it is each individuals choice whether to participate. Some people have been waiting for the invitation for years and will come immediately; others may take years to acknowledge the invitation at all.

As someone is deciding whether to embrace a workplace's culture, surprising things may come up. People express their feelings, especially those that have been bottled up for a long time, in a variety of ways. While library leaders may be most familiar with stress, anxiety, or sadness as responses, anger and indignation can also be common. Leaders have a choice: do they want people putting more effort into the content of their comments or the form their comments take? Put another way, do leaders want their team members worrying more about how they are being perceived than about the value of the information the team member is providing? The emotions of the team members should be acknowledged; however, these emotions do not have to be shared by the supervisor. When people are invited to be their authentic selves, supervisors must take what they get. A person cannot be told to act authentically while simultaneously being told "not in that way." Instead, supervisors engaged in the activity of creating cultures of belonging can act as quasi-sin eaters: hearing people out, acknowledging their feelings, and helping those people redirect those emotions into more positive outcomes for the team and organization.

IMPACTS AND OUTCOMES

The impacts of this work are still ongoing; the authors live with the ongoing outcomes every day. But anecdotally, this approach to the work seems to be working. Turnover is relatively low with people mostly leaving for better opportunities. Contribution to library initiatives among team members is high. Interpersonal conflicts are addressed and moved past. As the Tech Library works to move into the future, it is hiring a more diverse team of staff, faculty, and leaders than ever before. This increase in diversity creates new opportunities for a more robust culture of belonging as a greater variety of people are incorporated into the overall milieu of the organization.

At the Institute level, the leadership has also become more diverse and more engaged in creating a positive and supportive culture for learning and working. This commitment to continuous improvement has resulted in multiple surveys surrounding climate and culture over time. The results of the Institute's surveys, as well as more informal surveys and feedback opportunities, provide more solid evidence that the Library culture has and continues to change in a meaningful and desired direction.

Administered by Institute Diversity, Equity, and Inclusion and the Office of Academic Effectiveness every four years, the Georgia Tech Climate Survey shows that the Library has improved in the following areas: sensitivity to cultural differences; people's comfort with sharing thoughts, ideas, and differing opinions; people being treating fairly; and day-to-day work experiences. It has also moved the needle up in mentoring for career and leadership positions and professional development opportunities. One of the strongest positive trends found in the climate survey for the Library outcomes was that diversity is valued. The Institute's cultural alignment surveys (administered several times from 2020 to 2022) that focus on the Georgia Tech values also show that the Library is making positive gains. Like the Climate Survey, the alignment surveys show that the Library is making progress in the areas of psychological safety, trust, and culture. For the leadership, this is a big win, especially compared to results of earlier surveys (namely the 2014 ClimateQual and 2019 Ethical Culture Survey) that identified problems in these realms. The authors are hopeful that the increased participation rates in employees taking the surveys, i.e., approximately 80% of the Library faculty responded to the 2022 Climate Survey and over half of the Library staff, is also evidence that people are more comfortable and willing to share their opinions and thoughts.

The survey results are not uniformly positive. There is still much work to be done and more learning to understand what the results mean. For example, even with all of the emphasis on creating job categories with clear expectations and salary studies, there is some angst in this area, as well as in our efforts to recruit and retain employees. Despite this, though there have been significant improvements. Are these examples of rising expectations setting the bar higher or are there new problems that need to be addressed? The Library leadership is committed to exploring these areas to find the root cause(s) of the findings to facilitate moving forward. This is part of the journey in creating a stronger culture of belonging.

Proposed Model

Figure 4. A proposed model for a nested responsibility for building a culture of belonging

A Nested Responsibility for a Culture of Belonging

Institution	Administration	Team Supervisor
• Set standards, strategic plans, and values.	• Interpret strategic plan into context.	• Manage day-to-day implementation of cultural work.
• Create broad context and support for DEI initiatives that can be interpreted as needed at the unit and team levels.	• Set standards for unit action and behavior.	• Mediate issues on a one-to-one basis to encourage belonging.
	• Create structure for cultural change.	• Relay systemic issues to administration as needed for help.
	• Provide resources.	

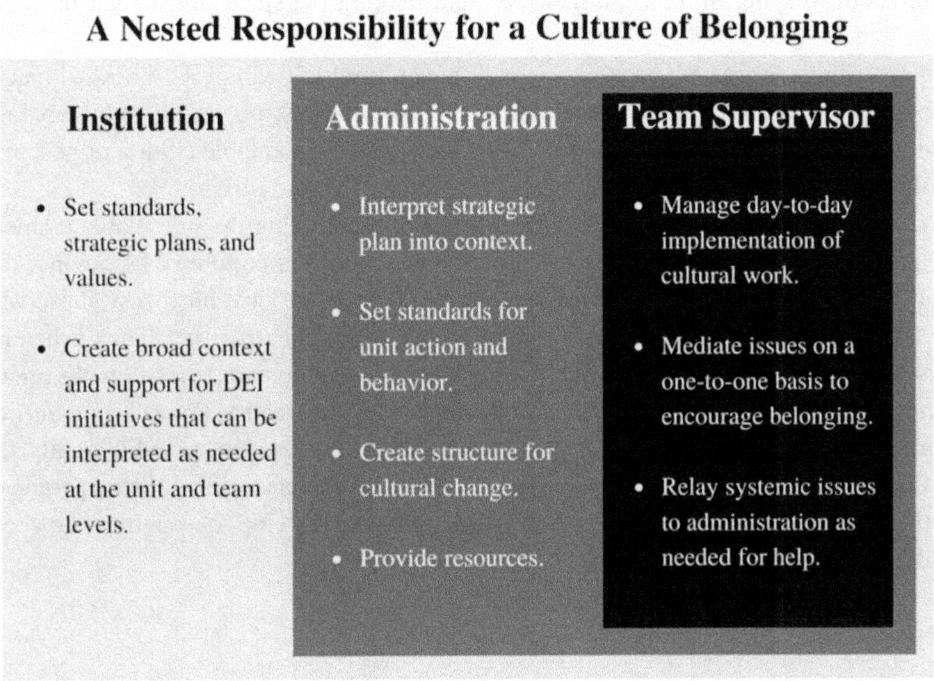

The actions of the team supervisor sit within the actions of the library administration which in turn sit within the institutional context.

The authors' proposed model for creating a culture of belonging calls for a two-tiered approach. In creating a culture of belonging, the Tech Library utilized a model that the authors refer to as nesting, which is a metaphor that plays on the various meanings of the word nesting (Figure 4). The unit-level manager's actions were nested in the Library's structural changes, and the Library's actions were nested in the Institute's strategic plan and values. This seemingly unintentional stacking of values and mission-driven actions created a nest for people to develop, grow, belong, and thrive. The full power of any layer of this cannot be unlocked by itself. Institutional and Library leadership must create a suitable structure for growth and belonging, but that structure is nothing if individual teams do not buy into it. Conversely, a direct supervisor can work to create a hospitable environment encouraging people to bloom, but this work can be undercut by a toxic overall environment.

Organizational leaders have the role of creating the scaffolding that a culture of belonging rests on. They create and embody the organization's values, they articulate the vision that provides the direction for the organization, and they hold people accountable for violations of trust that occur in the creation of culture. Additionally, leaders are responsible for unlocking the vital resources that are necessary for the ongoing work of cultural change. Metaphorically, their job is to design and build the nest.

Direct supervisors have the role of making the broad ideals of the organization real on an individual level. They use the structure set up by administrators and the tools that administrative sponsorship makes available to connect individuals to the culture of belonging. Their work may take the form of empowering individuals, providing feedback and praise, creating opportunities for growth, and deeply engaging with individuals about how they can contribute. They also work on the individual level to remove more personalized barriers to full community belonging. In the nest-building metaphor, the direct supervisor's role is more about weaving in the right materials and making the space an inviting place that people want to stay.

The two contributions are both necessary in creating cultures of belonging. A nest with no protection is a cold shell that does not fulfill its promises; materials with no structure are vulnerable to elements and outside interference. The two must come together to create sustainable culture or nest of belonging where employees can actively engage, feel safe, be comfortable, and thrive.

The other element of this model is the importance in recognizing the unscalable element of time. Wherever a team member is in their journey towards inclusion in a culture of belonging, there are no shortcuts. If there have been previous wrongdoings or actions that have hurt trust, these will not heal overnight. It takes time for people to forgive, but it is rare for people to forget. Thus, when leaders and supervisors attempt to create a culture of belonging, they must understand that all paths are unique and that the time needed (both by the individual and by supervisors in creating the environment) will simply take the time that it takes. This work cannot be rushed, and it is never linear. Additionally, the work of creating cultures of belonging is never-ending as attrition and the onboarding of new people create new dynamics that institutions must harness to maintain, grow, and develop their cultures to accommodate new and different members.

Next Steps

The joy and frustration of DEIB work is that it is never done; success in one area plants the seeds for future endeavors to make the workplace more successful. As such, this initial work of creating a culture of belonging was primarily focused on the matters of gender and race. However, the Library acknowledges that further work needs to be done related to LGBTQ+ issues, accessibility, and other areas of potential bias.

As for the functioning of the nested model, future research would show how a model like this behaves as it becomes more mature. Items such as how turnover might affect a culture of belonging, how tenure of leadership at various levels affects outcomes, and how an organization matures beyond the initial successes of DEIB work to continue to do the harder work that may provide more incremental gains. While the work continues to be challenging, those involved in this work are up for the challenge.

CONCLUSION

How to measure progress remains a challenge. Anecdotally, there seems to be improvement. Meeting with small groups, encouraging feedback and conversation, and asking people what is on their minds provide informal avenues to ascertain mood and tone. These interactions are trending more positively with fewer tears and more forward-looking conversations. The climate and culture surveys demonstrate there has been progress in many critical areas related to engagement, psychological safety, career development, appreciation of differences, and feelings of belonging. However, there are still people who are hesitant to come forward when there are issues and others who cite past wrongs that pre-date current leadership

Co-Creating the Start of a Culture of Belonging at the Georgia Tech Library

by years, if not decades. There is a recognition at the Georgia Tech Library that this culture change will be a process and that it will take whatever time that is needed.

A culture of belonging is not static. It is not a set of steps that someone can accomplish, check off a list, and then move on to the next thing. Instead, creating a culture of belonging is an ongoing, often unspoken conversation between leaders, supervisors, and team members. Each person has a role to play and can contribute. The specific example of the Tech Library shows an organization on an upward trajectory, but also an organization that still has great work to do. It is the authors' hope that this specific example can illuminate one salient point above all others: even organizations that have gone through dark times and have experienced trauma and a poisoned culture can recover and begin to build something new with room for all. Culture happens whether an organization pays attention to it or not; a culture of belonging only happens when leaders and supervisors mindfully pursue actions that work to include everyone in an environment of mutual respect, consideration, openness, and growth.

REFERENCES

Ashikali, T., Groeneveld, S., & Kuipers, B. (2021). The Role of Inclusive Leadership in Supporting an Inclusive Climate in Diverse Public Sector Teams. *Review of Public Personnel Administration, 41*(3), 497–519. doi:10.1177/0734371X19899722

Ayala, M. J., Carter, J. K., Fachon, A. S., Flaxman, S. M., Gil, M. A., Kenny, H. V., Laubach, Z. M., Madden, S. A., McDermott, M. T., Medina-García, A., Safran, R. J., Scherner, E., Schield, D. R., Vasquez-Rey, S., & Volckens, J. (2021). Belonging in STEM: An interactive, iterative approach to create and maintain a diverse learning community. *Trends in Ecology & Evolution, 36*(11), 964–967. doi:10.1016/j.tree.2021.08.004 PMID:34561090

BetterUp. (2021). *The value of belonging: New frontiers for inclusion*. BetterUp. https://grow.betterup.com/resources/the-value-of-belonging-at-work-the-business-case-for-investing-in-workplace-inclusion

Bolton, A., de Figueiredo, J. M., & Lewis, D. E. (2021). Elections, Ideology, and Turnover in the US Federal Government. *Journal of Public Administration: Research and Theory, 31*(2), 451–466. doi:10.1093/jopart/muaa051

Boon, J., Wynen, J., & Kleizen, B. (2021). What happens when the going gets tough? Linking change scepticism, organizational identification, and turnover intentions. *Public Management Review, 23*(7), 1056–1080. doi:10.1080/14719037.2020.1722208

Burrell, D. N., & Rahim, E. (2018). Developing inclusive leaders with religious literacy in the workplace. *Leadership, 14*(5), 567–584. doi:10.1177/1742715018793745

Deci, E. L., & Ryan, R. M. (2012). Self-Determination Theory. In P. Van Lange, A. Kruglanski, & E. Higgins, Handbook of Theories of Social Psychology: Volume 1 (pp. 416–437). SAGE Publications Ltd. doi:10.4135/9781446249215.n21

Driskill, G. W., & Brenton, A. L. (2019). *Organizational culture in action: A cultural analysis workbook* (3rd ed.). Routledge.

Edmondson, A. C. (2019). *The fearless organization: Creating psychological safety in the workplace for learning, innovation, and growth*. John Wiley & Sons, Inc.

Efron, L. (2022, July 26). What Drives a Culture of Belonging? *Gallup.Com*. https://www.gallup.com/workplace/395102/drives-culture-belonging.aspx

Ferdman, B. M., Avigdor, A., Braun, D., Konkin, J., & Kuzmycz, D. (2010). Collective experience of inclusion, diversity, and performance in work groups. *RAM. Revista de Administração Mackenzie, 11*(3), 6–26. doi:10.1590/S1678-69712010000300003

Georgia Institute of Technology. (2020). *Georgia Tech Strategic Plan*. Georgia Institute of Technology. https://strategicplan.gatech.edu/sites/default/files/georgia-tech-strategic-plan-2020-2030.pdf

Georgia Tech Library All Staff Meeting in Atlanta, GA. (2019, March 6). [Personal communication].

Ghosh, R., Reio, T. G. Jr, & Bang, H. (2013). Reducing turnover intent: Supervisor and co-worker incivility and socialization-related learning. *Human Resource Development International, 16*(2), 169–185. doi:10.1080/13678868.2012.756199

Harris, R. B., Harris, K. J., & Harvey, P. (2008). An Examination of the Impact of Supervisor on the Relationship Between Job Strains and Turnover Intention for Computer Workers. *Journal of Applied Social Psychology, 38*(8), 2108–2131. doi:10.1111/j.1559-1816.2008.00383.x

Jansen, W. S., Otten, S., van der Zee, K. I., & Jans, L. (2014). Inclusion: Conceptualization and measurement. *European Journal of Social Psychology, 44*(4), 370–385. doi:10.1002/ejsp.2011

Joyce, J. (1922). *Ulysses*. https://www.gutenberg.org/cache/epub/4300/pg4300-images.html

Kennedy, J. T. (2020). *Key findings: The power of belonging: What it is and why it matters in today's workplace* (Belonging Series). Coqual. https://www.google.com/url?sa=t&rct=j&q=&esrc=s&source=web&cd=&cad=rja&uact=8&ved=2ahUKEwj_56bnofH5AhU9mmoFHfKcBxQQFnoECAsQAQ&url=https%3A%2F%2Fcoqual.org%2Fwp-content%2Fuploads%2F2020%2F09%2FCoqualPowerOfBelongingKeyFindings090720.pdf&usg=AOvVaw3Irq-XOpMB5pEP-PvKtu15

Kennedy, J. T., & Jain-Link, P. (2021, June 21). What Does It Take to Build a Culture of Belonging? *Harvard Business Review*. https://hbr.org/2021/06/what-does-it-take-to-build-a-culture-of-belonging

Knapp, J. A., Snavely, L., & Klimczyk, L. (2012). Speaking Up: Empowering Individuals to Promote Tolerance in the Academic Library. *Library Leadership & Management, 26*(1). Advance online publication. doi:10.5860/llm.v26i1.5508

Mor Barak, M. E. (2019). Erecting Walls Versus Tearing Them Down: Inclusion and the (False) Paradox of Diversity in Times of Economic Upheaval. *European Management Review, 16*(4), 937–955. doi:10.1111/emre.12302

Ortega, A. C. (2017). *Academic libraries and toxic leadership*. Chandos Publishing, an imprint of Elsevier.

Pitts, D., Marvel, J., & Fernandez, S. (2011). So Hard to Say Goodbye? Turnover Intention among U.S. Federal Employees. *Public Administration Review*, *71*(5), 751–760. doi:10.1111/j.1540-6210.2011.02414.x

Re, G. work Project. (2018). *Re:Work*. https://rework.withgoogle.com/print/guides/5721312655835136/

RuPaul [@rupaul]. (2014, October 4). *Know who you are and deliver it at all times* https://t.co/3wO0iohWcv [Tweet]. Twitter. https://twitter.com/rupaul/status/518235173159456769

Schein, E. H. (2017). *Organizational culture and leadership* (5th ed.). Wiley.

Seung-Ho, A. (2019). Employee Voluntary and Involuntary Turnover and Organizational Performance: Revisiting the Hypothesis from Classical Public Administration. *International Public Management Journal*, *22*(3), 444–469. doi:10.1080/10967494.2018.1549629

Shore, L. M., Randel, A. E., Chung, B. G., Dean, M. A., Holcombe Ehrhart, K., & Singh, G. (2011). Inclusion and Diversity in Work Groups: A Review and Model for Future Research. *Journal of Management*, *37*(4), 1262–1289. doi:10.1177/0149206310385943

Stanley, D. J., Meyer, J. P., & Topolnytsky, L. (2005). Employee Cynicism and Resistance to Organizational Change. *Journal of Business and Psychology*, *19*(4), 429–459. doi:10.100710869-005-4518-2

Whorton, J. W., & Worthley, J. A. (1981). A Perspective on the Challenge of Public Management: Environmental Paradox and Organizational Culture. *Academy of Management Review*, *6*(3), 357–361. doi:10.2307/257371

Winters, M. F. (2013). From Diversity to Inclusion: An Inclusion Equation. In B. M. Ferdman & B. R. Deane (Eds.), *Diversity at Work: The practice of inclusion*. Jossey-Bass., https://learning.oreilly.com/library/view/diversity-at-work/9781118415153/c07.xhtml doi:10.1002/9781118764282.ch7

Witwer, R. F. (2021). *DEI and Belonging: Changing the Narrative and Creating a Culture of Belonging in Nonprofit Organization* [University of San Francisco]. https://usfblogs.usfca.edu/nonprofit/files/2021/05/witwerrakiya_6199833_68188178_Rakiya-Witwer-622-Capstone-Report.pdf

ENDNOTES

[1]   See https://strategicplan.gatech.edu/ for more information about the Georgia Tech Strategic Plan. Its mission is "The Georgia Institute of Technology is a public research university established by the state of Georgia in Atlanta in 1885 and committed to **developing leaders who advance technology and improve the human condition**." Its vision is "Over the next decade, Georgia Tech will be an example of inclusive innovation, a leading technological, research university relentlessly committed to serving the public good; breaking new ground in addressing the biggest local, national, and global challenges of our time; making technology broadly accessible; and developing exceptional leaders from all backgrounds ready to produce novel ideas and create solutions with real human impact." Its values are Students are our top priority; we strive for excellence; we thrive on diversity; we celebrate collaboration; we champion innovation; we safeguard freedom of inquiry and expression; we nurture the well-being of our community; we act ethically; and we are responsible stewards.

[2]   In this sense, referring to the faculty/staff divide, not the all-encompassing term for employees.

[3]   For more information about the LibraryNext initiative, see *Library Next: Seven Action Steps for Reinvention* (2021) by Catherine Murray-Rust

[4]   The portfolio is a project management system used to track all Library projects that require monetary resources or the collaboration of multiple Library departments.

[5]   In addition to requiring at least one faculty and one staff member on each search committee, Sharp required that all members of any search committees have implicit bias training, expanding Georgia Tech's policy that faculty on search committees be trained to all members—faculty and staff—must take training. A diversity advocate was also a member of each committee.

Section 2
Information Resources and Collections

Chapter 4
Citation Power:
Overcoming Marginalization One Citation at a Time

Jodi H. Coalter
Michigan State University, USA

ABSTRACT

Emerging from research dating back to the 1980's, citation justice is the practice of citing research based on both content and an author's identity. Due to citation gaps that exist across disciplines, citation practice is changing to cite authors of more diverse genders, races, and other marginalized identities. Librarians are uniquely situated in academic institutions to teach and encourage students and faculty to adjust their citation practice to close these gaps. This chapter describes citation justice in detail and describes the evidence for the need adjust citation practice to include identity. In addition, this chapter explores why librarians can effect the most change, and how this change needs to begin with students, before discussing the various ways librarian instruction can incorporate citation justice into their work.

INTRODUCTION

Citation justice is a fairly new concept, emerging in the 2010's from research on citation gaps between dominant and oppressed communities that dates back to the 1980's. The practice is rapidly spreading throughout academia, in fields as varied as neuroscience and English literature. Defined as the deliberate act of citing more work authored by people from marginalized communities in society and in academia, citation justice seeks to help correct an imbalance in citation practice. Multiple bibliometric analyses have discovered scholars from Black and Brown communities and women are cited less often than their white, male counterparts.

As research and citation experts, librarians are in an excellent position to support citation justice by introducing new researchers to the practice and teaching about tools to help writers track and manage citations. Our unique set of skills, including knowledge of when and how to cite, how to find diverse voices and their work, and our familiarity with citation management lend themselves well to this pursuit. With a reach across multiple disciplines, and our ability to work with a wide variety of researchers, from

DOI: 10.4018/978 1 6684 7255 2.ch004

Copyright © 2023, IGI Global. Copying or distributing in print or electronic forms without written permission of IGI Global is prohibited.

Citation Power

undergraduate students to faculty, we can support this movement quickly, efficiently, and thoroughly. This effort can help rebalance academia to be more inclusive and more equitable.

This chapter will explore the topic of citation justice, as described above, and will begin by further defining citation justice and laying out some of the foundational evidence for the need to develop the practice, and will discuss why librarians should take up this work.

The body of the chapter will focus on how librarians can incorporate citation justice into their instruction, including a thorough discussion of how to teach citation justice while still encouraging authoritative sources and citing for content. This section will be broken into three main parts. The first part will explore how to develop assignments, in conjunction with classroom faculty and instructors, that encourage and build a robust citation justice practice. This material might also be helpful for "train-the-trainer" workshops or faculty instruction sessions.

The second part of this section will describe a series of workshops that cater to different audiences. A workshop designed for undergraduates who are just beginning their academic careers should focus on the power inherent in citation practice; this workshop is designed to demonstrate how a student's voice is important to scholarly communication, and how choosing who to cite is often just as important, if not more important, than how to cite. For upper-level undergraduates, focusing on why citing different voices is important and exploring where those voices can be found is more appropriate. Graduate students, including both master's and PhD students, may have a more developed citation practice; workshops can focus on organizing citations, tagging sources with metadata for easy reuse, and auditing complete bibliographies. Finally, workshops for faculty examine their gestalt practice and provide encouragement for incorporating the practice into their own writing, and into the assignments they provide for students.

The third part of this section will explore how small changes to the infamous library one-shot workshop can encourage diverse citation practice with or without being explicit about citation gaps. This section will focus on developing short instruction modules on how to find diverse voices in one's own field, where marginalized communities are gathering their work for broader dissemination, and even simply choosing and demonstrating examples that encourage students to think about citation in their lives more broadly.

Ultimately, this chapter will introduce the concepts behind and evidence supporting the need for citation justice. It will explore why librarians are uniquely suited and situated in academia to teach these concepts, and why researchers at all levels should be encouraged to practice citation justice. Finally, it will offer guidance for instruction sessions of various types to help librarians interested in teaching citation justice to do so.

What is Citation Justice?

As mentioned previously, citation justice is a recently developed concept that primarily refers to citing authors based on identity and not solely on content. According to many bibliometric analyses explored below, authors from marginalized communities tend to be cited less frequently than those with more privileged identities. The definition of an identity can include, but is not limited to, race, gender identity and expression, sexuality, class/status (both inside and outside of academia), age, etc. According to many of those studies, this gap in cited research is growing, despite gains in diversifying faculty. When the research products from these underrepresented authors are ejected from the citation stream, long lasting implications for a variety of issues in higher education begin to emerge such as who gets promoted or tenured, who is teaching in the classroom, and differences in pay, among others. The problems can even lead to people from these marginalized communities leaving academia altogether. This, in turn, can result in a less diverse student body; research shows that students who do not see themselves at an institution leave that institution (Main et al., 2020).

Although the core of citation justice is incorporating more diverse voices into a bibliography, the entire concept is much broader, touching on not just literature reviews but also everyday conversations, lectures, discussions in the classroom, and research production from start to finish. This means not just the act of citing and creating or changing authority based on citations. That's the easier and more straightforward part. The harder part is incorporating these perspectives into the gestalt academic practice. All elements of citation justice are important, but this chapter will focus mostly on the core practice of considering bibliographical citations, since this aspect is what librarians are likely to be able to affect the most.

What does citation justice look like in practice? Aside from affecting the actual citations that appear at the end of a research product, such as an article or a chapter, citation justice can also mean simply choosing subjects, papers, and discussion topics from a wide variety of authors. For example, in *Data Feminism*, the authors describe not only how they chose to cite diverse authors, but also how the example case studies they chose to use, were selected based on a set of predetermined goals (D'Ignazio & Klein, 2020). In other words, the research they based their own research on was chosen from a diverse pool. But this can also mean including these voices in classroom teaching examples, in search examples using library databases, even in the formation of a research question.

Many leaders of the citation justice movement, including Christen Smith from the Cite Black Women. Collective, also encourage authors to internalize the arguments that they are citing, to explore the topics more deeply (Kwon, 2022; Smith). They list five core principles in their citation practice: read Black women's work, integrate Black women into the core of your syllabus (in life & in the classroom), acknowledge Black women's intellectual production, make space for Black women to speak, and give Black women the space and time to breathe. In other words, these authors need to not only be cited more frequently but also discussed in class and included in broader conversations. Essentially, if these scholars are not showing up in academic articles, it's also likely they aren't showing up in the classroom and elsewhere.

As awareness grows about the movement, citation justice initiatives are appearing in publications. Several journals are either requiring citation diversity statements, including the *Biomedical Engineering Society* ("Citation diversity statement in BMES journals," 2021), *Cell Press Reviews* (Zurn et al., 2020), and *Issues in Science & Technology Librarianship* (Hansen, 2022), or are asking authors to disclose race and ethnicity when they publish an article to better track publication trends (Else & Perkel, 2022). A typical citation diversity statement can appear in two forms. A longer form includes information on the state of citation gaps in a particular field, any goals the authors set to address those gaps, how well they achieved these goals, and how they attempted and/or will attempt to alter their citation practice to decrease these gaps. These statements can be quite lengthy and can include a bit of statistical analysis. A brief statement may simply acknowledge the issue, and state that the authors took steps to mitigate this in the research product. These are not only meant to acknowledge and account for the gaps in citation, but also act to spread awareness among other authors that the gap exists and that they can change their practice to close these gaps.

While it shouldn't have to be said, it bears repeating that citing based on identity does not mean that content is no longer relevant. Content should still be evaluated, in terms of methodology, results, and, ultimately, final conclusions. However, citation justice recognizes the fact that all research projects, from the most "objective" of engineering products to the subjective literature interpretation, are created by, and therefore biased by, the humans that produce them. Acknowledging this, and then consciously ac-

Citation Power

counting for this bias in citations, can lead to a more equitable academic community, and a more robust area of research.

Evidence for Citation Gaps

Evidence for citation gaps has been presented in bibliometric analyses since the 1980s, with gender as the most studied identity. Currently, many studies focus on citation gaps tied to gender, racial, or ethnic inequity. However, scholars have argued for more research on the effects of other systems of oppression such as ableism, classism, and colonialism. More research is needed in many of these areas, as there is much we still don't know about how works from authors within these communities are being cited. However, as each of these communities are affected by institutional systems of oppression, especially in the United States, it's likely that the evidence will point to gaps here as well. Still, as the body of evidence for disparity is large and growing, this section will provide a very brief overview of gender studies and racial/ethnic studies. For a more complete review, please see Coalter, J. 2023.

While the effect of gender on citation gaps is more regularly studied, there is very little research that looks beyond the binary of women/men. This lack of research not only gives us an inaccurate view of who is being cited, but also completely erasing an entire population of people (Plett, April 11, 2016). One notable article that addresses this gap suggests that studies investigating issues related to the transgender community have vastly different findings when they cite people from that community versus when they cite cisgender authors, and that such studies should take their cues from the trans community itself on who and how to cite (Thieme & Saunders, 2018). In addition, it should be noted that many studies' methodologies that use a "threshold" to assign gender based on an author's remove names that don't fit neatly into the binary (such as Jodi, Alex, etc.). For example, if 80% of people named Maria in a given year identify as female, then everyone named Maria is assigned female. If a name falls below that threshold, the name is removed. As many folks from the trans community choose names for themselves that do not fit into the traditional gender binary, this further removes their voices from the conversation. Despite the issues with the gender binary that limits most studies, the studies can still shed some light on the inequitable citation practices across multiple fields.

According to most studies that have investigated gender imbalance in citation practice, women are often cited much less frequently than their male counterparts (Chen et al., 2016; Davenport & Snyder, 1995; Dworkin et al., 2020), even when accounting for the number of women in a given field (Murphy, 2017). It should be noted that the number of times women are cited fluctuates within a field; one subfield may highly cite women while another may barely cite them (Dworkin et al., 2020; King et al., 2017). This has been observed in multiple fields including (but not limited to) physics (Teich et al., 2022), astronomy (Caplar et al., 2017; Trimble, 1993), neuroscience (Bertolero et al., 2020), communications (Chakravartty et al., 2018), economics (Chen et al., 2016), sociology (Davenport & Snyder, 1995), anthropology (Lutz, 1990), tourism (Nunkoo et al., 2019), geography (Mott & Cockayne, 2018), and engineering (Murphy, 2017). On the other hand, some fields more heavily cite women. For example, nursing, which is made up predominantly of women, sees a significant increase in citations of women (Kozlowski, Larivière, et al., 2022).

It should also be noted that men tend to cite themselves more regularly than their women colleagues cite themselves. One study found that men tend to cite themselves more often than their women colleagues (approximately 70%) more, that women were 10% more likely than men to not cite any of their previous work, and that these rates varied widely across field and subfield (King et al., 2017). This

65

self-citation gap can have a great impact on citation counts, as 9.4% of all citations in their study were self-citations. The authors also note that the proportion of women in a field did not correlate with the rates of self-citation.

When considering race or ethnicity, and the intersectionality of race/ethnicity and gender, we see similar trends where researchers who are white, or white and male, are cited more frequently than their non-white or non-white male colleagues. In a recent, large study that examined citations across multiple disciplines, women who are white, Black, or Latinx are undercited (cited less than expected based on the number of women in science) across multiple fields. While they are more equally cited in lower-cited fields, the gap persists. It should be noted that white women tend to have higher citations than either Black or Latinx women authors in almost all fields. Asian men tend to be more highly cited in engineering, technology. and physics, whereas they are severely undercited in the humanities where Black men tend to be overcited (Kozlowski, Larivière, et al., 2022).

It's notable that subfields within a large subject area, such as medicine, have vastly different citation outcomes depending on both the composition of those subfields, as well as the importance of citation within that subfield. For example, in clinical health, a field where citation is vastly important and citations are used extensively, Asian women tend to be overcited, and Black men tend to be undercited. However, both of these groups see a significant drop in citation counts in health, which tends to be less citation heavy (Kozlowski, Sugimoto, et al., 2022).

Overall, the trends tend to show that men and white authors are being overcited in most fields, especially when the proportion of men to women and white to BIPOC authors are factored in.

Why Librarians and Why Students?

The presence of inequity in citation does not automatically mean that librarians should take an active role in changing citation practice, so why should librarians step up to this particular plate? There are several reasons it makes sense for citation justice to be built into our instruction (and into our everyday teaching and reference). First, inequitable citations in any field can and do lead to inequitable departments in our academic institutions. Because citations are factored in so heavily to the hiring, promotion, and tenure processes, any inequity in the way citations are created and disseminated leads to inequity in our institutions. For example, a person receiving fewer citations due to gender might be rejected for a position as a result. Even if they are hired, they might be slower to be promoted, leading to unequal pay, and may be late receiving tenure, or might not be awarded tenure at all.

Librarians are perfectly suited to combat this trend. Academic librarians, particularly liaison librarians who have robust relationships with their departments, are often embedded within the campus community at all levels, from first year students through PhDs and faculty. This reach, and, in the case of liaison librarians, the subject expertise, perfectly positions academic librarians to effect change at all levels of academia, leading to a more robust response in a timely manner.

In addition, academic librarians already have citation materials ready, and connections with multiple on-campus groups that would facilitate a quick rollout of new citation materials. In some cases, changes can be small. For example, simply mentioning the fact that citation inequity exists and tools that can help locate diverse authors can lead students to start thinking about how they are citing and why they are citing. Adjusting or expanding current standalone workshops can encourage the maturation of a citation practice to include citation justice through simple modules that account for identity as well as content when evaluating a source.

Citation Power

However, this doesn't answer the question: if this is a problem with promotion and tenure, why teach students about citation justice and not faculty? Arguably, it's best to teach both, and this chapter does contain a section on promoting citation justice to faculty. In fact, many authors investigating citation inequity strongly affirm that the burden to change lies squarely with those who are in a position of power to do so (for example, white and/or male authors with institutional power). However, a mature citation practice takes years to develop. As with many aspects of citation practice, it can take a long time for equitable citation practice to become habituated within the student's writing. Starting instruction early in a student's post-secondary education means there's a higher likelihood that citation justice will become part of that student's practice, and, eventually, lead to more academics with a mature practice that includes citation justice.

Perhaps even more importantly, changing citation habits can have lasting impacts beyond academia, even for students. The way that people cite sources, even on social media or in information-based websites like Wikipedia, can have long lasting consequences in and out of academia. Encouraging strong use of citations, the development of a robust citation practice, and a focus on citing diverse voices can empower students to change the world around them. It can be difficult to be a first-year student and to feel relatively helpless to change the surrounding system. This can be an excellent way to not only teach citation, but to empower students to use their voices to create the world they wish to see. Empowering students creates investment in high quality citations which, in turn, can lead to long term retention of citation practice.

Developing Class Materials for Citation Justice

Encouraging a change in citation practice to include citation justice doesn't require massive overhauls in current citation assignments. Librarians already discuss evaluating the content of sources, so including information on how to evaluate sources based on author's identity can be relatively seamless. However, encouraging change in citation practice, even a small one, requires buy-in from the student on the value and necessity of the change. This is more easily accomplished when citation practice is discussed over the various stages of a research project, from planning to the final product Conversations about citation practice should take place over time but laying a foundation of understanding regarding citations before introducing an assignment can help set expectations. Encouraging discussions on what citations look like and mean, not only to research but the individual student, can create the buy-in and investment needed to build a strong citation practice. For example, starting with a preliminary exercise (perhaps like the one used in the Freshman/Sophomore Standalone Workshop described below), can encourage students to think more fully about what is important to a citation format. Would they include authors? If so, where would the author go in a citation? Why is that important? Discussion can then revolve around the importance of individual perspective in art and why the artist was cited first, before leading into citation justice. In another exercise, students might be encouraged to think about social media sharing as citation. Students can review one of their own social media accounts and to try and evaluate whose content they shared the most. They can be asked to consider why they thought sharing the content creator's name when they share their work was important.

The main point of these initial exercises is to encourage students to start thinking about why citing is important to them. The exercises might change depending on academic level. For example, juniors and seniors might already know why citing is important to both their field and to them but talking about how they choose a source can lead to excellent discussions on author identity. Students often describe

67

choosing sources based on content, but further guided discussion might reveal their choices are just as often based on the whims of the databases they are searching. Exploration of how results are presented to a searcher, and whether a searcher can filter results, can lead to excellent discussions on what types of papers are returned in the search results. For example, if the students are encouraged to sort results based on citations, an exercise could examine how certain papers become over inflated with importance because they are controversial or disproven, or because the experiment is poorly conducted. Exercises can also introduce topics such as authors who are ejected from the citation stream due to race or gender.

During the planning stages of a paper or project, encourage students to think about who they want to cite and why. Writing out a simple philosophy statement or setting specific goals they want to achieve can be an excellent way to encourage students to think more about the topic. For example, having students state that they want 50% of their citations to be from female authors and why they chose that percentage can be an excellent start to a project plan. This can also be a great opportunity to discuss why choosing higher percentages for female authors can help close the citation gap. Demonstrating different ways of finding those authors can also be helpful, whether it's searching for academics on a social media plat-form or by using database resources, such as citeblackauthors.com ("Cite Black Authors – A database for academic research by Black authors," n.d.).

The planning stage is also a great time to discuss definitions, important considerations, concepts, and issues related to identity. For example, this is an excellent time to introduce the difference between race and ethnicity, and the importance of tracking both for authors you are citing. It might also be beneficial to discuss how students are going to determine if an author belongs to a certain population that they are intent on tracking. For example, because race is a social construct based on visual determination, determining if an author is Black can be accomplished visually in many cases (though, an author stating their identity should always take precedence). This cannot be done in the same way if a student wants to track LGBTQ+ authors. However, in most cases, it's best to determine if an author is upfront or open with their identities. This can make categorizing authors easier. (A note on tracking authors from the LGBTQ+ community: it's always best not to out an author unless they themselves have already done so. When tracking authors within this community, take direct cues from the community itself, and not from those who write about the community but who do not belong to it. (Mott & Cockayne, 2017)) Depending on the audience, you can also discuss the gap in citations between the Global North and the Global South, or gaps based on language (for example, English language papers tend to be cited more frequently than Spanish language papers, or how papers written in Chinese tend to be neglected here in the United States) (Mott & Cockayne, 2017).

Finding and citing diverse authors is the logical next step in a paper or project, but one that can be difficult to complete. Having students find even one or two sources that are relevant based on content, but also written by an author from a marginalized community, can help students become more familiar with the resources that are available to them. Encouraging students to network within their field is one great way to locate authors from diverse communities. By following scholars' work on academic platforms such as Research Gate or OrcidID or on social media platforms, students can keep up to date with new articles as they are published. In some fields, social media is a vital resource for communicating new in-formation. For example, practitioners publishing mainly in trade publications often create robust networks for sharing information and new publications on social media. Being plugged into those publications as well as more traditional outlets for distributing research can connect students with more diverse authors.

Including an audit of author identities in the student's citations is an excellent way to wrap up discus-sions on citation justice. If goals were set in the planning stage, have students reflect on how they did

Citation Power

in terms of reaching those goals, some of the problems they encountered along the way (such as trouble finding relevant topics from diverse authors, especially in fields that might be predominantly white, male, etc., or perhaps reflecting on how hard it is to keep track), and what they might do to continue or promote citation justice in the future. It's important to note that many students might not be able to reach the goals they set in the beginning. Reflecting on the systems of citation and academia that prevented them from attaining their goals is more important than actually reaching a certain percentage.

Finally, if this is a large project with many citations, introducing tools and methods that larger projects use for determining race and gender specifically, and some of the problems inherent in those tools, might be a good idea. These might include the Diverse Bibliography code or the Gender Citation Balance Tool. Methodology for these tools relies on census counts and data analysis of race and gender by name. Discussing whether it is easier or more justifiable to manually keep track of authors as they publish new articles or to use these tools can lead to robust conversations on other areas of citation analysis.

Standalone Workshops for Developing a Citation Justice Practice

Standalone workshops can, and do, supplement formal learning that happens in the classroom. Ultimately, classroom instruction is likely to leave a few gaps, and library workshops give students an opportunity to fill those gaps, or simply add to their knowledge on topics they care about. In some cases, these workshops may be presented through campus organizations and student groups, or simply offered regularly throughout a semester. Having these workshops established can also be helpful to "plug-in" when confronted with an impromptu instruction request.

Given that a mature citation practice can take years to develop, it's important to create a series of workshops that meet the student where they are in their development. One workshop that tries to pack in all citation justice concepts will likely not be adequate, and may even be confusing, especially for those with less advanced citation skills. Having said that, the workshops described below can be reformatted or taught together; some can even be abridged, to meet the needs of different institutions.

Overall, these workshops tend to focus less on the philosophy of citation and focus instead on the problem of citation gaps and potential solutions. Exercises that give participants an opportunity to practice, to ask questions, and to explore the world of citation gaps themselves can lead to increased investment in citation justice practice. Discussions can focus on tools, strategies, and resources that will help participants seamlessly integrate this practice into their writing.

Regardless of what the workshop ultimately focuses on, and as with developing assignments, it's incredibly important to encourage younger students to invest in quality citation practice that focuses not just on getting the correct format (or, dare it be said, not focusing on that at all), but on the importance of citation in a world bursting with information. Citing is a form of power, of lifting up a person's voice and acknowledging that they should be part of the conversation. Each citation, therefore, is a student's voice on who should be heard, both in the classroom and outside of it, a vote in favor of those they think deserve a voice, whether that be a formal citation in an academic research paper or a share on TikTok. Encouraging students to invest the time and attention required to practice citation justice can be difficult, but it's not impossible. Grounding these workshops in student experiences is key.

Freshman and Sophomore Undergraduates: Planting the Seed of How and Why We Cite

Workshops that focus on those who are just beginning to develop their citation practice should help students develop their own philosophy of citation. What should be included in a citation and where should it be included? Why should that element be included? What is the importance of even having a format to begin with? These foundational questions can encourage students to start thinking about why identity in citation matters. For this reason, beginner workshops should be interactive and should encourage participants to share out some of their thoughts, often and repeatedly, about citation.

For example, during one workshop for freshman and sophomores, a group of students were encouraged to create their own citation style. Students were introduced to a website that showed photos of DC graffiti that they were encouraged to cite. They were broken into small groups and discussed the most important elements they wanted to include in their citation style, such as artist, intersection where the graffiti could be found, materials used, or even the date of the creation. These elements were compiled and the importance of including that element was voted on in the workshop. The elements were then put in order in the workshop's "citation style" by number of votes received. In every iteration of this activity, artist inevitably rose as the first element to be included in the citation. This focus on artist in turn lead to discussions surrounding the importance of attribution to artists, scientists, and creators of all kinds. It's fairly easy to explain, in America, why attribution is important to intellectual property, as much of our economy is based off intellectual property that can be monetized. At this point in the workshop, it's important to start thinking about how citations in the real world, in the form of links on websites, mentions in social media, or reviews in popular cultural mediums, can reflect the biases in society at large. Participants were then encouraged to count the number of women being mentioned in the first 5 or 10 posts of their social media feeds. Are more women being mentioned, or more men? What about the number of white or Black people?

Ultimately, the goal of this workshop is to ground participants in the importance of citation, not just to their work on campus, but to sharing information in the broader world. By reflecting on how citations can play a part in their everyday lives, and not just their school lives, students start to invest in the idea of a more robust citation practice, one that focuses on the importance of thoughtful citation, regardless of where they are.

This workshop is ideal for an audience that has just started their citation practice. It was most often presented to groups of freshmen or first-year students when librarians were invited into non-academic units, such as student clubs or multicultural community centers, or when librarians offered general department workshops. Having a specific organization on campus supporting and offering the workshop encouraged much higher attendance than having workshops held exclusively in the library. The workshops ran for around 1 to 1 ½ hours and were presented on request.

Junior and Senior Undergraduates: Tending a Robust Citation Practice

Upper-level undergraduates are often starting to become familiar with the fields that they will eventually join. A small portion of them will go on to graduate school, but many will be facing professional careers outside of academia. This makes for an interesting mixed audience and can make creating an effective workshop difficult. One possible way to address this issue is to plan workshops for more specific audiences; as mentioned previously, partnering with other campus organizations to address smaller segments

Citation Power

of the student population with shared interests can increase the success of these workshops. Regardless of how the workshop is planned and organized, continuing to encourage the importance of thoughtful and engaged citation practice, regardless of where their careers take them, is vitally important.

Key components of the workshop should include reiteration of the importance of citation, both professionally and in participants' everyday lives, as well as reminding them of where citation is a factor online, such as in social media, as well as in trade and academic journals. In addition, it's important for developing citation justice practice to remind students that citation goes beyond the simple act of putting names and dates in parenthetical or endnote citations, but also includes engagement with the piece in the form of discussing the quality and content, incorporating the information into their larger body of knowledge, and being able to expand into an engaged conversation with other works. This is also an excellent time to introduce students to other ways that academics keep in touch, and how they track their citations, through databases like Web of Science, Scopus, and Google Scholar, and through academic groups such as OrcidID and ResearchGate.

It's helpful if these workshops follow one that introduces a citation manager; however, it's not required. Having a passing familiarity with citation managers can help students organize communities of citations that they may want to use again, or citations that they may want to go back to later. They can also keep track of citations from authors they want to support more regularly, or even tag a citation with an identity that they can search for. This work can also be done manually, in a simple Excel sheet with appropriate labels, such as author, identity, title, publication, and DOI.

Finally, this workshop can also explore finding diverse voices. Juniors and seniors can benefit from demonstrations of searches, websites, databases, and other resources that help authors locate diverse sources. As with other workshops, definitions and concepts may need to be described, such as the difference between race and ethnicity, the dangers of outing those in the LGBTQ+ community, and other concepts that are important for students and anyone practicing citation justice. Being open and clear about what these issues are can make the search easier.

Master's and PhD Students

For graduate student workshops, one can assume that they are at least mildly invested in citation. They can more easily articulate why citation is important to them and to their field. It's also likely that, if they plan to continue to work in academia, they have a vested interest in learning more about citation practice, both how it can affect their careers as well as how it can affect their standing in their field. However, it's possible they haven't thought much about long term impacts of citation or how those impacts touch their own lives, both in and out of academia. For example, it's possible they haven't thought about how their citation choices may have an impact on the faculty mentors and professors they have to choose from when applying to grad school, how citation can be a tool to support faculty in their pursuit of tenure, or how their papers can uplift diverse voices. Graduate students may not need a semester long project to understand these ramifications, and a brief introduction and a discussion on the topic will often encourage a more robust citation practice.

Once graduate students are aware of the issues related to citation justice, discussion can focus on how to adapt their citation practices to correct for these issues. Workshops can focus on the minutia of citation practice that will have a broad effect. Topics can include advanced citation management techniques that allow for tracking of diverse voices and ease of use when writing papers, advance search techniques, how to maintain networks of diverse voices, updating their research when new articles are published by target populations, and the process of auditing citations. The workshop is more effective if the conversation is steered by the students to the topics that most interest or affect them; giving a brief overview of citation justice topics is helpful but encourage student participation by asking questions related to their field, setting up small group discussions, and tailoring the workshop to the audience and their disciplines as much as possible.

The process of auditing citations can be fraught, as previously mentioned. Not only do methodologies and processes differ, but some fields expect graduate students to cite the "greats" or the well-known experts; if they do not, they may be seen as failing to cover the required texts. For example, in many fields, citing already highly cited articles (those often written by white men) is expected to demonstrate that a student knows the research literature. Citing these already well-known authors is a demonstration of the knowledge they've gained. Mentors and committees may question why an author was not included. In this scenario, less is not more. Often I encourage students to include those citations, but to use the "SHINE" method, as proposed by Rigoberto Lara Guzmán (Guzmán & Amrute, 2020). Guzmán recommends using in line citations only for authors that should be highlighted, authors whose voices may have been minimized in the past. Parenthetical citations or footnotes should be reserved for authors who already have the weight of citations behind them and who do not necessarily require any more push from you.

This method is also highlighted in Mott and Cockayne's excellent paper on citation in geography. They stress that "reference lists that do not adhere to a journal or editors' impressions of 'successful performativity' should not be grounds for rejection" (Mott & Cockayne, 2018). While graduate students may be a long way from being editors themselves, this is an important point to drive home as they are more firmly and conscientiously developing their own citation practice. Mott and Cockayne go a step further, encouraging collaboration and partnerships with researchers from marginalized communities as the act of having an author with a privileged identity on a paper can significantly reduce or even remove the citation gap.

As mentioned previously, one method graduate students can be encouraged to practice more is self-citation. Self-citation is a remarkably controversial topic and one that elicits strong opinions from many well-established academics. However, it is clear that those with privileged identities are citing themselves. Encouraging students to cite themselves and their graduate student peers or their new faculty members can be a way to rebalance that citation gap. This makes sense from both a traditional citation practice, as well as from a citation justice practice. It's likely that their current research grew from previous research they've conducted. Therefore, both content and identity are considered when they cite themselves.

Graduate workshops can also include pointers on how to craft citation statements and what can or should be included in those citation statements. Having a general template or examples of citation statements can be a good way to get conversations started. The merits of a short or long statement can also be discussed. It can also be beneficial to discuss how to present the idea of a citation statement to a new journal, or whether to include one in the initial manuscript, noting that some journals can be particular about what can and cannot be included in an article. Choosing a long or short statement may depend on what is appropriate for the journal they choose to publish in.

All of these topics can take up an entire hour discussion alone, especially as students become aware of the nuances in publishing and citation practice. For this reason, encouraging students to both continue the discussion throughout their academic careers and to continue discussions with their librarians is crucially important. Developing a robust citation practice can be a long road but having contacts who can act as a resource when questions arise will help them overcome any hurdles they encounter.

Citation Power

Faculty Workshops

Faculty workshops offer a unique opportunity to effect change at the heart of the problem. While citation is important in undergraduates, those who can (and should) minimize citation gaps now are faculty. However, it can be difficult to convince those with fully developed citation practices to change the way they are citing, especially if they have been taught previously that citing is an objective practice. For example, those faculty in the sciences may be more resistant to change given the "objective" nature of their research philosophy, though there can be a surprising amount of pushback across disciplines.

The most effective faculty workshops for inspiring change are those in which citation specialists are invited in, especially from leaders in a department or institution, but to which faculty are encouraged, not required, to attend. In fact, requiring faculty to attend is not only contentious within a department, but often creates hostile, if not outright negative, instruction sessions. Grounding citation justice within their own institution can be helpful for encouraging engagement. For example, discussing how many faculty are women or BIPOC, how those numbers relate to peer institutions, and how citation plays a role in promotion and retention at their institution can encourage faculty to start reflecting immediately on how their own practice has real implications.

Focusing on the ease of tools to audit citations, and how to track citations within citation managers, can be practical. There can be problems if different managers are used across departments, but citation managers are similar enough that faculty can often find correlated features regardless of which manager they are using. Demoing tools that allow faculty to audit their already completed bibliographies can be enlightening, and even noteworthy. However, most of the questions encountered at these workshops tend to focus on how faculty and instructors can encourage citation justice practice among their students, especially among their graduate students. Having guides, offering workshops, or partnering on assignments based on citation justice is a great way to begin these conversations. Offering help from the libraries encouraged one engineering department's faculty to implement citation justice assignments across the graduate program, starting with a workshop mandated for graduates.

In other words, faculty workshops often require instructors to be flexible in what and how they teach based on the needs that faculty bring up within the workshop. Taking the materials found in the "Developing Class Materials for Citation Justice" section can be a simple and easy way to create a train-the-trainer workshops on how to create citation justice assignments. During one Teaching & Learning Conference workshop, instructors were asked to come prepared with an assignment they wanted to revise to include more citation justice work. After an initial presentation on the topic and common pitfalls in citation justice, participants then spent time working in small groups brainstorming ways that their assignment could expand, change, or adjust, to include citation justice.

For librarians offering these faculty workshops, it's strongly encouraged to examine the collections most used by faculty to determine if these resources already have tools available for tracking down diverse voices. For example, some databases have taken time to curate collections of materials that focus on diverse authors. Becoming familiar with these resources and gathering them together into a research guide can be a highly effect tool for building departmental relationships. It's highly likely that someone will ask where to find these resources, and it does take some time to track them all down; completing this work ahead of time is most useful to the faculty in the workshop, and also will save a lot of stress for the librarian after the workshop is completed.

The (Infamous) One-Shot

The one-shot instruction session that many librarians provide can also incorporate components of citation justice. Instruction doesn't have to be explicit, though it can be. Citation justice can be embedded into many one-shot sessions by adjusting instruction modules to include conversations on evaluating content or authority and author identity. Discussing how women have been and are currently undercited in the natural sciences, for example, and focusing on papers that are written by women in examples can be a quick way of incorporating citation justice.

Before investigating ways that one-shot instruction sections can be modified to include citation justice, it's important to note that the one-shot format is far from an ideal platform to teach citation justice. In fact, as Sofia Leung points out in her excellent article, one-shot instruction sessions are far from ideal in teaching any type of information literacy, and may do very little good in terms of EDI instruction (Leung, 2022). She argues that one-shots act more as a band-aid that simply prop up white supremacy in academia, and, as such, should be abandoned. Information literacy and equity, diversity, and inclusion topics, like citation justice, should not simply be an add on, an afterthought that is tacked haphazardly into a course, but should be incorporated into a full course, embedded deeply within an assignment, and connected to a student's classes throughout their time in their educational program. This is also a core of citation justice mentioned earlier. *Cite Black Women.* state explicitly that citations alone aren't enough. These works need to be explored and incorporated fully into a student's education. Therefore, it is strongly encouraged that instruction policy surrounding citation justice include the stipulation that these information literacy concepts be embedded from start to finish in an assignment or throughout a semester course. One-shot instruction on these concepts should be avoided. However, since one-shot instruction sessions are currently the standard by which much of information literacy instruction is conducted, making adjustments to the current model can, at the very least, start some conversations across campus on how to change citation practice.

Many instruction sessions discuss how to evaluate authority of the author(s) of a text to determine whether information can and should be trusted. This is an excellent opportunity to incorporate different ideas about why some communities are cited less, and how individual biases may impact who is being cited and what works are being shared. This can be a simple statement of fact, followed by options for changing this practice. Evaluating authority should almost always include an assessment of identity. Why is one author being cited more than another? Should that change? Why? An instruction module that incorporates authority should often, if not always, touch on author identity.

Even if a full authority module isn't called for, simply incorporating EDI topics in a search strategy example can be an excellent way to incorporate citation justice. For example, if one searches for information on civil engineering principles, design the topic to include how engineering can incorporate feedback from the community in which a project is based (Coalter et al., 2022). Using search terms that return diverse search results can be an excellent opportunity to mention that searching for different perspectives from the academic community is important. Again, this need not be a full module, simply a topic brought up and incorporated into the search.

Finally, when discussing citation in general, whether in relation to plagiarism or citation managers or simple formatting, always take the opportunity to discuss citation justice principles. This can include tools for managing diversity of citations (using tags in citation managers such as Zotero or EndNote to keep track of diverse authors) or where to find diverse voices. Again, incorporating these principles doesn't require a complete overhaul of existing information literacy modules. Ultimately, there are ample

Citation Power

opportunities to introduce the topic, and even initiating the discussion can lead to great conversations about adapting a more inclusive citation practice.

CONCLUSION

While citation justice is a relatively new concept, and while further research can offer more insight on citation gaps and how to address them, the existing work makes the importance of this topic clear. Further investigation of citation justice might examine fields in greater detail or examine fields that have not been explored yet in order to develop a greater understanding of the issues. Current evidence makes it abundantly clear; however, that a more proactive and mature citation practice is needed across many fields that incorporates not just content of a research product but the author's identity and perspective as well. By developing a robust citation practice, students, faculty, and librarians can all change who is included and who stays in academia. Because librarians are experts in both research and citation practices, and due to their robust relationships with departments across campus, librarians are uniquely situated to effect change across the face of academia. By making small and large adjustments to citation practice and instruction, and by advertising their skills as search experts, librarians can incorporate citation justice in many areas of academia. The workshops and ideas outlined in this chapter offer a framework to begin integrating citation justice into library instruction and can serve as a starting point to be adjusted and developed as needed. The need for justice in citation practice is there and is crucial to the equity of academia across all fields. Librarians are well-positioned to take the lead on effecting this change and can choose to make a significant contribution in this important component of good research .

Citation Diversity Statement

Recent work in several fields has demonstrated that scholars from marginalized communities have been routinely undercited relative to the number of works published by members of those communities. The author of this chapter chose to cite authors from these communities to proactively address this issue. Author identity including race and gender was considered in addition to content when evaluating content and authority. Approximately 59% of the citations listed in the bibliography have a woman first author, and approximately 31% of first authors are scholars of color.

REFERENCES

Bertolero, M. A., Dworkin, J. D., David, S. U., Lloreda, C. L., Srivastava, P., Stiso, J., Zhou, D., Dzirasa, K., Fair, D. A., Kaczkurkin, A. N., Marlin, B. J., Shohamy, D., Uddin, L. Q., Zurn, P., & Bassett, D. S. (2020). *Racial and ethnic imbalance in neuroscience reference lists and intersections with gender.* https://www.biorxiv.org/content/10.1101/2020.10.12.336230v1 doi:10.1101/2020.10.12.336230

Caplar, N., Tacchella, S., & Birrer, S. (2017). Quantitative evaluation of gender bias in astronomical publications from citation counts. *Nature Astronomy, 1*(6), 0141. doi:10.103841550-017-0141

Chakravartty, P., Kuo, R., Grubbs, V., & McIlwain, C. (2018). #CommunicationSoWhite. *Jo urnal of Communication, 68*(2), 254–266. doi:10.1093/joc/jqy003

Chen, J., Kim, M., & Liu, Q. (2016). Do Female Professors Survive the 19th-Century Tenure System?: Evidence from the Economics Ph.D. Class of 2008. SSRN *Electronic Journal*. https://doi.org/ doi:10.2139/ssrn.2885951

Citation diversity statement in BMES journals. (2021). *Journal of Biomedical Engineering, 49*(3), 947-949. https://doi.org/https://doi.org/10.1007/s10439-021-02739-6

Cite Black Authors – A database for academic research by Black authors. (n.d.). Cite Black Authors. https://citeblackauthors.com/

Coalter, J., Durden, D., & Dunewood, L. A. (2022). Equitable from the Beginning: Incorporating Critical Data Perspectives into Your Research Design. In K. Getz & M. Brodsky (Eds.), *The Data Literacy Cookbook* (pp. 140–144). Association of College and Research Libraries.

D'Ignazio, C., & Klein, L. F. (2020). Our Values and Our Metrics for Holding Ourselves Accountable. In *Data Feminism*. MIT Press. doi:10.7551/mitpress/11805.003.0011

Davenport, E., & Snyder, H. (1995). Who cites women? Whom do women cite? An exploration of gender and scholarly citation in sociology. *The Journal of Documentation, 51*(4), 404–410. doi:10.1108/eb026958

Dworkin, J. D., Linn, K. A., Teich, E. G., Zurn, P., Shinohara, R. T., & Bassett, D. S. (2020). The extent and drivers of gender imbalance in neuroscience reference lists. *Nature Neuroscience, 23*(8), 918–926. doi:10.103841593-020-0658-y PMID:32561883

Else, H., & Perkel, J. M. (2022). The giant plan to track diversity in research journals. *Nature, 602*(7898), 566–570. doi:10.1038/d41586-022-00426-7 PMID:35197624

Guzmán, R. L., & Amrute, S. (2020). How to Cite Like a Badass Tech Feminist Scholar of Color. *Medium*. https://points.datasociety.net/how-to-cite-like-a-badass-tech-feminist-scholar-of-color-ebc839a3619c

Hansen, S. personal communication, November 10, 2022

King, M. M., Bergstrom, C. T., Correll, S. J., Jacquet, J., & West, J. D. (2017). Men Set Their Own Cites High: Gender and Self-citation across Fields and over Time. *Socius: Sociological Research for a Dynamic World, 3*, 2378023117738903. doi:10.1177/2378023117738903

Kozlowski, D., Larivière, V., Sugimoto, C. R., & Monroe-White, T. (2022). Intersectional inequalities in science. *Proceedings of the National Academy of Sciences of the United States of America, 119*(2), e2113067119. doi:10.1073/pnas.2113067119 PMID:34983876

Kozlowski, D., Sugimoto, C. R., Larivière, V., & Monroe-White, T. (2022). *Intersectional Inequalities in Science*. https://sciencebias.uni.lu/app/

Kwon, D. (2022). The rise of citational justice: How scholars are making references fairer. *Nature, 603*(7902), 568–571. doi:10.1038/d41586-022-00793-1 PMID:35318470

Leung, S. (2022). The Futility of Information Literacy & EDI: Toward What? *C&RL, 8*(5), 751. https://doi.org/https://doi.org/10.5860/crl.83.5.751

Citation Power

Lutz, C. (1990). the erasure of women's writing in sociocultural anthropology. *American Ethnologist, 17*(4), 611–627. doi:10.1525/ae.1990.17.4.02a00010

Main, J. B., Tan, L., Cox, M. F., McGee, E. O., & Katz, A. (2020). The correlation between undergraduate student diversity and the representation of women of color faculty in engineering. *Journal of Engineering Education, 109*(4), 843–864. doi:10.1002/jee.20361

Mott, C., & Cockayne, D. (2017). Citation matters: Mobilizing the politics of citation toward a practice of 'conscientious engagement'. *Gender, Place and Culture, 24*(7), 954–973. doi:10.1080/096636 9X.2017.1339022

Mott, C., & Cockayne, D. (2018). Conscientious disengagement and whiteness as a condition of dialogue. *Dialogues in Human Geography, 8*(2), 143–147. doi:10.1177/2043820618780575

Murphy, F. (2017). Engineering a gender bias. *Nature, 543*(7646), S31–S31. doi:10.1038/543S31a PMID:28328907

Nunkoo, R., Hall, C. M., Rughoobur-Seetah, S., & Teeroovengadum, V. (2019). Citation practices in tourism research: Toward a gender conscientious engagement. *Annals of Tourism Research, 79*, 102755. doi:10.1016/j.annals.2019.102755

Plett, C. (April 11, 2016). Zucker's "Therapy" Mourned Almost Exclusively By Cis People. *Harlot.* https://web.archive.org/web/20160607175210/http://harlot.med ia/articles/2582/zuckers-therapy-mourned-almost-exclusively-
by-cis-people

Smith, C. (n.d.). *Cite Black Women.* Cite Black Women Collective. https://www.citeblackwomencollective.org/

Teich, E. G., Kim, J. Z., Lynn, C. W., Simon, S. C., Klishin, A. A., Szymula, K. P., Srivastava, P., Bassett, L. C., Zurn, P., Dworkin, J. D., & Bassett, D. S. (2022). Citation inequity and gendered citation practices in contemporary physics. *Nature Physics, 18*(10), 1161–1170. doi:10.103841567-022-01770-1

Thieme, K., & Saunders, M. A. S. (2018). How do you wish to be cited? Citation practices and a scholarly community of care in trans studies research articles. *Journal of English for Academic Purposes, 32*, 80–90. doi:10.1016/j.jeap.2018.03.010

Trimble, V. (1993). Patterns in citations of papers by American astronomers. *Quarterly Journal of the Royal Astronomical Society, 34*(2), 235-250. <Go to ISI>://WOS:A1993LF43800007

Zurn, P., Bassett, D. S., & Rust, N. C. (2020). The Citation Diversity Statement: A Practice of Transparency, A Way of Life. *Trends in Cognitive Sciences, 24*(9), 669–672. doi:10.1016/j.tics.2020.06.009 PMID:32762966

Chapter 5
The Power of Collaboration in Creating and Sustaining Anti-Racism Resource Guides:
A Case Study From Binghamton University Libraries

Jennifer K. Embree
Binghamton University, USA

Megan L. Benson
Binghamton University, USA

Rachel Berman Turner
Virginia Commonwealth University, USA

Sharon Bunch-Nunez
Binghamton University, USA

Elise Ferer
Binghamton University, USA

Amy Gay
https://orcid.org/0000-0001-8136-9296
Binghamton University, USA

Neyda V. Gilman
Binghamton University, USA

Laura Christine Haynes
Broome County Public Library, USA

Lauren Loewen
Binghamton University, USA

Rennae Robinson
Binghamton University, USA

ABSTRACT

In this book chapter and case study, the authors tell the story of how they created and sustained the Binghamton University Libraries' Anti-Racism and Resource Guide. They discuss how they first came together on this project to develop their vision of the guide and how they were able to evolve and adapt the project over time so that it remains updated, relevant, and sustainable. They also highlight the extremely collaborative nature of their work in this guide, and reflect on how bringing together their varied voices to collectively develop a resource on the topic of anti-racism led to the creation of an extremely unique and dynamic guide.

DOI: 10.4018/978-1-6684-7255-2.ch005

Copyright © 2023, IGI Global. Copying or distributing in print or electronic forms without written permission of IGI Global is prohibited.

The Power of Collaboration in Creating Anti-Racism Resource Guides

In the summer of 2020, several of Binghamton University Libraries' faculty and staff were filled with an authentic desire to bring more awareness to issues of racial and social justice within their academic community. Inspired by the George Floyd protests, a group of passionate individuals came together to form a task force focused on advancing anti-racism initiatives within the Libraries. This task force eventually developed several subcommittees, one of which included a team of library faculty and staff who were especially interested in anti-racism education and research. This team, officially named the Anti-Racism Resources & Education subcommittee, spent the next two years utilizing their diverse expertise to collectively develop, build, and maintain the Binghamton University Libraries' Anti-Racism Research & Resource Guide.

In this book chapter, the creators of the Binghamton University Libraries' Anti-Racism Research & Resource Guide present a case study on how they worked together to create and maintain their guide over the past two years. They discuss how they developed their vision of the guide, how they made design choices and selected resources, and how they evolved and adapted their project so that it could remain updated, relevant, and sustainable. They document the setbacks and challenges that they faced when creating the guide, and provide recommendations for library and information professionals who may be interested in creating social justice guides or updating existing ones at their own institutions. Most importantly, they highlight the collaborative nature of their work and reflect on how they harnessed their individual strengths, perspectives, and experiences to ultimately build a dynamic anti-racism resource guide.

LITERATURE REVIEW

Libguides is a content management system created by the company Springshare in 2007 and is frequently used by libraries to create digital guides that provide information, resources, links, and research help on a variety of topics ("Libguides", n.d.). These guides can vary widely in scope and purpose, but in the academic library field, the Libguides tool is often used by librarians to create curated guides that provide resources and research help specific in certain subject areas, courses, or assignments (Bergstrom-Lynch, 2019).

Libguides have become ubiquitous in the field of librarianship over the past fifteen years. Springshare currently states that they are used by 6,100 libraries and 130,000 librarians across 82 countries as of February 2023 ("Libguides", n.d.), and this has led to the publication of countless research articles, usability studies, and opinion pieces focused on how to best utilize the software tool to meet user needs, particularly in the areas of guide design, resource curation, and organizational structure (Neuhaus et al., 2021). Several usability studies that evaluate Libguide designs, for instance, have found that participants more often preferred side-navigation menus over top-level horizontal navigation menus (Ouellette, 2011; Thorngate & Hoden, 2017; Barker & Hoffman, 2021), were often distracted or turned-off by big blocks of text and cluttered-looking guide pages (Stonsteby & DeJonghe, 2013; Barker & Hoffman, 2021), and were most drawn to minimalist guides that required less scrolling and fewer tabs to navigate (Conerton & Goldenstein, 2017; Barker & Hoffman, 2021). Some user studies have also sought to determine the most effective methods of content organization. Both Lee & Lowe (2018) and Barker & Hoffman (2021) found that students seemed to prefer pedagogical-style guides (i.e. guides organized by research processes and learning outcomes) over more traditional "pathfinder" guides (i.e. guides organized by resource type).

However, despite the abundance of studies that address Libguide design, usage, and organization in a general sense, there is a significant lack of literature that examines the use of Libguides to create social justice and anti-racist resource guides. One of the few articles that have been published on the topic is Twanna Hodge's (2020) "Using LibGuides to support racial justice & create inclusive communities," in Springshare's online newsletter *SpringyNews*. In this article, Hodge provided valuable guidance, tips, and examples of how libraries can create high-quality social justice-oriented resource guides. Hodge's recommendations were then used to help create a rubric in Piper, Ameen, and Lowe's (2021) ground-breaking study, in which the authors evaluated 66 anti-Black racism libguides that met their criteria from 61 ARL institutions. After evaluating the libguides, their findings indicated that guides scored higher in areas of design and resource suggestions, but were significantly lacking in two content areas: "Framing of Social Justice" and "Pedagogy" (Piper et al., 2021). They determined that guides were more likely to omit definitions of key social justice terms, solidarity statements, and contextual information that engaged more directly with social justice theory and learning goals for the guide (Piper et al., 2021).

What the authors of this publication believe to still be missing from the literature, and what they hope to add to this small but growing body of research, is a case study that thoroughly documents the many complex, challenging, and rewarding processes that have to take place in order to create and maintain a social justice libguide. As the calls for creating more impactful social justice guides continue to be made (Hodge, 2020; Piper et al. 2021), several librarians and information professionals may want to more thoroughly engage in this process. However, building and sustaining high-quality social justice LibGuides can be strenuous, time-consuming, and exhausting. The authors of this case study hope that by offering an in-depth account of their collaborative journey to create an anti-racism resource guide they can provide valuable insights to library and information professionals planning to create social justice guides of their own or looking for effective ways to sustain the guides they already operate.

Case Study: Creating and Implementing the Binghamton University Libraries' Anti-Racism Research and Resource Guide

Background

The idea for the guide was first mentioned to the Dean of the Libraries by a Subject Librarian in June 2020 in the wake of the George Floyd protests. The Subject Librarian believed that creating such a guide would be a great opportunity for the Libraries to provide support for more anti-racism education, awareness, and research within the campus community. At the time, there were several conversations happening amongst the Binghamton University Libraries workforce about ways in which employees could engage in more anti-racism initiatives, and the Dean suggested bringing up the idea of the guide to the Library faculty in a meeting to gauge interest in the project. However, before the opportunity arose to discuss the guide in a faculty meeting, the entirety of the library staff held a special assembly and discussed creating a department-wide Anti-Racism Task Force. This action was approved, and the University Libraries' Anti-Racism Task Force came into being in the early summer of 2020. The task force was initially organized very organically. Individuals proposed and created subcommittees within the task force based on personal interests and sent out calls for participation. The Task Force ended up forming multiple subcommittees, such as an Anti-Racism Collections Audit subcommittee and an Anti-Racism Statement subcommittee.

The Subject Librarian that initially pitched the idea for a guide to the Dean formed a subcommittee under the new Anti-Racism Task Force called the Anti-Racism Resources & Education subcommittee. The subcommittee's main charge was to create an anti-racism resource guide for the Binghamton community that would support teaching, learning and research in topics related to anti-racism and racial justice. When the initial call for committee volunteers was sent out six additional library faculty and staff members joined the subcommittee. The volunteers that made up this committee came from several different departments across the Binghamton University Libraries system, including cataloging, instruction & outreach, subject librarianship, digital scholarship, and reader services. It was reflected upon later that bringing together a team that had such a diversity in expertise really strengthened the Anti-Racism Research & Resource Guide and ultimately made it a more unique and dynamic guide.

Planning and Initial Steps

After the initial team of seven collaborators was formed, the next step was mapping out the anti-racism resource guide project and developing its overall vision and scope. From the beginning, the subcommittee knew they wanted to create an anti-racism guide that offered something unique and different from other, pre-existing anti-racism library guides. When they began looking at examples from other academic institutions for inspiration, they noted that several were already maintaining excellent guides with well-informed and thoughtful content. One example is the Simmons University Anti-Oppression LibGuide, which provides extremely thorough information on several forms of oppression and lists countless resources and educational tools to help educate oneself further on these topics. Instead of trying to recreate guide content like this that was already available and of high quality, the committee members thought it best to create a resource guide that filled in gaps in the current nationwide guide content on anti-racism, while also still creating a guide that met the educational and research needs of their own campus community.

To do this, they began evaluating anti-racism guides from other academic libraries around the country. During this process committee members noted that many other guides at the time seemed to have a more generalist approach to providing resources on anti-racism. A typical anti-racism guide might provide a general overview of anti-racism, sometimes including a few definitions of terms, and then a general book/resource list of popular titles and places where people could get started in educating themselves further about a variety of issues. A couple of guides would provide information about specific topics or movements relevant to anti-racism, such as racial justice or political movements. However, the committee members were not able to find any anti-racism guides at the time that contained comprehensive, in depth lists of resources on several subject-specific areas that were geared towards anti-racism study and education. In addition, the focus of most of the guides seem to be general education on anti-racism, not specifically on how to incorporate these resources into academic or student research and not on how to actively utilize these resources in the classroom or course curricula. These were the two particular areas that the committee members decided they wanted to center in their own anti-racism resource guide.

Overall, the committee members decided that they wanted to create an anti-racism resource guide that provided a curated selection of academic-level resources and materials on topics related to anti-racism, racial justice, and systemic racism from their collections for those in the Binghamton University community. At the same time, the members were aware that not all Binghamton University community members inhabit the same intellectual space, and so more popular material for early researchers was also included. They wanted the guide to provide support for students, faculty, or staff members that are interested in learning more about these topics, as well as provide a starting point for those that are interested in conducting research on topics related to this area of study. In addition, they wanted the guide to serve as a resource for instructors on campus who are interested in diversifying or decolonizing their course readings and resources, and to help amplify historically marginalized voices in their classroom curricula. In order to do this in the most effective manner possible, they decided to organize the guide into subject-based categories. Each category would include a variety of resources that would help support research and learning, such as relevant books, articles (both scholarly and popular), databases, reading lists, a/v selections, and additional resources. The guide would also have a general "Anti-Racism: Where to Start" page that would provide more generalized information about the topic of anti-racism for those looking for more introductory material.

They also wanted to ensure that the guide was situated as a living, community document, meaning that it was expected to be consistently changing, adapting, and evolving based on feedback from the Binghamton community. They wanted to ensure that there were easy mechanisms to gather feedback on the guide from a variety of individuals and organizations on campus and planned to always be open-minded and receptive to adapting the guide to fit the needs of those that wanted and planned to utilize it.

Creation and Considerations

Once the scope and vision of the Anti-Racism Research & Resource Guide had been established, the next step was planning out and doing the work to create a comprehensive, subject-specific guide. Because there were so many committee members, the team knew it would be a challenge to balance consistency in the guide's layout and design with ensuring that there was still opportunity for each individual to incorporate their own expertise, voice, and unique perspective into their contributions.

The committee members met to discuss the subject areas that they wanted to include in the guide's first draft. The core areas that the committee decided upon were the following: Environment, Gender & Sexuality, Healthcare, Housing, Policing & The Justice System, Politics & Voter Suppression, and Technology & AI. The committee members also wanted to make sure there was a "Where to Start" page, "Celebrating Black Voices" page, and a "Decolonizing Curricula" page included in the guide as well. These subject areas were decided upon both based on the committee members' general agreement on topics that were essential to the study and education of anti-racism and their individual interests. Additional pages were added to the guide after launch, including Arts & Culture, Food, Food Justice, & Food Insecurity, and Latinx Anti-Racism. A comprehensive chart describing each of the guide's pages in more detail, including how content was selected and reflections from the page creators, can be found in Appendix 3.

After selecting the main pages and subject area topics that the committee wanted to include in the guide, the chair wanted to ensure that the work spent creating the pages would be as streamlined as possible. In order to do this, she created a workflow chart (see Appendix 1) that allowed all committee members to sign-up to become a page manager for the page(s) that interested them most. Once a committee member had signed-up to be the page manager of a certain page, they then became responsible for building that page, including searching for and adding resources, adding additional resources that were provided via feedback from other committee members/outside organizations to the page, and maintaining the page after the guide became live (i.e. fixing broken links, adding newly recommended resources, re-evaluating and updating content, etc.). All of these responsibilities were outlined in the workflow chart document.

The Power of Collaboration in Creating Anti-Racism Resource Guides

In addition, the committee chair experimented with a few different layouts and designs for organizing the resource guide pages in order to create a template that all committee members could follow. This would make it easier to guarantee a consistent look throughout the resource guide's many subject pages.. After running these design ideas by the committee members and getting positive responses, the committee chair created the <u>Anti-Racism Resource Formatting Guide</u> (Appendix 2), which provided detailed instructions and guidelines to all committee members on how to organize, format, and add resources to their assigned guide pages.

Generally, the organization for the pages all followed a similar flow. The core resource types that were required of each page were books (in a gallery-type setting), articles (both popular and scholarly), podcasts and videos, and additional resources. Other potential resource areas that could be included, but were not required, were reading lists, hot topics, and resources for research. Each page was also required to include an "Are We Missing Anything" blurb that asked the community to provide feedback if there were any resource recommendations they wanted to make. There was no set amount of resources that each section was required to include on any individual page - this was left up to the discretion of the page manager. However, there were efforts made to ensure that there wasn't an overabundance of resources included, so that a page would not overwhelm a user browsing on the page.

The creation of the Anti-Racism Resource Formatting Guide was extremely effective in establishing more cohesion and consistency amongst the pages, despite so many individuals working on the project simultaneously. Committee members were all able to reference the guide as they built their pages to make sure that formatting matched, but still were given a lot of creative leeway in the types of resources they researched, selected, and added to the guide. It then became easy to set and check up on deadlines at the committee's regularly scheduled meetings.

Formatting consistency was not the only issue. Committee members also wondered how they could recommend resources for other topics and pages outside of their own. Redundancy was also a concern, given the interdisciplinarity of topics. For instance, there may be a book that addresses both technology and politics/voter suppression. In this case, where does that resource get highlighted? How does one determine where this resource gets placed and how does the committee know where to ultimately find it?

To address these issues, a resource tracking Google document was created. Using the organization flow mentioned above, the committee members used this tracking sheet to document all of the resources that they were finding in their own research, so that they could be reviewed before being added to the libguide page. Other committee members were then able to add in suggestions or recommended resources for other pages beyond their own in this document, and committee members could also make notes, add comments, etc. to decide where resources that straddled interdisciplinary lines should end up living once the official pages were created in the libguide.

A deadline was set by which all resources needed to be added to the document and reviewed by all; this had to be done before work officially started on libguide pages. Once the resources were all approved by the group, this tracking sheet served the added benefit of notifying committee members that resources they were considering were already added to the guide.

One of the last kinks that arose during this organization process was the realization that several of the books that committee members found and wanted to add to the guide were not owned by the library. At Binghamton, purchasing monographs is the responsibility of individual subject librarians. Originally, it was suggested that if the committee came across an unowned book, they should reach out to the appropriate subject librarian to request it for purchase. This workflow quickly became too overwhelming,

83

both for committee members and for subject librarians, since the number of unowned books members wanted to add to the guide was quite numerous.

To remedy this issue, the chair of the committee reached out to the Dean of the Libraries, the Head of Collections, and the Head of Acquisitions to propose the creation of a small Anti-Racism collection fund. This fund would be managed by the committee, so that they could purchase books immediately without having to go through any additional approval channels. Its primary purpose would be to supplement the Library's collection with titles about anti-racism that would also be featured on the guide. All of the parties included in this discussion loved the idea, and a new collection fund of $2,000 was created. This accomplishment of establishing an anti-racism fund was very exciting for all of the committee members; However, the committee now had the added responsibility of tracking and documenting spending to stay within budget.

In order to do this most effectively, an Anti-Racism Recommendation List was created by the chair. This recommendation list was used to track all of the books that were not currently owned by the Libraries, but that committee members wanted to purchase and feature on the guide. Information was collected in this list, such as title, author, print vs. ebook pricing, etc. so that informed purchase decisions could be made by the group at our scheduled meetings. Additional tracking information was also included, such as a checkmark to indicate whether or not the book had been purchased, whether or not that resource had been added to the guide yet (and where it was added), and a color-coding system that let all committee members know where in the stage of purchasing/being added to the guide that particular resource was. The chair would monitor this list periodically and add it to the agenda of the next meeting, where recommendations would be discussed and approved. Once the recommendations were approved the chair would purchase the books.

Utilizing all of these workflows and documents, the committee worked together to meet the deadlines that they set for releasing this guide. The committee's first meeting took place in June of 2020. They set a goal to try and release the guide by September 1st, 2020, so that the guide could be promoted and made accessible to the campus community at the start of the fall semester. They committee members were on track to meet this deadline. However, before the guide was officially launched, they wanted to share a draft version of the guide with various community members and stakeholders to gather feedback.

Response and Feedback

As the committee continued to make good progress building the guide through the summer of 2020, they began to turn their attention towards planning a "soft launch" to gather feedback from various stakeholders within the campus community. In early August of 2020, the committee chair shared a draft version of the guide with the Dean of the Libraries and the Deputy University Librarian for initial feedback and to get approval to soft launch the guide and share it with others outside of the Libraries. Both were very supportive of the guide and had no additional feedback to share.

The committee members then made a list of additional stakeholders with whom they wanted to share a draft version of the guide. Utilizing the campus connections that were already established amongst the committee members, they decided to share the guide with representatives from the Multicultural Resource Center, the Anti-Racism Pedagogy Working Group, and the organizer of a collective discussion group amongst faculty and staff on campus that focused on having weekly discussions about issues related to equity, diversity and inclusion, called Conscious Conversations. Both the Multicultural Resource Center and the Anti-Racism Pedagogy Working Group expressed great enthusiasm for the guide, and had very minimal feedback to share beyond that they thought it would make an excellent resource for the campus. The lead organizer of Conscious Conversations also expressed strong support for the guide, and provided additional helpful feedback. In the original version of the guide, the committee members had a page for Decolonizing Curricula that contained information related to anti-racism pedagogy. The organizer of Conscious Conversations suggested having an additional page that discussed anti-racism efforts and issues across higher education more broadly. For example, having resources that different professional organizations and departments across campus could use, such as Resident Life, Student Services, and Athletics. This feedback was noted, and at the start of the 2021 semester, a new page was added to the guide called "Anti-Racism in Higher Education" to address this feedback directly.

With this feedback gathered, the committee felt that they were ready to make the guide officially live at the start of the 2020 fall semester, with plans to incorporate more extensive projects based on feedback recommendations over the course of the semester. Throughout the beginning of September, they finished gathering feedback from the stakeholders listed above, worked out the logistics of where the guide would be visible on the Libraries' homepage, prepared promotional materials, such as a blogpost announcing the guide, and then officially launched it in full on September 17th, 2020.

After the guide was launched on September 17th, 2020, there was an immediate positive reaction from the Binghamton University community overall. Just a few days after the launch a student writer for the University's campus newspaper, Pipe Dream, reached out with an interest in writing an article on the resource guide and the recent Anti-Racism statement the Libraries released. The article was published on September 21, 2020 and included information about the guide and its overall purpose. In addition, the Director for the Center of Civic Engagement reached out directly to the Dean of Libraries to state that, "the anti-racism resource guide will be a tremendous asset to our community. I…promise to help to promote these resources to our faculty, staff, students, and community members."

The Student Affairs Divisional Diversity Officer also let the committee chair know that they added the resource guide to their own website as a suggested resource for students to consult. In addition to this positive feedback, several committee members heard additional praise for the guide through word of mouth, and the guide has been mentioned by other SUNY schools as a reference that they used when creating some of their own anti-racism themed guides.

Since its launch date, the Anti-Racism Research & Resource Guide has been viewed 8,014 times over the course of 27 months, for an average of 297 views per month. Its peak views were in March and April of 2021, with over 550 views for each month.

Looking to the Future: Sustaining the Guide and Adding in New Voices and Perspectives

Sustaining the Guide

After the successful launch of the guide, the committee members transitioned their efforts to look more towards ways in which they could sustainably maintain the guide as a committee. Every semester, they met to discuss new ideas for pages that they wanted to create, how to incorporate feedback from outside organizations, general maintenance reminders (i.e. checking broken links, updating content on the guides to more timely materials and resources, add new purchases, etc.), and approve recommended purchases using the anti-racism fund.

The committee added four additional pages to the guide over the course of October 2020-December 2021, including two new subject pages (Arts & Culture and Food, Food Justice, & Food Insecurity), the Anti-Racism in Higher Education page, and a Get Involved page that provides links to local, regional, and national resources for those interested in engaging in anti-racism activism. In addition, the committee decided in the spring of 2021 to create a "hot topics" section of the guide, where more specialized content on timely topics related to anti-racism could be highlighted. Under this new heading, they added two new pages: Covid-19 & Anti-Asian Racism and Voter Suppression Efforts Post-2020 Election.

Despite all of these milestone developments, in the fall of 2021 the committee was beginning to feel a bit overwhelmed with the responsibilities of maintaining the guide long-term in the fall of 2021. The Libraries underwent a reorganization in the spring of 2021 and also started a massive strategic planning process in the summer of 2021, so job responsibilities were shifting, priorities were changing, and committee work was becoming difficult to sustain for several staff and faculty members within the Libraries during this transitional period. However, all committee members still believed in the importance of maintaining this resource and were devoted to making sure that it was sustained. They began discussing ways in which workflows could be adjusted and new avenues could be explored to make sure that the resource guide stayed updated while not overburdening the committee members.

One workflow that was altered was how the committee approached maintaining the anti-racism fund. After the 2020-2021 fiscal year, the anti-racism fund was given a huge boost in funding. This was very welcome and exciting for the committee members. However, since the Resource Guide had already been launched, there were not as many immediate recommendations and cost needs as there were when the guide was initially being created. The purpose of the fund had shifted from being a "start-up" fund for supporting the guide to being a more general fund for the Libraries to purchase any resources related to Anti-Racism. Because of this, it became more of a challenge for the committee to manage this fund in the way they had previously had–by adding books that were recommended for specific pages that the Libraries did not have and having regular meetings to discuss and approve the purchases. The committee was not meeting as frequently, and there were not enough resources needed for the subcommittee to expend their allocated budget. Therefore, it became very hard for the committee to spend down the money collectively, without someone being specifically responsible for doing outside research and collection development for the fund. The chair began doing this work, and the committee decided at a meeting in early 2022 that she would take on the responsibility of managing this collection fund as part of her official job duties instead of a responsibility through the committee. However, the committee collectively agreed that recommendations from the committee would always hold the highest priority when making purchasing decisions, and the chair would still track all purchases made using the fund and share them with the committee so they could see and provide feedback, if they so desired.

In addition to adapting the way the committee handled the Anti-Racism Collection Fund, they also began to explore ways in which they could empower graduate students working in the libraries to help maintain, sustain, and revitalize the guide.

New Voices and Perspectives

The committee recognized that one of the original strengths of the Anti-Racism Research & Resource guide was the diversity in expertise that its team members brought to the project. The committee brought many distinct and diverse voices and perspectives together from several different departments across the Libraries, and this led to more innovative ideas being shared, more creativity being infused into the

The Power of Collaboration in Creating Anti-Racism Resource Guides

process, and more perspectives being represented in the creation of the guide. The committee members realized that to keep the guide relevant, new and varied perspectives would be necessary long-term. Below are personal reflections from librarians, staff, and students that share how they were able to provide new perspectives and approaches to the Anti-Racism Research & Resource Guide over the past two years.

Perspectives of Library Staff

Assistant Head of Reader Services for UDC; Coordinator for Libraries' High Impact Student Program

A healthy commitment to inclusion is at the heart of Binghamton Libraries' Anti-Racism efforts. From its birth, all of the Libraries' staff were encouraged and afforded the time to be a part of the Anti-Racism Task Force and its various subcommittees. Faculty, Clerical and Professional Staff took part in scripting our Anti-Racism statement. All members of staff were invited to propose and/or lead subcommittees dedicated to investigating and implementing antiracist strategies into the work of the Libraries. When the Anti-Racism Research & Resource Guide was proposed, being a part of the effort was natural.

As is typically the case with academic library subject guides, Binghamton Libraries' subject guides are curated with the thoughtful and expert lenses of Subject Librarians. The Subject Librarians' expertise in the discipline of the respective subject guide ensures the inclusion of foundational texts, relevant databases, and emerging trends. For that reason, the invitation to all of the staff members to contribute to an antiracism resource guide was a unique, inclusive, and potentially intimidating challenge for those who have never had the opportunity to curate a subject guide. As a professional staff member situated in public services, taking on this challenge was exciting.

Through Binghamton University's Student Affairs Administration program, this author has developed a keen understanding of the vital role student affairs professionals serve in enhancing college student success. Professionals who work in the offices that serve Binghamton's international students, students with disabilities, first-generation students, LGBTQ and BIPOC students, and beyond, must dedicate time and energy to better understanding how to uphold the commitment to equitable and inclusive support of all students. An antiracist lens can offer tools to meet that charge. To complement the robust selection of resources that support antiracist classroom instruction, it was important to offer student services and professional resources that primarily extend beyond the confines and standards of the classroom.

Given the nature of the collaborative effort to create a cohesive Anti-Racism Research & Resource Guide, the Librarians who contributed to the guide compiled a tremendously thorough set of supporting documents that included formatting guidelines, responsibility workflows, and a clearly articulated charge. As a first-time subject guide contributor, these tools were pivotal. The inclusive and supportive attitudes of the team of librarians who contributed to this guide not only equipped this author with the confidence to overcome the ugly specter of imposter syndrome, they also demonstrated the level of effort that is necessary to make equitable inclusion a real possibility.

Utilizing Graduate Students

Instruction and Outreach Librarian & Supervisor of Research Help Desk Graduate Students

In early 2022, Binghamton University Libraries launched a Research Help desk staffed by graduate students in a variety of disciplines (Binghamton does not have a library science program). These graduate students brought diverse perspectives to the Libraries through their own identities and past experiences and their disciplinary knowledge. While the primary responsibility of these students is staffing a service point that offers research assistance, they were also offered hours off the desk in which they would work on special projects for the Libraries. One of those off desk projects became the maintenance of the library's Anti-Racism Research & Resource Guide.

The primary responsibility of the graduate students is to check links and replace links when possible, but members of the Anti-Racism Resource Group also wished to gather feedback on the guide from a student perspective. Based upon this, graduate students began their work by evaluating the guide itself. The committee, along with the supervisor of the Research Help Desk, drafted questions for the graduate students to reflect upon while exploring the guide for the first time. These questions asked students to comment on what they liked and disliked about the guide, the overall organization of the guide, resources they found interesting, resources that were missing, missing subject areas, as well as general comments on the guide.

During this time, two of the graduate students at the Research Help Desk began reviewing the guide, with the intention that the links on the guide would be reviewed once a semester both to check broken links and review all resources for timeliness, and quality. These graduate students were given the opportunity to add new content to the guide and the comprehensive list of resources maintained by the Anti-Racism Resources & Education subcommittee. In order to complete this work, graduate students were given instructions on Springshare's LibGuides platform, focusing on checking and revising links and building new pages within a guide. They were also encouraged to make book recommendations to be purchased using the Anti-Racism collection fund. As a result of this initial process, several resources were added to the guide and the Latinx Anti-Racism page was created by a graduate student during their off-desk work hours.

All of these efforts have expanded the scope of the guide and added new voices to the conversation. It has been helpful to have the perspective of two students who are not accustomed to the LibGuide format and who bring their own identities to this work. The work of graduate students has expanded the scope of the guide and their involvement may assist in continuing to maintain and expand the guide itself.

There have been some noticeable challenges in giving this work to graduate students, the first of which was orienting them to the LibGuides format and teaching them how to build guides. The other main challenge is that off desk work does not always happen on a recurring basis. Off desk work depends upon the ability of graduate students to make time for it in their schedule. Their first responsibility is staffing the Research Help Desk; after that graduate students may elect to do a set number of off desk hours per week. Depending upon the preferences of these students, there may be a lot of off desk work happening or little-to-no off desk work. Summer and break periods when the Research Help Desk is open fewer hours is often when much of the off desk work happens. Because of this it can be difficult to make sure links are checked every semester.

Additionally, student workers eventually do graduate, so most of the graduate students are employed with the libraries 2 years or less. This means that a graduate student who creates a page on the guide will not be the one to maintain it. But at the same time this can add some variety to the voices and viewpoints represented in the guide.

In the future, there are plans to have graduate assistants continue their work with the Anti-Racism Research & Resource Guide, checking links, suggesting resources, and building pages on the guide. As stated above, this will add diversity to the guide itself as well as keep the guide up to date. Based upon the amount of off desk time that graduate students are available to work, these updates may not happen

The Power of Collaboration in Creating Anti-Racism Resource Guides

every semester, but will be performed at least once a year to keep the guide current. Overall, the graduate students have already made valuable contributions to the Anti-Racism Research & Resource Guide.

As the supervisor of the graduate students who worked on the guide, this author supported the work that was necessary to maintain the guide. She was excited to gather student perspectives on the guide and to see their ideas and additions. Her greatest contribution was drafting questions that the graduate students could answer as they reviewed the guide. From past experience, one receives better feedback when asking targeted questions, so it was crucial to have questions that could serve as a starting point for review.

Once the graduate students had the opportunity to review the guide and reflect on the resources, they were able to suggest valuable additions to the guide. As a relative newcomer to the project, this author wanted to understand the purpose and intention behind the guide before suggesting any changes. She worked to explore the guide on her own, along with the materials supporting the guide, and met with the Anti-Racism Resources & Education subcommittee to understand their perspectives. Some of the suggestions did not fit neatly into the structure of the guide, so working with others on the Anti-Racism Resources & Education subcommittee to understand their perspective and discuss how to incorporate new ideas was important. This helped guide the graduate students in their work on the guide, meaning that they could come to the author with questions and/or to talk through ideas.

As changes and additions were being proposed and made, the author served as the intermediary between the graduate students and the Anti-Racism Resources & Education subcommittee. Because of her relationship with the subcommittee she was able to answer questions posed by the graduate students and help them brainstorm and develop their contributions to the guide. As the guide is hosted in Springshare's LibGuides platform, she introduced the graduate students to the LibGuide platform and helped them do everything from fix broken links to build new pages for the guide.

This work is very important and the author does not think that full time library employees should be the only ones contributing to this work. She has been very happy to incorporate student voices into Anti-Racism work and is interested in how the subcommittee can continue to find ways to involve others in this work. Below are personal narratives from both graduate students as they reflected on their own contributions to the Anti-Racism Research & Resource Guide.

Graduate Student 1

The opportunity to review and help maintain the Anti-Racism LibGuide was simultaneously daunting and exciting. As per usual procedure with any assignment that asks for assessment and feedback, the author came armed with their pen and notebook. The initial hours (spread across several days in the Spring 2022 semester) of poring through the guide were an intense experience. Something akin to being inundated with powerful information and tools that took some time sitting with and processing. Unsure of how to structure a review, the author turned to the questions provided by their supervisor for guidance. They remember moving through the pages strategically, tab by tab, sub-section by sub-section. And with each area reviewed they considered the questions given— What do you like or not like about the guide? Does the organization make sense to you? Did you find any resources that were interesting to you? etc. Overall, closing feedback highlighted the academic and personal benefits of having such a wide-ranging source organized into approachable categories. The author also offered a few podcast suggestions and possibly a subsection within the guide that aims to help students and faculty navigate the emotional and mental process of exploring such an impactful resource.

89

Graduate Student 2

The author's work on the anti-racism subject guide began when they were tasked with looking through the guide. The main goals were to check and update the links on the web page, and add additional relevant resources. They did this by filling out a form provided by the supervisor that allowed the author to reflect and create suggestions based on these evaluations. During this process, they noticed that there was no page dedicated to anti-immigrant or anti-Latinx racism. The author finished updating the links on the pages and included a few new and relevant resources discovered. After this, their supervisor granted approval to create a Latinx Anti-Racism page, which was discussed above.

REFLECTIONS ON THE CREATION OF THE GUIDE: CHALLENGES, LIMITATIONS, AND RECOMMENDATIONS

The creation of this guide is a result of the passion, dedication, and interest of several individuals within the Binghamton University Libraries community. Each member of the team reflected on their experience working on the guide, sharing challenges they faced, limitations they encountered, guide improvements they recommended, and personal stories of growth and self-evaluation. The authors believe that these reflections provide valuable insights and recommendations for other librarians and institutions that may be interested in creating their own anti-racism guides.

Challenges

The creators of the guide noted several challenges that they encountered while creating the resource. One of the most frequently mentioned challenges was curating the overwhelming amount of information that was discovered during researching and evaluating sources for the guide. The creator of the healthcare page on the guide stated that she was seeing potentially good sources everywhere she looked everyday due to the overlap of the COVID-19 pandemic and the George Floyd protests. At times, she felt that navigating and evaluating all of these resources was impossible. Both the creators of the Food Justice page and the Policing & The Justice System pages also expressed challenges when selecting resources for their sections. The Food Justice page creator felt that there were so many different avenues and nuances to the topic of food justice that it was difficult to determine what to cover. The Policing & The Justice System creator shared that there were so many conversations in the media surrounding her topic that it was difficult to determine which resources would not lead to misinformation or confirmation bias for those visiting the page.

In order to address these challenges, each page creator came up with their own solutions or suggested improvements for their pages. The Healthcare page creator decided to share a PubMed search on her page because she believed it was extremely important to educate the guide's visitors on finding their own research and resources, especially in a field where information is constantly being updated on a daily basis. On the Healthcare page, she provides the search she used to find articles (That search was: (health AND (("Race Factors"[Mesh]) OR "Racism"[Mesh] OR "Ethnic Groups"[Mesh])).) and describes it as a good place for people to start their own search. To supplement the idea of searching in PubMed, she also provided the link to the MEDLINE/PubMed Search and Health Disparities & Minority Health Information Resources to encourage more independent research on this topic. The creator of the

The Power of Collaboration in Creating Anti-Racism Resource Guides

Food Justice page approached the challenges she faced by focusing on the current conversations related to the topic of food and food justice that were coinciding with the Black Lives Matter movement. She also suggested that in the future, the page could include more concrete definitions and explanations of the various terms that are frequently used in discussions of food justice topics, such as food sovereignty, food insecurity, etc. Lastly, the creator of the Policing & The Justice System page addressed her concerns about counteracting misinformation and confirmation bias by linking to several external and credible resources, such as The Innocence Project and the Sentencing Project, and a variety of reading lists.

Additional challenges that were shared by the guide creators were ensuring that the resources selected were appropriately varied, accessible, and also able to hold the interest of as many interested guide visitors as possible. The guide creators knew that making the guide as accessible as possible was important, but this became complicated when they wanted to highlight research-oriented resources, such as databases and subscription journals. These are often only accessible behind paywalls, making these desires contradictory. Several of the guide creators discussed how important they felt it was to provide practical and freely accessible information on their pages in conjunction with research resources, so that patrons of all backgrounds, interest levels, and research needs could find useful resources on the page. For instance, the creator of the Voter Suppression page discussed how, since this page was created in the months leading up to the 2020 election, this page had an immediate need to educate patrons on practical issues. She chose to focus many of her selected resources on voter ID laws to elucidate for patrons the actual regulations and rules around voter ID laws and to combat misinformation that was circulating related to voting and voter suppression.

Limitations

In addition to challenges that the creators faced while creating the Anti-Racism Research & Resource Guide, they also reflected on the limitations of the guide. Both the creators of the Food Justice page and Gender & Sexuality page felt that a lack of clear definitions for the variety of complex areas discussed on their pages could be viewed as a limitation, and that future iterations of the guide could benefit from including definitions and contextual information throughout the guide to help ground users in core concepts related to important anti-racism topics. Another limitation of the guide that is significant to note is that the majority of the guide creators identify as cis-gender, white women. Several of the guide creators acknowledge that their identities result in limitations when creating and curating content for the Anti-Racism Research & Resource Guide, and can therefore lead to unintentional harm and biases because of the privileges that they themselves have benefited from due to the racist and oppressive systems that are enmeshed in virtually every aspect of society.

Recommendations

The creators of the guide have several recommendations, both for improving the Anti-Racism Research & Resource Guide, and for any individuals who may be interested in creating an Anti-Racism Resource Guide for their own institutions. The first recommendation is adding more definitions and contextual information to the guide. This was suggested to help patrons who may not be as familiar with certain core terms and concepts used in a particular area of anti-racism research, such as food justice or reproductive justice. Another recommendation is creating ways to encourage patron participation in the selection of resources. A potential avenue that could be explored is having a highlighted patron-suggested resource section on the guide to help encourage more interaction with the community. Another is hosting workshops or presentations aimed at students and faculty that can teach them how to use the guide for research or teaching, and encourage them to provide feedback on how to improve the guide to suit their needs and interests.

The creators of the guide also recommend anyone looking to create or update an Anti-Racism libguide encourage as much participation as possible across diverse sectors of their community and/or organization. While it was often challenging to work with such a large number of team members, the guide creators strongly feel that the diversity of perspectives resulting from such a large group led to its success. However, because this was such a large group, it took some trial and error to determine the best way to communicate and organize the group and its ideas. Notes and comments were made in Google Docs, and Google Sheets was utilized to keep track of purchases and other tasks. Flexibility and experimentation in finding the best methods of communication and documentation for your organization is encouraged.

It is also important to note that this guide was created during a moment of heightened focus. Graduate assistants have since aided in the maintenance, currency, and longevity of the guide. The guide creators recommend that people interested in creating similar guides consider the time and energy necessary to not only create but also sustain their own guides.

For additional recommendations and best practices for creating social justice libguides found in the literature, both Hodge's (2020) "Using LibGuides to support racial justice & create inclusive communities" and Piper et al.'s (2021) "An Investigation of Anti-Black Racism LibGuides at ARL Member Institutions" provide essential guidelines that are well worth referencing.

CONCLUSION

Creating the Binghamton University Anti-Racism Research & Resource Guide was a multistep, time consuming, but ultimately very rewarding experience. The events of 2020 that galvanized this subcommittee required a resource that was thoughtful and thorough, intentional in its teaching, and which did justice to the turbulence that necessitated its creation. The members of the subcommittee that worked on this guide did their best to create such a resource by bringing together and incorporating their diverse expertise, strengths, voices, and lived experiences into the making of this guide. It is the hope of the subcommittee that this case study will provide information to help other librarians collaborate on similar anti-racism guides that are curated to the needs of their communities.

REFERENCES

Anti-Oppression: Anti-Oppression. (n.d.). Simmons University Library. https://simmons.libguides.com/anti-oppression

Barker, A. E., & Hoffman, A. T. (2021). Student-centered design: Creating LibGuides students can actually use. *College & Research Libraries*, *82*(1), 75. doi:10.5860/crl.82.1.75

Bergstrom-Lynch, Y. (2019). LibGuides by design: Using instructional design principles and user-centered studies to develop best practices. *Public Services Quarterly*, *15*(3), 205–223. doi:10.1080/15228959.2019.1632245

Chatterjee, L. (2020). *BU Libraries aim to advance anti-racist practices by creating resources for students*. Pipe Dream. https://www.bupipedream.com/news/117857/auto-draft-380/

Conerton, K., & Goldenstein, C. (2017). Making LibGuides work: Student interviews and usability tests. *Internet Reference Services Quarterly*, *22*(1), 43–54. doi:10.1080/10875301.2017.1290002

Food Justice. (n.d.). FoodPrint. Retrieved December 15, 2022, from https://foodprint.org/issues/food-justice/

Goodsett, M., Miles, M., & Nawalaniec, T. (2020). Reimagining research guidance: Using a comprehensive literature review to establish best practices for developing LibGuides. *Evidence Based Library and Information Practice*, *15*(1), 218–225. doi:10.18438/eblip29679

Hodge, T. (2020). Using LibGuides to support racial justice & create inclusive communities. *SpringyNews*. https://buzz.springshare.com/springynews/news-49/libguides-tricks

Lee, Y. Y., & Lowe, M. S. (2018). Building positive learning experiences through pedagogical research guide design. *Journal of Web Librarianship*, *12*(4), 205–231. doi:10.1080/19322909.2018.1499453

Libguides. (n.d.). Springshare. https://springshare.com/libguides/

Neuhaus, C., Cox, A., Gruber, A. M., Kelly, J., Koh, H., Bowling, C., & Bunz, G. (2021). Ubiquitous LibGuides: Variations in presence, production, application, and convention. *Journal of Web Librarianship*, *15*(3), 107–127. doi:10.1080/19322909.2021.1946457

Ouellette, D. (2011). Subject guides in academic libraries: A user-centred study of uses and perceptions. *Canadian Journal of Information and Library Science*, *35*(4), 436–451. doi:10.1353/ils.2011.0024

Piper, G., Ameen, M., & Lowe, M. S. (2021). An Investigation of Anti-Black Racism LibGuides at ARL Member Institutions. *Communications in Information Literacy*, *15*(2), 188–207. doi:10.15760/comminfolit.2021.15.2.3

Sonsteby, A., & DeJonghe, J. (2013). Usability testing, user-centered design, and LibGuides subject guides: A case study. *Journal of Web Librarianship*, *7*(1), 83–94. doi:10.1080/19322909.2013.747366

Thorngate, S., & Hoden, A. (2017). Exploratory usability testing of user interface options in LibGuides 2. *College & Research Libraries*, *78*(6), 844–861. doi:10.5860/crl.78.6.844

KEY TERMS AND DEFINITIONS:

Anti-Racism: This is the committed practice of identifying racism in all areas of life, including ourselves, and then actively working to break down racism.

Decolonization: This is the work of de-emphasizing the influence of colonial powers, particularly US-centric and Eurocentric influences, from our institutions, governments, arts, and culture in general. A large part of this work is amplifying the influence of those cultures muted by colonization.

Libguides: These are library resource guides that use a particular software created by the company Springshare. These resource guides are created by libraries to provide detailed information and resources for specific topics.

APPENDIX 1: WORKFLOW CHART

The Anti-Racism Resource: Workflow of Responsibilities

Introduction:

This document outlines the varying responsibilities for managing and maintaining the Anti-Racism Resource Guide among participating committee members.

Table 1. Assigned Guide Pages:

Page Title	Page Manager
Welcome & How to Use This Guide	
Anti-Racism Resources: Where to Start	
Resources By Subject: Home Page	
Arts & Culture	
The Environment	
Gender & Sexuality	
Healthcare	
Housing	
Policing & The Justice System	
Politics & Voter Suppression	
Technology & AI	
Celebrating Black Voices	
Decolonizing Curricula	
Resources in Higher Ed	
Food Justice	
Activism	

Responsibilities of Page Managers

The page managers are primarily responsible for creating, editing, and maintaining their pages on the Anti-Racism Research & Resource Guide. Below are some guidelines for managing these responsibilities: (**NOTE:** for every resource that you add to your guide, make sure to also note it in the **COMPREHENSIVE LIST** as well.)

For Pages that are Live:

1. **Check & Fix broken links (at least once a semester):** Check links to ensure that they are still working. Fix any broken links or issues that may arise from content on their pages.
2. **Add newly recommended resources to guide (every 2-3 months):** Check the "Additional Resources Recommendation List" spreadsheet, and add the resources to your pages that you think

seem fitting. Not all recommendations have to be added to the guide - if you do not want to add it, just put a note in the column of the spreadsheet. **NOTE:** for every resource that you add to your guide, make sure to also note it in the **COMPREHENSIVE LIST** as well.

3. **Re-evaluate & update content on pages (at least once a semester):** Look through the overall contents on the website and re-evaluate/update resources. Update older articles with newer content, if needed, add new books, and change out the content highlighted in the "Hot Topics" areas, etc. **NOTE:** for every resource that you add to your guide, make sure to also note it in the **COMPREHENSIVE LIST** as well.

For Pages that are in the process of being created:

1. **Search for & Add resources that will be included in the live category page to the <u>Subject Categories Spreadsheet</u>:** This <u>spreadsheet</u> will track all resources that you plan to add to the page. Keeping all resources in this spreadsheet will be useful to see if other committee members want to suggest resources to add to the page as well.

2. **Add resources for your page from the Subject Categories Spreadsheet to the libguide:** For more details on how to format/organize new pages in the anti-racism resource guide, see the **<u>Anti-Racism Formatting Guide</u>.**

3. **Transfer the list of all resources to the Comprehensive List once the resources have been added to the page:** The Comprehensive List can be found **here**.

Responsibilities for all Committee Members

This section outlines the general responsibilities that all committee members can contribute to.

1. **Making Book Purchasing Recommendations (anytime):** All committee members can suggest books to purchase using our ANTIRAC collection fund. If members want to suggest books to purchase, they can visit the <u>Anti-Racism Book Recommendation List Spreadsheet</u>, and then enter in the book that they'd like to recommend under the "New Recommendations" section. The only info they need to add is title and author.

2. **Evaluating Book Purchase Recommendations (1-2 times a semester):** The committee chair will gather all the purchasing info for the book recommendations and then send out a spreadsheet to all committee members to ask for final feedback/recommendations before the books will be purchased.

3. **Recommending additional materials, content, or new pages for the guide (anytime):** Committee members can recommend new materials to add to the guide at any time.

When Recommending new materials for a specific page, committee members can either: 1) Email the page manager with the recommendation to see if they want to add it to their page or, 2) Add the resource to the page themselves.

When Recommending new general content, pages, etc., committee members can email the chair (Jen) or bring up suggestions during a committee meeting, for discussion.

The Power of Collaboration in Creating Anti-Racism Resource Guides

APPENDIX 2: FORMATTING GUIDELINES

The Anti-Racism Resource Formatting Guide

Introduction:

This guide provides the formatting guidelines for the Anti-Racism Resource Guide.

Table of Contents:

1. Guide Organization
   a. Guide Organization Overview
   b. Section/Box Heading Titles & Their Order
2. Formatting Headings
   a. Formatting the Headings Under each Section/Box
3. Formatting the Book Gallery
   a. Creating a Book Gallery Box
   b. Creating Assets & Adding Books Titles to the Gallery
   c. Formatting the Look of the Book Gallery
   d. Making the Book Gallery Readable to Screen Readers
4. Formatting Articles
   a. Article Sections
   b. Adding an Article to a Section/Box
   c. Article Formatting Requirements
5. Formatting Podcasts & Videos
   a. Podcasts & Videos Sections
   b. Adding a "Podcast" or "Video" Link to a Section/Box
   c. Embedding Videos
   d. Podcasts & Videos Formatting Requirements
6. Additional Information
   a. Formatting Descriptions

Guide Organization

Guide Organization Overview

This guide is currently organized into three primary sections:

I. Anti-Racism Resources: Where to Start
II. Resources by Subject
III. Resources on Decolonizing Curricula in Higher Education

While the "Where to Start" page and "Decolonizing Curricula" page may have different layouts than the Resources by Subject page, the subject-specific pages will all follow the same format.

97

Section/Box Heading Titles & Their Order

There are several section/box headings that can be included in each "subject-specific" page. **Below is the list of subject headings that can be included, the order in which they should appear on each page, and the way in which the section/box heading should be written. The highlighted sections are the ones that each subject page *should* include, if at all possible.** The other sections are optional, depending on material that can be found on the topic.

I.   Hot Topics
    A.   This section is optional--can be added to a page when there are topics from that subject area that are particularly relevant to the current times.
II.   Books (Click on Books for More Information)
III.   Articles
    A.   Popular/News Articles
    B.   Scholarly/Academic Articles
IV.   Podcasts & Videos
    A.   Podcasts
    B.   Videos
V.   Resources for Research
    A.   Databases
VI.   Reading Lists
VII.   Additional Resources
    A.   Additional Media Sources (ex: digital humanities projects, interactive articles, etc.)
VIII.   Are We Missing Anything? (Feedback Form - in the Left-Hand Column)

Formatting Headings

Formatting the Headings Underneath Each Section/Box

Within each section/box (see above), there are additional headings that can be used to organize links and/or resources. For instance, under the section/box heading "articles", there should be two additional headings of "Popular/News Articles" and "Scholarly Articles".

I.   Each of the headings within the sections/boxes should be **formatted as "Heading 5"**.

    a.   To do this, first click on the "add/reorder" button at the bottom of the box.
    b.   Select the "Rich Text/HTML" option
    c.   Once the Rich Text box appears, go to the top of the text box and select the drop down menu that says "Normal" and change it to "Heading 5"
    d.   After selecting "Heading 5", type in the name of the heading in the text box and click "Save & Close." Now, when you preview the guide, your section headings should look like this:

The Power of Collaboration in Creating Anti-Racism Resource Guides

Formatting The Book Gallery

Creating a Book Gallery Box

I. To create a book gallery, first click on the "Add Box" link at the bottom of the page.
II. Once the pop-up screen appears, click on the "Type" drop down menu and select "Gallery".
III. A Gallery box will then appear. To edit the gallery, select the gear symbol in the upper right-hand corner of the box. It will take you to a new page where you can begin adding in books and edit the look and formatting of the book gallery.

Creating Assets and Adding Book Titles to the Gallery

I. To add books to the gallery, you will need to turn the books into **assets** first.
II. To do this, click on the "Content" tab at the very top of the LibGuides page (found on the gold bar). Then, click on "assets."
III. Once on the "assets" page, click on the button that says, "add content item" and select the "book from the catalog" option.
IV. After clicking on the "Book from the Catalog" button, a pop-up window will appear so that you can add the book in as an asset. You can fill in the book's information manually, or you can find the ISBN number for the book you want to add, copy and paste it into the ISBN section, and hit the "Get Book Info" to autofill the entire form.
V. Once all the information has been added, click the "Save" button at the bottom of the window, and the asset will be added to LibGuides.
VI. Now, go back to the edit gallery page. Once here, you can begin adding in books that you have turned into assets by clicking on the "add a new slide" button, and selecting "book." Once you have selected "book", just start typing in the title of the book you want to add, and select it to add it to your gallery.
VII. Once you have added books to your gallery, you can edit them in a few different ways. To change the order of the books, you can click on the up and down arrow icon on the left-hand side of a book entry, then drag the title where you'd like it to be. To delete a book entry, click on the "x" on the right-hand side. To edit the contents of the book entry, click on the pencil/box icon on the right-hand side.
VIII. **To add in the Catalog URL for each book, click on the "edit" icon (seen above). A new window will appear, and there will be a section to add in a URL.** This will allow users to click on the books in the gallery and be led to the catalog record of the book.

99

Formatting the Look of the Book Gallery

I. Once you've finished adding in all your books to the book gallery, the last step is formatting the look of the gallery. Look over the menu on the right hand side.
II. Below is a picture of how to format the gallery. **The categories to change are:**
   a. Max image height: 300C
   b. Slides per row: 5
   c. Slides to show: 5
   d. Slides to scrolls: 5

Making the Book Gallery Readable to Screen Readers

I. In order to make the book galleries readable on screen readers, an "alternative tag" needs to be added to each book.
II. To do this, click on the gear button on the book gallery
III. Then click on the edit button for and individual book:
IV. Next, find the section that says "image alt text"
V. Add in the **title of the book and the author's name.** Then click save.

Formatting Articles

Article Sections

Each "Articles" section should have two categories:

I. Popular/News Articles
II. Scholarly/Academic Articles

Adding an Article Link to a Section/Box

I. To add an article entry to the "articles" section, first click on the "add/reorder" button at the bottom of the box, then select the "link" option.
II. Clicking on this link will take you to the pop-up window where you can add in the metadata for the article entry. See the "Article Formatting Requirements" below to see exactly what information to include for each article entry.

The Power of Collaboration in Creating Anti-Racism Resource Guides

Article Formatting Requirements

Each article entry should contain the following same pieces of information in the same order:

I. **Title of the article** - the title of the article should be the linked portion of the article entry
II. **Author, Source, & Year of Publication** - this information should be placed in the "description" section of the article in the following order and format:
III. **Optional:** If the article warrants a deeper description, a sentence or two can be added in the "more info" section of the article entry form.
IV. **Note: For Scholarly/Academic Articles,** if there are several authors, the "et al." abbreviation can be used to shorten the list of authors.
V. Below is an example of the article entry form, filled out:
VI. Below is an example of the article section completed in the correct format:

APPENDIX 3

Table 2. Subject pages chart

Subject Page Title	Description of Page	How was Content Selected	Reflections from the Page Creator
Welcome Page & Anti-Racism Resources: Where to Start	The Welcome page provides a brief snapshot of all of the content that can be found on the guide. At the bottom of the welcome page, the guide also provides a link to a publicly shared Google spreadsheet called the "Comprehensive List of Resources." This spreadsheet provides a searchable list of all of the resources included across all of the pages in the guide. The Anti-Racism: Where to Start page serves as a starting point for those that may just be beginning to learn about anti-racism and as a place that houses the seminal works on anti-racism.	Seminal works on topics of anti-racism and racial justice were chosen to feature on this page. Resources that covered more introductory material and provided more broad and general coverage of anti-racism research topics were also included.	The main author of both of the above pages was driven by a strong desire to make the overall guide as accessible and easy to use as possible. There was great emphasis placed on including clear, concise, and open language in both pages of the guide. The creator of these pages also relied on helpful feedback and recommended resources from other committee members to make these pages as comprehensive and navigable as possible.
Arts & Culture	This page aims to address racism in art and art history, including the performing arts, and to provide a celebration of BIPOC art.	Content was selected by using specific search terms in the library's catalog. Some examples of search terms used include "racism in art," "art and race," and "African Americans in art." Other resources came from the author's previous research into how race functions within the art historical record. There were many resources in the news that were applicable, and those resources were included on the guide as well.	The guide could be updated to include more recent content, as well as fill in leftover gaps in the collection of resources.
The Environment	This page contains resources about environmental justice related to issues of race.	Search terms such as "environmental racism" and "environmental justice" were used to find resources in the library's catalog. Using the internet was also helpful in finding other sources for the page. Looking at pre-established book lists on environmental racism was helpful in creating the book section.	This page was interesting to develop as the author had little knowledge of the details of environmental racism, but had interest in the topic. By working on this page, the author gained knowledge which they hope continues to spread to others.
Food, Food Justice, & Food Insecurity	This page highlights food justice, "a holistic and structural view of the food system that sees healthy food as a human right and addresses structural barriers to that right" (Food Justice, n.d.)"	Resources were chosen to highlight those with lived experience and/or actively engaging in the work of food justice, food sovereignty, and food insecurity. Resources discussing food insecurity were chosen with the local Binghamton and Broome County in mind.	Future editions of this guide could have clearer definitions and explanations of food justice versus food sovereignty. Local resources that combat food insecurity and promote food justice and food sovereignty should be added.
Gender & Sexuality	This page aims to highlight resources that explore the intricate intersectionalities between race, gender, and sexuality.	The main focus of this page was on amplifying the voices, perspectives, and personal experiences of BIPOC individuals with gender and/or sexual identities and expressions that are often marginalized, underrepresented, or overlooked even in conversations, research, and discussions directly related to anti-racism.	One of the challenges encountered when creating this page was trying to most effectively bring attention to how significantly gender and sexuality impacts and influences issues of race, racism, and anti-racism. There are resources that draw connections between gender and sexuality to all of the other subject areas included in the guide. The author really wanted to bring attention to these connections.
Healthcare	This page covers systemic racism in healthcare, providing information on racial and ethnic health disparities for current and future healthcare providers, as well as the general public. COVID-19 is a 'hot topic' on the page.	Content was initially selected by referencing resources other libraries had already created. Irrelevant items were removed and new content was added. The additional content was found through numerous updates from medical journals, doing literature searches in medical databases, and finding resources recommended or suggested by members of the BIPOC community. News sources were utilized for COVID-19.	Healthcare affects personal health, but is also a critical component to a successful society. Systemic racism has affected what one's healthcare looks like. It was the author's goal to provide resources that could be used to educate the next generation of healthcare providers and help patients better understand and advocate more for themselves.

Continued on following page

Table 2. Continued

Subject Page Title	Description of Page	How was Content Selected	Reflections from the Page Creator
Latinx Anti-Racism	This page is dedicated to anti-immigrant and anti-Latinx racism. It was added later (summer 2022) because there was an identified gap in this area; the author thought it could expand on the resources for other minority groups.	The anti-Latinx racism page was modeled after the others on the guide. The author used a combination of their own experience, the relevant resources in the library catalog, and the compiled databases put together by the librarians in their subject guides. The author combined the resources in a sheet for review, gathering and incorporating feedback from their supervisor and colleagues.	Including a page on this subject was important to the author as a first-generation Latinx immigrant and college graduate because the Latinx population in the US is a large minority group. By creating this page, the author hoped to incorporate another perspective in the dialogue uplifting marginalized and underrepresented perspectives. The author personally enjoyed working on the Anti-racism subject guide and learned a lot about themself and the gaps in their knowledge surrounding this issue.
Policing & The Justice System	This section provides resources for faculty to provide context and history of the American social justice system.	This page highlights experts who spoke out after the murder of George Floyd. It also uses resources shared in *Just Mercy: A Story of Justice and Redemption* by Bryan Stevenson. It also provides several databases available to the Binghamton University community, as well as external resources such as the Innocence Project and the Sentencing Project.	In the future, this guide could include scholarship and conversations about the long-term impact of George Floyd's murder on the justice system in the United States and the continued racism-fueled abuses in the police and judicial systems despite the outcry and desire for change.
Politics & Voter Suppression	This page was created to help patrons understand the ramifications of racism on politics and voting, with an immediate goal of helping voters navigate the 2020 election.	Content was selected based on two main concerns: access and interest. First, it was important to make the page as freely available as possible, including content that is not behind the Binghamton University paywall. Learning accessibility was also considered; audiovisual resources were included. Popular resources such as podcasts, popular videos, and news articles from popular publications were also used.	One of the author's goals when creating this page was to inform voters in the 2020 election, battle misinformation, and provide practical information for election day. Beyond this, the author wanted to create a page that was a good mixture of academic and popular resources.
Technology & AI	The Technology and Artificial Intelligence (AI) section of the libguide highlights content focused on how these areas impact and raise issues on race and racism.	This section includes non-fiction books related to biases within technology and software, sharing both data and real-life examples where these biases occur within the AI programming. There are also links to news and media articles, scholarly research articles, and other linked sources and databases. Audio and video content and podcasts were also included.	Facial recognition systems are biased toward white men; biased algorithms extend to healthcare systems, job applications, and multiple other areas. Human judgment used when building data for AI causes continued challenges with hidden bias as more and more daily life processes are automated.
Celebrating Black Voices	The "Celebrate Black Voices" section of the libguide is a place to highlight resources and multi-media content that celebrates black culture, creativity, and literary works.	This page focuses on Black stories and heritage, using content within the Binghamton University Libraries' collection, as well as freely available media. The Libraries purchases books for this section of the collection. There is also a section labeled "digital humanities projects," which shares links to digital exhibits, interactive content telling stories through digital media, oral histories, data visualizations, and more.	It is important to note that the current content for this page has been curated by a group of mostly white women. As the libguide continues to grow and evolve, the Libraries hope to have more recommendations for content submitted from the community through the linked feedback form on the guide.
Decolonizing Curricula	This section was intended to aid faculty in incorporating more voices of color into their syllabi.	This guide was curated in part from the author's personal experience as a former community college professor. Many resources were included in the guide to help faculty improve class discussions and incorporate the lived experiences of students.	This guide could continue to grow by working with the campus' Center for Learning and Teaching to add assignment and assessment ideas and examples, as well as scholarship that addresses the evolving needs of students.

Chapter 6

Starting and Sustaining JEDI Acquisitions and Collections in Academic Libraries:
Considerations and Strategies for Success

Colleen S. Mullally
https://orcid.org/0000-0002-0643-215X
Pepperdine University, USA

Jeremy Whitt
University of California, Los Angeles, USA

Kayla Valdivieso
Wellesley College, USA

ABSTRACT

Academic libraries are increasingly seeking to incorporate Justice, Equity, Diversity, and Inclusion (JEDI) initiatives at their institutions. While many librarians recognize these as important values, the process of implementing them into daily workflows proves to be more challenging. In this chapter, the authors provide recommendations intended for those at all levels within an academic library to initiate and enact JEDI initiatives within library collections and acquisitions. These steps include creating an action plan, communicating with fellow constituents, and considering different vendor selection criteria in acquisitions. The authors also address how to navigate challenges that may arise while conducting this work such as budget constraints, staffing shortages, and the limited diversity within the library and publishing fields.

DOI: 10.4018/978-1-6684-7255-2.ch006

Copyright © 2023, IGI Global. Copying or distributing in print or electronic forms without written permission of IGI Global is prohibited.

INTRODUCTION

Working toward justice, equity, diversity, and inclusion (JEDI) initiatives contributes to the creation of spaces that are welcoming for all people in the community. While this work has been documented and put into action in academic libraries for many years, the push for participation accelerated in May 2020 as over 150 libraries and library organizations throughout the United States released statements regarding the murder of George Floyd and the subsequent protests against systemic racism (G. Price, 2020). The events that immediately followed the murder of George Floyd served to motivate professional librarians, a group that is largely White (Rosa & Henke, 2017; see also Figueroa & Shawgo, 2021; A.C. Price, 2021), across the United States to increase their commitments to JEDI. Librarians pledged support for marginalized communities by creating and carrying out plans within their libraries to address inequities, exclusivity, and a lack of diversity. For many, it led to open conversations that highlighted how complicity with existing systems conflicts with the perceived ideals of libraries—namely, that they are inclusive and welcoming to all. The moment was also a turning point for many in terms of seeking action and meaningfully addressing systemic bias built into library systems, processes, and values. In expressing support for the Black, Indigenous, and People of Color (BIPOC) community and as part of a larger movement of racial reckoning, academic libraries and their associated institutions quickly issued statements and earnest pledges of solidarity and commitment to change (G. Price, 2020).

Libraries have achieved important JEDI work through deliberate decisions about their offerings and services for patrons; training for employees; resources acquired; and recruitment, hiring, and retention practices. This chapter shares guidelines for small and medium-sized academic libraries on how to develop and implement JEDI efforts specifically in collections and acquisitions. Drawing from their own experiences, the authors consider collection-building initiatives that decenter Whiteness and actively work toward equity, inclusion, and accessibility through a diversity of voices, subjects, publishers, and vendors. The chapter begins by addressing how to get started and build momentum for creating change by establishing JEDI collections initiatives. Next, the authors offer recommendations on work that can be accomplished with limited institutional guidance that aims to have lasting impact; this includes creating a collections action plan, involving colleagues in collection building, and acquiring resources from diverse vendors. The authors have found that the creation of an action plan is crucial as it sets forth specific actions librarians can take regarding JEDI collection development efforts. As plans can only succeed with the needed action and support behind them, this chapter calls for the widespread inclusion of stakeholders and colleagues from across the library and institution to broaden involvement in JEDI collection-building efforts. Joint participation increases the odds of carrying out a successful JEDI initiative and maintains the momentum needed to achieve goals. The chapter also provides thoughts on putting the plan into practice with respect to the opportunities, challenges, and decisions related to the acquisition process. While the budget for academic collections should primarily focus on supporting the evolving research, teaching, and learning needs of the community, Lori M. Jahnke et al. (2022) echoed Ellen Finnie and Michael A. Arthur (2016) stating that "collection decisions should also reflect community values and priorities of openness, diversity, and inclusion" (p. 179). Finally, the authors examine major factors that hinder these goals, namely that the overwhelmingly White library profession in the United States is lacking diversity and that libraries may face limitations in collecting diverse materials as a result of external market forces within the publishing industry. These limitations are connected to larger systemic issues that society is facing, and libraries are not immune. By raising awareness of these challenges, this chapter discusses ways of broadening collection-building efforts in order to overcome wherever possible the problems of limited input and options.

BACKGROUND

Academic institutions and non-profit organizations have responded to the general call to increase diversity in libraries by forming task forces and publishing their findings in reports. The Association of Research Libraries SPEC Kits have provided many examples of diversity and inclusion plans since 2010 (Anaya & Maxey-Harris, 2017; Maxey-Harris & Anaya, 2010) for how to address this challenge. Guidance on implementation of diversity plans within academic libraries has also been available in the literature (Edwards, 2015), though few such studies have focused on the topic of this chapter, collections and acquisitions. The recently released Ithaka S+R Report *Leading by Diversifying Collections: A Guide for Academic Library Leadership* (Bledsoe et al., 2022) was unique as it was written for senior library administration and aimed at situating the importance of this topic. While pointing out the main issues surrounding JEDI collection building, the report also provided practical examples, exercises, and takeaways for those looking to initiate, increase, and assess the efforts made by their library in diversifying collections.

Until the 2022 release of the Ithaka S+R report, practical guidance on collections and acquisitions occurred more at the institutional level. The *MIT Report of the Collections Directorate Diversity, Inclusion, and Social Justice Task Force* (Baildon et al., 2017) offered several strategies and ideas for change in the areas of scholarly publishing in the areas of representation of marginalized perspectives, community outreach, and organizational infrastructure for JEDI initiatives. The embodiment of diversity, inclusion, and social justice work within MIT's technical services department was outlined in a case study several years later by Rhonda Y. Kauffman and Martina S. Anderson (2020) that also included potential applications of departmental work by job functions and responsibilities. More recently, the University of Washington Libraries (Caruso et al., 2022), in alignment with the organization's strategic plan, released a report based on the results of a Task Force on DEI and Anti-Racism in Collections, which recommended budget reallocation to JEDI materials, infrastructure investments supporting JEDI collections, and staff training. The report also shared findings on the state of JEDI within the scholarly publishing and academic library marketplace. Casey D. Hoeve and David Macaulay (2022) identified local and consortial initiatives focusing on JEDI collections actions, which served as a roadmap for these initiatives at the University of Nebraska. For those seeking practical advice on how to create plans for collections and acquisitions and incorporate JEDI initiatives into daily workflows, these cases have represented emerging information on the topic.

Barriers to this work go beyond the issue of locating an adoptable framework for building JEDI collections or creating one's own structure. Even though diversity has been an ongoing theme within the library literature for decades, Apryl C. Price (2021) observed that there has been much less emphasis placed on diversity within general academic collections. Echoing this sentiment while writing about assessing collections diversity, Jahnke et al. (2022) noted that the literature on collection management and defining diversity is "relatively sparse" (p. 167). In their writing, A.C. Price (2021) and Jahnke et al. (2022) addressed common roadblocks that prevent libraries from moving toward more diverse and inclusive collections. Both authors discussed biases in the publishing industry, and A.C. Price (2021) cited a lack of diversity within academic publishing as well as within the librarian profession. These two

Starting and Sustaining JEDI Acquisition, Collection in Academic Libraries

articles (A.C. Price, 2021; Jahnke et al., 2022) also discussed the matter of insufficient staff time and shrinking library budgets as common issues that create additional hurdles, further limiting the ability of libraries to build JEDI collections. Megan Bresnahan (2022) interviewed academic librarians to understand how libraries have implemented JEDI plans. Noting barriers and challenges, Brenahan (2022) found a range of concerns among those interviewed, including concerns about inconsistent support from library leaders, a lack of resources to carry out JEDI plans, and a sense among librarians that the work was performative in nature. Nevertheless, A.C. Price (2021), Jahnke et al. (2022), and Bresnahan (2022) maintained that a commitment to action is essential and necessary work despite these barriers.

Within much of the existing literature, there has been a greater focus on assessment and/or development of collections and less written on how to build JEDI purchasing strategies into existing acquisitions workflows or develop and carry out a JEDI collections plan. Much of the recent library literature has explored ideas tangentially related to the topic of this chapter, such as collection development, collection assessment, collections diversity, and JEDI task force findings, but there has been much less emphasis on the mechanics of developing and sustaining JEDI acquisitions and collections plans. The authors of this chapter aim to provide a variety of actionable ideas that can be employed by those carrying out technical services work and that do not necessarily require a larger library-wide JEDI action plan.

PREPARING AND ENACTING SUCCESSFUL JEDI COLLECTIONS AND ACQUISITIONS

The Issue of Developing or Maintaining Momentum of JEDI

While academic libraries quickly issued statements and pledges of solidarity and commitments to change in the summer of 2020, challenges remain in carrying out JEDI initiatives. Librarians engaging with efforts wrestle with how complicated they can be to carry out. It is easy to become complacent with the status quo, and in the face of challenges it can be difficult to maintain momentum on fulfilling plans and achieving goals.

One such issue that presents itself is how to continue to sustain this effort when JEDI topics are no longer the high point of focus within the mainstream media and among institutional leadership. For some libraries, JEDI initiatives were already part of the fabric of strategic planning and in motion before the Black Lives Matter protests in the summer of 2020 (Anaya & Maxey-Harris, 2017; Maxey-Harris & Anaya, 2010). There are some librarians who witnessed this outward embracing of action plans by senior library leadership and are now left wondering how they can ensure that this interest remains genuine and alive for the long term (Bresnahan, 2022). Notwithstanding issues around shifting political winds and matters of donor support (Bresnahan, 2022) at the institutional level, librarians seeking sustainable JEDI practices around collection building and acquisitions may question whether programmatic support will wane in the future due to budget constraints and staffing turnover. Especially when the work is not explicitly a part of a library's strategic plan, it can be a challenge for all library employees to maintain interest, awareness, and engagement with JEDI initiatives. Inclusive collection building is not an initiative that is achieved in a one-, two-, or three-year period: it is ongoing work requiring steady commitment.

Key Players in JEDI Initiatives

Although leadership on this initiative need not come from the top for the work to take place, the role and support of senior library leadership has been shown to have a direct impact on the sustainability and trajectory for JEDI initiatives (Geiger et al., 2023), including collection building (Bresnahan, 2022). The newly released "Guide for Academic Library Leadership on Leading by Diversifying Collections" (Bledsoe et al., 2022) from Ithaka S+R provided strategies and guidance aimed at senior library administration seeking support.

For those outside of library administration, there are still opportunities to lead JEDI initiatives. The members of the library who are responsible for acquisitions can play a pivotal role in building JEDI collections by the nature of their involvement in selecting the vendor for book purchases and adding the items to the catalog. While acquisitions departments may not have influence over the titles selected, they do have control over selecting the most appropriate vendors from which to purchase these selected titles. Heidy Berthoud and Rachel Finn (2019) advocated for "rethinking how and when to shift purchases to local, independent bookshops," and library staff in acquisitions should feel equipped to carefully assess the available vendors, prioritizing those that are diversely owned and local.

While acquisitions work is process-oriented and limited to only those few library employees whose responsibilities include ordering materials, the work of collection development is more open and nebulous. Collection building is significant in its reach and its potential lasting impact on the community. The volumes within a library serve as artifacts revealing what has been valued by the community throughout different parts of its history. Just in browsing a library's stacks, it is easy to see the evidence of many decades of deliberate selection. One can also spot areas that have not been evaluated or seen recent use. Whereas many university libraries once had subject bibliographers with distinct collection-development responsibilities, collection building in today's libraries is far more dependent on approval plans. Title selection is not typically carried out by a subject bibliographer or collection development librarian, but instead by a librarian who may serve as a subject liaison to several departments and who often has multiple responsibilities including reference and instruction. It takes collective effort to make well-informed and impactful decisions that provide for diverse collection building. Staff with selector responsibilities may not already be consciously carrying out attempts to diversify collections. It is imperative to involve each staff member with those responsibilities as well as to consider input from other key community stakeholders.

Pre-Planning: Defining Terms and Building Consensus

Beyond the issues of finding partners within and beyond the library, agreeing on terms and defining outcomes can easily derail action and stall momentum for initiating JEDI collections efforts among librarians active in collection building. There are many different ideas about how to define DEI, EDI, and JEDI–Is it BIPOC? LGBTQIA+? Does it include women and disabled communities? –and it may not be easy to get support or interest among all library stakeholders. To get started with these discussions, library colleagues can explore how other institutions are utilizing a shared vocabulary around DEI terms (e.g., University of Minnesota Libraries' Diversity, Equity, and Inclusion Leadership Committee, 2021). Librarians can extend the conversation around defining these terms with a social justice frame by considering responses to the questions contained in the toolkit for collections and acquisitions from the University of Colorado Boulder (Aguilera et al., 2022). Furthermore, library leadership may be interested

Starting and Sustaining JEDI Acquisition, Collection in Academic Libraries

in investing in staff development programs—such as the 21-day racial equity challenge undertaken at the UNC Chapel Hill Library (Figueroa & Shawgo, 2021)—that aim to deepen personal awareness of issues around systemic racism and the impacts on marginalized communities. These options are more accepted and relevant at some academic libraries than others depending on the institutional climate. If arriving at a common set of definitions would stall or hinder critical support for the project, it is advisable to develop less prescribed plans that will still allow for progress toward inclusive collection building.

Once support has been established for this type of focused collection development, time and consideration should be focused on determining how the work will be carried out. Library stakeholders should establish a scope around which areas of the collection should be prioritized, whether the breadth or depth or recency of work should be the focus, and how growth should be measured—by dollars spent, titles purchased, or another method. There are many approaches in the near and longer term that can help guide the development of a plan. Determining who will be responsible for certain areas, the frequency of title evaluation and selection, and how funds are to be allotted are all points that need to be addressed, with special consideration given to ensuring commitment and accountability.

Writing and Executing a JEDI Action Plan

Components and Content

In July 2020 the authors developed a focused plan, the JEDI Action Plan for Collections, which formed the basis of guidelines outlining the steps necessary to make progress on JEDI initiatives within the realm of library collection development. The formulation of such a plan is advantageous because it provides a single reference point for the unique details and data directly related to a library's particular JEDI collections initiatives. As a self-contained, micro-collection development plan, a JEDI Action Plan for Collections should include components (Table 1) that define its purpose and need, outline its scope, record major progress, and list relevant resources. Development of the background, scope, and guiding principles section of the plan allows liaisons to take action and advance JEDI collections initiatives.

Table 1. Components of a JEDI collections action plan

Component of Plan	Content
Background and Guiding Principles	Overview of the plan's objectives
Scope	Defined parameters for selection and budget
Timeline of Actions	Log of major activities identified and a list of those accomplished by year; Acquisition summary of resources purchased along with outreach strategy
Resources	Further reading; professional standards and guidelines

A single document to reference assists stakeholders in maintaining focus on achieving JEDI goals and desired outcomes. The plan can be referenced in meetings with liaisons throughout the year and over time it can document different actions taken along with their outcomes. This approach is meant to build a foundation for establishing JEDI collections initiatives, from which more large-scale, transformative efforts can emerge on an individual or group level.

Background and Guiding Principles

While formulating a JEDI collections action plan, the authors sought to provide background information for its creation while also providing broader context by indicating how the plan aligned with the library's overarching JEDI plan and broader institutional efforts on diversity. As they were writing the collections action plan, the authors affirmed the progress that had been accomplished to date on JEDI efforts, recognizing that the current state of a collection is the product of decades of rotations around the collection lifecycle, and that transformation does not occur overnight. Instead of pointing fingers at the past or adopting a deficit mindset, the authors saw this instead as an opportunity to build JEDI collections proactively and intentionally via the plan's articulation of a set of formal strategies and values. The first section of the action plan details the scope and guiding principles of the JEDI collections effort and provides useful institutional memory by acting as a historical record when viewed years later. When crafting this section, library staff should consider the overall charge for the library and any organizing principles behind a JEDI effort. The inclusion of institutional statements on diversity, standards from professional organizations, and references to policies created by other institutions ensures alignment with an institution's practices and the profession at large.

To help define goals and ambitions the authors initially looked to plans, standards, and policies adopted by professional organizations, academic libraries, and library consortia. In 2012 the Racial and Ethnic Diversity Committee of Association of College and Research Libraries (ACRL) developed 11 standards known as the "Diversity Standards: Cultural Competency for Academic Libraries" to advocate for diversity in academic libraries. The fourth standard of the diversity standards addressed collections: "Librarians and library staff shall develop collections and provide programs and services that are inclusive of the needs of all persons in the community the library serves" (American Library Association, 2012). While this document has since been rescinded by the ACRL Board of Directors in 2022 following the joint approval of "Cultural Proficiencies for Racial Equity: A Framework" by two professional organizations, the American Library Association (ALA) and Association of Research Libraries (ARL) (2022), the diversity standards provided valuable professional guidance at the time. It was also helpful for the authors to define the terms diversity, equity, and inclusion to stay on course in achieving their stated goals. The definitions from MIT Libraries in their "Creating a Social Justice Mindset" document (Baildon et al., 2017) were especially instructive: "Diversity means difference"; "inclusion means creating and actively sustaining an organization and community in which all can participate fully, be respected, and be treated in an equitable manner"; and "social justice is a commitment to recognizing, addressing, and correcting systemic power imbalances that privilege one group at the expense of another" (p. 8). Additionally, the Consortium of Academic and Research Libraries in Illinois (CARLI) shared a list of sample JEDI language used in collection-development policies, which is another informative resource to reference (CARLI, 2022).

Scope

In this section of the plan, libraries should seek to answer the question, "Which collecting areas will be the focus of our JEDI efforts?" This question provides the opportunity to define, at least initially, which areas or selection criteria the library will focus on with this collection development effort. The demographics of an institution's student body can be one source of inspiration to use when identifying JEDI collecting areas; Veronica A. Wells et al. (2022) conducted a DEI audit at the University of Pacific Libraries and

Starting and Sustaining JEDI Acquisition, Collection in Academic Libraries

involved paid student employees throughout the process with the goal "to make the library collection more representative of Pacific's student body" (p. 335). Aligning JEDI goals with student demographics supports the goal for students to see themselves represented in the library's collection. Another option is to take a topical approach in which librarians collect materials focusing on historically marginalized or underrepresented groups such as BIPOC, LGBTQIA+, neurodiverse people, people with disabilities, and incarcerated individuals, to name a few, and/or collect works written by diverse authors and related topics. Berthoud and Finn (2019) offered two innovative and noteworthy models for building collections and filling in gaps, known as "spiral collecting" and "expansive scope collecting" (p. 165). The former method relies on identifying a topic of interest and then finding related, intersecting materials to collect, while the latter employs a broader approach, in which one chooses a topic and then collects JEDI materials on that topic across many disciplines. There is much flexibility here, but a key to success is ensuring the inclusion of stakeholders' voices and building a consensus for the chosen focus area, either as assented by liaison librarians and selectors or affirmed by overarching institutional JEDI plans.

Timeline of Actions

The following section of the plan, which details approaches and initiatives by year, is updated annually with budget information, format distribution of materials collected (print or online), the year's collecting focus, and lists of any major resources acquired by year. The authors composed this section by first setting forth a budget and then allocating the budgeted funds to formats of resources to be acquired. In the authors' plan covering the first year, half of the JEDI collections budget was allocated to books and the remaining half was dedicated to databases requiring a one-time purchase.

In addition to serving as a timeline, this section of the JEDI collections action plan details the library's guiding principles on review and selection of JEDI collections. The authors deemed it prudent to begin by detailing preliminary actions to take in order to guide future selection activities. In the authors' plan, this section contained a list of action items and concrete steps to take to achieve the stated objectives of the action plan. It also assigned and delegated responsibility to parties in charge of carrying out those stated actions. These actions appear in non-sequential order in the below table (Table 2).

Table 2. Preliminary actions for JEDI collection building efforts

Aspect	Materials Needed	Objective	Primary Party
Diversity of library approval plan	Current specifications of the library's approval plan	Review publishers on auto shipment lists	Collections and acquisitions
Publishers excluded from approval plan	Current specifications of the library's approval plan; JEDI acquisitions lists	Locate trade publishers, independent presses, small publishers not on approval plan	Collections and acquisitions
Existing collections	ILS collections conspectus map; ILS inventory report	Review collections areas by copyright year, subject area and most recently published (10 years); review interlibrary loan reports to identify gaps in JEDI collections	Collections and acquisitions
Expenditure tracking	ILS acquisitions data	Create a JEDI fund code	Collections and acquisitions
JEDI Collection building requests	New online form for all library employees	Expand access to requesting purchases for collection building beyond librarians	Collections and acquisitions
JEDI funds for new title selection	Budget for new acquisitions	Assign a monetary goal for new JEDI library materials	Library administration

This section will vary by library, depending on the specifics of a library's collection, staff, and data availability. The authors found it helpful to enumerate goals and evidence of success for each goal.

Listing collections coverage areas with criteria and objectives for subject liaisons is another aspect of providing directional guidance and should be included in this part of the plan. Actions for selectors to take in this area include reviewing, identifying, evaluating, and locating:

- JEDI materials in liaisons' respective subject areas;
- books identified to be diverse;
- titles within interdisciplinary topics;
- collection gaps by geographical publication area;
- publisher ebook packages focusing on JEDI;
- self-published book award winners (University of Toledo Libraries, 2022);
- JEDI monograph series for possible standing order;
- areas for JEDI growth in primary sources and databases for purchase;
- free or open access JEDI resources for inclusion within the library's complete alphabetical listing of electronic resources and relevant research guides.

While the quantity of actions related to reviewing and selecting resources may sound daunting, the authors found it effective to sketch out the landscape of many possible actions to take, with some action items being more time intensive than others. Since this action plan has been regularly updated, the authors viewed the list of action items as a resource that would provide long-term guidance. If initiatives were not completed initially, the authors revisited them the following year. In addition to crafting guiding principles on review and selection, the authors developed strategies for outreach to broadcast the impact of JEDI efforts. These efforts are more fully discussed in the following section of this chapter and include:

- seek feedback and recommendations from students, student groups, and faculty;
- continue book displays and tie-in displays with JEDI programming on campus;
- highlight JEDI ebook collections on library website and share with faculty;
- promote new acquisitions.

Resources

The final sections of the collections action plan serve as appendices providing further reading and professional standards and guidelines guiding JEDI collections work. The authors cited ALA's "Diverse Collections: An Interpretation of the Library Bill of Rights," (2019) and a number of policies written by libraries referenced in the initial sections of the plan, such as Columbia University's "Diversity in and of Collections" policy (2019). This section of the plan provides a contextual reference back to different principles within the plan. It serves as a valuable resource not only for key team members, but for future stakeholders as well.

Regular Plan Review and Updates

Just as significant as initiating a new JEDI collection-development plan is ensuring the long-term sustainability and viability of this work. Revisiting, revising, and updating the plan's contents regularly,

Starting and Sustaining JEDI Acquisition, Collection in Academic Libraries

such as on a semi-annual or annual basis, in collaboration with other colleagues who are involved ensures that JEDI efforts stay on track and do not lose steam. The authors also found it helpful to take the long view. The collection of data along the way, such as expenditures on JEDI materials, gaps filled in the collection, and titles added, is extremely helpful in demonstrating the impact of a JEDI collections effort to campus colleagues both inside and outside of the library. Studying these results also presents opportunities to take stock of the effort as a whole, look for further areas of growth, and identify any necessary additions or changes to the collections action plan.

Broadening Participation in JEDI by Communicating Internally and Externally

Following the creation of a JEDI collections action plan, communicating with all those who will be involved in selecting titles is an essential part of the implementation process. JEDI titles span across many disciplines, and their scope is not limited to a small area or specific subject within the library collections. Thus, it is helpful to get buy-in from those who have experience building collections and who currently serve as subject selectors because they can look for JEDI titles in their subject areas. Action-oriented JEDI collections meetings with library liaisons proved to be a helpful practice for the authors. At several points in the year, the authors met with library liaisons to discuss and review ongoing and upcoming work, share expenditure information, identify individuals who would lead the selection of JEDI titles, and provide space for dialogue. In preparation for those meetings, they also reviewed expenditures on JEDI titles to date. The authors also consulted with liaisons on upcoming scheduled book displays to help plan for new acquisitions that celebrated the lived experience of specific marginalized groups. These two points helped to shape conversations throughout the meetings and provided touchstones to serve as references.

Selection of JEDI titles also includes more than just the work of subject selectors in a library, and there are advantages to an "it takes all of us" approach. A foundational principle within the report from Bledsoe et al. (2022) was that "meaningful contributions to collections work can come from library staff at all levels" (p. 6). If one of the goals of collection building is to be more expansive and involve other library personnel beyond those who typically request library titles, it is essential not only to consider the parameters and criteria for their title recommendations, but also to communicate the goals for this more inclusive collection-building process. For those in the library who do not regularly interact with acquisitions staff to place orders, the authors found it helpful to share guidelines clarifying how requests are received, reviewed, and selected.

While library employees should carry responsibility for building JEDI collections, it is also critical to look for input from outside of the library. There are many different strategies for broadening involvement in building JEDI collections to connect librarian subject selectors with the community, student groups, faculty members, and other university employees. These approaches depend on the context of one's institution, and it is vital to look for opportunities that align with institutional JEDI efforts. Using existing partnerships or developing new relationships with faculty can bring to life collaborations that may enhance "library collection development criteria, curated resource guides, and instructional strategies for searching and identifying relevant library resources" (Sappington et al., 2022, p. 45). In the authors' own experience, engaging in new partnerships meant supporting a student-led collections project aimed in part at expanding the voices of marginalized communities. Students involved in this project received advising from faculty and were paid through a fellowship award from the university.

Additionally, staff from other departments on campus may wish to be involved in contributing to the inclusivity and accessibility of the library's collections building efforts. For example, the authors have been engaged in conversation with academic support staff about the importance of accessibility compliance for content licensed by the library. The dialogue has been beneficial in developing a better understanding of the needs of students with disabilities within the library and has highlighted the importance of the library's role in providing equity and promoting accessibility. The authors have also collaborated with the university's chief diversity officer, who offered support and engagement on the library's collection development efforts. Members of the chief diversity officer's staff recommended titles for the library to purchase in order to promote a better understanding of the lived experiences of marginalized voices. The library has also collaborated with this office on numerous physical and virtual book displays.

As Jahnke et al. (2022) pointed out, "curating a diverse collection is a difficult task with constantly evolving goals" (p. 173). It is beneficial to check in on progress and communicate periodically what achievements have been made, especially with subject liaisons who are most closely tied to building collections. Recognizing and celebrating milestones is an important part of JEDI collections meetings, as it ties together all that has been accomplished and helps build momentum to continue upcoming work. In advance of meeting with liaisons, compile a list of recent achievements within JEDI collections and acquisitions regardless of whether they had been a part of the existing collections action plan. Periodically reviewing the plan and communicating updates helps to ensure that the subject areas, processes, and work remains applicable to one's situational context. By meeting to review progress and discuss new developments within the plan, library liaisons are informed and active partners in advancing upcoming JEDI collections initiatives.

Strategies and Considerations for JEDI Acquisitions

In addition to building diverse collections, libraries should consider structural changes to internal acquisition processes, including how and where library resources are purchased (Morales et al., 2014). Some acquisition strategies for incorporating JEDI efforts include purchasing from booksellers that are diverse-owned, independent, and/or local when possible, as well as advocating for change among publishers. Shifting preferred vendors away from large corporations when making JEDI acquisitions is one process-oriented change that libraries can make. While the authors found success in locating new booksellers for the procurement of JEDI materials, this may not be a feasible option for all libraries, due to local limitations such as insufficient staffing or institutional policies. Cost is another consideration in making this change; libraries that opt for this approach may not be able to purchase as many books in the event that a switch from large corporate book suppliers results in a loss of discounted pricing. Such a situation raises the issue of how libraries choose to balance competing values, such as financial stewardship and support for marginalized communities within collection development and acquisition policies. For some libraries, this conundrum requires a paradigm shift and for others it generates an articulation or reprioritization of values (Aguilera et al., 2022; Baildon et al., 2017; Kauffman & Anderson, 2020). Libraries are advised to reassess the factors driving their collection development decisions in addition to considering the possible impacts of capital in supporting their JEDI efforts.

Despite the possible difficulties involved, sourcing JEDI materials from diverse-owned vendors remains a strategy worth considering. It helps libraries support efforts toward building bibliodiversity within their collections. Additionally, by purchasing directly from these booksellers, libraries are also positively contributing to the businesses in a way that allows them to continue to be accessible in their

Starting and Sustaining JEDI Acquisition, Collection in Academic Libraries

local communities. Some independent bookstores have their own websites and online stores where new titles can be purchased directly. Others may instead use Bookshop.org, an online storefront where selectors can choose a bookstore to "purchase" from with 30% of the retail price going to the selected bookstore (About Us, 2022). Ordering from this platform allows for the same ease of use as a larger company while still supporting independent bookstores.

Invariably, libraries will encounter situations where purchasing materials from diverse-owned businesses is not possible due to lack of availability in ebook format or because the product is only sold by one corporation. Libraries have opportunities in these situations to convey expectations that support a library's JEDI initiatives. Elizabeth Speer (2022) discussed how Gilson D. Lewis Health Science Library at the University of North Texas sent formal communications to vendors expressing their commitment to creating a collection that espouses JEDI values. Through this communication, the library informed vendors of their requirements. Other opportunities for action from libraries include advocating for publishers to prioritize the accessibility of their electronic resources. Along with providing practical negotiation suggestions, Michael Rodriguez (2020) listed several names of organizations from which to draw standardized accessibility language in license agreements, including:

- American Association of Law Libraries (AALL)
- California Digital Library (CDL)
- Canadian Research Knowledge Network (CRKN)
- Center for Research Libraries (CRL)
- JISC (formerly the Joint Information Systems Committee)
- Library of Congress (LOC)
- NERL (formerly NorthEast Research Libraries)
- Ontario Colleges Library Service (OCLS)

Libraries can also push for the publication of more content from diverse authors within academic publishing. For example, The Royal Society of Chemistry now provides standards for diversity and inclusion, including a commitment to review recruitment of editors to attract a diverse group and to report on their diversity initiatives progress (Royal Society of Chemistry, n.d.). Finally, libraries can apply JEDI principles to expanding open access by participating in transformative agreements with publishers, providing funding for article and book processing charges for their faculty authors, and advocating for the expansion of self-archiving within their institutional repository. The work of acquisitions and open access intersects when opportunities arise for libraries to participate in publishers' funding initiatives such as the "Subscribe to Open" model from Annual Reviews and the "Direct to Open" membership model from MIT Press. It is advantageous to follow the terms and details of publishers' new and existing open access funding models, evaluate the financial feasibility for one's own institutional participation, and communicate these opportunities to library leadership for institutional participation.

Navigating Challenges: Unplanned Limitations and Balancing Priorities

Even the best JEDI collection-building plans can go awry when funds dry up or staffing challenges arise. These two problems may happen without advance notice and cause disruptions. They threaten sustainability and have a real impact on remaining staff's ability to participate, stay motivated, or contribute. Should these unplanned situations arise, it is essential to reference the core principles of the action plan and to identify to what extent this work can be carried out in the face of these challenges. Resourcefulness and pragmatism are key components to staying committed and making progress, even if progress is reduced.

Restrictions in funding may mean lessening the library's allocations for new JEDI materials. While a loss of funds would not impact opportunities for collection building through donated materials, it may not be feasible to employ as many JEDI acquisition strategies. Libraries that are part of a larger network can work with other consortial members at developing plans that benefit regional collection-building efforts while minimizing the financial burden on one's institution. In fact, "collaborative collection development may further allow for respective institutions to concentrate on better representing their local populations in their collections, rather than depending on established diversity lists" (Jahnke et al., 2022, p. 178-9). Additionally, redirecting attention to audits of diversity within existing collections (Jahnke et al., 2022; Kristick, 2019; Sappington et al., 2022; Wells et al., 2022) is a recommended strategy so that when funds become available again, target areas for growth are already identified.

Another way of making strides toward JEDI collection-building initiatives if faced with cuts to funding is to direct attention to existing JEDI acquisitions. Librarians can focus on evaluating the quality of these collections and how well the titles fit particular needs within the curriculum. Emphasis can be on promoting specific titles that either align with institutional areas, programs, courses, or celebratory periods such as Black History Month. While the authors of this chapter maintained a dedicated JEDI fund code that was not impacted by budget cuts, they also continued to highlight strengths within existing collections when promoting materials for display. For example, they drew on the strengths of their art collection to collaborate on a physical book display of library books about the African American experience that related to a temporary installation in the university's art gallery.

If it is not a budget issue but rather a staffing shortage that is the most pressing concern, it is critical to identify which JEDI collections and acquisition strategies can be maintained during vacancies. Considering which practices can be continued despite short staffing helps to continue the momentum of JEDI initiatives in collections and acquisitions. Staffing shortages can mean having fewer librarians who participate in collection development. Where expertise in certain areas is lacking, it is helpful to fall back on other ways of supporting collection growth. One strategy is to identify one or more faculty partners who teach in relevant subject areas, look at their research interests, and more directly engage them in collection-building collaborations. Ultimately, it is beneficial to have realistic, pragmatic approaches that maintain the forward momentum no matter what circumstances unfold. Keeping current on the relevant literature helps sustain energy, and crowd-sourced resources that are expanded by other librarians concerned with building JEDI collections, such as a public DEI Assessment group on Zotero and an Assessing Diversity in Collections folder on Box, are useful. Joining the listserv ASSESSDIVCOL--request@LISTSERV.UGA.EDU is another way of sharing ideas and approaches with others who are actively involved in collection initiatives around JEDI.

Two Immutable Restrictions Facing Libraries: Content Published and Space Constraints

One issue for librarians is that they are limited in what they can purchase by the content made available by publishers. Publishing remains principally centered in Whiteness. Lack of diversity is a problem shared by large publishing companies (So and Wezerek, 2020) as well as university presses (Association of University Presses, 2019). Prominent voices such as Leslie Chan (2020), director of the Knowledge Equity Lab at the University of Toronto Scarborough, have also highlighted the problems of centering

Starting and Sustaining JEDI Acquisition, Collection in Academic Libraries

Whiteness in knowledge production. But how can libraries grapple with this problem and effect positive change? Certainly, library purchasing power and the demands of libraries for these materials have an impact on the bottom line. However, libraries and librarians should also continue to support publishing and peer review efforts that work to bring diversity to publishing. Librarians have opportunities to raise questions about authorship and representation within publishing at conferences and meetings where those in the publishing industry are present (e.g. Charleston Conference, Society for Scholarly Publishing). The lack of diversity among those who work in the publishing industry plays a part, and this is not a new topic to be addressed in public forums (Roh, 2016). It is necessary to keep raising, discussing, and addressing questions like the one posed by librarian Matthew Noe during a Health Sciences Lively Lunch discussion during the 2020 Charleston Conference: "How many of our 'core' texts are primarily written by those in the West, and what issues arise because of that?" (Bernhardt et al., 2021). Librarians also have the opportunity to bring to the attention of publishers the need for diversity within content both in direct one-on-one communication (Speer, 2022) as well as in venues with librarians and vendors present (Barnett, 2022). These concerns should continue to be a focal point for librarians and publishers because publishing is centered in Whiteness and this impacts the levels of diversity attainable within library collections.

One hard constraint that libraries face is the finite space and the footprint of existing physical collections. Space availability limits the physical size of the collection and necessitates a periodic evaluation and deaccessioning of materials by librarians. The legacy left behind by physical collections is intended to have enduring value, and it outlasts most librarian tenures at an institution. What can or should librarians do to anticipate future collection development decisions around deaccessioning that have at least a partial basis in usage? As Jahnke et al. (2022) noted, overreliance on usage statistics for developing and weeding "risks amplifying existing representational inequalities" (p. 174). As a way to provide more nuanced data to those tasked with reviewing and making deselection decisions, librarians within technical services may consider flagging JEDI acquisitions by adding a staff note in the local holdings record. Alternatively, librarians can supply a list of all titles tied to the JEDI fund code whenever called upon to gather usage statistics reports for colleagues engaged in collection evaluation. This type of information serves as a useful data point when circulation statistics are gathered to provide context and help inform collection evaluation and deaccessioning decisions.

FUTURE RESEARCH DIRECTIONS

When examining what research on JEDI acquisitions and collections is needed going forward, librarians must continue to measure the outcomes of their efforts and demonstrate their impacts. Documenting the outcomes of one's own library JEDI collections plan provides contextual understanding of the impact made by those who are working to diversify their collections. Ultimately, conducting a large-scale assessment will demand significant time and involve an extensive data collection process. The nature of such large-scale studies necessitates a longer tail of collection usage data in order to document progress toward JEDI goals within acquisitions and collections. While important, a longitudinal assessment may not be as achievable for smaller institutions facing staffing shortages and budgetary constraints without the provision of additional resources from library administration or institutional leadership.

On a broader level, one of the largest areas for future research on the topic of starting and sustaining JEDI initiatives is tracking the measurement of progress made toward JEDI goals in plans written by stakeholders and leaders within the library profession. This is a challenging task because JEDI plans vary by institution, and progress is not always transparent or easy to track. Moving forward, it also remains to be seen how recent state legislation that affects funding for JEDI at public universities will impact the work of library JEDI initiatives, including efforts on acquisitions and collections. Nonetheless, the question remains; have libraries, library leaders, and publishers made meaningful progress on the JEDI initiatives they first set out to achieve? What measures or tools will be used to assess the outcomes and the impacts on student learning? Additionally, there are many opportunities for future research on the questions of whether there is a consensus among library leaders regarding the sustainability of JEDI efforts and whether leaders envision these efforts as being incorporated within library strategic plans for the foreseeable future. Library-wide diversity plans for ARL libraries have been examined at a higher level, but a similar review of plans merits study and review for smaller colleges and universities.

CONCLUSION

For many years libraries have been committed to issues of justice, equity, diversity, and inclusion and have developed new ways of integrating these values into their daily work. However, it has proven challenging to maintain momentum and continue to advocate for change in a majority White profession. Despite its difficulties, the work must continue to be advanced. When initiating JEDI collections and acquisitions efforts within an academic library, the authors recommend identifying partners and determining the best way to move forward. Ideally, this will include support from all levels of employees within the library, though this will certainly not always be the case. Whether group efforts include the entire library staff or a select few, the authors assert that it is helpful to begin by creating a collections action plan. Throughout the execution of this plan, including and communicating with as many constituents as possible is vital to its success. Providing opportunities for new participants in collection building emphasizes the value of diversity and reflects the needs and wants of many perspectives. When purchasing materials for the collection, it is imperative to consider the choice and responsibility that comes with vendor selection. Regular assessment and frequent reference to the plan allows the document to fit the changing contexts, available resources, and support. When faced with barriers, the authors recommend seeking out alternative methods for executing the established action plan and consider how the overarching goals can be advanced through modifications to this plan. Whatever direction is taken or challenges that are faced, the values of justice, equity, diversity, and inclusion should be integrated into the thought and planning process. The work that is done to include voices from the margins will have an impact for the academic community. While not always easy or acknowledged, it is important and enduring.

REFERENCES

Aguilera, A., Carey, F., Dommermuth, E., Li, X., Koob, A. R., Swanson, J., Tingle, N., & Watkins, A. (2022, June 14). *Anti-racist library collection building*. University of Colorado Boulder Libraries research guides. https://libguides.colorado.edu/anti-racist-collections-review-acquisitions/home

Starting and Sustaining JEDI Acquisition, Collection in Academic Libraries

American Library Association. (2012, May 4). *Diversity standards: Cultural competency for academic libraries (2012)*. Association of College & Research Libraries (ACRL). https://www.ala.org/acrl/standards/diversity

American Library Association. (2019, June 24). *Diverse collections: An interpretation of the library bill of rights.* ALA. https://www.ala.org/advocacy/intfreedom/librarybill/interpretations/diversecollections

American Library Association. (2022, February 28). *Cultural proficiencies for racial equity: A framework*. Public Library Association (PLA). https://www.ala.org/pla/initiatives/edi/racialequityframework

Anaya, T., & Maxey-Harris, C. (2017). Diversity and Inclusion, SPEC Kit 356. Association of Research Libraries., doi:10.29242spec.356 doi:10.29242pec.356

Association of University Presses. (2021, March 18). University press numbers from the Lee & Low Diversity Baseline Survey 2.0. *Association of University Presses.* https://aupresses.org/news/up_data_lee_and_low_dbs_2/

Baildon, M., Hamlin, D., Jankowski, C., Kauffman, R., Lanigan, J., Miller, M., Venlet, J., & Willer, A. M. (2017). *Creating a social justice mindset: Diversity, inclusion, and social justice in the collections directorate of the MIT Libraries.* MIT Libraries. https://dspace.mit.edu/handle/1721.1/108771

Barnett, E. (2022). Collection and vendor relationships: Diversity evaluation and communication. *Serials Review*, *48*(3–4), 253–255. doi:10.1080/00987913.2022.2119058

Bernhardt, B., Hinds, L., Meyer, L., & Strauch, K. (Eds.). (2021). *Charleston Conference Proceedings, 2020*. Charleston Information Group. 10.3998/mpub.12470905

Berthoud, H., & Finn, R. (2019). Bringing social justice behind the scenes: Transforming the work of technical services. *The Serials Librarian*, *76*(1–4), 162–169. doi:10.1080/0361526X.2019.1583526

Bledsoe, K., Cooper, D. M., Schonfeld, R. C., & Rieger, O. Y. (2022, November 9). Leading by diversifying collections: A guide for academic library leadership. *Ithaka S+R.* doi:10.18665/sr.317833

About Us. (n.d.). Bookshop.org. https://bookshop.org/info/about-us

Bresnahan, M. (2022). Library diversity and inclusion statements in action. *Journal of Library Administration*, *62*(4), 419–437. doi:10.1080/01930826.2022.2057125

Caruso, M., Christenberry, F., Davis, A., Gascon, L., Henchy, J. A. N., Kenny, C., Schroeder, S., Shen, Z., & Sullivan, M. (2022). *UW Libraries Task Force on diversity, equity, inclusion, and anti-racism in collections final report*. UW Libraries https://digital.lib.washington.edu:443/researchworks/handle/1773/49181

Chan, L. (2020, November 9). *Decentering the White gaze of academic knowledge production: A paper presented at the Critical Knowledge Forum* [Presentation slides]. Zenodo. 10.5281/zenodo.4289243

Columbia University Libraries. (2019, April). *Collection development policies & strategies: Diversity in and of collections.* Columbia University Libraries. https://library.columbia.edu/about/policies/collection-development-policies-strategies.html

Consortium of Academic and Research Libraries in Illinois (CARLI). (2022, April). *Sample DEI language used in collection development policies.* Consortium of Academic and Research Libraries in Illinois. https://www.carli.illinois.edu/products-services/collections-management/Sample_DEI_Language_Used_in_Collection_Development_Policies

Edwards, J. B. (2015). Developing and implementing a diversity plan at your academic library. *Library Leadership & Management, 30*(2), 1–11. doi:10.5860/llm.v30i2.7129

Figueroa, M., & Shawgo, K. (2021). "You can't read your way out of racism": Creating anti-racist action out of education in an academic library. *RSR. Reference Services Review, 50*(1), 25–39. https://doi.org/10.17615/zs2n-bs65 doi:10.1108/RSR-06-2021-0025

Finnie, E., & Arthur, M. A. (2016). Being earnest with collections—voting with our dollars: Making a new home for the collections budget in the MIT Libraries. *Against the Grain (Charleston, S.C.), 28*(4), 90–92. doi:10.7771/2380-176X.7496

Frederick, J. K., & Wolff-Eisenberg, C. (2021, March 17). National movements for racial justice and academic library leadership: Results from the Ithaka S+R US Library Survey 2020. *Ithaka S+R.* doi:10.18665/sr.314931

Geiger, L., Mastley, C. P., Thomas, M., & Rangel, E. (2023). Academic libraries and DEI initiatives: A quantitative study of employee satisfaction. *Journal of Academic Librarianship, 49*(1), 102627. doi:10.1016/j.acalib.2022.102627

Hoeve, C. D., & Macaulay, D. (2022, June 10). *Bringing DEI to the Forefront in University of Nebraska-Lincoln Libraries' Collections* [Poster presentation]. Joint Spring Meeting of the College & University Section and the Technical Services Round Table of the Nebraska Library Association, online. https://digitalcommons.unl.edu/libraryscience/431

Hopkins, E. (2022, March 18). *Zotero Groups: DEI Assessment.* Zotero. https://www.zotero.org/groups/4633903/dei_assessment/

Jahnke, L. M., Tanaka, K., & Palazzolo, C. A. (2022). Ideology, policy, and practice: Structural barriers to collections diversity in research and college libraries. *College & Research Libraries, 83*(2), 166–183. doi:10.5860/crl.83.2.166

Kauffman, R. Y., & Anderson, M. S. (2020). Diversity, inclusion, and social justice in library technical services. In S. Marien (Ed.), *Library technical services: adapting to a changing environment* (pp. 213–236). Purdue University Press., doi:10.2307/j.ctvs1g8h5.17

Kohn, K. (2022, August 10). *Assessing Diversity in Collections.* Box. https://app.box.com/s/i8kqp7lacv1uuvolktqrx16vcy8izjho

Kristick, L. (2020). Diversity literary awards: A tool for assessing an academic library's collection. *Collection Management, 45*(2), 151–161. doi:10.1080/01462679.2019.1675209

Maxey-Harris, C., & Anaya, T. (2010). *Diversity Plans and Programs, SPEC Kit 319.* Association of Research Libraries. https://doi.org/10.29242/spec.319

Morales, M., Knowles, E. C., & Bourg, C. (2014). Diversity, social justice, and the future of libraries. *portal. Portal (Baltimore, Md.)*, *14*(3), 439–451. doi:10.1353/pla.2014.0017

Price, A. C. (2021). Barriers to an inclusive academic library collection. *Collection and Curation*, *41*(3), 97–100. doi:10.1108/CC-05-2021-0018

Price, G. (2020, July 1). Statements from libraries and library organizations re: racism, Black Lives Matter, and increased violence. *InfoDocket*. https://www.infodocket.com/2020/06/01/statements-from-library-organizations-re-racism-and-increased-violence/

Rodriguez, M. (2020). Negotiating accessibility for electronic resources. *Serials Review*, *46*(2), 150–156. doi:10.1080/00987913.2020.1760706

Roh, C. (2017). Library publishing and diversity values: Changing scholarly publishing through policy and scholarly communication education. *College & Research Libraries News*, *77*(2), 82–85. doi:10.5860/crln.77.2.9446

Rosa, K., & Henke, K. (2017). 2017 *ALA member demographics study*. American Library Association Office of Research and Statistics. https://www.ala.org/tools/research/initiatives/membershipsurveys

Royal Society of Chemistry. (n.d.). *Minimum standards for inclusion and diversity for scholarly publishing*. Royal Society of Chemistry. https://www.rsc.org/new-perspectives/talent/minimum-standards-for-inclusion-and-diversity-for-scholarly-publishing/

Sappington, J., De León, E., Schumacher, S., Vardeman, K., Callender, D., Oliver, M., Veeder, H., & Heinz, L. (2022). *Library impact research report: Educating and empowering a diverse student body: Supporting diversity, equity, and inclusion research through library collections*. Association of Research Libraries., doi:10.29242/report.texastech2022

So, R. J., & Wezerek, G. (2020, December 11). Just how white is the book industry? *The New York Times*. https://www.nytimes.com/interactive/2020/12/11/opinion/culture/diversity-publishing-industry.html

Speer, E. (2022). Communicating with vendors in support of DEI collection evaluations. *Online Searcher*, *46*(1). https://www.infotoday.com/OnlineSearcher/Articles/Features/Communicating-With-Vendors-in-Support-of-DEI-Collection-Evaluations-150915.shtml

University of Minnesota Libraries' Diversity, Equity, and Inclusion Leadership Committee. (2021, February 1). *Our approach to inclusion, diversity, equity, and accessibility*. University of Minnesota Libraries. https://www.lib.umn.edu/about/inclusion

University of Toledo Libraries. (2022, September 27). *Diversity equity, inclusion & accessibility @ UToledo Libraries: DEIA bookshelf*. LibGuides at University of Toledo Libraries. https://libguides.utoledo.edu/diversity-equity-inclusion-accessibility/DEIA-bookshelf

Wells, V. A., Gibney, M., & Paris, M. (2022). Student learning and engagement in a DEI collection audit: Applying the ACRL Framework for Information Literacy. *College & Research Libraries News*, *83*(8), 335–340. doi:10.5860/crln.83.8.335

KEY TERMS AND DEFINITIONS

Accessibility: The material's availability in a format that allows users with disabilities to view, read and engage. This consideration should form a part of collections and acquisition strategies.

Acquisitions: The process of procuring or purchasing materials.

Bibliodiversity: The amount and variety of materials being published. Publishers, especially those that are small, independent, and academic help contribute to this concept in more deliberately and consciously choosing what content to publish. Small publishers and others in the field of scholarly communication see the threat to diversity within the book publishing field by those larger publishers that are capable of publishing a far greater number of books. These large publishers are gaining a concentrated share of the market with more mergers and are concerned more about the profitability of the books being published; thus, they are less likely to publish a book that is not expected to generate a high volume of sales. Small publishers recognize the need beyond bestsellers and the struggle for diversity in the corpus of books produced and made available to readers.

Collection Development: The selection of materials usually in a specific subject area, format, or physical library location. The responsibility for this job function is now typically carried out by liaison librarians but was historically a separate and full-time position in academic libraries by subject bibliographers.

JEDI: The acronym Justice, Equity, Diversity, and Inclusion. Variations without the J include DEI and EDI. Another variation of this acronym incorporates Accessibility and is expressed as IDEA and DEIA.

Liaison: Also referred to as a library liaison, this is a librarian who is responsible for one or more academic departments or divisions and is the point of contact for faculty and students in that area. This librarian is frequently charged with collection development, reference, instruction, research support, and outreach to all faculty and students in that area. The liaison may or may not have a degree in the associated subject area.

Selector: Sometimes used synonymously with the term liaison, this is a librarian who has responsibilities for identifying materials for the library to acquire and may also have instruction, reference, or other liaison responsibilities

Subject Bibliographer: A full-time librarian responsible for developing the library's collections in a particular subject or subjects within an academic department or departments or across academic divisions. This role is much less common in current academic libraries and the work is usually now carried out by library liaisons.

Technical Services: The department in the library responsible for acquiring, collecting, licensing, cataloging, maintaining, and ensuring access to all general library materials in various formats.

Section 3
Programmatic Approaches

Chapter 7
Challenging the Silences:
Leading Change to Support Indigenous Representation and Priorities in Australian Libraries

Kirsten Thorpe
(iD) https://orcid.org/0000-0002-2844-168X
University of Technology Sydney, Australia

Monica Galassi
University of Technology Sydney, Australia

Lauren Booker
University of Technology Sydney, Australia

Tracy Barber
University of Technology Sydney, Australia

ABSTRACT

The complex history of Indigenous and colonizer relations in Australia has significantly impacted the terms of engagement between Indigenous peoples with libraries and archives. The library and archive sectors are now being challenged to be responsive to Indigenous calls for action for better representation and engagement with institutions and within collections. This chapter discusses developing and evaluating an Indigenous-led staff capability program designed to increase Indigenous representation and priorities in Australian libraries. By responding to the historical gaps of Indigenous perspectives and worldviews in library, archive, and information studies curriculum, the program provides learning opportunities for participants to activate support for Indigenous self-determination and sovereignty in libraries. The program aims to increase support for implementing protocols and practices that engage appropriately with racist and offensive legacy materials in library collections.

DOI: 10.4018/978-1-6684-7255-2.ch007

Challenging the Silences

INTRODUCTION

Aboriginal and Torres Strait Islander peoples[1] in Australia have a conflicted relationship with libraries. While often seen as places of vital support for learning and education, libraries are simultaneously places of tension and distrust for Aboriginal and Torres Strait Islander peoples. The recently launched report of the *National Survey on Aboriginal and Torres Strait Islander employment in Australian Libraries* (Thorpe, 2021) outlined the critical lack of representation of Aboriginal and Torres Strait Islander peoples in Australian libraries and the subsequent cultural load that Indigenous library workers face. The report identified that systemic and structural issues are pervasive in the Australian library and archives fields, including Indigenous workers having to deal with institutional racism, racist and offensive collections, and challenges of managing Indigenous knowledges with respect for appropriate protocols (Thorpe, 2021). A lack of Indigenous worldviews and perspectives in formal library studies has meant that many libraries, archives and information workers across Galleries, Libraries, Archives and Museums (GLAM) are ill-equipped to support Indigenous priorities.

In response to the silences of Indigenous representation in library, archive and information studies, the Jumbunna Institute for Indigenous Education and Research (Jumbunna Research) at the University of Technology Sydney (UTS) designed and delivered a staff capability program, in the form of a short course, to activate and inspire change to support Indigenous priorities and worldviews in Australian libraries. As an Indigenous-led institute, Jumbunna Research was uniquely positioned to undertake the course, and to understand current trends and gaps in relevant skills across the library workforce and contextualize this in line with principles of Indigenous self-determination. The Jumbunna Research team, comprised of Indigenous and non-Indigenous allies, undertakes the highest quality participatory research to achieve societal change and positive outcomes for Indigenous people informed by Indigenous research methodologies.

The authors of this paper, Indigenous and non-Indigenous researchers based at Jumbunna Research, discuss the rationale and approach to designing and delivering the staff capability program to support decolonial and anti-racist approaches within libraries. They describe the focus areas of the program's content and the support for embedding and implementing other Indigenous sector-appropriate protocols. The paper describes the research methodology and approach, and reports on the research findings. In doing this, the paper highlights the vital need to provide professional learning that will enable workers to respond to and support Indigenous social justice initiatives in libraries, particularly in developing Indigenous led approaches for providing appropriate care for Indigenous cultural materials. It describes the gaps in knowledge for supporting Indigenous peoples' information needs and highlights findings on how incorporating Indigenous worldviews and perspectives into libraries can assist in dismantling systems and structures of oppression to better support Indigenous peoples' representation in the library, archive and information sector[2].

BACKGROUND

Libraries are considered vital access points for every local community, supporting information literacy and opportunities for engagement in lifelong learning. Australian public libraries are positioned as upholding democratic values, providing a public service and as being 'vital contributors to our national communities and to our national economies' (NSLA, 2022). However, for Aboriginal and Torres Strait

Islander peoples, libraries have not always been welcoming places of intellectual and creative expression. Libraries are troubling and complicated spaces that raise distrust and deep tensions, but also hold significant cultural and personal materials (Thorpe and Galassi, 2014). Australian libraries, alongside archives and museums, hold large collections of Aboriginal and Torres Strait Islander peoples' cultural heritage, personal information and other forms of surveillance and documentation. These collections have historically been held at a distance from Aboriginal and Torres Strait Islander peoples and contain vital information to support the reconnection of communities to languages, cultural practices and family histories. Much of these materials have been created about Indigenous peoples rather than by Indigenous peoples, which raises questions regarding the accuracy and appropriateness of legacy materials and publications held by libraries. Issues of ongoing colonialism, discriminatory research and publications, and racism have affected both engagement with libraries and employment within the sector, with Aboriginal and Torres Strait Islander peoples greatly underrepresented in the library sector workforce (Thorpe, 2021).

The Aboriginal and Torres Strait Islander population across Australia is rich and diverse. Aboriginal culture is recognized as one of the oldest continuing cultures in the world, existing for over 60,000 years, a land comprised of over 250 different language groups across the nation. According to the 2021 *Australian Census of Population and Housing*, Aboriginal and Torres Strait Islander peoples represented 3.2% of the population, with a total of 812,000 people identifying as being Indigenous (Australian Bureau of Statistics, 2022). Indigenous peoples in Australia still feel the impacts of British colonization. The ideologies of colonialism are embedded in the processes of the settler-state, and they continue to impact the ability of Indigenous people to recover and revitalize their communities. Libraries and archives have supported the ideologies of colonialism through their institutional systems and practices. Nationally across Australia, the GLAM sector is being challenged to engage in more critically reflexive practice about their role in the colonial project of the dispossession and erasure of Aboriginal and Torres Strait Islander peoples. There is greater dialogue about the need to consider methods for the decolonization and Indigenization of libraries.

While national reports, including the 1991 *Royal Commission into Aboriginal Deaths in Custody* (Royal Commission into Aboriginal Deaths in Custody, 1991) and 1997 *Bringing Them Home Report* (Human Rights and Equal Opportunity Commission, 1997), brought critical attention to the importance of libraries and archives for Aboriginal and Torres Strait Islander people, there remains a lack of literature on understanding the links between Indigenous social justice and the library sector and many complexities and challenges remain. Much of the literature that exists on Indigenous priorities in the library, archive and information sector – including research that is led and supported by Indigenous peoples - relates to the development of protocols (Barrowcliffe et. al., 2021; Nakata, et al, 2008; Thorpe, 2013; Garwood-Houng & Blackburn, 2014), increased access to digital collections including materials for language and cultural revitalisation (Christen, 2018; Thorpe and Galassi, 2014) and reflections on the dominance of western perspectives in libraries and archives (Masterson, Stableford, & Tait, 2019; Nakata, 2007). More recently, there has been a growing body of reflection written on areas of cultural competency from non-Indigenous practitioners (Blackburn, 2020; Galassi, 2019; Galassi, 2022) as well as demands for change from Indigenous peoples engaged in the sector (Sentance, 2018; Thorpe, 2019; Barrowcliffe, 2021). The 2022 article *Co-creating Public Library Futures: An Emergent Manifesto and Participatory Research Agenda* argues that the field of social justice offers a critical view for imagining libraries as a place of community networks and creative spaces for community engagement (Swist, et al, 2022). For the purposes of this paper, we have identified four primary areas of concern on the complexities of Indigenous engagement with libraries in Australia drawn from the literature.

Challenging the Silences

Indigenous Self-Determination and the Management and Ownership of Data and Collections

The first area relates broadly to the concerns of Indigenous people about the lack of ability to manage and control their cultural heritage materials. The principles outlined in the *United Nations Declaration on the Rights of Indigenous Peoples* (UNDRIP) guide progressive action and support for Indigenous people to control and maintain their knowledge and culture (General Assembly of the United Nations, 2007). There is limited implementation of UNDRIP, and its principles of Indigenous self-determination across all social, cultural and political spheres, within libraries and, more broadly the GLAM sector. Indigenous peoples' inherent collective and individual rights in access and participation in the preservation and management of their cultural heritage outlined in UNDRIP, are however, being addressed now in the work of the international Indigenous Data Sovereignty movement. In 2016, the publication *Indigenous Data Sovereignty: Toward an Agenda* (Kukutai & Taylor, 2016) drew attention to the need for Indigenous people to control the data relating to their communities and, importantly, their cultural heritage. The publication highlighted how Indigenous people are demanding and asserting their data rights in the context of Indigenous sovereignty and self-determination. Drawing on this, Walter and Sunia (2019) discuss the lack of data being created and framed through "Indigenous Lifeworlds" arguing that "Indigenous self-determination relies on data self-determination" (p.236). Earlier work in GLAM settings include discussions on issues of Indigenous self-determination and tensions regarding ownership of institutionally held collections of Indigenous cultural heritage and personal information (Anderson, 2005; Fourmile, 1989; Janke, 1998; Janke, 2021; Nakata et al, 2008).

Managing Racist, Offensive, and Derogatory Information and Materials

The second area relates to dealing sensitively and effectively with materials developed in the context of the colonization of Australia, including the management of racist, offensive and derogatory information and materials. The emergence of protocols for libraries, archives and information services helped bring awareness to issues of racist, offensive and derogatory information (ATSILIRN, 2015, n.p). Thorpe (2019) discusses the challenges of institutions managing offensive collections in open access paradigms and the intergenerational trauma and harm that this may cause Indigenous peoples. Additionally, Wright argues that challenges are found not only in the collection's content but also in the descriptions, metadata and cataloguing (Wright, 2019). In Australia, the Aboriginal and Torres Strait Islander Library, Information and Resource Network (ATISLIRN) *Protocols for Libraries, Archives and Information Services* discuss the need for appropriate Indigenous representation, including discussion on materials that are offensive and racist. Protocol 7 'Offensive' notes that Libraries, archives and information services must respond and manage appropriately materials that are offensive to Aboriginal and Torres Strait Islander peoples, including materials that are racist, sexist, derogatory, abusive or offensively wrong. (Aboriginal and Torres Strait Islander Library, Information and Resource Network, 2012) Thorpe and Galassi (2018, p.187) used "explanatory statements and sensitivity notices" to implement the protocols to support the management of offensive or culturally sensitive collections. The literature argues that although guidelines are vital as frameworks to guide practice in the sector; awareness of their existence can fluctuate. Citing research by Nakata and colleagues (2005), Alana Garwood-Houng and Fiona Blackburn noted that although the ATSILIRN Protocols make a significant contribution to the library profession, their use was not widespread and the implementation of the ATSILIRN Protocols was reliant on "the commitment and goodwill of individuals" (Garwood-Houng & Blackburn, 2014, p.5)

Privileging of Non-Indigenous Peoples' Narratives

A third area of concern is the presence of biases, silencing and the privileging of narratives of non-Indigenous people in Australian library and GLAM collections. According to Barrowcliffe, the materials held in institutional collections are frequently incomplete and biased (Barrowcliffe, 2021) and sometimes contain information that has been fabricated, or is inaccurate (Indigenous Archives Collective, 2021). Most of these collections and their narratives were created in contexts that were intrusive and racist (Thorpe, 2022; Faulkhead, 2009; Nakata, 2007; Russell, 2005). Evans and colleagues reflect on issues of bias and representation and the impacts on Indigenous people's wellbeing asserting that, "Positive narratives of Indigenous peoples, culture and history assists the wellbeing of the represented communities, whilst bolstering the education of next generation Australians to question the colonial, hegemonic and assimilatory narratives of the past." (Evans, et al, 2020, p.136) The research conducted as part of the *National Survey on Aboriginal and Torres Strait Islander employment in Australian Libraries* (Thorpe, 2021) demonstrated how many library workers have come to the sector without the opportunity to engage with Indigenous peoples' worldviews and perspectives, nor engage in dialogue about the impacts of colonization and how these tools and systems might continue to be embedded in systems and structures of libraries. Recently, Kerry Klimm (Gugu Yalanji and Koko Lamalama woman), journalist and communications specialist called attention to the existences of offensive and derogatory book held in her son's primary school library. Taking to social media, Klimm's advocacy demonstrated the lack of attention to the material being acquired that portrayed Indigenous peoples as "nomadic" and "uncivilized" (Klimm & Robertson, 2021). Often these library experiences of working in Indigenous contexts spur on moments of learning, however, often this is done as a reaction to a situation or incident.

Silencing Indigenous Peoples' Worldview and Perspectives

The fourth and final area of concern identified in the literature relate to the dominance of the settler-state and the prevalence of Eurocentric values that silence Indigenous worldviews and perspectives in Australian libraries and GLAM institutions. This dominance relates both to the existence of collections and the metadata and information sources and engagement related to them. Citing, Sentance (2018) and de Jesus (2014), Wright notes that "… archives (and museums and libraries) were established as part of the settler-colonial state, and thus reinforcing this paradigm is built deep within these structures" (2019, p.341). The dominant western paradigm also involves accessing materials that are catalogued and available through western knowledge systems, such as the Library of Congress headings (Masterson, Stableford, & Tait, 2019) There is limited literature on this area of scholarship in Australia. However, internationally, there is discussion and critique about the lack of Indigenous ontologies being incorporated into the design of information systems (Duarte and Belarde-Lewis, 2015), incorporating the use of traditional knowledge labels and licenses to support Indigenous data sovereignty in documentation processes (Montenegro, 2019) and a focus on relationships between people rather than a focus merely on information and records (Christen, 2018). In an Aotearoa/New Zealand context, Māori academic Spencer Lilley (2021) writes about the need for Indigenizing libraries for "'Indigenous constructs become part of the core structure of an institution or organization" (p. 306). Ulia Gosart (2021) suggests adding the

Challenging the Silences

notion of "living knowledge" to traditional librarianship theories in North America; or the Hawaiian approach, that positions Hawaiian natural resource management principles to explore their application in the library sector (Komeiji et al, 2021).

In the United States discussions on Justice, Equity, Diversity and Inclusion (JEDI) initiatives are active in #critlib library practice and literature to encourage dialogue about social justice in libraries (Leung & López-McKnight, 2021; Cooke, 2020). A systemic review of library and information science literature undertaken by Jones and colleagues (2022), identified that the range and scope of initiatives focused on anti-racism, inclusion and social justice in libraries had increased in the literature over the past ten years (p. 92). According to the authors, although the literature demonstrates a range of initiatives have been undertaken, further research is required to investigate how changes in library approaches have served marginalized communities (Jones et al, 2022, p. 97). As another example, the American Library Association (ALA) have produced an Equity, Diversity, and Inclusion series of initiatives to include multiple perspectives in library services (ALA, n.d.).

In an Australian context, it is clear that current library initiatives highlight goodwill in the profession to support Indigenous priorities, and several projects have been developed to respond to the gaps in Indigenous worldviews and perspectives across practice (e.g. Australian Library and Information Association et al, 2019; National and State Libraries Australasia, n.d.). However, a review of scholarly literature shows that there are significant gaps in research on the course curriculum and approaches for increasing the skills of library, archive and information workers to deliver on advancing support for Indigenous priorities, particularly in the frame of supporting Indigenous self-determination. Underexplored areas include gaps in data about identifying and eradicating structural issues such as biases, racism, and the lack of knowledge of the impacts of colonization on Aboriginal and Torres Strait Islander people in the library and information sector. Issues of diversity are not limited to Aboriginal and Torres Strait Islander inclusion. The *ALIA Workforce Diversity Trend Report* in 2019 exposed that the library profession in Australia was largely a "homogenous profession, characterised by a white, middle-class staffing base". (Muir, et al., 2021. p.10)

DEVELOPING AND DELIVERING THE INDIGENOUS PRIORITIES AND ENGAGEMENT SHORT COURSE

In recognizing the critical need for developing education and professional skills in libraries that will benefit Aboriginal and Torres Strait Islander peoples, the Jumbunna Research team developed a short course focused on Indigenous priorities and engagement in 2019. The team, composed of Indigenous peoples and non-Indigenous allies, was uniquely positioned to design a course focused on libraries and Indigenous social justice in Australia. The one-day Indigenous Priorities and Engagement course focused on methods to engage and support Indigenous peoples and communities with their information needs. These information needs relate broadly to Aboriginal and Torres Strait Islander peoples having access to culturally appropriate and relevant information sources that are free from bias and racism and that acknowledge Indigenous worldviews, ways of knowing, being and doing. By establishing a foundation of knowledge to support and promote Aboriginal and Torres Strait Islander histories and culture, the course's fundamental aim was to equip participants to build engagement programs and collections responsive to Indigenous peoples' diverse needs. The audience of the course represented different age groups, gender, nationality, and professional roles. Most attendees worked in public libraries, but there was also interest from people who worked in academic libraries, local councils, museums and small archives.

The course's pedagogical approach was unique in combining learnings and insights from Indigenous research methodologies and the 8ways learning framework (2011). Collectively this ensured that Indigenous peoples voices, knowledge and priorities informed all aspects of the course's design, delivery and evaluation. The 8ways framework provides a basis for understanding learning as a holistic process involving non-linear, visual, kinesthetic and social dimensions, with story sharing a key element throughout. It provides a culturally safe entry point for Indigenous and non-Indigenous educators to actively engage in cross-cultural dialogue and shared learning about Aboriginal knowledge and worldviews, including the interconnectedness of people, land, culture, language and spirit. Importantly, for the course development, national and international mandates were drawn upon as a roadmap to better frame and support Indigenous peoples' priorities and information needs.

In alignment with Indigenous worldviews, which see one's standpoint as the starting point of any relationship, the course focused on the vocalized sharing of experiences and reflections by both the facilitators and participants as key to its success. As Behrendt has written, where you are placed – your positioning or standpoint - "Will fundamentally influence the way you see the world" (Behrendt, 2019, p. 176). Acknowledging and sharing the point where one was positioned in a journey of learning about Indigenous worldviews and histories laid the foundations for honest and productive conversation during the course. Indigenous Research staff members led sharing of their stories, followed by non-Indigenous ally team members. This encouraged course participants to reflect on and consider their standpoints.

The key learning objectives for the course, in addition to focus on supporting decolonial and Indigenizing approaches within libraries, were aligned with the recent Australian Library and Information Association (ALIA) *Professional Pathways Project* (ALIA, 2019). The key learning objectives were developed across four key topics: (1) understanding the context of Indigenous peoples' engagement with libraries and examples of Indigenous communities' information needs; (2) becoming aware of Aboriginal and Torres Strait Islander sovereignty and self-determination in the context of library and information needs; (3) gaining insight into protocols for libraries, archives and information services and principles and practices relating to Indigenous-led engagement and decolonizing practices; and (4) understanding strategies for developing welcoming spaces, programs and collections that support Indigenous peoples' wellbeing.

METHODOLOGY AND METHODS UTILIZED FOR THE RESEARCH AND EVALUATION

The research and evaluation utilized qualitative methods, informed by an Indigenous research paradigm (Wilson, 2008; Kovach, 2021). Indigenous research methodologies have become an established element of qualitative research and are increasingly utilized by both Indigenous and non-Indigenous researchers (Singh and Major, 2017, p. 6). Indigenous research methodologies seek to ensure that research is conducted in culturally appropriate and respectful ways, through centering Indigenous self-determination and Indigenous worldviews, whilst also focusing on the accountability of the researcher (Archibald et al, 2019; Singh and Major, 2017, p. 5; Rigney, 1999, p. 119). In addition, the research approach was aligned with the *AIATSIS Code of Ethics for Aboriginal and Torres Strait Islander Research* (2020), as a key framework for ethical and responsible conduct in research that centers respect for Aboriginal

Challenging the Silences

and Torres Strait Islander peoples "values and worldviews, acknowledging the wisdom and diversity of Indigenous knowledge systems" (AIATSIS, 2020). The research approach was also informed by critical library and archival studies which provide opportunities for understanding more about the concerns of Indigenous peoples in information and archival contexts. Authors Nicholson & Seale (2018) argue that a critical lens enables librarians to "use a reflexive lens to expose and challenge the ways that libraries and the profession consciously and unconsciously support systems of oppression" (p. 2). Furthermore, the course was designed and delivered to support decolonial (Smith, 2012) and anti-racist approaches within libraries (Leung and McKnight, 2021).

The research approach was developed to open dialogue and gather data by enabling a circular feedback loop to study the effectiveness of the short course as a staff capability program. The research aims were to:

- Understand course participants' experiences, including whether the course is effective in achieving its stated objectives and whether the content, teaching and learning processes are effective in engaging participants and meeting their learning interests and needs
- Identify ways in which the course could be strengthened or adapted to improve its effectiveness and responsiveness to participants' needs and interests
- Identify the longer-term impact of the course upon participants' own work practices in relation to building Indigenous services and collections
- Identify other wider impacts of the course, including upon developing Indigenous services and collections and impact on local communities
- Identify further opportunities for building upon the course with other programs and resources that will lead to the improvement of Indigenous services and collections in libraries.

Participants were recruited by invitation and on a voluntary basis after completion of the course. The inclusion criteria for the research were that the participant had undertaken the short course run by Jumbunna Research on building Indigenous priorities in libraries, archives, and GLAM institutions. There were no exclusion criteria. Participants in the course came from various roles in GLAM organizations, including public and academic galleries, libraries, archives and museums. The cohort of participants involved in the follow-up study collectively represented a diversity of individual experiences, insights and institutional contexts. Participants were both Indigenous and non-Indigenous.

Semi-structured interviews were used to gain insights from participants on their experiences of the course. The interviews were conducted via online conference tools (Zoom), and participants were provided with open-ended questions prior to the interview to support their reflections. The questions used as a guide in the semi-structured interview were as follows:

1. How has the course impacted upon participants' understanding of processes and strategies for building Indigenous services and collections in libraries?
2. Are the course pedagogical resources, strategies and processes effective in engaging participants, providing a positive learning experience and supporting learning around the course topics?
3. Has course participation impacted upon participants' professional practices on return to the workplace, and if so in what ways?
4. Has course participation contributed to other changes in the participants' workplaces in relation to building Indigenous services and collections?
5. Has the course contributed to other changes in the library or local community?

6. What more could be done to strengthen staff capacity in building Indigenous services and collections in libraries, either during the course or through other related programs/resources?
7. What other opportunities are there to utilise the building of Indigenous services and collections to contribute to empowering Aboriginal and Torres Strait Islander peoples and achieving sovereignty and self-determination?

The in-depth data analysis using the interview transcripts enabled the team to achieve the research aims of understanding individual participants' experiences and whether their needs and interests were met by the short course. In addition, the interviews sought participants' ideas for strengthening the course and how the course might have impacted their own work experiences and the experiences of their institutions. All data collected in the interview process was treated as confidential, and the use of participant quotes were anonymised. With the consent of the participants, the research interviews were recorded and the transcripts were analyzed using methods of coding and thematic analysis. Knott et al (2022) have described how "Interviews are especially well suited to gaining a deeper insight into people's experiences" (n.d.) and how analysis of transcript is not a straightforward process but allows the researcher to "Create something new when analyzing the data by applying their analytic lens or approach to the transcripts" (Knott et al., n.d.).

The impact of the Covid-19 pandemic resulted in a smaller pool of participants being recruited for the interviews. Initially, the research estimated 15-30 participants in the study; however, a lesser amount of six in-depth interviews were achieved. The researchers intend to build upon the learnings from the sample within this study, by continuing to research into this area of how to develop the capacity of libraries, and more broadly GLAM institutions, to support Indigenous peoples' engagement and information needs.

FINDINGS

The analysis identified five main themes, each with multiple subthemes as summarized in Table 1.

Table 1. Summary of themes

(a) Tensions and limited focussed action to support Indigenous priorities	• A lack of Indigenous employment • Harms of unsafe practices on Indigenous library workers • Need to work respectfully with Indigenous communities
(b) Lack of Indigenous representation and the existence of racist and offensive materials	• Existence of racist and offensive collections • Lack of representation of Indigenous histories and perspectives in collections • Lack of awareness and foundational knowledge about the history of colonization
(c) Proper Indigenous community engagement and the building of relationships and trust	• Institutional timeframes are different to Indigenous communities' timeframes • Learning about methods and approaches for engaging respectfully
(d) Recognizing the role of power and the need for political will	• Awareness of Indigenous priorities and failure to act • The need political will and the support of leadership
(e) Decolonization and time for change	• Importance of policies and the need for frameworks, protocols and tools • Benchmarking and learning from others • Understanding of how to be an ally to take action • Need for decolonizing approaches in library practice

Challenging the Silences

Tensions and Limited Focused Action to Support Indigenous Priorities

Interview participants, both Indigenous and non-Indigenous, described their frustration at the low rates of Indigenous staff working across libraries in Australia. A lack of Indigenous staff was seen as a core issue for participants in being able to support Indigenous priorities. There was a shared view and a recognition that Aboriginal and Torres Strait Islander library workers opened up opportunities for engagement with communities and that they needed this support to activate relationships and connections. The gaps were described by one participant in the following blunt terms:

"So, at the moment, there is no Indigenous employment in the in library...and that's just not good enough".

Participants described how the sector was currently in a period of change, but with no Indigenous staff to help drive the change, the work was difficult. There was also a desire expressed for institutions to have more Indigenous staff in the workforce across a range of roles, including for example, curatorial roles and roles that support community consultation. The rationale for increasing Indigenous staff in libraries differed from the perspective of non-Indigenous and Indigenous participants. Non-Indigenous participants expressed concerned about their lack of cultural competency and community connections, while Indigenous participants spoke of the significant opportunities for Aboriginal and Torres Strait Islander representation and associated opportunities to increase decision-making and agency. Also, it was noted that in the current situation the lack of staff resulted in Indigenous staff becoming burnt out from their need to respond to every Indigenous enquiry coming into their institution.

However, the lack of Indigenous staff also led non-Indigenous participants to experience fear and inertia. Non-Indigenous staff felt worried about getting things done "right", which led to a failure to act.

"Allowing people to have an opportunity to get employment in the sector is one of the first steps, because we're not going to get engagement unless we have [Aboriginal people] working there."

One non-Indigenous participant described these tensions as follows:

"We really feel that this work is most appropriately done by Aboriginal people, but without Aboriginal staff to turn to we find ourselves needing to try and do this ourselves via consultation with the community ... it's hard to do ethically."

These responses echo a common theme in practice that a lack of resourcing and support for Indigenous staff impacts a library's ability to build appropriate forms of community engagement and support for Indigenous staff. While the discussion on the lack of Indigenous employment in the research spoke to gaps and opportunities, it was also discussed that any opportunities for increases in Indigenous employment need to be aligned with decolonizing projects that sought to minimize the existing harmful approaches of libraries. For example, stopping the sharing of racist and offensive materials, or engaging appropriately to ensure adequate acknowledgements of local Indigenous people and languages in their library's operations.

The discussion of bias was a repeated theme in the interviews and statements were continually made about the need for library workers to have their assumptions tested about library neutrality. When discussing racist and offensive collections, participants expressed concern that not enough was being done to

133

reduce the harm connected to holding racist and offensive materials, which portrayed Indigenous people with negative stereotypes. However, as was the case with the Kerry Klimm calling out racist materials in a school library collection, most library approaches were considered as being at best, reactionary. Overall, participants perceived their organizations to be unsafe and, because of this, felt it was harmful if Indigenous people took up roles. One non-Indigenous participant noted that:

"[We] don't want Aboriginal employees to face the burden of cleaning up the mess."

The research identified a lack of cultural competence in the profession, particularly with issues related to a lack of action to respond to racist and biased materials and the need to work respectfully with Indigenous people and communities about the management and use of cultural materials. It was evident within the research interviews that library workers had limited opportunities to engage previously with Indigenous perspectives in libraries, and that it was a missing ingredient in both foundational library and information studies curriculum and within workplace organizational culture. For the Jumbunna Research team this further emphasized the need for the short course, however it also demonstrated the problematic nature of how Indigenous cultural competency training was being used as an approach to fill the gaps in education. Although programs have been run within the National and State Libraries of Australasia (NSLA), for example, in supporting the *Culturally Safe Libraries* project, which engaged over 2000 library workers in online cultural competency training from 2019 to 2021 (NSLA, n.d.), and with the Australian Society of Archivists (ASA) developing the *Indigenous Recordkeeping and Archives* course (Booker, 2020), they represent a "filling of the gaps" rather than a focused approach to action. The insights shared by participants, both Indigenous and non-Indigenous demonstrate the large-scale lack of appropriate education on Indigenous priorities and information needs at the core of library and archival studies curricula.

Overall, participants both Indigenous and non-Indigenous expressed emotions of being angry and upset about the harms of unsafe library practices. The lack of focussed strategy and action to support Indigenous priorities was made clear, as was the need for library institutions and staff to work respectfully with Indigenous community to bridge these gaps. The importance of building trust – and responding to issues of distrust - was seen as the most critical part of building relationships. Participants also recognised that their libraries had to do community engagement correctly and that more time needed to be given to relationship building, particularly connecting with Indigenous Elders.

Indigenous Representation and the Existence of Racist and Offensive Materials

Issues of racist and offensive collections were discussed, and one non-Indigenous participant suggested that they now "had to look at things more carefully" than they had previously done so, and that there was more institutional awareness of how Aboriginal and Torres Strait Islander representation was an issue in library collections. Examples were shared of libraries having online content that participants described as offensive, including one specific example where collections held overtly racist content in local studies collections, and that the collection had been noted as problematic for some time. There was acknowledgement by non-Indigenous participants that those racist and offensive collections supported white supremacy and racism in the community, and that sharing any changes to the content would incite a "White racist backlash" as the collection was "a safe space for white supremacists". In this particular example, it was acknowledged that library processes had not sufficiently addressed issues of racism de-

Challenging the Silences

spite people being aware of the problem. The research showed that although there are multiple initiatives focused on understanding and improving Aboriginal and Torres Strait Islander people's cultural safety, aiming to interrogate issues of marginalization, discrimination and representation across Australian libraries, these initiatives have failed to address the systemic and structural issues that Thorpe (2022) has identified as existing in the sector.

A persistent theme emerged about the lack of Indigenous-authored representations of Indigenous histories and perspectives in library collections. Participants were asked whether course attendance had led to changes in their work environment and an increased focus on Indigenous priorities. In response, many of the participants reflected on the issues related to Indigenous representation, especially the lack of Indigenous peoples' visibility in collections and the lack of public and staff knowledge of local histories. Feedback about the benefits and impact of the course showed that the program helped increase participants' understanding of issues of representation. According to one non-Indigenous respondent:

"There's a lot of community interest and interest ourselves in the colonial and Indigenous origins, stories that are related to area as well. […] we've got migrant histories, but we've also got these Indigenous histories that are not really well recorded by us in our collection".

Critically, participants regarded acquiring more Indigenous materials and resources for the library without community engagement as being insufficient. Libraries should first consider "what did [local Indigenous communities] want to see about themselves or about other Indigenous people within the collection". According to some non-Indigenous participants, there is a general lack of public and institutional awareness of local Aboriginal histories and their intergenerational impacts, and a lack of foundational knowledge on the history of colonization. This includes recognizing the concept of Indigenous peoples' sovereignty on the land where the library stands and the different histories and experiences between Aboriginal and migrant communities. As one non-Indigenous participant stated, referring to how the media depicts these issues: "There's actually some people before you in the queue, and you seem to be talking about them as almost as a migrant population, you know, quite strange, some of that language". This aspect unravels bias and assumptions about diversity and equity:

"within [our council area], in particular, the [local migrant] population has a lot of prominence. So in some ways that eclipses Indigenous issues, just because of the actual weight … if you walk around here, for example, it has a very, very [migrant community] flavour, quite literally, to it. You know, that's what it is. That's great. It's awesome. It's a very diverse place. But the strength of that [local migrant] community, also, you know, say, if you do something that addresses that community, it's like diversity tick, done […]. […] it's very easy to get [Indigenous priorities] to be an afterthought, in that sense."

Indigenous and non-Indigenous participants discussed how it was essential to understand the history of colonization and be aware of the reality that many Aboriginal people had been forcibly moved or relocated from their communities. Many people who live in local council areas and visit the library might be reluctant to speak on local topics as they do not represent the interests of those communities. This area of tension speaks of a gap in education in the study of Aboriginal history. It dramatically influences how relationships are established between the library and local Aboriginal communities:

"So the Indigenous people who live locally …do they represent the Indigenous people, […], a lot of other places in in urban, metropolitan areas where the local Indigenous population is so displaced, …

it's a little bit hard for people to feel like they can speak on behalf of the people who do or once lived in this area, and, you know, decisions to be made about their country. Sometimes I think there's a bit of ambivalence, because people feel like, you know, it's not necessarily our country to speak about"

Speaking about challenges of engaging with the local Aboriginal communities at a Council level, another issue that was raised by a participant related to the [perceived] "Invisibility of the local Indigenous population" as one of the reasons that motivated the lack of engagement.

Proper Indigenous Community Engagement and the Building of Relationships and Trust

Difficulties of libraries having the skills to engage with local Aboriginal communities were raised, especially with the specific example of realising how timelines may be different between communities and institutions:

"We didn't have great results ... results are sometimes good, sometimes not so good. Sometimes just silence. I feel like ... maybe there's a cultural gap or a timing gap or an approach that we could, we could accidentally be putting [the local Indigenous community] offside just because we're a Council and the way we do business, and our requirements, and our timelines, and the way we write emails ... I don't know. I wonder about that for myself, ... I don't want to accidentally miss out on feedback because I'm trying to get the feedback in the wrong way or ... I don't think we ...do it in ...an intentional way – but I do [wonder] about that because historically [engagement] hasn't gone well"

This area of tension speaks of the challenges participants faced when determining priorities and finding opportunities to bring Indigenous voices in at the planning stages of projects or seek feedback on initiatives.

Participants saw the course as an opportunity to learn about the facilitators' experiences and hear their views on respectfully engaging with communities. A key outcome of the course was that participants were able to learn about methods and approaches to engage with Indigenous communities respectfully. Having both the perspectives of Indigenous facilitators and allies who come from diverse backgrounds and who now work in this context was helpful. One attendee said:

"It's not so much there's a right or wrong, but there's actions that need to be taken that take time to get a result ... one of the important things is starting that process and talking to the right people ... the stories that that you both shared as presenters helped us understand that day to day aspect of it .. the [action] and talking to the right people and building trust and relationships with elders is the way to move forwards ... that we can't just move forwards we need to start that journey."

Recognising the importance of improving this aspect, one of the non-Indigenous participants raised the need of focusing some of the course content on this:

"Maybe one of the things that would be reassuring, is [sharing] some of those consultation and engagement pieces, because I know there's a way to do it ... There's a way that you can do it, [that is] effective and there's a way to do it that accidentally is wrong on all levels, and you just make a terrible impression."

Challenging the Silences

Again, a repeated theme was that the learning style, and the approach to hearing about the importance of Indigenous standpoint and the sharing of stories, helped develop a trusted and welcoming learning environment. Through this were reflections about people being engaged in reflexive practice about their work, learning from others, and learning from the content and stories shared by the facilitators. One participant shared feedback on the relaxed and safe space shared, noting:

"it's really a really, really great workshop. I don't often feel that comfortable speaking out in workshops and … even then, I was fairly quiet anyway. It was a very comfortable space that you will created … I think that's really powerful …I don't know how you do it must just be you guys. But thank you very much for that."

Recognizing the Role of Power and the Need for Political Will

Some participants discussed the challenges of Indigenous priorities being absorbed into broader inclusion and equity initiatives, including engagement with multicultural communities. It was thought that Indigenous priorities required their own agenda and that a commitment should be made to embed support that was not tokenistic or, as some expressed, a "tick the box" effort. The sentiment was expressed that Aboriginal people have always been here, but sometimes libraries approach Indigenous engagement under the frame of 'multiculturalism'. There was a clear need stated that library's needed to increase their awareness of Indigenous priorities and build appropriate implementation strategies to activate support.

Additionally, participants discussed feelings of fear and inertia in their workplace as a result of staff feeling vulnerable and not having the skills to work appropriately in Indigenous contexts. These feelings of uncertainty were felt alongside a genuine commitment to act.

"We are taking tentative steps forward and hopefully doing the correct things, but without expert advice, how do you know that what you're doing is the right thing?"

"[not supporting Indigenous priorities] It's a collective failure of Australian institutions"

Participants expressed their emotions about their lack of awareness of protocols for managing Indigenous collections. One person mentioned that "personally, I feel a lot of shame…these protocols ..these ideas have been around for a long time, haven't they? … There's been a failure to implement things."

Access to power and resources was a constant theme in the interviews. There was recognition that the political will to act needed to exist so that Indigenous perspectives were included more formally across library functions and projects. There needed to be more political will offered up by Library's and Library leadership teams needed to offer their support for Indigenous priorities. Additionally, it was expressed that this work had to be formalized. Comments were made that the GLAM sector is broadly conservative, and participants expressed interest that they wanted to be a part of changing the status quo of how institutions work.

"It's not just a matter of resources. Its political will …. And why am I still working in contexts where I can't seem to make these things real?"

Decolonization and Time for Change

Policies supporting Indigenous priorities were seen as a real strength as they enabled libraries and institutions to make recommendations based on input and direction from community engagement. The importance of having access to frameworks, protocols and tools was also evident. Examples of key policies include having Indigenous input into library collection development policies, whilst implementing established and relevant protocols already existing in the field. For example, the interviews showed that there was a gap in awareness of the ATSILIRN protocols.

"having worked in libraries for that many years it was the first I'd heard of the [ATSILIRN] protocols ... I hadn't known about those before ...They've obviously been around for quite a long time, but they either hadn't come up, I hadn't come across them ... I guess [that] shows the state of play in a lot of libraries, how these protocols are there, but unless you're specified to look at them and use them, they become part of what you do. You just sort of come across them. I find that quite amazing that that they've been around for such a long time, and I didn't know that then."

There was an acknowledgment that Aboriginal and Torres Strait Islander histories were not taught at school for many people, so there is a sense of catching up through workplace training to fill these gaps in knowledge. Indeed, there was recognition that further education was needed and that frameworks such as the ATSILIRN protocols could assist in leading change. The tools provided and additional readings discussed in the course were valuable for people to dive deeper into topics and follow up on their own self-learning. Sentiments such as "I wrote down all of these notes" and "I got a lot out of it personally" were descriptions shared as feedback on participating in the course. The research team observed a lack of awareness of the principles articulated in documents such as the UNDRIP and those associated with the Indigenous Data Sovereignty movement.

A reoccurring theme from participants was that the course structure enabled peer-to-peer learning, which encouraged people to learn and benchmark their organization against others. One participant talked about how the course enabled a vision of what work could be achieved, while another described feelings of being daunted.

"I thought it was really interesting how some institutions are way ahead of us, and some are on the same sort of level. And so [there is] obviously a lot of variation out there. So these sessions, and having them as group sessions with people from other institutions, I think is a great idea. Because you get to see, I guess, where you stand and what is possible."

"being able to see that [the ATSILIRN protocols] and see what we hadn't achieved was scary"

Having the opportunity to listen to other organizations and hear what they were doing gave people what was described as "food for thought".

One oarticipant commented that the principles of inclusion discussed in the course are still in their infancy in terms of being implemented in their library context. Additionally, non-Indigenous participants raised questions about they could be more effective allies. How could allyship support Indigenous self-determination, for example in being able to identify resources and budgeting to support Indigenous priorities? The challenge of insufficient resources was consistently discussed, and comments were made

Challenging the Silences

that allyship is an excellent first step. However, challenges were raised when working in an organization without Indigenous employment and no budget for engaging Aboriginal and Torres Strait Islander community members. It was felt that it was hard to make firm decisions without input from community. One participant summed up their feelings about resourcing, saying:

"institutions and organizations have to start putting their money where their mouth is."

Several respondents highlighted the need for further conversations and learning regarding decolonization of GLAM work and collections. There was a real desire expressed for further resources and tools to be developed to support decolonizing approaches in library practice. For example, one participant spoke about the difficulties of it:

"Because it's such a difficult thing to do for [staff], who don't have ... [experiences based on your own cultural background] ...our worldview is, is what it is, and helping us get outside of that. I think that's one of the benefits of the course really helped us kind of see our focus that there might be a gap for council that we need to, you know, pursue thoughtfully".

In the context of decolonization, participants noted that the course helped move people from thinking about Indigenous engagement through deficit approaches to aligning more with views of Indigenous self-determination and agency. There were also comments about the levels of people's understanding of Indigenous ways of knowing, being and doing and that the notion of "cultural care" is invisible if you do not know it exists.

DISCUSSION

The themes discussed above and summarized in Table 1 show that participants are committed to supporting Indigenous priorities and engagement in their library context. However, the research identified a deep level of fear and inertia felt by non-Indigenous people concerned about getting things wrong. This was often expressed alongside the view that they could not develop pathways for support because there needs to be more Indigenous employment across the libraries and information settings they work in. Indigenous employment was identified as necessary to activate and support the engagement of Indigenous communities. However, the questions raised by some non-Indigenous participants regarding concern over 'who has the right to speak' indicates a lack of understanding of how the library can support Indigenous self-determination. Additionally, there was a lack of knowledge and skills of participants being able to work in Indigenous cultural contexts, including understanding engagement by connecting with local Indigenous cultural authorities through local Indigenous community governance structures. Instead, the focus on community engagement remained primarily focused on supporting the library's institutional goals and drivers.

Further, there was a lack of clarity around combining broader 'diversity and inclusion' priorities with Indigenous priorities, creating much conflict and confusion for some participants. There is a need for a defined and stand-alone agenda based on concepts of Indigenous sovereignty that is at present not visible in the library sector. A position of Indigenous sovereignty would support negotiations and agreements to be made between the library and Indigenous communities to support self-determination in a way that

Challenging the Silences

moves beyond tokenism and the need to 'tick the box'. The discussion of inclusion in the context of multiculturalism demonstrates the normative patterns that 'white' services are the norm, whereas other 'non-white' communities are on the margins.

The research has shown that many course participants were beginning to build Indigenous priorities and community engagement. Participants shared that they had positive learning experiences from hearing the facilitator's stories of community engagement and relationship building. However, despite the goodwill and the display of foundational learnings, there was a significant lack of maturity in developing engagement and programs that support Indigenous people's self-determination. One of the most critical goals expressed by participants was building trust and relationships with Indigenous clients and communities, and an overarching focus existed on wanting to engage appropriately. Insights gained from the research evidence how essential it is for libraries to be more proactive in embedding Indigenous perspectives, prioritizing Indigenous engagement, and including these priorities more formally across all services and departments. It was evident that the principles of inclusion and engagement addressed by the course are still at the beginning of being applied in practice by participants and their library and information settings.

There were distinct gaps of awareness of Indigenous histories and concerns regarding how these histories and experiences were recorded and shared in libraries and their collections. The research found that there needs to be further development of Indigenous collections that represent the perspectives and worldviews of Indigenous peoples. Appropriate resources also need to be made available for all clients and users of the library and information setting. The research demonstrated participant's awareness of the importance of Indigenous people not being represented and referred to in racist, offensive and derogatory ways. Furthermore, it was understood that libraries need to ask Indigenous people how they want to see themselves represented in collections.

The research also found that participants did not have the skills and frameworks to respond to racism in their library, archive and information contexts. This included seeking support for removal of racist information from circulation whether in books, catalogues, or descriptive material on websites. The research responses overall described challenges in reporting these issues up to management and leadership teams. Therefore, it was unclear how issues of racism and representation were managed in organizational contexts.

The question of the longer-term impact of participants' learning, including the impact on their work practices, needs further consideration. It was not clear from the data collected how work practices in relation to Indigenous initiatives, engagement and collections in libraries, including the impacts of the course on developing local projects, would develop. Going forward, methodological improvements, including options for follow-up research interviews, must be considered in the future delivery of the course. It was clear that the approach to encourage participants to be reflexive practitioners whilst drawing on the resources shared about protocols for embedding decolonial and anti-racist frameworks were beneficial for participants. Overall, it was found that the staff capability program benefited from undergoing research and evaluation, as it provides further opportunity to ensure the course content and approach is effective in assisting the library, archive and information sectors to better support Indigenous self-determination and Indigenous sovereignty.

Challenging the Silences

CONCLUSION

This paper has discussed library and information professionals' gaps in knowledge and skills of understanding Indigenous people's information needs. These gaps are known to exist because of a lack of specialization and appropriate Indigenous content in library and archive course curricula. The research identified that the staff capability program is a temporary solution for a much more significant gap in the education and training of library, archive and information workers.

Aboriginal and Torres Strait Islander peoples have distinct information needs in relation to accessing library services. By designing a short course for increasing awareness of Indigenous people's priorities, the team at Jumbunna Research have been able to engage with participants of the course to gain insights into the real-world challenges that exist and contribute to current debates about furthering support for Indigenous priorities across the GLAM sector.

This study responds to a gap in research and literature, and it aims to benefit Aboriginal and Torres Strait Islander peoples who wish to engage with libraries and information services. The research uncovered several key themes that highlight deeper understanding of how a staff capability program can assist to deliver culturally appropriate services and collections. Libraries provide important societal benefits and the impact on their communities can be profound. This research opens up the potential for libraries to be more accessible and culturally safe for Aboriginal and Torres Strait Islander peoples in Australia.

Competing Interests

The research outlined in this paper has been approved by the University of Technology, Sydney Human Research Ethics Committee (UTS HREC reference number ETH20-4681).

All authors of this article declare there is no competing interest.

Funding

This research received no specific grant from any funding agency in the public, commercial, or not-for-profit sectors. Funding for this research was covered by the author(s) of the article.

ACKNOWLEDGMENTS

The authors acknowledge the Traditional Owners on the land on which this paper was written and acknowledge their ongoing connection and custodianship of land. Always Was, Always Will Be Aboriginal Land.

The authors also would like to thank the GLAM workers who participated in the course and enthusiastically shared their views with our team. Some wording in the interviews have been slightly edited to ensure the participants can remain anonymous.

REFERENCES

Aboriginal and Torres Strait Islander Library Information Resource Network. (2015). ATSILIRN Protocols for Libraries Archives and Information Services. AIATSIS. http://atsilirn.aiatsis.gov.au/protocols.php

American Library Association (ALA). (n.d.). *Equity, Diversity, and Inclusion*. ALA. https://www.ala.org/advocacy/diversity

Anderson, J. (2005). Indigenous knowledge, intellectual property, libraries and archives: Crises of access, control and future utility. *Australian Academic and Research Libraries*, *36*(2), 83–94. doi:10.1080/00048623.2005.10721250

Archibald, J. A., De Santolo, J., & Lee-Morgan, J. (2019). *Decolonizing Research: Indigenous Storywork as Methodology*. ZedBooks.

Australian Bureau of Statistics. (2022, July*). Australia: Aboriginal and Torres Strait Islander population summary*. ABS. https://www.abs.gov.au/articles/australia-aboriginal-and-torres-strait-islander-population-summary

Australian Institute of Aboriginal and Torres Strait Islander Studies. (2020). Code of Ethics. Australian Institute. https://aiatsis.gov.au/research/ethical-research/code-ethics

Australian Library and Information Association. (2019). *Professional Pathways Project*. ALIA. https://professionalpathways.alia.org.au/

Barrowcliffe, R. (2021). Closing the narrative gap: Social media as a tool to reconcile institutional archival narratives with Indigenous counter-narratives. *Archives and Manuscripts*, *49*(3), 151–166. doi:10.1080/01576895.2021.1883074

Behrendt, L. (2019). Indigenous Storytelling: decolonizing institutions and assertive self-determination: implications for legal practice. In J. Archibald, J. De Santolo, & J. Lee-Morgan (Eds.), *Decolonising Research. Indigenous Storywork as a Methodology* (pp. 175–186). Zedbooks.

Blackburn, F. (2020). Cultural Competence: Toward a More Robust Conceptualisation. *Public Library Quarterly*, *39*(3), 229–245. doi:10.1080/01616846.2019.1636750

Booker, L. (2020). 'Indigenous Recordkeeping and Archives Course' goes Live. *Indigenous Archives Collective*. https://indigenousarchives.net/2020/09/30/indigenous-recordkeeping-and-archives-course-goes-live/

Christen, K. (2018). Relationships, Not Records. Digital Heritage and the Ethics of Sharing Indigenous Knowledge Online. Pp. 403-412. (Ed) Sayers, J. The Routledge Companion to Media Studies and Digital Humanities. New York. Routledge.

Cooke, N. A. (2020). Critical library instruction as a pedagogical tool. *Communications in Information Literacy*, *14*(1), 7. doi:10.15760/comminfolit.2020.14.1.7

de Jesus, N. (2014). Locating the library in institutional oppression. *In The Library With The Lead Pipe*. https://www.inthelibrarywiththeleadpipe.org/2014/locating-the-library-in-institutional-oppression/

Duarte, M. L., & Belarde-Lewis, M. (2015). Imagining: Creating Spaces for Indigenous Ontologies. *Cataloging & Classification Quarterly*, *53*(5-6), 677–702. doi:10.1080/01639374.2015.1018396

Evans, J., Faulkhead, S., Thorpe, K., Adams, K., Booker, L., & Timbery, N. M. (2020). Indigenous archiving and wellbeing: surviving, thriving, reconciling. *Community archives, community spaces: Heritage, memory and identity*, 129-164.

Faulkhead, S. (2009). Connecting through records: Narratives of Koorie Victoria. *Archives & Manuscripts*, *37*(2), 60–88.

Fourmile, H. (2020). Who owns the past? Aborigines as captives of the archives. In *Terrible Hard Biscuits* (pp. 16–27). Routledge. doi:10.4324/9781003137160-2

Galassi, M. (2019). My Cultural Competency Journey. An Italian perspective of working with Aboriginal and Torres Strait Islander Collections and Services in GLAM. *Indigenous Archives Collective*. https://indigenousarchives.net/2019/06/27/my-cultural-competency-journey-an-italian-perspective-of-working-with-aboriginal-and-torres-strait-islander-collections-and-services-in-glam/

Galassi, M. (2022). Reflections on shaping leadership across LIS. *Civica Journal*. https://www.civica.com/en-au/thought-leadership-library/reflections-on-shaping-leadership-across-lis/

Garwood-Houng, A., & Blackburn, F. (2014). The ATSILIRN Protocols: A twenty-first century guide to appropriate library services for and about Aboriginal and Torres Strait Islander peoples. *The Australian Library Journal*, *63*(1), 4–15. doi:10.1080/00049670.2014.890018

General Assembly of the United Nations. (2007). *United Nations Declaration on the Rights of Indigenous Peoples*. UN. http://declaration.humanrights.gov.au/

Gosart, U. (2021). Indigenous librarianship: Theory, practices, and means of social action. In IFLA Journal, Special Issue: Indigenous Librarianship, 3(47), pp. 293-304

Human Rights and Equal Opportunity Commission. (1997). *Bringing Them Home. Report of the National Inquiry into the Separation of Aboriginal and Torres Strait Islander Children from Their Families*. HREOC. https://humanrights.gov.au/our-work/bringing-them-home-report-1997

Indigenous Archives Collective. (2021). The Indigenous Archives Collective position statement on the right of reply to Indigenous knowledges and information held in archives. *Archives and Manuscripts*, *49*(3), 244–252. doi:10.1080/01576895.2021.1997609

Janke, T. (1998). *Our Culture, our Future: Report on Australian Indigenous Cultural and Intellectual Property Rights*. Aboriginal Studies Press.

Janke, T. (2021). *True Tracks. Respecting Indigenous Knowledge and Culture*. UNSW Press.

Jones, E. P., Mani, N. S., Carlson, R. B., Welker, C. G., Cawley, M., & Yu, F. (2022). Analysis of anti-racism, equity, inclusion and social justice initiatives in library and information science literature. *RSR. Reference Services Review*, *50*(1), 81–101. doi:10.1108/RSR-07-2021-0032

Klimm, K., & Robertson, D. (2021). *How an old book created a commitment to better represent First Nations Australians*. Schools Catalogue Information Service. https://www.scisdata.com/connections/issue-117/how-an-old-book-created-a-commitment-to-better-represent-first-nations-australians/

Knott, E., Rao, A. H., Summers, K., & Teeger, C. (2022). Interviews in the social sciences. *Nature Reviews. Methods Primers*, *2*(73), 73. doi:10.103843586-022-00150-6

Komeiji, K., Long, K., Matsuda, S., & Paikai, A. (2021). Indigenous resource management systems as models for librarianship: I waiwai ka ‘aina. In IFLA Journal. Special Issue: Indigenous Librarianship. 3(47), pp. 293-304

Kovach, M. (2021). *Indigenous Methodologies. Characteristics. Conversations and Contexts* (2nd ed.). University of Toronto Press.

Kukutai, T., & Taylor, J. (2016). *Indigenous data sovereignty: Toward an agenda*. ANU press. doi:10.22459/CAEPR38.11.2016

Leung, S. Y., Jorge, R., & López-McKnight, J. R. (2021). *Knowledge Justice: Disrupting Library and Information Studies through Critical Race Theory*. The MIT Press. doi:10.7551/mitpress/11969.001.0001

Lilley, S. (2021). Transformation of library and information management: Decolonization or Indigenization? In IFLA Journal. Special Issue: Indigenous Librarianship, 3(47), 305-312

Masterson, M., Stableford, C., & Tait, A. (2019). Re-imagining Classification Systems in Remote Libraries. *Journal of the Australian Library and Information Association*, 3(68), 278–289. doi:10.1080/24750158.2019.1653611

Montenegro, M. (2019). Subverting the universality of metadata standards: The TK labels as a tool to promote Indigenous data sovereignty. *The Journal of Documentation*, 75(4), 731–749. doi:10.1108/JD-08-2018-0124

Muir, B., Qayyum, A., & Thompson, K. (2021). Jumping hurdles: ‘Hurdle wording’ and hiring for diversity and inclusion. *Incite*, 42(4), 10–11.

Nakata, M. (2007). *Disciplining the Savages Savaging the Disciplines*. Aboriginal Studies Press.

Nakata, M., Nakata, V., Gardiner, G., McKeough, J., Byrne, A., & Gibson, J. (2008). Indigenous digital collections: An early look at the organisation and culture interface. *Australian Academic and Research Libraries*, 39(4), 223–236. doi:10.1080/00048623.2008.10721360

National and State Libraries of Australasia. (2022). *Strategic Plan 2020-2023*. NSLA. https://www.nsla.org.au/index.php/about-nsla/strategic-plan

National and State Libraries of Australasia. (n.d.). *Culturally Safe Libraries*. NSLA. https://www.nsla.org.au/our-work/culturally-safe-libraries

Nicholson, K., & Seale, M. (2018). The Politics of Theory and the Practice of Critical Librarianship, 1-18. Litwin Books.

Rigney, L. I. (1999). Internationalisation of an Indigenous anticolonial cultural critique of research methodologies: A guide to Indigenist research methodology and its principles. *Wicazo Sa Review*, 14(2), 109–121. doi:10.2307/1409555

Royal Commission into Aboriginal Deaths in Custody. (1991). *National Report*. UTS Library. http://www.austlii.edu.au.ezproxy.lib.uts.edu.au/au/other/IndigLRes/rciadic/

Russell, L. (2005). Indigenous Knowledge and Archives: Accessing Hidden History and Understandings. *Australian Academic and Research Libraries*, 36(2), 161–171. doi:10.1080/00048623.2005.10721256

Challenging the Silences

Sentance, N. (2018, November 28) Diversity means disruption. *Archival Decolonialist*. https://archivalde-colonist. com/2018/11/28/diversity-means-disruption/

Singh, M., & Major, J. (2017). Conducting Indigenous research in Western knowledge spaces: Aligning theory and methodology. *Australian Educational Researcher*, *44*(1), 5–19. doi:10.100713384-017-0233-z

Smith, L. T. (2012). *Decolonizing Methodologies: Research and Indigenous Peoples* (2nd ed.). ZedBooks.

Swist, T., Hendery, R., Magee, L., Ensor, J., Sherman, J., Budge, K., & Humphry, J. (2022). Co-creating public library futures: An emergent manifesto and participatory research agenda. *Journal of the Australian Library and Information Association*, *71*(1), 71–88. doi:10.1080/24750158.2021.2016358

Thorpe, K., & Galassi, M. (2014). Rediscovering Indigenous Languages: The Role and Impact of Librar-ies and Archives in Cultural Revitalisation. *Australian Academic and Research Libraries*, *45*(2), 81–100. doi:10.1080/00048623.2014.910858

KEY TERMS AND DEFINITIONS

Aboriginal and Torres Strait Islander Peoples, Aboriginal peoples, Indigenous peoples: In this chapter, the terms *Aboriginal and Torres Strait Islander*, *Aboriginal* and *Indigenous* are respectfully used interchangeably in reference to First Nations peoples across the lands and waters of Australia. The authors recognize the self-determination of individuals, communities and nations in naming oneself and their community. The authors do not intend to homogenize First Nations peoples by using the terms chosen for this paper.

Colonial Project: The term *colonial project* is in reference to the ongoing colonial occupation and exploitation of Indigenous peoples, lands and waters. The authors use this term in alignment with Watson's (2016) outline of the *colonial project* as the maintenance of 'unequal relationships' between Indigenous peoples and the colonial state (p.30).

Country: The term *Country* refers to the lands and waters with which Aboriginal and Torres Strait Islander peoples have a sovereign connection. *Country* is a complex term that encompasses the physical lands and waters and the cultural, social and spiritual connections and practices connected to these places.

Racism: The term *racism* is used in this paper to refer to the discriminatory treatment of Aboriginal and Torres Strait Islander peoples due to their identity as First Nations peoples. This racism is systemic in the colonial project of Australia and is apparent in both overt and covert forms.

ENDNOTES

[1]   Acknowledging the different ways in which Aboriginal and Torres Strait Islander peoples refer to themselves and their communities, this paper uses the terms *Aboriginal and Torres Strait Islander peoples* and *Indigenous peoples* to refer to First Nations peoples in Australia.

[2]   While the staff capability building program was developed specifically for libraries, it has broader application across the library, archive and information sector, and more broadly into GLAM con-texts. We use *the library, archive and information sector* throughout the paper acknowledging that Indigenous knowledges are held and managed across a range of institutional settings across GLAM.

Chapter 8
Forging Alliances for Reparative Documentation and Revitalization of Marginalized Communities:
Reclaiming the African American Heritage of Southern Illinois

Anne Marie Hamilton-Brehm
https://orcid.org/0000-0002-9160-3477
Southern Illinois University, Carbondale, USA

Pam Hackbart-Dean
https://orcid.org/0000-0002-4071-4281
University of Illinois, Chicago, USA

Walter Ray
Southern Illinois University, Carbondale, USA

Aaron M. Lisec
Southern Illinois University, Carbondale, USA

Melvin "Pepper" Holder
Southern Illinois University, Carbondale, USA

ABSTRACT

Describing efforts to uncover the largely undocumented history of African Americans in southern Illinois, this case study demonstrates how universities and activists can empower local communities to preserve and share their heritage. The Special Collections Research Center (SCRC) of Southern Illinois University's Morris Library, SIU faculty, and community partners have substantially increased knowledge about many extraordinary individuals and communities by actively pursuing digitization of correspondence and images collected by families and organizations and conducting oral histories and preservation workshops. New plans for a coordinating center aim to radically expand revitalization efforts.

DOI: 10.4018/978-1-6684-7255-2.ch008

Copyright © 2023, IGI Global. Copying or distributing in print or electronic forms without written permission of IGI Global is prohibited.

INTRODUCTION

Educational institutions have a responsibility to serve the communities that sustain them. Doing so benefits the institution by making the region a better place for living and working. Institutions willing to accept responsibility for their impact on the community and potential to do good rather than neglect or harm engage with their communities in various ways, from inviting the community to participate in institutional activities to conducting focused and sustained outreach programs. Regardless of the approach, institutional efforts to connect with and provide aid to communities come from the institutional mode of doing business, which is often highly orchestrated and production oriented, with allocation of labor and resources controlled by grants, boards, and administrators. Without institutional support, community engagement is likely to be an uphill battle. On the other hand, even well-intentioned administrators who fail to comprehend the needs of a community may cause more harm than good by operating programs out of step with community culture and rhythms.

In contrast with institutional initiatives accomplished with formal allocations of funds and paid staff, community activism depends mainly on volunteers whose enthusiasm often surpasses their lack of resources. Although volunteers' passion can be leveraged to significant effect by community leaders, community initiatives inevitably depend on the limited time volunteers can lend, and efforts may be slowed by disagreements between project members, especially in the absence of deadlines. Although they approach work differently, the complementary strengths and experience lent by community members and institutional partners can accomplish goals greater than either could achieve alone.

The biggest hurdle for collaboration is the orientation of the institution toward engagement, particularly the ability to commit meaningful staff time and energy rather than funding alone. Southern Illinois University Carbondale (SIUC) is an institution committed to enabling and encouraging its staff to engage with the communities that it serves. However, the Black community of Carbondale, along with those in other regions of the state, has been underserved historically, and reparative efforts are a relatively recent development. Only in the past two decades has the rich regional history of the Underground Railroad, for example, been substantially documented by archaeologists. At the same time, professors at SIUC increasingly support the efforts of local communities to demonstrate chronic harm to historically Black neighborhoods from dangers such as industrial waste. Forces are gathering to effect meaningful change in southern Illinois.

Launched in 2017, the project *Reclaiming the African American Heritage of Southern Illinois* (RAAHSI) is an effort to engage closely with community activists across the region to acknowledge and share the extensive contribution of Black people to the history and culture of southern Illinois. Progress made since then has proven the fundamental value to SIUC of investing meaningful time and energy in getting to know and working alongside the communities the university serves.

Literature Review

Although libraries and archives may be viewed as neutral and objective spaces, as Betts (2021) reminds us, "librarians and archivists of color have long argued that given their institutional history, policies, and practices of exclusion, archives and libraries are in fact not neutral, transparent, comprehensive, nor easy to access even today" (p. 21). The reparative efforts of SIUC are part of a rather recently growing movement in libraries and archives to engage with and preserve the history of silenced communities. Archival activism is centered on issues of social justice, particularly diversity, equity, and inclusion. The importance to communities of representation in archives is highlighted by Caswell, et al. (2017) in their study of community archives and staff in southern California: while the combination of absence and misrepresentation in media and archives amounts to *symbolic annihilation*, representation in community constructed collections provides *representational belonging*. The Mellon Foundation (2019) notes that self-documentation by community members can provide "an anchor and a sense of permanence and legitimacy among a population that faces constant uncertainty". Essays and case studies in *Community Archives, Community Spaces: Heritage, Memory and Identity* (Bastian & Flinn, 2020) expand the theoretical framework for community archives, acknowledging their important role in preservation and access and formal recognition in the United Kingdom. Assessing rural community archives in South Carolina, Wagner & Bischoff (2017) note the lack of case studies and models for supporting community archives in the United States compared with the United Kingdom. Partly addressing that shortfall, *Archives and Special Collections as Sites of Contestation* (Kandiuk, 2020) examines stewardship of archives within a social justice framework, illuminating the limits of theory versus practice in institutional settings and professional practice in essays examining cases of colonialism, commodification, and erasure of voices in archives of the United States and Canada.

As they accept responsibility to redress historical gaps and seek greater engagement with local communities by offering to preserve their history, institutions are in fact walking in the footsteps of a longer tradition of self-documentation and grass roots efforts. The Wilson Library at University of North Carolina has noted (2019) that community archives are based on the collective effort of a group of people organizing to preserve and share their history. As SIUC archivists learned, Black churches in Southern Illinois have traditionally preserved the history of their communities. In fact, the practice of self-documentation is widespread and considered urgent among churches and other community groups everywhere. Hopkins (2022) explains how St. John [Colored] Missionary Baptist Church, established by former slaves in Fort Bend County, Texas, reconstructed its history after church records were lost in a 2006 fire by examining records outside the Black community. More broadly, Mondésir, Tummino, & Wong (2021) address preservation and engagement programming supporting diverse groups across the community of Queens, New York. Hetland, et al. (2020) build a framework based on research in Europe, Canada, Australia, and the United States for understanding how museums and archives increase relevancy of cultural heritage by engaging with communities.

Institutions can help document diverse histories in many ways. Oral histories have become more popular in recent decades to provide a vehicle for highlighting diversity. Craft (2018) shares how oral history projects at institutions in North Carolina document campus and community diversity and suggests further resources for institutions interested in pursuing or growing oral history programs. Another way for academic archives to support documentation is by publishing information about community and family histories. *The Bridgwater Family: A History of an African American Family in the American West from Slavery to the Civil Rights Era* (Williams, 2020), describes more than a century of history documenting Black life in the West collected by the family matriarch and her daughter. "A Survey of the African American Records in UK's Special Collections" (McDaniel, 2011) offers information on ten collections documenting Black history in Kentucky, including equal rights activism and the role of women in the Black community. Assistance with digitizing photographs may be one of the most important services institutions can provide to communities. Porter (2020) describes collaboration between the Chicago State University Archives and the International Sons and Daughters of Slave Ancestry, a Chicago-based genealogy society, to digitize and provide access to more than 350 historic photographs of formerly enslaved Black people and more than ninety family histories submitted by descendants. The case study describes creative, flexible approaches to collaborative digital projects between an academic institution and a community organization, including balancing metadata standards with community goals for a collection.

Trust in an institution takes time to establish, often requiring demonstration that the institution will not take materials away from the community. In addition to access, institutions must ensure that the community can control how their history is portrayed. Flinn, Stevens, & Shepherd (2009) explore the response of Black communities in the United Kingdom to preservation initiatives, suggesting that some communities may resist preservation in an effort to maintain control over their history. Archives may be viewed as perpetuating colonial practices. Local heritage societies and educational institutions benefit by engaging with and learning from each other before approaching communities. Bastian, Sniffin-Marinoff, and Webber (2015) explore how archives and libraries can work together to better serve their communities.

If a collaborative relationship can be established, heritage and educational institutions can engage with community members to raise awareness of the value of preserving heritage. In *The Routledge Companion to Media and Activism* (Meikle, 2018), essays on media activism and social movements speak to the supporting role archives play in documentation. Another compilation edited by Hill (2011), *The Future of Archives and Recordkeeping: A Reader*, addresses the societal role of archives in addition to such topics as digital preservation and community engagement. Cifor, et al. (2018) describe roles of community archives and archivists in social justice activism in southern California.

In addition to amplifying voices of historically silenced groups, dismantling the digital divide has become more urgent for librarians and archivists over the past decade. The increasing use of digital technologies is moving archival outreach toward creating online resources accessible to everyone, particularly those who may not be able to visit archives in person. Digitization also helps archives address the challenge of acquiring collections from community groups. Communities not wishing to part with their historical records may request that archives digitize and return them. As smartphones become more prevalent in communities, archives can build community relationships through social media links to digital collections and online exhibits. The role of libraries and archives in enabling digital access has become even more vital since the COVID-19 pandemic. In 2021, the Digital Empowerment and Inclusion Working Group, including representatives from a number of broadband providers, issued a report acknowledging the monetary and infrastructure challenges faced by libraries providing online access to their communities. The working group noted that the key role of libraries in providing online access was highlighted by school closures during the pandemic (Brioche et al., 2021).

The importance of addressing the digital divide cannot be ignored since communication is foundational to learning and growth of opportunities. Anderson, Jackson, & Trogden (2021) emphasize that intercultural communication is vital not only globally but within regional, local, and virtual spaces. Each region faces its own reparative challenges. Communities stand to benefit most when initiatives are grounded in the historical record particular to the region, acknowledging a socioeconomic and cultural context not only of trauma but more importantly of agency and courage. Reparative work then serves further to amplify the contribution of the formerly silenced.

History of Black People in Southern Illinois

Although institutional projects to historically document and support local communities are becoming more common, they are driven not only by wider attention to social justice but more specifically in response to local injustice and triumph over adversity. RAAHSI in particular seeks to illuminate and celebrate the contributions of Black people to southern Illinois throughout its history and plans to support cultural heritage tourism drawn to that history.

Black people played significant roles in the growth and prosperity of southern Illinois, from farming and industry to business administration and politics. Located at the convergence of two great rivers, between the former slave states of Kentucky and Missouri and on main routes of the Underground Railroad and the Great Migration, southern Illinois has a long tradition of Black activism and community building, dating back to antebellum free Black communities such as Lakeview and Miller Grove. Southern Illinois also attracted Black people moving north as refugees during the Civil War and in the upheaval of its aftermath. However, as with many underrepresented communities worldwide, this community and its contributions to social and political change have remained largely invisible and unacknowledged in historical accounts (Ray, 2022). As one former SIUC history professor has written:

Forgetting lies near the heart of community life by sustaining a shared sense of identity. It is the silent and indispensable partner of remembering. By connecting their present to the past—by remembering—neighbors fix themselves in place and time, affirm who they are, and thereby create for themselves a usable past. In doing so they keep what they deem significant—useful—and sweep aside other portions of the past as irrelevant. But by forgetting, they make themselves vulnerable to experience and to dissenting voices on the edge. The process demands work and is forever meeting resistance (Batinski, 2021, p. 1).

Early Settlement and Slavery

Southern Illinois continues to struggle with the enduring trauma of its historical role in slavery. Slavery in Illinois predated the arrival of Europeans. Entering the Illinois region in 1673, French explorers Louis Jolliet and Jacques Marquette discovered that the Illinois tribes enslaved people they captured from other tribes, such as the Pawnee. The Illinois were a loose confederation of at least thirteen kinship groups distributed throughout the region. They were recent arrivals themselves, having moved west of the region south of Lake Erie and in the Ohio River Valley during the 16th and 17th centuries (Chamberlain, 2015).

Africans arrived in southern Illinois early in the 18th century after it became part of the French colony of Louisiana. Around 1723, Philippe Renault brought hundreds of enslaved Africans from what is now the Dominican Republic to support his mining operations in Missouri and Illinois. When Renault's mining operation failed, farmers bought some of the people he enslaved (Allen, 1963). By the mid-18th century, enslaved Africans made up nearly a third of the population in Illinois settlements (Davis, 1998). The French king legalized slavery and issued laws to control enslaved people and the slave trade, allowing disobedient enslaved people to be killed (Allen, 1963). French colonists acquired enslaved Native Americans and Africans and freed some of them. A few free Black people lived among the French; they could engage in commerce, bear arms, and make contracts (Davis, 1998). Historical records document, for example, that Jacques Duverger bought a house at Kaskaskia, hired a Frenchman to go on a winter hunt and travel to New Orleans, and received payment for working as a surgeon (Brown, 1991).

Although enslavement of Native Americans became less common over time, enslavement of Africans increased (Davis, 1998). France ceded Illinois to Britain in 1763 following the French and Indian War. Britain continued to permit slavery in the region. Some enslaved people gained their freedom by serving as soldiers in the American Army during the American Revolutionary War from 1776 to 1783 (Russell, 2012).

Forging Alliances for Repairing and Revitalizing Marginalized Communities

The newly formed American government claimed the region of Illinois in 1778, later making it part of the Northwest Territory. While the 1787 Northwest Ordinance prohibited slavery in the Northwest Territory, it allowed capture of fugitive enslaved people, and the territorial governor decided that enslaved people in the territory could remain enslaved (Russell, 2012). After Illinois became part of the Indiana Territory in 1800, lengthy terms of indentured servitude prevented enslaved people from gaining their freedom (Davis, 1998). Unsuccessful in petitioning the United States to permit slavery, the Indiana Territory also retaliated with laws limiting the rights of free Black people. Created in 1809, Illinois Territory continued to enforce laws requiring Black people to provide proof of freedom and limiting their rights to own property and conduct business (Dexter, 2011). However, antislavery sentiment was rising, inspired by the American Enlightenment movement and religious leaders from the East.

The first antislavery movement in southern Illinois began when Virginian minister James Lemen promoted the ideals of Emancipation Baptists in 1809 near Waterloo (Russell, 2012). Attracted to Illinois since it had not become a slave state, free Black settlers began to arrive from Virginia and the Carolinas after Native American conflict diminished in 1815. Black people faced increasing restrictions in southern states and came to southern Illinois seeking a better life (Russell, 2012).

Some slaveholders, like future second Illinois Governor Edward Coles, moved to Illinois to free people they enslaved and provide them with opportunities. A planter from Virginia, Coles became an antislavery advocate at the College of William and Mary, where ideals of the American Enlightenment considered slavery morally indefensible. Because Virginia law required formerly enslaved people to leave the state within a year and restricted the ability of free Black people to make a living, Coles relocated to Edwardsville, Illinois, in 1819, freeing nineteen people his family had enslaved and acquiring land for them. Coles continued campaigning against slavery in Illinois as governor (1822-26), leading the successful fight against a pro-slavery constitution in 1824 (Russell, 2012).

After statehood in 1818, Illinois continued to permit slavery in the salt mines and allowed current slaveholders to keep the people they already enslaved. The salt works near Shawneetown exploited more than a thousand enslaved people contracted from slaveholders in slave states. Illinois law permitted importation of enslaved Africans to the salines until 1825. When the exemption expired, indentured servitude replaced enslavement (Myers, 1922). So-called *term slaves* agreed to serve for a certain number of years in exchange for food, clothing, and shelter (Dexter, 2011). Since slavery was allowed only for those who had settled in the region of the Northwest Territory prior to 1787, indentured servitude was offered to entice slaveholders to immigrate. While indentured Europeans typically agreed to serve seven years to pay for their passage to America, an 1803 "Law concerning servants" established that any indentured servants who came into what was by then Indiana Territory could be made to serve for any number of years specified in their contract (Dexter, 2011). Although the law specified care for the servant and the provision of clothing and a blanket at the end of the term, there was no punishment for masters who failed to comply. Indentured servitude was further offered as a way to avoid prison or chattel slavery, but the threat of physical abuse to indentured servants was no less. Servants found guilty of a crime for which a free person would be fined were punished at the whipping post (Dexter, 2011). Indenture laws also reflected racism. Black people and Native Americans could purchase servants of their complexion or darker, but if they presumed to purchase a white servant, the law would consider that servant free (Dexter, 2011).

From 1822 to 1824, James Lemen worked with other Emancipation Baptists and Governor Coles to prevent Illinois from becoming a slave state. Later, eastern ministers John Mason Peck and Elijah Parish Lovejoy contributed to the movement. From 1833 to 1836, Lovejoy served as editor of the *St. Louis*

Observer, publishing articles critical of slavery. When threats of mob violence in St. Louis escalated, Lovejoy moved his press across the river to Alton, Illinois. Challenging the efforts of abolitionists in January 1837, the Illinois Legislature almost unanimously adopted a resolution condemning abolition societies. Abraham Lincoln was one of only six opposing state representatives. That year, Lovejoy died in Alton, Illinois, defending his printing press from a pro-slavery mob (Allen, 1963).

Abolitionists faced mounting opposition. In 1853, the Illinois General Assembly proposed legislation spearheaded by southern Illinois Representative John A. Logan limiting the rights of free Black people living in the state and discouraging further migration of free Black people with exorbitant fines and threats of indentured servitude. The bill passed in 1855, becoming known as "Logan's Black Law." Logan later became one of the most prominent Union generals in the Civil War, switched to the Republican Party, and staunchly supported Black rights in Congress and the Senate during Reconstruction, in stark contrast to his early career as a state legislator (Russell, 2012).

Black Settlements in Southern Illinois

Black settlement in Illinois predates statehood and demonstrates the historically courageous and enterprising behavior of Black people who came to Illinois for a better life. The stories uncovered by archaeological investigation and historical research have the potential to inspire us all and change lives. Though never easy, Black settlement burgeoned following statehood, ranging from northeastern Lawrence County to southern Union County. LaRoche (2013) identifies shared characteristics of early Black communities in southern Illinois. Due to racist policies and economic limitations, Black settlements were usually situated on inferior farmland but had access to abundant natural resources. Intermarriage strengthened family connections. A church was often also used as a school, and communities had a cemetery. White abolitionists and missionaries usually lived close to the community and documented their visits with its members, which may have worked as part of the Underground Railroad.

Historical narratives are often silent on the involvement of Black people in resisting slavery due to the bias of white participants, the need for secrecy, the Black tradition of sharing history orally rather than in writing, and the omission and distortion of Black voices in the nineteenth and twentieth centuries in regional histories (Wagner, 2019). Public records and oral history have helped trace some knowledge about early Black settlements. Participation in Underground Railroad activities emerges from a combination of archival and archaeological data, geographical and natural features, and oral history. Together, such information can reveal free Black communities' contributions to the Underground Railroad on their own and in collaboration with white abolitionists (Wagner, 2019).

La Roche (2013) suggests that the proximity of Black settlements in southern Illinois to bordering slave states indicates involvement in the Underground Railroad. Black residents faced danger from kidnappers who would sell them into slavery. The pursuit of fugitives and kidnapping of free Black people continued in Illinois through the early 1860s (Wagner, 2019). Despite such threats, communities grew and thrived. Settlement increased after the Civil War when Black soldiers made southern Illinois their home. Granted citizenship by the 13th Amendment, newly arrived Black people developed farms, worked in coal mining and other industries, and owned businesses. Forming small communities, they worked as tradesmen, preachers, businesspeople, and teachers.

Russell (2012) offers a descriptive overview of some Black communities formed in the early nineteenth century. As early as 1812, Black people and white settlers sheltered together at Russellville in Lawrence County when Native American hostility threatened. Afterward, some of the Black families eventually

Forging Alliances for Repairing and Revitalizing Marginalized Communities

settled in Lawrenceville Township. Black innkeeper Cornelius Elliott formed a community in Saline County in the 1820s. Formerly enslaved salt mine workers who had purchased their freedom established another. Farmers Arthur and Patience Allen, from North Carolina, founded the Black settlement of Allen in eastern Union County in 1828. Fugitive enslaved people and free Black people settled Brooklyn in St. Clair County around 1829. Formerly enslaved Joseph Higginbotham bought land and founded a settlement in Clay County around the 1830s, attracting other free Black people. Harry Dougherty, a freed fugitive who became a landowner, joined with those freed by Illinois governor Edward Coles to establish Pin Oak.

Joseph Ivey, a successful businessman who purchased property before 1830 near Jonesboro, amassed four hundred acres in Union County. Commissioned by Jonesboro, Ivey built a bridge over the Running Lake waterway, leading to his grist mill. By 1835, thirty-five free Black people and their white friends lived in the informally named settlement of "Ivey." It was not long, however, before their community was forced to move on when two of its members were indicted for allegedly planning to murder a nearby racist politician. The charges were dropped, but no residents remained by the 1840 census (Russell, 2012).

Formerly indentured servants and formerly enslaved people founded the settlement of Africa near the line between Franklin and Williamson County. When they considered abandoning their community in response to threats, white Methodists convinced them to remain and establish a school. In Hamilton County, white settlers engaged a Black preacher as their first schoolteacher. While the law forbade interracial marriage in Illinois, marriages still took place, and free Black people could win court cases (Russell, 2012).

The system of routes used to help enslaved people escape from the Southern states became known as the Underground Railroad by the 1830s. Fugitives traveled mainly on foot, resting at safe havens in the homes of abolitionists and others, known as stations. Those who helped fugitives reach the next station were known as operators and conductors. Greater restrictions on both enslaved people and free Black people increased with the success of the Underground Railroad. Slave states hired patrols and bounty hunters to recapture fugitives, and northern newspapers advertised rewards for fugitives from southern slaveholders (LaRoche, 2013).

Bordered by slave states Missouri and Kentucky and dipping farther south than other free states, Illinois was an essential part of the Underground Railroad. Routes in southern Illinois began on the Mississippi River in Randolph County at Chester and at the junction of the Ohio and Mississippi rivers in Cairo. These two lines merged at Centralia and extended north to Chicago. Another route followed the Illinois River from the Mississippi River at Alton, opposite St. Louis, to Chicago. From Chicago, fugitive enslaved people could take a boat to Canada (Gale, 2018). Newspaper articles on the horrors of slavery and sensational tales of fugitives escaping to Canada increased public awareness of the Underground Railroad in the 1840s (LaRoche, 2013).

Miller Grove

In recent decades, archaeological and archival evidence has suggested the vital role of Miller Grove in the Underground Railroad, both honoring the valor of early social justice activists and greatly expanding the potential for heritage tourism in southern Illinois. Northwest of Golconda, Miller Grove was founded in 1844 by a small group of free Black people from Bedford and Marshal Counties in south central Tennessee (LaRoche, 2013). The settlement had a school, church, and cemetery in addition to farmsteads. Some of the Black settlers had been born free, but others had recently been freed from enslavement.

153

Named for the Miller family, whom Andrew Miller and his sister Matilda had freed, the community included other families from Tennessee and some of their former masters, who assisted with paying bonds for families to enter and remain in Illinois. During the 1840s, the Dabbs, Millers, Sides, and Singletons emancipated sixty-eight people. Edward Dabbs and Dolly Sides celebrated the earliest wedding at Miller Grove in 1848 (McCorvie, 2002). Charles and Clarissa Dabbs were the first to purchase 160 acres of public domain land in Pope County in 1849.

Early settlers began by occupying unpurchased public land and improving it to attempt to claim certain rights. The Dabbs purchased land just four years after Miller Grove was established, but further purchases were limited until 1854 when the United States Congress reduced the price of unsold public land to as little as thirteen cents an acre. As a result, almost all of the families at Miller Grove owned their land by 1856 (Wagner, 2019). Many residents increased their land ownership over time, and their children continued farming in the area. The original one-room log building that served as their church and school was on land belonging to Harrison and Lucinda Miller, later owned by their daughter, Frances Miller Sydes (McCorvie, 2002).

Local history, geographical features, and archaeological evidence suggest that Miller Grove also provided a waystation for the Underground Railroad. Remoteness from well-traveled roads would have afforded protection (Wagner, 2019). Crow Knob, a sandstone ridgetop to the north of the Miller Grove community, may have served as a lookout point. Nearby rock shelter Sand Cave reportedly served as a hiding place for fugitives crossing the Ohio River.

Correspondence between American Missionary Association ministers James Scott Davis and James Madison West alludes to abolitionist activities in the area. Living near the Miller Grove community, James West often visited and spent the night with Henry Sides, documenting contributions to the "Canada Refugee Fund" and distributing Bibles. In 1857, West praised Miller Grove residents receiving antislavery literature as "messengers who seem to be doing a work that would otherwise be hard to accomplish" (McCorvie, 2009). Lead type recovered by archaeologists from one of the homesteads suggests that Miller Grove may also have had a press for printing abolitionist literature or forging freedom papers (Wagner, 2019). The *Chicago Press & Tribune* reported in 1860 that West had been threatened with lynching by *The Golconda Herald* for "circulating incendiary documents" (McCorvie, 2009). Davis was staying with West in 1861 when a mob attacked West's home with rocks, demolishing the windows and breaking down the door. West's wife fled with her youngest baby to a nearby farm for help (McCorvie, 2009).

Everyday activities carried out in Miller Grove were extraordinary in light of the repressive Black Codes that had restricted the freedom of earlier Miller Grove settlers. Tennessee had required freed Black people to leave the state, while Illinois and neighboring states required those entering to post a bond of $1000 to ensure they would not become a financial burden to the state (McCorvie & Devenport, 2004). Henry Sides paid the bonds for many freed families from Tennessee. He and his wife Barbara moved from Tennessee to Miller Grove with the original four Black families. A former slaveholder in Tennessee, Sides freed all his enslaved people and posted their bonds to enter Illinois. In 1846, a gang broke into the Sides' home, beat Henry and Barbara severely, and stole silver coin which may have been bond money (LaRoche, 2013). Henry and Barbara, who reportedly lost an eye in the attack, courageously continued to post bonds for incoming Black settlers. In his will, Henry bequeathed all of his property to Abraham Sides. McCorvie and Devenport (2004) observe that while white people like Henry Sides and Joseph Dabbs assisted with the bonding process and provided some economic support, Black settlers seized opportunity for themselves in southern Illinois and ensured a thriving future for their children.

Recovered artifacts depict everyday life and the material choices available to Black settlers. Archaeologists discovered part of a pistol, a horse harness hook, broken plates, a bottle, a doll leg, and a piece of a slate writing board at Abby Miller's house (Educating with Evidence, 2017). Remnants of ceramic vessels reflect material choices available to Black women after they gained freedom and joined the Miller Grove community. Shawnee National Forest Archaeologist Mary McCorvie (2002) considers these ceramic sherds the most durable and striking evidence of Black women's freedom of choice in Miller Grove. Public records document how cottage industries grew into businesses for the women of Miller Grove. The 1860 agricultural census reports that Belzora Williams and her daughters made fifty pounds of butter; ten years later, they produced 250 pounds (McCorvie, 2002). Pope County tax records in 1856 document that Miller Grove residents owned livestock, including horses, cattle, sheep, and hogs. By 1860, Harrison and Lucinda Miller owned livestock worth $500 and more than 420 acres of land worth $1500. They made butter and grew wheat, beans, corn, peas, and tobacco along with their son Bedford. Although by 1870 their farmland had decreased in value to $1000, their products had diversified to include molasses, potatoes, and wool (McCorvie & Devenport, 2004).

The 1860 census documents that Miller Grove had a Black school teacher, Julia Singleton, who was formerly enslaved in Tennessee (Wagner, 2019). She taught in a one-room log structure that also served as Mt. Gilead AME Church. The AME Church was active in the abolitionist movement and Underground Railroad; both white and Black neighbors met there for community celebrations (Wagner, 2019). The community rebuilt the structure after a fire destroyed it in 1918. Wagner (2019) comments that the fire occurred a year after the East St. Louis race riots, during which more than 200 Black people were murdered. Archaeological investigation of Miller Grove discovered writing slates; oral history suggests literacy was higher at Miller Grove compared with surrounding white communities (LaRoche, 2013).

In 1900, there were twenty families with 108 people in Miller Grove, but by 1920, only eight families remained, and the population had fallen to twenty-one. Farming had become unprofitable due partly to soil exhaustion, and opportunities in coal mining and major cities enticed younger generations to move on. The community was completely abandoned by the early 1930s (Wagner, 2019). Most of the unproductive land was sold to the federal government, becoming part of the Shawnee National Forest. However, Wilbert McClure, a Bedford and Abigail Miller descendant, maintains twenty acres of their original land.

Archaeologist McCorvie has conducted several investigations of Miller Grove, and SIUC holds part of its summer archaeological field school there. An Educating with Evidence project of SIUC Curriculum and Instruction provides 3D images of artifacts discovered at Miller Grove that reveal the activities of its residents (Educating with Evidence, 2017).

The Bostick Settlement and Civil War Veterans

John Bostick and his daughter had enslaved brothers Hardin, Dudley, Stephen, and their cousin William. Soon after Lincoln's Emancipation Proclamation in 1861, William enlisted in the Union Navy with his cousins, beginning military service aboard the USS General Bragg (Jones, 2017). After completing their military service, Hardin and Dudley Bostick settled five miles south of Murphysboro in Jackson County with fellow veteran Isaac Morgan. Stephen Bostick joined them in 1866 along the boundary between Murphysboro and Pomona Townships. Hardin Bostick provided land for the cemetery, the only surviving feature. Farms, a church, a school, and a cemetery appear in the 1907 Jackson County atlas, along with a photograph of Stephen Bostick, a successful farmer. Although he paid to have his portrait included in the atlas, his photograph is separated from the rest because of his race (Jones, 2017).

Fellow veteran Adolphus Isom, formerly enslaved by John Isham in Tennessee, was another member of the Bostick Settlement. While serving in the 4th US Colored Heavy Artillery, he was wounded in a skirmish near Clinton, Kentucky. Isom married Lucy Stovall in 1876 and moved to the Bostick Settlement around 1887. The 1900 census reports that he rented a farm and lived near Dudley Bostick. His wife died in 1924, just a year before he died along with nearly 700 others in the Tri-State Tornado of 1925. A headstone placed in 1994 memorializes Isom in Bostick Cemetery (Jones, 2017).

Dudley attempted to join Murphysboro Grand Army of the Republic Worthen Post No. 128 in 1887 but was refused membership because of his race. In 1890, the Bosticks and their friends established Murphysboro Grand Army of the Republic Post No. 728 (Colored). When Post No. 728 dissolved due to declining membership in 1899, Worthen Post voted unanimously to accept its former members (Jones, 2017).

Each year on May 30, the General John A. Logan Museum of Murphysboro, Illinois, celebrates Memorial Day, established by Logan in 1868, with a presentation at Woodlawn Cemetery in Carbondale, where Civil War soldier Lewis Chambers was eventually laid to rest. The only Black person in the cemetery identified by name, Chambers was born in Kent County, Maryland, in 1839 and enlisted in the Union Army in 1864. During the war, he fought in a segregated Black regiment of Illinois (Voigt, 2021).

Black People at Southern Illinois University

As the intellectual center of Southern Illinois, Carbondale has benefitted from the progressive reputation of Southern Illinois University. From its founding as a teacher's college in 1869, SIU admitted small numbers of Black students, including two women in the first class. The first male student, Alexander Mills Lane, was born in 1860 in Mississippi. Brought north after the war by a Union officer, Lane enrolled at SIU in 1876. By the early 1880s he was principal of Carbondale's segregated Black school. By the end of that decade he moved to Chicago, where he graduated from Rush Medical School, established a practice on the city's South Side, and served two terms as an Illinois state legislator before his death in 1911 (Smoot, 2012). Alexander Lane's success reflects the university's earliest efforts to create and support a diverse student body. Yet his remarkable story was nearly lost forever. Although Betty Mitchell's 1993 *Southern Illinois University, A Pictorial History* includes Black students, Lane is not among them. Lane's connection to SIU was only recently brought to light by historian Pamela Smoot after his name appeared in a 2011 library Black History Month exhibit, "The History of African-American Students at Southern Illinois University Carbondale."

The small Black contingent on campus can be seen in glimpses during SIU's first half century, singly in a turn-of-the-century photo or in twos and threes here and there in the yearbooks that began appearing about 1915. In 1925, Black students established the Dunbar Society, named for the poet Paul Laurence Dunbar. It became the center of Black life on campus until the 1940s, when Black fraternities and sororities began to take over that role. The campus newspaper, *The Egyptian*, had an ongoing column written by Black students during World War II, "Dark Musings," which tackled such controversial subjects as racism in the military (examples can be found in the Daily Egyptian Diversity News Archive, a digital collection accessible through the library's webpage).

While social life on campus remained largely segregated, sports was an arena that saw early movement toward inclusion. The university initially allowed Black athletes only in track and field, which did not involve bodily contact (Batinski, 2021). Gradually, SIU integrated other sports. In 1950, the football

Forging Alliances for Repairing and Revitalizing Marginalized Communities

team made news when it refused to compete against all-white opponents who demanded SIU leave its Black players at home.

Throughout SIU's gradual evolution, Carbondale remained a segregated city, where Black residents attended segregated schools and lived in their own neighborhood. They could not eat at downtown restaurants and were relegated to the balcony of the local theater. Black students had no access to campus housing and usually boarded at private homes in the Black neighborhood, facing a long walk to class and no place to eat along the way. After World War II, returning Black veterans chafed at such discrimination. Along with white allies among the student body—rapidly growing in the postwar education boom—they began to tackle the issue. An early target was Carter's Café, a favorite student hangout just steps from campus. A picket drive in early 1947 set the tone for later efforts in an ongoing struggle (Batinski, 2021).

Cosmopolitan-minded Delyte Morris, who presided over SIU's transformation from sleepy teacher's college to major research university, arrived on campus in 1948. Morris was a charismatic and visionary leader. One of those he inspired was SIU track star Dick Gregory, later a famous comedian and activist. Raised in deeply segregated St. Louis, Gregory had low expectations when he arrived for freshman orientation in 1952. Then, as he recalled a half century later, he heard Morris address an assembly. During an interview in 2002, Gregory reflected:

It's the first time I'd ever been somewhere where a powerful white man is talking to me from a friendly standpoint. The only powerful people I see in Saint Louis that was white was the storekeepers that was ripping us off and selling us bad food and short weight or the cops or the people in authority. And I heard [Delyte] Morris say, 'I don't care what kind of grades you make. Can be straight As. You can be a perfect student. If you don't understand God, you're a failure.' And I walked out of there a changed person. Black women couldn't live in the dormitory. Black fraternities, sororities couldn't be. And we changed it. We organized and busted that school. And I can sit here today and say SIU was the first school, major school, that had a black athletic director, Gale Sayers. It was the first major school that had a black vice president. As we sit here now, the president of the whole systems are black, and SIU has 16 percent black folks. That's the seed that was planted (Goodman, 2017).

Still, progress in Carbondale was slow. In the late 1950s, several Black students confronted Morris about continued discrimination at downtown businesses. One of these was Roland Burris, who became the first Black to win statewide office in Illinois. Since the businesses claimed to be integrated, Morris encouraged the students to bring him proof. Jewish students worked as witnesses with the Black students to document the informal discrimination practices. Hearing their testimony, Morris summoned the local business owners. Using the university's economic power and moral authority, he convinced all but one to integrate (R. Burris, personal communication, April 29, 2022).

Despite successful efforts to expand civil rights, economic inequality persists, and Carbondale remains largely racially divided. Northeast Carbondale, long the center of Black life, is also close to the city's industrial sites where many residents worked, notably the Koppers Wood-Treating plant. Living and working in such proximity increases residents' exposure to environmental toxins. Some in the university community have helped to expose these environmental issues in recent decades. Koppers shut down after contamination in Glade Creek may have killed fish and cows. In June 2022, the Centers for Disease Control and Prevention opened an investigation of the cancer cluster in the Tisdale family, who grew up next to and played in a pond bordering the Koppers plant.

Origins of RAAHSI

In 2017, representatives of the Black community in Carbondale and SIUC's Morris Library joined forces to address the legacy of "forgetting" and acknowledge the rich contributions of Black people to southern Illinois by helping communities and individuals preserve and share their heritage. The initiative became known as Reclaiming the African American Heritage of Southern Illinois (RAAHSI). While similar efforts have been made elsewhere that could have provided a model to follow, like many community-based projects, RAAHSI evolved organically from the urgent local desire for reparations, beginning with action at the community level rather than emerging from academic theory. It was truly a joint initiative of SIU and local communities.

Archival collecting in general depends on developing relations between archivists and potential donors. Donors need to feel confident that the documents and artifacts they place in an archival repository will be appropriately cared for and used. The need to cross social boundaries that have led to communities' marginalization can complicate relationships between archivists and members of marginalized communities. In their work, Michelle Caswell, Marika Cifor, and Mario H. Ramirez suggest "communities can make collective decisions about what is of enduring value to them, shape collective memory of their own pasts, and control the means through which stories about their past are constructed" (Caswell, et al., 2016).

Building relationships between SCRC archivists and the Black community of Southern Illinois began with the RAAHSI project team. The project grew out of a relationship between Melvin "Pepper" Holder, a community activist, radio personality, and lifelong resident of southern Illinois, and SCRC archivist Walter Ray. Through the interviews Holder conducted on his radio program, he became aware of many stories that he thought should be made more widely available and preserved.

The idea began to take shape when the director of SCRC met with SIUC history faculty, archival faculty, and community members to organize and determine a mission for this project. From the start, the goal was to create a joint community-SIUC project. Holder acted as a contact, identifying interested members of the community and making introductions. Holder also suggested approaching local Black pastors to connect with the Black community and generate interest in the project. The Black community's history can be traced through its religious organizations. Pastors also know who is interested in collecting and preserving history among their congregations. A luncheon for local pastors and other community leaders at SIUC led to invitations to present the project at other venues, such as the Mount Olive Baptist District meeting in Mount Vernon and the anniversary celebration of Paul's Chapel in Marion. With community involvement, it is important to talk with a cross-section of individuals to be inclusive.

A contact by Holder in the community of Colp, Illinois, resulted in the first major donation to the project, the research files of a local Colp historian who had retired to Phoenix after a long career in the IRS. Holder also contacted the Black community of Lakeview, near Carrier Mills, which originated as a free Black community before the Civil War. Holder arranged an oral history interview with the 98-year-old compiler of *Memories of Lakeview* (1976), a collection of documents and memoirs from the community. Holder and Smoot then attended the community's annual Memorial Day reunion. These efforts resulted in another significant donation. Holder also arranged a meeting with the local NAACP branch, which led to depositing the branch records in SCRC.

Building Community Relationships

The familiar adage that ninety percent of success is showing up is undoubtedly true when developing archival relationships. It is necessary to be present in the relationship, which means being present for the community's events. Project team members have attended annual Martin Luther King Jr. breakfasts, Juneteenth events, Christmas programs, and other community events. Team members bring brochures and often present the project to audiences.

There are frictions within any community. An important benefit of partnering with community members is that they know the fault lines within their community. They know whom to approach, when, and how. They can help avoid missteps in the relationships between archivists and communities and repair relations when missteps occur. For example, Holder smoothed friction when RAAHSI sought historical information online. A Facebook post noted the story of a Black Civil War soldier from the area, sharing documented information about him and suggesting some historical possibilities. A soldier's descendant mentioned her displeasure with the storytelling. Holder was able to serve as a mediator, explaining the donor's concern to the archivist and the archivist's intentions to the donor. Archivist and donor were able to agree on new wording for the post.

Documents are the products of discourses and mediate stories (Holland, 1998). As members of historically marginalized communities, Black people are sometimes reluctant to part with their documents for important reasons. The documents are meaningful to them because of the stories they mediate. The physical documents themselves symbolize survival against overwhelming odds over generations. Moreover, the families are often concerned about how others will use the documents to tell their stories. The ability to tell one's own story is a mark of freedom and power over oneself (N'Diaye, 2021). The archivists have addressed these concerns by being open to copying or digitizing documents for preservation, allowing donors to retain the originals, and emphasizing the risk of losing unpreserved documents and stories. The desire to tell one's own story can be accommodated through oral history to place the documents in context.

A good example of how archivists work with families is the recent acquisition of a collection that predates the Civil War. Allen (or McAllen) Dinwiddie was born in slavery in Missouri in 1846. His father, Lorren, was a formerly enslaved person who followed his enslaved wife from place to place as one slaveholder sold her to another. After Emancipation, Allen worked as a farm laborer in Missouri. In 1873 he married Mary Ellen Russell (1851-1944), another formerly enslaved person. Allen brought his growing family to Illinois, drawn by cheap land, eventually purchasing 100 acres near Woodlawn in 1880. Allen and Ellen had seven children, including one daughter, Polly Eva, who attended SIU but died before completing her studies. The 1910 census reported only one child still living. Effie Pearl (b. 1883) had married Harry Young, who owned the neighboring farm in Woodlawn. Harry and Pearl had at least three daughters: Zola, Bessie Edna, and Jennie Louise. Jennie married John Jones of Carbondale. They had four children: Johnetta, Jerald, Harry, and Dan, at least two of whom attended SIU. Jennie Louise taught early childhood education at SIU and helped establish Head Start programs throughout the country. Their daughter Johnetta Jones earned her Master's in history from SIU in 1971 with a thesis titled "Negroes in Jackson County, 1850-1910."

The last of the siblings, Dan Jones, passed away in 2020. His son is the current owner of the Dinwiddie-Young-Jones Family papers, which include 200-300 documents and at least 175 photographs dating back to the 19th century. The photographs include tintypes and cartes de visite. There was a professional photographer in the family around the turn of the century. The photos are in excellent condition and are well-identified. A large portion of the documents consists of the business records from the farm, which date to 1880. There are also family memoirs and artifacts, including quilts and a wood carving by Lorren Dinwiddie.

The collection owner, a friend of an archivist at SIU, asked if SCRC could digitize his family's collection so they could have easier access to the data and the ability to share it with other members of their family. The owner and archivist agreed that the best solution for this collection was to digitize the papers for preservation and return them to the family. The archivist would oversee the digitization but lacked adequate staff for the project. As it happened, SCRC had been asked to provide a summer internship for a student in the Historic Preservation Program at nearby Southeastern Missouri State University. This project proved a perfect fit and afforded the student a valuable learning experience while allowing SCRC to complete the digitization and promptly return the originals to the family. Going forward, the archivists plan to create an online exhibit or other digital humanities products featuring items from the papers.

In the course of its relatively brief existence, the RAAHSI initiative has resulted in a dozen new collections that document this forgotten history. They include church records, town histories, and SCRC's oral history project. A common thread through many of these collections is the importance of funeral programs in documenting local Black history and genealogy. Leah Fleming, Morning Edition host for National Public Radio, notes that "funeral programs are more than brochures passed around during a funeral service. They are a snapshot of the deceased's life, and for several Black families, also serve as a genealogical piece of ancestry and heritage" (Fleming & Bermas-Dawes, 2021).

In the absence of more traditional history and biography, or even contemporary newspaper coverage, the funeral program is a vital record that chronicles the life and connections of an individual who might otherwise slip through the historical cracks. A funeral program is in some ways a sacred object that is not thrown away but carefully stored in a drawer or a file folder. A large number of these have made their way into the RAAHSI collections where they will serve as a valuable resource for future historians.

Outreach

Outreach to other Black community members who might be interested in reclaiming their histories and spreading the word is vital to this project. In addition to word-of-mouth, RAAHSI first created a pamphlet to provide background information about the project, along with suggestions for types of materials to save, how to work with an archives, and contact information.

A quarterly e-newsletter was launched to foster more connections across southern Illinois. It was first sent to those who attended the initial community events, donors, and interested community members. It updates subscribers about newly donated materials, recently processed collections, related community archives in the area, and upcoming events that may be of interest.

A research LibGuide—an online tool to highlight resources available in the library related to study of Black history in southern Illinois—has also been created (Ray, 2022). This guide identifies manuscript collections, university records and rare books related to Black history and culture in southern Illinois.

Furthermore, a community Facebook page was developed for the RAAHSI project, to publicize the project, share information about community events and provide an open forum to discuss the rich history of Black people in southern Illinois.

Forging Alliances for Repairing and Revitalizing Marginalized Communities

Future Plans

Although the 2020-2022 pandemic impacted outreach, reducing opportunities to hold community events, RAAHSI has remained committed to community engagement. SCRC continues to solicit donations of family papers to add more stories to a growing historical narrative. Special Collections and RAAHSI members have taken steps to promote those stories and to ensure transparency and open communication.

RAAHSI is currently exploring the possibility of establishing a center at SIUC to coordinate the expansion of archival services to communities, installation of historical markers, creation of a lecture series, and other programming celebrating Black history and culture throughout southern Illinois. While planning to expand its reparative service to local communities in 2022, the RAAHSI steering committee reached out to the library's development officer for funding guidance. The officer recommended identifying five projects supported at various levels of giving. The steering committee generated service ideas from placing historical markers to hosting regional tours and speaker series. After identifying the projects, the steering committee realized that dedicated ongoing coordination would be required to manage all the projects. Furthermore, only a perpetually funded center could maintain the momentum required to pursue such initiatives and provide a dependable presence that truly supports community welfare. Ultimately, even if it were to receive state funding, the center will require significant donor support to endow the director and staff positions and operations to protect against budget shortfalls. RAAHSI and SIU staff are beginning to explore avenues such as private donations, state funding, and grant funding.

Black communities everywhere stand to benefit from reparative support and cultural resources that enable them to thrive now and in the future. The center will act as the hub of a network of resources serving diverse constituencies according to their needs. Although the steering committee members passionately support the RAAHSI project, they know that a director and staff paid to dedicate their full effort and attention to achieving the initiative's goals will best serve the community's needs.

The center will catalyze engagement. Preserving and sharing Black culture will be a primary goal. Working with Morris Library, SCRC, and the University Museum, the center will spearhead revitalization and education by coordinating art installations, interactive exhibits, and provocative works by prominent visual and performing artists. RAAHSI envisions providing Black people in southern Illinois a platform to address contemporary issues facing their communities. If it can be based in Morris Library, the hub of SIUC campus life and a destination for alums and other visitors, the center will draw heritage tourism, genealogy researchers, and many students who will be inspired and empowered by cultural engagement and expression. The center will also support instruction at SIU, particularly in the School of Education and History Program. SIU offers the only Africana Studies bachelor's degree in Illinois and a graduate certificate in Africana Studies.

In addition to documenting heritage, the RAAHSI project aims to acknowledge the university's impact on community welfare. While the university welcomes and supports Black students, the enduring harm of segregated neighborhoods in Carbondale and the suffering of families impacted by nearby industrial facilities deserve more attention (Gaston & Lewis, 2022). The RAAHSI board is planning to hold a professionally facilitated strategic planning retreat with southern Illinois community members to learn how the planned center might best collaborate in healing and supporting communities. Twenty-five community representatives from southern Illinois will join the steering committee in 2023 for the workshop. RAAHSI is considering producing a program for the workshop with advertising by local businesses to increase reach and engagement.

Progress made by the initiative has already demonstrated how the resources of libraries and archives can amplify voices and begin to address systemic damage to communities. The experience of RAAHSI participants has proven the value of consistently and earnestly working to build connections with Black communities for the benefit of all in southern Illinois. There will be many steps toward establishing the center, but the rewards of dedicated community engagement promise an enriching journey for all participants.

REFERENCES

Allen, J. W. (1963). *Legends & lore of southern Illinois*. Southern Illinois University.

Anderson, K. D., Jackson, M., & Trogden, B. (2021). Looking back, moving forward: Intercultural communication must be part of all learning. *Liberal Education, 107*(1), 32–39.

Bastian, J. A., & Flinn, A. (Eds.). (2020). *Community archives community spaces: Heritage memory and identity*. Facet Publishing.

Bastian, J. A., Sniffin-Marinoff, M., & Webber, D. (2018). *Archives in libraries: What librarians and archivists need to know to work together*. Society of American Archivists.

Batinski, M. C. (2021). *Forgetting and the forgotten: A thousand years of contested histories in the heartland*. Southern Illinois University Press.

Betts, V. (2021). Imagining Futures Through the Archives. *American Studies (Lawrence, Kan.), 60*(2), 19–22. https://doi-org.proxy.lib.siu.edu/10.1353/ams.2021.0005

Brown, M. K. (1991). Documents and archaeology in French Illinois. In J. A. Walthall (Ed.), *French colonial archaeology: the Illinois country and the western great lakes*. University of Illinois Press.

Caswell, M., Cifor, M., & Ramirez, M. (2016). "To suddenly discover yourself existing": Uncovering the impact of community archives. *The American Archivist, 79*(1), 56–81. doi:10.17723/0360-9081.79.1.56

Caswell, M., Migoni, A. A., Geraci, N., & Cifor, M. (2017). 'To be able to imagine otherwise': Community archives and the importance of representation. *Archives and Records (Abingdon, England), 38*(1), 5–26. https://doi-org.proxy.lib.siu.edu/10.1080/23257962.2016.1260 445. doi:10.1080/23257962.2016.1260445

Chamberlain, C. (2015). *Illinois Indians made a bid for power in early America, based on bison and slavery*. Illinois News Bureau. https://news.illinois.edu/view/6367/298688#:~:text=blog%20po sts-,Illinois%20Indians%20made%20a%20bid%20for%20power%20in% 20early,based%20on%20bison%20and%20slavery

Cifor, M., Caswell, M., Migoni, A. A., & Geraci, N. (2018). "What we do crosses over to activism": The politics and practice of community archives. *The Public Historian, 40*(2), 69–95. https://doi-org.proxy. lib.siu.edu/10.1525/tph.2018.40.2.69. doi:10.1525/tph.2018.40.2.69

Craft, A. R. (2018). Creating connections, building community: The role of oral history collections in documenting and sharing campus diversity. *Serials Review*, *44*(3), 232–237. https://doi-org.proxy.lib.siu.edu/10.1080/00987913.2018.1513 750. doi:10.1080/00987913.2018.1513750

Davis, J. E. (1998). *Frontier Illinois*. Indiana University Press.

Dexter, D. (2011). *Bondage in Egypt: Slavery in southern Illinois*. Center for Regional History, Southeast Missouri State University.

Educating with Evidence. (2017). *Using artifacts as evidence: Blacks and the Miller Grove, Illinois settlement*. Southern Illinois University. https://educatingwithevidence.siu.edu/_common/documents/the-underground-railroad-pdfs/ewe-miller-grove-artifacts.pdf

Fleming, L., & Bermas-Dawes, S. (2021). Digitized funeral programs document Black history. *GPB News*. https://www.gpb.org/news/2020/10/29/digitized-funeral-progra ms-document-black-history

Flinn, A., Stevens, M., & Shepherd, E. (2009). Whose memories, whose archives? Independent community archives, autonomy and the mainstream. *Archival Science, 9*(1-2), 71–86. doi:10.100710502-009-9105-2

Gale, N. (2018). In Illinois, the Underground Railroad began in Cairo (at the confluence of the Mississippi and Ohio Rivers), Illinois' southernmost point. *Digital Research Library of Illinois History Journal*. https://drloihjournal.blogspot.com/2018/02/illinois-undergro und-railroad-began-in-cairo-at-illinois-southern-most-point.html

Gaston, J., & Lewis, J. (2022, January 14). Contaminated wood treatment site still hurting Carbondale community 100 years later. *The Daily Egyptian*. https://dailyegyptian.com/111347/news/contaminated-wood-trea tment-site-still-hurting-carbondale-community-100-years-later/

Goodman, A. (2017). Dick Gregory in his own words: Remembering the pioneering comedian and Civil Rights activist. *Democracy Now*. https://www.democracynow.org/2017/8/21/dick_gregory_in_his_o wn_words

Hetland, P., Pierroux, P., & Esborg, L. (Eds.). (2020). *A history of participation in museums and archives: Traversing citizen science and citizen humanities*. Routledge. doi:10.4324/9780429197536

Hill, J. (2011). *The future of archives and recordkeeping: a reader*. Facet Publishing. http://public.eblib. com/choice/publicfullrecord.aspx?p=1167408

Holland, D. C. (1998). *Identity and agency in cultural worlds*. Harvard University Press.

Hopkins, P. D. (2022). Finding place in the archive: A case study of St. John [Colored] Missionary Baptist Church, 1866–1900. *History (London)*, *107*(375), 337–355. https://doi-org.proxy.lib.siu.edu/10.1111/1468-229X.13270. doi:10.1111/1468-229X.13270

Jones, P. M. (2017). *Forgotten soldiers: Jackson County's African American Civil War veterans* [Exhibit]. General John A. Logan Museum.

Kandiuk, M. (Ed.). (2020). *Archives and special collections as sites of contestation*. Library Juice Press.

LaRoche, C. J. (2013). *Free black communities and the underground railroad: The geography of resistance*. University of Illinois Press. doi:10.5406/illinois/9780252038044.001.0001

McCorvie, M. R. (2002). *Women of color in southern Illinois: Free African American women in rural ante-bellum communities in southern Illinois*. Paper presented at the Annual Conference on Historical Archaeology, Mobile, Alabama.

McCorvie, M. R. (2009). *Archaeology and abolitionists: Ardent spirits, riotous mobocrats, Wide Awakes, Egypt and the presidential election of 1860*. Illinois Archaeological Awareness Month presentation, July 15, 2009.

McCorvie, M. R., & Devenport, V. (2004). *Miller Grove: An introduction*. Paper presented at the 2004 Conference on Historical and Underwater Archaeology, St. Louis, Missouri.

McDaniel, K. R. (2011). A Survey of the African American Records in UK's Special Collections. *Kentucky Libraries*, *75*(4), 8–12.

Meikle, G. (2018). *The Routledge companion to media and activism*. Routledge. https://www.routledge.com/The-Routledge-Companion-to-Media-and-Activism/Meikle/p/book/9780367659967

Mellon Foundation. (2019). *Community archives empower through access and inclusion*. Mellon Foundation News. https://www.lapovertydept.org/wordpress/wp-content/uploads/2019/08/2019-Community-Archives-Empower-through-Access-and-Inclusion-The-Andrew-W.-Mellon-Foundation.pdf

Mondésir, O., Tummino, A., & Wong, J. (2021). Uplifting diverse and marginalized voices through community archives and public programming. *Urban Library Journal*, *27*(2), 1–9.

Myers, J. W. (1922). History of the Gallatin salines. *Journal of the Illinois State Historical Society*, *14*(3-4), 337–349.

N'Diaye, D. B. (2021). Telling our own stories: Reciprocal autoethnography at the intersections of race, class, and gender. *Journal of American Folklore*, *134*(533), 252–257. https://www.muse.jhu.edu/article/800148. doi:10.5406/jamerfolk.134.533.0252

Porter, G. (2020). Freed faces, our past Americans: Collaborations to create, digitize and describe the "Former Slaves in Freedom" collection. *Collaborative Librarianship*, *12*(1), 20–51.

Ray, W. (2022). *Resources for the study of African American history in southern Illinois: Overview of Special Collections*. LibGuide. https://libguides.lib.siu.edu/c.php?g=936792&p=6751751

Russell, H. K. (2012). *The state of southern Illinois: An illustrated history*. Southern Illinois University Press.

Smoot, P. (2012). Alexander Lane: From slavery to freedom: The life of Alexander Lane, educator, physician and Illinois state legislator, 1860-1911. *The Simon Review (Occasional Papers of the Paul Simon Public Policy Institute)*. https://opensiuc.lib.siu.edu/ppi_papers/29

Voigt, J. (2021). *Site of the first memorial service in Illinois*. The Historical Marker Database. https://www.hmdb.org/m.asp?m=163493

Wagner, M. J. (2019). *"The place where no one ever goes": A landscape study of the Miller Grove community.* Paper presented at the Society for Historical Archaeology Annual Meeting, St. Charles, Missouri.

Wagner, T. L., & Bischoff, B. (2017). Defining community archives within rural South Carolina. *Advances in Librarianship*, *43*, 155–180. doi:10.1108/S0065-283020170000043007

Williams, C. (2020). The Bridgwater family: A history of an African American family in the American west from slavery to the Civil Rights era. *The Western Historical Quarterly*, *51*(4), 349–380. https://doi-org.proxy.lib.siu.edu/10.1093/whq/whaa115. doi:10.1093/whq/whaa115

Wilson Special Collections Library. (2019). *Creating and growing community-based memory projects.* The University of North Carolina at Chapel Hill. https://library.unc.edu/preservation/creating-and-growing/

Chapter 9
The Foundation of and Future Directions for JEDI @ University of Massachusetts Amherst Libraries

Michael W. Mercurio
https://orcid.org/0000-0002-3891-4946
University of Massachusetts, Amherst, USA

Adam Holmes
University of Massachusetts, Amherst, USA

Carole Connare
University of Massachusetts, Amherst, USA

Nandita S. Mani
https://orcid.org/0000-0002-0955-1066
University of Massachusetts, Amherst, USA

Jennifer Friedman
University of Massachusetts, Amherst, USA

ABSTRACT

This chapter per the authors provides an in-depth overview of how the University of Massachusetts Amherst Libraries has leveraged historical connections and special collections to provide a robust foundation for justice, equity, diversity, and inclusion programming and initiatives on campus, in the community, and worldwide. Readers will be provided with examples that will inform conversations about JEDI efforts at their own libraries and on their own campuses, as well as insights gleaned during the process of doing this work at University of Massachusetts Amherst Libraries.

DOI: 10.4018/978-1-6684-7255-2.ch009

This chapter published as an Open Access Chapter distributed under the terms of the Creative Commons Attribution License (http://creativecommons.org/licenses/by/4.0/) which permits unrestricted use, distribution, and production in any medium, provided the author of the original work and original publication source are properly credited.

Foundation and Future Directions for JEDI at U. of Massachusetts Libraries

INTRODUCTION

The focus on justice, diversity, equity, and inclusion (JEDI) efforts in libraries predates the public murder of George Floyd on May 25, 2020, though that event became a clear turning point in the attention paid to the systemic inequities inherent in the United States of America. Americans were unable to look away from what the writer Wendell Berry (1970) described as a "hidden wound" in his deeply personal book of that title, and concepts like institutional racism and white privilege became regular topics of discussion among the American populace. In addition, institutions of all sorts, from private companies to public libraries, scrambled to affirm their support for Black lives and to acknowledge the need for real, substantive changes to occur both internally and across American society.

Now, several years past the immediate reactions to Floyd's murder, it is possible to reflect on the ways such reactions have played out in academic libraries and to understand the scholarly and intellectual foundations upon which they were built. This chapter will focus on the ongoing work at the University of Massachusetts Amherst Libraries, including the work of the W. E. B. Du Bois Center, whose mission is to carry on the critical inquiry pioneered by Du Bois himself, and to apply that lens to the ongoing challenges of our time.

ABOUT THE UMASS AMHERST LIBRARIES

The UMass Amherst Libraries are the largest publicly supported academic research library in New England, with a budget of $20 million (plus endowments and gift funds), and over 100 staff. With more than 8 million physical and digital items, the Libraries include the W. E. B. Du Bois Center and the Robert S. Cox Special Collections and University Archives Research Center (SCUA), which contains the papers and memoirs of W. E. B. Du Bois, Horace Mann Bond, Daniel Ellsberg, Kenneth R. Feinberg, the Irma McClaurin Black Feminist Archive, and hundreds of other collections documenting the lives and work of activists, innovators, political figures, spiritual leaders, writers, and more.

The University of Massachusetts Amherst acknowledges that it was founded and built on the unceded homelands of the Pocumtuc Nation on the land of the Norrwutuck community.

We begin with gratitude for nearby waters and lands, including the Kwinitekw – the southern portion of what's now called the Connecticut River. We recognize these lands and waters as important Relations with which we are all interconnected and depend on to sustain life and wellbeing.

The Norrwutuck community was one of many Pocumtuc Indian towns, including the Tribal seat at Pocumtuc (in present day Deerfield), Agawam (Springfield), and Woronoco (Westfield) to name just a few. The Pocumtuc, who had connections with these lands for millennia, are part of a vast expanse of Algonqiuan relations. Over 400 years of colonization, Pocumtuc Peoples were displaced. Many joined their Algonquian relatives to the east, south, west and north—extant communities of Wampanoag, including Aquinnah, Herring Pond, and Mashpee, Massachusetts; the Nipmuc with a reservation at Grafton/Hassanamisco, Massachusetts; the Narragansett in Kingstown, Rhode Island; Schagticoke, Mohegan and Pequot Peoples in Connecticut; the Abenaki and other Nations of the Wabanaki Confederacy extending northward into Canada; and the Stockbridge Munsee Mohican of New York and Massachusetts, who were removed to Wisconsin in the 19th century. Over hundreds of years of removal, members of Southern New England Tribes would make the journey home to tend important places and renew their connections to their ancestral lands. Such care and connection to land and waters continues to the present day.

Today, Indigenous Nations in southern New England continue to employ diverse strategies to resist ongoing colonization, genocide, and erasure begun by the English, French, Dutch, Portuguese and other European Nations, and that continued when Tribal homelands became part of the United States. Native Americans from Tribal Nations across the U.S. and Indigenous peoples from around the world also travel into these Pocumtuc homelands to live and work. This land has always been and always will be, Native Land.

We also acknowledge that the University of Massachusetts Amherst is a Land Grant University. As part of the Morrill Land Grant Act of 1862, Tribal lands from 82 Native Nations west of the Mississippi were sold to provide the resources to found and build this university.

This Land Acknowledgement is the first step in the university's commitment to practice intellectual humility whilst working with Tribal Nations toward a better shared future on Turtle Island. We aim to foster understanding, deep respect, and honor for sovereign Tribal Nations; to develop relationships of reciprocity; and to be inclusive of Native perspectives and thriving Native Nations far into the future. Members of Massachusetts-based Tribal Nations who are kin to the historic Pocumtuc contributed their insights in composing this acknowledgement – namely Tribal representatives from Mashpee, Aquinnah, and Stockbridge Munsee. As an active first step toward decolonization, we encourage you to learn more about the Indigenous peoples on whose homelands UMass Amherst now resides on and the Indigenous homelands on which you live and work.

Why Du Bois?

William Edward Burghardt Du Bois was born in Great Barrington, a small town in western Massachusetts, on February 23, 1868.

In 1903, W. E. B. Du Bois published *The Souls of Black Folk*, a collection of essays that transcends any academic field or literary genre to present a stirring, poetic, honest, and profoundly modern portrait of the history of Black America and the continuing problem of the color line. The book was an immediate sensation and still ranks as one of the seminal works in American literature. In this book, Du Bois departed from the strictures of academic writing to present his readers with fiction that was used to illustrate fact, an accompanying 'soundtrack' of sorrow songs and other musical pieces, snatches of memoir that force the reader to see with Du Bois's own eyes, and a host of indelible images all drawn in magisterial and sweeping language.

The Souls of Black Folk brought Du Bois national acclaim; it also laid him open to criticism from a variety of quarters. There was the predictable racist backlash from white supremacist writers, including Thomas Nelson Page, but there was also a sizeable amount of condemnation from those who also strove for Black liberation and civil rights yet took different approaches. Most notable among these voices was the by now world-famous Booker T. Washington, a man whom Du Bois had not been afraid to criticize in the book. The disagreement between Du Bois and Washington was one which would continue until the latter's death in 1915 and has been intensely studied and debated by scholars ever since.

The realization that the Du Bois archive would have enormous value to scholars, researchers and, indeed, the public came while Du Bois was still alive. The effort to collect and organize these papers was begun by the man himself, encouraged by Shirley Graham and comrades like Herbert Aptheker. When Du Bois died the bulk of the papers stayed with Shirley, but no institution had yet emerged as a place for them to reside. This changed when Randolph Bromery, the first Black person to serve as Chancellor of UMass Amherst, led the effort to bring the papers back to Du Bois's home state. The University acquired the papers in 1973 and they were opened to the public in 1980. At the dedication ceremony, in his keynote address, Lerone Bennett Jr. (1980) said that "no one can understand Massachusetts or the United States of America without some understanding of the man who turns and twists and challenges and dreams in the papers collected here" (p. 2).

The Du Bois collection, housed in the Robert S. Cox Special Collections and University Archives Research Center, consists of 294 boxes and nearly 100,000 individual items. This trove of letters, manuscripts, speeches, photographs and realia is the centerpiece represents the bulk of the archival legacy of one of the defining intellects of the 20th Century, a thinker whose work set the stage for addressing justice, equity, diversity, and inclusion in American society.

A Brief History of the Du Bois Center

As early as 1974, the aforementioned Chancellor Randolph Bromery was advocating for the foundation of a "W. E. B. Du Bois Center for Intellectual Leadership" as "a fitting tribute to America's foremost Black scholar" and as a "catalyst to start a more reasoned and effective approach to solving some of the mounting social, economic, and political problems of the country." Du Bois Center Scholar-in-Residence Phillip Luke Sinitiere writes that Bromery was "both perpetually intellectually curious and historically minded. His commitment to the life of the mind prompted him to puzzle out ways to activate the Du Bois manuscripts for maximum intellectual production and to find ways for them to impact the community beyond the university" (P. L. Sinitiere, personal communication, December 20, 2022).

Bromery's lofty ambitions would not be realized for decades, but the objectives set down by Bromery have informed the work of the Du Bois Center since its founding in 2009. The responsibilities of the Center in its early years were primarily to support the activities of a small number of visiting research fellows and to organize the annual W. E. B. Du Bois Lecture. It continued to grow, occupying a larger footprint within the building, and adding book giveaways and student events to its range of activities.

In 2016 the Center's director successfully applied for a major grant from the Andrew W. Mellon Foundation that led to a dramatic expansion of the Center's work. This influx of funding allowed the Center to justify the hiring of a full-time Program Manager in 2018; due to the increased volume of work and outreach conducted by the Center's staff, this position has been reclassified as Assistant Director. Even before this increase in staffing, the Center was running a fuller range of programs, including day-long workshops for local community college students. It was also able to increase the number of research fellows and include graduate students from UMass Amherst in the fellowship program for the first time. As a complement to the Center's work, an accessible timeline of Du Bois's life has been installed in the Center's primary space. It includes text and physical and digital objects and images, so that visitors to the Du Bois Center will be able to move through a brief history of his remarkable achievements at their own pace.

Since its inception, the Center has striven not only to provide access to the work of Du Bois and his archive, but also to be a space of knowledge production and one that applies Du Bois's work to contemporary issues. These ideals form the basis of the Center's longest-standing and most impactful program, the weekly "Breakfast with Du Bois."

Breakfast With Du Bois

The idea for a weekly, Du Bois-focused reading group was first suggested by a Du Bois Center graduate fellow studying political science, Benjamin Nolan, in late 2018. Ben proposed the format and came up with the title, "Breakfast with Du Bois," while the Center arranged for UMass catering to deliver weekly consignments of coffee, fruit and muffins to the 22nd floor. He recollects that "the idea for the Breakfasts was inspired by the director telling the fellows about her practice of trying to read one short Du Bois text per day as a kind of personal practice that wasn't narrowly scholarly, but rather prioritized the cultivation of a broader and personal connection. I was in a liminal moment in my graduate studies, transitioning to the intense solitude of dissertation research and writing, and thought it would be amazing if we could come up with a way to develop a kind of community ritual in the same spirit" (B. Nolan, personal communication, December 19, 2022).

The first Du Bois Breakfast took place on Monday, February 4, 2019, and was attended by nine people, mostly other graduate students. The group read aloud a speech which Du Bois gave in 1890 as his baccalaureate disquisition at Harvard, "Jefferson Davis as a Representative of Civilization." The digitized version of the text came from the Du Bois papers and a copy was printed for each member of the group. The reading was followed by an open-ended and spirited discussion which covered topics ranging from Du Bois's early and excellent use of rhetoric and logic to persuade his audience of the validity of his point, the ways in which American society embraces the myth of the "strong man," and the racist distortions of American history in Du Bois's time and our own. It was agreed by all in attendance that this short text from the end of the nineteenth century had a tremendous amount of resonance in 2019. Upon the session's conclusion it was agreed that the breakfasts would continue on a weekly basis, meeting every Monday.

At the next session, the group read Martin Luther King's speech, "Honoring Dr. Du Bois," an address he gave on what would have been Du Bois's 100th birthday, and one of the last public speeches he would ever make. In the speech, King praised Du Bois's achievements as a scholar and civil rights leader, while paying particular attention to his work on Reconstruction. Again a handsome, digital copy of the text was taken from the Du Bois papers and printed out for the attendees. At a dozen pages, it was nearly twice as long as the previous week's text, but there was still ample time for discussion when the reading concluded. Texts of about this length have since proved to be the most effective for the Breakfast with Du Bois format as they allow the session to be almost evenly split between reading and discussion. A slightly larger group was in attendance for this second breakfast and a mailing list was started. Flyers were distributed via email and printed for display on campus notice boards to encourage others to join the group the following Monday.

The breakfasts continued on a weekly basis for the remainder of the academic year and grew in popularity, attracting undergraduate students, faculty members, and library staff. The format which had worked so well in the first two sessions was codified during these months and has stayed the same ever since. An email would be sent out each Friday by Ben, which introduced the text to be read the following Monday and included a PDF for people to read ahead of time if they felt so inclined. The group would then meet in the Du Bois Center on Monday morning and help themselves to coffee and breakfast snacks, taking this opportunity to catch up with other members of the group. Chairs and tables would be arranged so that the group could sit in a rough circle and face one another. After this brief fellowship, the reading would begin, with the convener reading the first paragraph or two and then passing to the next person, who would in turn read as much as they felt comfortable with before passing on to their

Foundation and Future Directions for JEDI at U. of Massachusetts Libraries

neighbor. The text would make itself round the table until it was concluded. A discussion would then follow which, facilitated – but not necessarily *lead* – by the convener. The group was always encouraged to take the discussion in whichever direction they wished, and this led to many stimulating conversations on a host of topics.

It was decided by a unanimous vote of breakfast attendees on the last Monday of the spring semester to keep up the breakfasts through June, July, and August of 2019, especially as so many local community members and library staff were now involved who would be in Amherst throughout the summer break. Between July and August that year's cohort of postdoctoral Du Bois Center fellows also joined many of the breakfasts and brought exciting new perspectives based on their research in the archives. Phillip Luke Sinitiere, now scholar-in-residence at the Center, found a copy and recording of the keynote speech given by Lerone Bennett at the dedication of the Du Bois papers in 1980. The breakfast group listened to, and read along with, the recording on July 21, 2019, and provided a second "audience," so to speak, for Bennett nearly forty years after the speech was originally given.

Ben received a fellowship to study in South Africa for the 2019-2020 academic year and another graduate fellow, Aaron Yates from the sociology department, stepped into the role as facilitator of the reading group. Aaron led the breakfast club into the new semester with aplomb, drawing on his own academic background to introduce new writings, both by Du Bois and scholars drawing on his work. A new group of friends and associates from the sociology department and others also joined the group that semester making up for the loss of the postdoctoral fellows, who had by then returned to their own institutions. New archival treasures were unearthed for the group to enjoy, including original speeches from the dedication ceremony for the Du Bois Boyhood Homesite in Great Barrington in 1969, which the group read and listened to on the fiftieth anniversary of that event.

The final in-person Breakfast with Du Bois for spring of 2020 took place on March 9, 2020. A week later all staff, students, and faculty at UMass Amherst were sent home, and campus closed. The pandemic forced a total change of plans for the Du Bois Center, the activities of which were, for the foreseeable future, to be run from the assistant director's kitchen table. The first virtual breakfast took place on April 12, 2020, and the weekly gatherings on Zoom have continued ever since. A major reason for the preservation of the online format has been that moving the breakfasts online has allowed people to join from beyond Amherst. Breakfasters have dialed in from all over the United States and from countries including Angola, Canada, South Africa, South Korea, and the United Kingdom. Although the food provided by UMass catering has disappeared, the format has remained the same. A volunteer puts themselves forward as the first reader then nominates the next person and the text makes its way around the group.

During the lonely and uncertain early days of the pandemic, the breakfasts with Du Bois proved an invaluable way for the community around the Center to keep in touch, share personal updates, and discuss the unprecedented times being lived through. The murder of George Floyd by police in the spring of 2020 brought an increase in attendance at the breakfasts as people began to feel a greater sense of urgency around questions of racist violence and anti-Blackness in America and around the world. Reading and discussing Du Bois together helped the attendees at the breakfasts to not just learn more about the long historical roots of the current crisis, but also to form bonds of solidarity and express collective feelings in a moment of extreme stress. In the summer of 2020, Aaron Yates stepped back from facilitating the breakfasts and handed over to Adam Holmes, the Center's assistant director, who has led the group since and always tried to find texts from Du Bois's canon that meet the moment. Fortunately, given the vastness and richness of Du Bois's written record, this has never been a challenge.

171

Whether in person or online, Breakfast with Du Bois has been the most effective way of introducing a wide range of people to the written words of W. E. B. Du Bois and interpretations of them. An attendee who joins the group over a dozen times will have read somewhere in the region of 150 pages of Du Bois's work from a range of sources. Someone who regularly attends the sessions for a year or more will have read the equivalent of an entire book. Only serious Du Bois scholars have spent a comparable amount of time with archival materials from the Du Bois papers as the breakfast club. Cheryl Townsend Gilkes, a regular attendee and professor of sociology at Colby College, states that, "The breakfasts have made it possible for me to be exposed to documents beyond my own narrow interests in a scholar who produced a vast published literature. Reading unpublished documents in a shared setting has been absolutely critical for providing a larger context to my own work" (C. T. Gilkes, personal communication, December 18, 2022).

The breakfasts demonstrate the value in the Libraries' decision to democratize access to the Du Bois papers, which are available to anyone with an internet connection or the ability to come to UMass Amherst and make their way to the Robert S. Cox Special Collections and University Archives Research Center on the 25th floor. The breakfasts have provided a free, inclusive, constantly evolving, yet structured way for people to study and learn from Du Bois and deepen their familiarity with a body of work that can feel intimidatingly vast. Ben states that it was always vital to him that the breakfasts be in the spirit of Du Bois and democratic. "That is accessible, empowering of each voice to be heard, and guided principally by the conversations it cultivated rather than by any given programmer. A big part of this democratic accessibility to me was to make sure that it never required homework, and that food would be involved. I forget how we came up with the idea of reading the texts aloud, but to me the significance of it is that it makes sure that everyone's voice is literally heard even before the open conversation begins. Moreover, it turns reading itself, which for me at least had become an overwhelmingly solitary practice, into a communal one, prompting each of us to engage with the text through the eyes and ears of every other reader in the circle" (B. Nolan, personal communication, December 19, 2022).

The experience of reading Du Bois aloud as a group is indeed a profound one. Cheryl Townsend Gilkes says that "Du Bois writes to be understood but so richly that skimming does him a great disservice. Every word matters and reading aloud makes us recognize that" (C. T. Gilkes, personal communication, December 18, 2022).

The poetic lyricism and rhetorical thrust of Du Bois's use of English are a pleasure to experience, but also give the texts a vividness and immediacy that is difficult to find in writers not blessed with Du Bois's talents. Reading aloud, and actively listening to others do so, is both an intimate and meaningful experience but it also opens up a text, revealing its many hidden subtleties. Du Bois, except when working on the most academic of his scholarly works, always intended his literature to be accessible, and to carry a message. In 1926, Du Bois wrote that "whatever art I have for writing has been used always for propaganda for gaining the right of black folk to love and enjoy" (p. 296). The experience of 181 (at the time of writing) Du Bois breakfasts has demonstrated the truth of this statement.

There is seldom a week that goes by where a member of the breakfast club does not remark on either the power of Du Bois's writing, the almost eerie relevance to our own moment, or both. As Phillip writes, "I have realized how relevant Du Bois's writings and ideas remain. There's always something in his writings that connects to contemporary history and current events. His observations often anticipated future trends or from the vantage point of the present provide insight into current political or cultural conditions. To sum it up: the Du Bois breakfast gatherings have demonstrated to me how durable Du Bois's thoughts and ideas are" (P. L. Sinitiere, personal communication, December 20, 2022).

Foundation and Future Directions for JEDI at U. of Massachusetts Libraries

People can rightly become exasperated by the fact that so many of the issues Du Bois elucidated in his writings of a hundred years ago have continued without abatement well into the 21st Century. More often than not, however, the sheer brilliance of Du Bois's arguments and formulations fortify the breakfasters, who gain not just insight, but have developed a moral, rhetorical, and intellectual framework based on the work of Du Bois for approaching issues related to racial and social justice. This was precisely Du Bois's own intention for his own audiences when he set his words down in print, and a large reason why he kept such a meticulous archive and worked to ensure its survival. He wanted his words and thoughts to echo beyond his lifetime and continue to do their work. They do precisely that every Monday morning on the 22nd floor of the library that bears his name.

Perhaps the most profound thing about the breakfasts, however, is not the work of Du Bois but the community that has grown around them. Laura Richards, who graduated from Smith College in 2022, is a regular breakfast attendee and says that "[e]veryone feels welcome and I think everyone can find something new in Du Bois's writing…Breakfast with Du Bois is inspiring and an opportunity to sit down and read Du Bois's work weekly with people whose knowledge enriches the experience. I get much more out of his work in this group setting, listening to his words read aloud, than I would reading Du Bois silently on my own" (L. Richards, personal communication, December 16, 2022).

The shared excitement about Du Bois, the affection and enthusiasm the group has for one another, and the collective dedication to pursuing justice is beyond inspiring. It shows what can be done when people are regularly gathered together to examine significant issues, and it underscores that other great theme of Du Bois's life - the importance of organizing groups dedicated to change. This community has coalesced not just around the Monday reading group but the many other activities of the Du Bois Center.

After Breakfast: Other Initiatives of the W. E. B. Du Bois Center

One of the Center's key functions from its earliest days has been the production of scholarship based on the archival collection. Archives like those of Du Bois do their greatest work when being explored by scholars making new discoveries and connections. The Center helps give scholars access to this collection through its fellowship program, which has not just produced a host of important books and articles on Du Bois but has also ensured that the Center's own approach to "teaching" Du Bois is in line with current scholarship. Huge national figures like Du Bois are in danger of having values projected onto them by audiences and institutions if the appropriate care is not taken. The Fellows help ensure that, through the papers, Du Bois's own values are reflected by the Center. Ben writes that "being part of the fellowship has transformed my academic work, validating my own commitment to internationalism and history as necessary to politically useful scholarship, and illuminating a wide variety of pathways by which to bring this commitment to bear. It also put me into a position to engage with questions of race in spaces that are not dominated by white voices, assumptions, and expectations" (B. Nolan, personal communication, December 19, 2022).

As part of the fellowship program, each scholar also agrees to return to UMass during the school year to give a public talk on their work at the Center. These lectures combine with talks by Du Bois Center staff and affiliated faculty and graduate students, not to mention the Annual Du Bois Lecture traditionally held around the time of Du Bois's birthday, to ensure that there is a year-round series of opportunities for people to learn about Du Bois at the Center. These lectures are all recorded and posted online to make sure they reach the widest possible audience. The last two annual lectures were also live streamed and watched live by hundreds online. In fact, the Du Bois Center became something of a hub of video production during the first year of the pandemic, with a mini-documentary on the history of the papers garnering nearly 1,000 views on YouTube. Even more successful was a video featuring different voices reading out Du Bois quotes which has since been watched over 4,000 times.

The Du Bois Center works closely with local schools and community colleges and organizes visits to the library for students and educators. As part of these visits the groups are introduced to the life and times of Du Bois in the Center before being led up to the 25th floors to visit the archives and handle original artifacts. These visits have a range of benefits for students, providing them with knowledge and information to support courses in history, Black studies, sociology, literature, civics, and other social sciences, as well as the experience of working with primary sources and the opportunity to learn about the functions of an archive and research library. For students from Massachusetts, these visits are also a reminder that local history is not just confined to the pilgrim fathers and the Revolutionary War.

In partnership with the Libraries' Digital Media Lab, the Du Bois Center created a resource specifically for younger audiences, examples of which have made their way to five schools across the state. The Du Bois "Museum in a Box" presents a selection of facsimiles from the papers and 3D-printed replicas of artifacts found at the Du Bois Boyhood Homesite in Great Barrington. Each object is affixed with an RFID contact sticker that plays an audio caption when held near a speaker. The resource is an accessible, tactile and, importantly, fun way for younger learners to get information on Du Bois and explore the wonders of the archive.

The Du Bois Center's approach to the Museum in a Box is informed by the same ethical commitment that it applies to all of its work. The Center is dedicated to always presenting a truthful and honest view of Du Bois as a historical figure and of his work. As stewards of his legacy and the first contact many people have with Du Bois, the Center has never, and must never, be guilty of whitewashing or romanticizing Du Bois and recognize the pain and violence that is present in his work. As a predominantly white institution, and a land grant college, UMass Amherst must also recognize its own institutional role in perpetuating unequal structures of power and supporting white supremacism and seek to make amends. One way it can do this is not falling into the trap of basking in the reflected glory of Du Bois's presence, but humbly allowing his work and those of the scholars and activists who draw on it to exist in the world without interference and with the maximum of support.

The Du Bois Center, formed to steward its namesake's legacy and stimulate scholarship in his spirit, has spun off many JEDI-focused activities. Within the constellations of Libraries JEDI programming, Du Bois events have the greatest depth and breadth, with a parallel narrative of continual audience expansion.

The longest-running activity is the annual Du Bois Lecture, during which, for the past 28 years, researchers have presented new scholarship on Du Bois to an audience of students and scholars. Until 2019, the event had been in person, open to all, and filmed for later sharing and viewing. The audience was primarily graduate students and faculty interested in the subject, rounded out by undergraduate students, independent researchers, and members of the campus and local community.

As the Du Bois Fellows program has grown—from two visiting fellows per year to more than 10 visiting graduates and posts-docs from 2017 on, and with engagement from an increasing number of academic disciplines—scholarly talks by returning fellows increased in frequency, to several each semester. The expansion of opportunities broadened audiences in size and scope and extended our reach into the home institutions and academic communities of visiting fellows.

With a goal to introduce every UMass student to Du Bois, the Du Bois Center has, since its inception in 2009, sought opportunities to increase engagement. Out of this came the annual Du Bois Birthday celebration open to every member of campus ("You're invited to stop by the library lobby for a cupcake, a free copy of *The Souls of Black Folk*, and to learn about Du Bois!"), a low-barrier entry to finding out about the life and work of the sociologist, activist, and author. Yet, despite Du Bois's birthdate of February 23, the Libraries sought to avoid relying on Black History Month to anchor JEDI efforts. Recognizing that Black history is American history, we continue to offer introductory events all year long.

During the same time period, the Libraries' collaborations with campus and community partners who were interested in Du Bois increased, such as the Du Bois in Our Time exhibit held from September 10 - December 8, 2013, a partnership between the libraries and the Fine Arts Center, and in 2020, a film celebrating the 40th anniversary of the papers coming to UMass, weaving together reflections from diverse Du Bois scholars. We worked with community members, librarians, and lawmakers to host a traveling Du Bois exhibit, which has been shown across the Commonwealth from Great Barrington Public Library to Boston City Hall. These collaborations have been invaluable in understanding what was important to the communities we serve and those with whom we seek to partner.

While many of these activities have increased our engagement with an ever-wider variety of audiences, they have largely been developed by the libraries in response to campus goals. To truly break down barriers, we need to be both more intentional and more collaborative with the audiences we want to engage—not just with Du Bois, but also JEDI programming for other spaces, resources, and services.

JEDI Collection Development, Access, and Assessment

In keeping with the intellectual legacy of Du Bois, the UMass Libraries work to develop collections that reflect the commitment to both the social justice mission and to the campus community. Students and faculty that see themselves represented in a respectful way in the libraries collections are more likely to be connected to the campus community and feel a sense of belonging.

Since the creation of the Collections Strategies Group in 2018, the libraries have prioritized adding materials to the collection that represent diversity regionally, nationally, and on a global scale, such as *History Vault: Black Freedom Struggle in the 20th Century, Historical Jerusalem Post, Shen Bao*, and *Early Arabic Books*. The libraries add materials in all formats and incorporate individual titles throughout the year as academic liaisons identify new resources to add to the collections.

In one specific example of our responsiveness to patron-driven requests, the Libraries recently added the movie *Powerlands* to support a campus viewing event focused on Indigenous peoples who have been displaced from their native lands by corporate America. In addition, the Libraries have also recently added *The 1619 Project: A New Origin Story* to our collections to support a spring reading event for our School of Social and Behavioral Sciences. In reviewing available platforms, Libraries staff determined that OverDrive was the best platform for this resource, as it would provide the broadest access for our community. OverDrive also includes JEDI in its indexing, making it easy to search and locate available titles on this platform, and offers over 100 titles as part of its own JEDI collection. In recent months, a small group of UMass Libraries staff has curated a UMass-specific JEDI collection on the OverDrive platform and has selected titles tailored for UMass users' needs and available in easily accessed e-book form.

Though representing the UMass Amherst community in library collections is important, it is equally important to make sure that collections are easy to locate and accessible, while also taking into account the manner in which classifications might display epistemological prejudices inherent in the minds of their creators. For example, in direct response to questions and concerns raised by members of the UMass queer community, the Libraries attention was drawn to the fact that subject headings for incest, child sexual abuse, and similar topics under call number HQ72 had been historically classed next to those for queer theory, suggesting an affiliation between these topics that sustains a long-standing rhetorical feint used to demean and diminish queer people and to portray queerness as a danger to families, communities, and children. In response to this input from the community, UMass metadata librarians have determined that HQ72 is not commonly in use, and so no recent books are being classed into this call number, while books from the 1970s, 1980s and a few from the early 1990s are being reclassed into the currently used call number areas, which are not shelved next to queer theory, and are instead predominantly in the HV or R schedules. New call numbers and any new subject headings identified during subject analysis are added to the WorldCat record for any future libraries to use or update their records. The UMass librarians involved in the project hope that this will allow these changes to have the maximum impact possible.

In addition to acquiring and making JEDI collections available, the Libraries are mindful of how patrons are represented in library systems. In early 2019, we began supporting the use of patrons' preferred names. By the end of 2020, as the Libraries approached full implementation of a new open-source library services platform (FOLIO), Libraries staff began integrating preferred names into library systems. By end of spring semester 2021, all edits were complete so that patrons who use their preferred names will see themselves properly represented in communications generated by most of the Libraries systems. As of this writing, patrons still have to manually update their name in the interlibrary loan system until there are appropriate systems connects, though this project is underway. The Libraries are not unique on campus in the need to integrate system interoperability to reflect preferred names, and it is an ongoing technological challenge, but it is a priority and will remain one in the future.

Overall, The Libraries are taking the necessary steps to represent JEDI across collections, though there is a goal to conduct a complete collection assessment to determine how collections reflect JEDI, where there are gaps, and how those gaps will be addressed. This will be a significant undertaking, but one that is critical to the Libraries commitment to the community.

FURTHERING LIBRARY JEDI EFFORTS THROUGH PROGRAMMING AND EVENTS

A Solid Foundation

The Libraries have a long history of producing programming in physical and digital spaces related to the topics of justice, equity, diversity, and inclusion. With the W. E. B. Du Bois Papers as the cornerstone, the Special Collections are most intentionally comprehensive and interconnected in the area of social justice. This concentration of resources has provided focus for JEDI events and programs.

UMass Amherst Libraries' social change collections have inspired events through the years, including colloquia on topics ranging from de-incarceration and communal living to Vietnam War activism, Quaker abolitionists, and disability rights. Likewise, issues of environmental equity have periodically been the focus for events and programs supported by the Libraries' Sustainability Fund, underwritten by alumni and friends. The Libraries' commitment to open access and the promotion of open scholarship have spawned JEDI-focused events, at times in partnership with student groups such as the Massachusetts Public Interest Research Group and the Student Government Association, since students directly benefit from access to free and low-cost academic resources, especially for learners from first-generation or from underrepresented populations.

New Strategic Directions

Prioritizing JEDI efforts means intentionally taking a new approach. The programming described above, while data-driven and effective, has been developed in response to library goals (e.g., providing support for students and faculty in sustainability research and practice, and communication with to donors who support the Libraries sustainability fund about the good things they help make happen) or reactionary (e.g., a donor funds a collection which is highlighted and used toward shared goals). While these efforts have been well-intentioned, they lacked an underpinning of intent that invited audiences to actively help the Libraries change and grow. The Libraries Leadership Team is working to set strategy for a JEDI-informed communications approach to reach all stakeholders.

In one example of what this might look like, the Libraries' student success and engagement team has been charged with co-creating programming in dialog with our diverse audiences. We want to launch all efforts by inviting input: asking what audiences need and want and then incorporating those ideas into subsequent programming. The Libraries are also focusing on discovering what audiences view as barriers and then removing them whenever possible.

For the annual Du Bois Lecture in 2023, this new approach means focusing on the widest possible audience; for example, live-streaming the lecture across platforms and captioning it to be freely accessible, to allow for maximum participation.

In the early stages of adopting a co-creative framework for JEDI programming, The Library Leadership Team worked with librarians and staff to find partners for JEDI initiatives. We researched what was already going on within communities, finding out what was already being planned and in need of broader support. Among the initial efforts included sponsoring the film *Powerlands* for Indigenous People's Month (as noted earlier in the chapter) and a dance lesson during Latinx Heritage Month, using our sponsorship to broaden the audience for the events and helping to remove financial barriers.

The Libraries' Outreach Series

The Libraries' Outreach Series and corresponding RECESS space (Recharge, Engage, Connect, Energize, Support, Succeed) has been established as the format in which the UMass student communities will partner with the Libraries for co-creating programming going forward.

The Libraries have long been focused on how to feel welcoming to all students, including finding creative ways to bring them through the doors. Before the pandemic, the Libraries offered Finals Fun with snacks and arts and crafts to de-stress and partnered with peer health educators on campus to provide canine companionship twice a semester in the W. E. B. Du Bois Library lobby with Bright Spot Therapy Dogs.

During the first pandemic phase of remote learning, connecting with students became even more important. The Libraries' hosted its first virtual Get Your Game On board game night. More than 70 students joined via Zoom and spent nearly two hours playing bingo, trivia, Pictionary, and Scattergories. As the event wrapped up, a number of attendees asked for more events like it.

In response to input from students craving opportunities for connection, the Libraries' Outreach Librarian and the Associate Editor for Digital Content formed the Library Outreach Team and collaborated to build out a bimonthly virtual game night series for the rest of the semester. The success of those events led to the development of the Libraries Outreach Series, which, in addition to games, offered weekly activities such as yoga, virtual concerts, open mic night, and online visits with the therapy dogs.

For the 2021–2022 school year, which saw the return of students to our residential campus, the Outreach Series moved to in-person, which allowed for even more types of events, including arts and crafts activities and an improv workshop.

Throughout the evolution of the Outreach Series, the act of co-creation with students as full partners has been key to this work. For the Libraries, this has taken the form of paper-based surveys, white boards with prompts for students to respond to at will, and a trial participatory design initiative involving first-generation students that will inform the co-creative efforts going forward.

Co-creating virtual and physical spaces where students feel they belong is an essential aspect of supporting student success. Feeling like they belong in the Libraries and on campus helps students make connections, which directly supports their mental health and their academic journey.

Equipped with survey data proving the impact of the Libraries' focus on well-being, and the types of events students favored, the Library Outreach Team proposed converting an underutilized room in the Du Bois Library into a study break space with games, crafts, and opportunities for connection; this space also provides a central and easily accessible venue for events held as part of the Libraries Outreach Series.

Of the more than 300 attendees initially surveyed, every student indicated the Libraries Outreach Series events helped with a combination of well-being, making connections, relaxing, and recharging. Many commented that they appreciated "being able to wind down and take my mind off things," "meeting new people, the chill environment," and "[relaxing] with friends in a space big enough for all of us." By creating a space **for** students, **by** students, and **with** students, the Libraries' goals were met, too: More than 90 percent of students surveyed said they would be more likely to use library services and resources after attending an Outreach Series event.

Having established this strong foundation for student interaction with library programming, the next phase that will be undertaken is focused on finding how best to incorporate diverse student voices into library planning. As educators and advocates, serving students must be at the center of the campus's planning, says Pearson, the monomial director of New Student Orientation and Transitions at UMass Amherst.

The creation of this library space is a testament to putting students first. The Libraries should be a liberating, inclusive environment where students can feel intimately connected and cared for, and that is what the creation of RECESS has done. Many incoming students have a limited perspective of what a library can provide. Student success, student well-being, and student belonging must be integrated, collaborative work from our entire campus. The Libraries' creation of RECESS demonstrates their commitment to student success, and to listening to the campus and institutional student needs.

Using Participatory Design

In line with educational institutions' emphasis on student well-being, many academic libraries, like the UMass Amherst Libraries, have been creating their own wellness initiatives. The growing involvement of libraries in supporting well-being on campuses has been identified as one of the 2020 top trends in academic libraries by the Association of College and Research Libraries (Research and Review Committee, 2020).

The emerging interest in developing library services, programs, and spaces that facilitate student wellness is an example of a social turn in library innovation, or a shift from collection-based to com-

Foundation and Future Directions for JEDI at U. of Massachusetts Libraries

munity-oriented service models. In this new framework, libraries take a holistic approach to the student experience, actively seeking partners and collaborators within and beyond the institution.

During the Fall semester 2022, the UMass Libraries Outreach Librarian collaborated with the Library Data Analyst to pilot a participatory design project involving first-generation students. The goal was for a small group to work together with Libraries staff over the course of eight meetings to create materials or messages that would assist other first-generation students in gaining familiarity with the Libraries' resources and services. The students were offered lunch and a stipend for their time. The students produced social media messages relevant to first-gen students and others who were new to academic library spaces and resources.

The first iteration of this effort produced other results that, while unexpected, have proven beneficial to planning future efforts of this sort. For example, the Libraries learned that student feedback groups need time to feel comfortable with each other, so having a semester-long cohort worked; convening the group over lunch, however, was not as successful, so future meetings will be in the afternoon with snacks instead of a meal. Compensation was the reason students were attracted to the opportunity to offer feedback to the Libraries; they continued to participate, however, because of the sense of importance and belonging they felt as part of the group's work.

Based on these results, the Libraries will engage a new set of students next year to provide input and feedback into events and programming. Specifically, students will be asked to share their ideas about an awards program the Libraries are planning that will showcase undergraduate projects and experiences. Libraries staff also ask students to provide input on the RECESS space, the Outreach Series, and potential pop-up ideas for marketing library services.

Connecting Library Expertise with Students: The Libraries Workshop Series

The Libraries Workshops Series has been a way for staff in the Libraries to offer short sessions on topics within their areas of expertise. In Fall 2020, when the campus was primarily remote, a small organizing group within the Libraries focused on pivoting the Libraries workshop series from in-person to online. This pivot was quite successful for the Libraries, both for increasing accessibility for patrons within and beyond the UMass Amherst community and encouraging more staff within the Libraries to develop workshops in their areas of expertise. Each academic year, the number of workshops offered has grown by semester, with 2020-2021 seeing 31 workshops in the fall, and 35 in the spring. The 2021-2022 series featured 47 workshops in the fall semester, and a significant increase to 87 in the spring, with the annual total more than doubling from 66 in 2020-2021 to 134 in 2021-2022. This growth seems to be holding steady, with 85 workshops offered in the fall semester of 2022 alone. When the Libraries returned to in-person services in Fall 2021, the workshops remained primarily online, though subsequent years have seen a hybrid approach to workshop offerings; this allows for workshops to be accessible to members of the community regardless of their location.

The organizing group worked closely with Development and Communications to improve the marketing of workshops. Analysis shows that people have registered from across all colleges and schools at UMass Amherst. There is often at least one registrant from each of the departments within a college or school. The workshops also have a broad reach across other departments and areas at UMass, including entities such as Foundation Relations, Information Technology, Office of Research Development, Student Affairs and Campus Life, UMass Cranberry Station, UMass Donahue Institute, University Health Services, and more.

Over time, the breadth of topics of the series has dramatically increased. Previous workshops were focused primarily on basic topics within information literacy. Each semester, more people within the Libraries taught within the program after they heard about their colleague's experiences and the positive feedback and suggestions for other topics from workshop participants. Topic areas now include area studies research methods, citation managers, citizen science, contemplative pedagogies, data services, literature reviews, open educational resources, open scholarship and managing one's researcher profiles, patents, science fun nights, software, technologies, and introductions to the libraries for different audiences such as first-generation students. These sessions help build connections with the community and the Libraries consistently receive feedback about the willingness of instructors to create a welcoming learning environment; e.g., "Sometimes it isn't just about the content of the workshop, but the feelings of camaraderie it helps to generate." Expanding the topics we teach is important for connection and belonging. We want our students and community to see the Libraries as a welcoming place to ask questions even if they are outside what people traditionally see as the bailiwick of libraries. The Libraries will continue to widen the breadth of topics within this series and use the evidence generated from consistent survey practices to further the program's reach. In the future, The Libraries envision inviting campus partners to teach workshops within the program as part of the goal to increase collaborations with the Libraries.

Portfolio Project

The Libraries have been exploring the relation of library usage to student success through the Portfolio Project, led by Libraries Assessment & Planning staff. This effort followed the class of 2021 from their freshman year through graduation by tracking their use of library services, such as use of physical materials, participation in library instruction and use of reservable library rooms. The results of the project suggest that the use of different library services correlates with higher graduate rates within four years and higher retention rates. The retention rate to the second year was 17% higher for students who had library instruction than students who did not. Graduation rates within four years were 63% higher for students who had library instruction versus students who did not. For students who checked out physical library materials, they had graduation rates (within four years) that were 10% higher than those who did not. Students using reservable library rooms graduated in four years 16% more than students who did not use the rooms. In the future, the Libraries would like to develop closer relationships with the entities on campus focused on student success to explore expanding this type of research and incorporating library services into student success measurements across campus.

Reconfiguration of Student Success and Engagement Department

The UMass Amherst Libraries experienced the same circumstances during the pandemic as others, including a high number of vacancies due to retirements and shifts in career focus. This opened the opportunity to re-imagine the Student Success & Engagement (SSE) department, which had previously focused on staffing the Learning Commons and included the Digital Media Lab. The newly revised department will instead partner with the departments and groups on campus that support student success and focus on connection and belonging, such as the UMass JEDI Collaborative, the Center for Multicultural Advancement and Student Success, Disability Services, New Students Orientation and Transitions, Off Campus Student Life, the Office of Equity and Inclusion, the Graduate School Office of Inclusion and Engagement, Residential Life Residence Education, Student Engagement and Leadership, and Student

Foundation and Future Directions for JEDI at U. of Massachusetts Libraries

Success. Staffed by a department head, two student success librarians, and the peer research consultant program supervisor, the department will not only collaborate with the aforementioned areas but, more importantly, will partner with students and student groups to help all areas of the Libraries enhance existing programs and services and develop new programs and services based upon their experiences and feedback.

The Peer Research Consultant program, a key initiative to increase inclusion among students who make use of the Libraries, had been a resounding success for the Libraries prior to the pandemic. Students in this program were stationed at the Learning Commons desk, where they answered or triaged reference questions, including those that came via email and chat, and were available for peer research consultations. Peer research consultants were taught the basics of research assistance, including reference interviews, as well as friendly customer service methods. They met weekly as a group and were continually trained in different resources and approaches. Librarians who previously staffed the desk were impressed by the dedication, curiosity, and competence of the student consultants. Anecdotally, it seemed that students were more likely to approach the desk and actually ask questions when the peer research consultants were present. Unfortunately, the previous peer research consultants graduated while the campus was closed for 18 months during the pandemic.

The program was resurrected in Fall 2022 upon the return to a primarily in-person campus experience, which concurred with the hiring of a new program supervisor. Under the guidance of this new staff member, training for peer research consultants has already been expanded to include more hands-on experience with services offered within the main library building by the Libraries, services offered within the building from other campus departments, as well as services and spaces at the branch Science & Engineering Library. The new department will work with the other peer consultant programs on campus, such as the Tutoring Center and the Writing Center, to explore opportunities for cross-training and cross-promotion of services rather than having each service operate in silos with only vague knowledge of each other. The Libraries' student success staff will also seek partnerships with Student Affairs and Campus Life to offer peer research assistance outside the Libraries that will reach students in the places where they gather to eat and socialize.

Open Educational Resource Efforts

UMass Amherst recognizes that that Open Educational Resources (OERs) represent an opportunity to address the financial challenge of ever-increasing textbook and material costs; it is a clear way to be inclusive and equitable for students who may not otherwise have easy access to high-quality course materials, or who may be disinclined to pursue particular educational paths due to cost. However, the Libraries have also faced challenges when trying to engage faculty in the process of developing OERs – a challenge better represented as benign disinterest rather than outright disdain on the UMass Amherst campus. The Libraries initial approach involved liaison librarians evangelizing broadly about the benefits of OER and trying to convince faculty of their value, which was admittedly unsuccessful in part due to a lack of targeted coordination and clear solid goals.

Currently the Libraries are focused on two efforts: the Open Education Initiative (OEI) Grant and strategic planning through participation in the 2022-2023 Association of Colleges & Universities (AAC&U) Institute on Open Educational Resources. The OEI grant is a collaboration with the Provost's Office that is coordinated by the Libraries, and which provides funding for instructors to adopt, adapt, or create OER. Grant recipients are selected by a cross-campus committee comprised of staff from the

Libraries, Center for Teaching and Learning (CTL), and Instructional Design, Engagement, and Support (IDEAS). In 2022, the committee focused on prioritizing projects that would impact large numbers of students, preferably in a General Education course. We will assess the changes to process in this year's grant cycle, along with the effectiveness of the grant to encourage faculty to engage with OER and creating a promotion plan for completed projects funded by the grant.

The AAC&U Institute on Open Education Resources has been an excellent opportunity for the Libraries to develop strategic goals for OER awareness and adoption in collaboration with other campus partners invested in OER. The team includes the Open Education Librarian, Peer Research Consultant Program Supervisor, and Associate Dean for Research & Learning from the Libraries, the Lead Instructional Designer and Faculty Support Coordinator from the IDEAS group, and the Student Services Coordinator from University Without Walls, a primarily online program for students returning to higher education to complete their bachelor's degrees. The Libraries participation in the Institute is helping to develop scaffolded realistic goals and a focused action plan for increasing awareness and usage of OERs to decrease barriers to education on campus. The first goal is to step back and assess the current landscape of OER use on campus. Once staff understand the current landscape, the group will focus on developing strategies to implement course marking in the course system, determine the feasibility and action plan for creating support structures across the Libraries, CTL and IDEAS to increase faculty adoption of open pedagogical approaches, and the most effective ways to engage students in understanding, promoting and possibly creating content for OER and co-creating strategies with the Libraries.

Addressing JEDI Through the Lens of Special Collections

The guiding principles for developing a robust set of special collections to support research, teaching, and learning will vary widely from institution to institution, informed as they are by the way each university defines its mission and decides to interact with the world. However, regardless of these differences, the aforementioned guiding principles are also a natural place to examine the philosophical approach of an institution to JEDI initiatives. The Robert S. Cox Special Collections and University Archives Research Center (SCUA) at UMass Amherst has been guided by the principle of documenting social change, with additional focuses on entrepreneurship and the local history of Western Massachusetts. As noted in the opening of this chapter, among the collections already contained in SCUA are the papers of W. E. B. Du Bois, whose importance as a multidisciplinary Black scholar and author cannot be overstated; as well as those of Horace Mann Bond, an influential scholar and educator who served in leadership roles at a number of historically Black colleges and universities (HBCUs) and wrote extensively on subjects involving race and education; and the "Visibility for Disability" set of collections, which document the history of individuals and groups engaged in the (ongoing) fight for disability rights protections. There are a great number of other SCUA collections and resources that intersect with or touch on the principles of justice, equity, diversity, and inclusion as well.

The existence of these collections, however, simply isn't sufficient to say that SCUA – or the UMass Libraries as a whole – is engaged in the necessary work of promoting JEDI at UMass Amherst; it is critical for these collections to be activated in the curriculum, where students and faculty may connect with – and be inspired by – the work and writing of those who grappled with questions of justice, diversity, equity, and inclusion prior to the present moment, and where researchers of today may encounter ideas and insights that have informed the global discourse. In both cases, the potential exists for a deepening

Foundation and Future Directions for JEDI at U. of Massachusetts Libraries

and a broadening of the JEDI conversation, on campus and beyond, but only if approached through the active and deliberate use of a JEDI lens.

In a practical sense, this means reviewing any extant collection development policy or guidelines for SCUA to identify what may already exist in terms of JEDI focus and revising the policy or guidelines as appropriate to provide a framework enabling both the current and future staff to include consideration of how particular gifts or strategic acquisitions would further the essential commitment to justice, equity, diversity, and inclusion. This is not to say that such a framework would become a rubric for turning away collections; rather, it would be used to evaluate where new or proposed accessions would fit in the larger context of the overall collections, to understand what gaps or omissions still exist in the growth and development of SCUA's holdings, and to set strategic priorities for addressing such omissions.

Expanding the Archive of Social Change

"There must come vast social change in the United States; a change not violent, but by the will of the people certain and inexorable; carried out 'with malice toward none but charity for all'; with meticulous justice to the rich and complete sympathy for the poor, the sick and the ignorant; with freedom and democracy for America, and on earth Peace, Good Will toward men."

W. E. B. Du Bois, Chicago, June 29, 1951

For more than a decade, the UMass Amherst Libraries' Robert S. Cox Special Collections and University Archives has intentionally focused collecting efforts on materials related to social change. The W. E. B. Du Bois Papers—the most-used collection within its care, 100,000 items documenting the life and work of the activist, author, and sociologist—serve as keystone.

Drawing upon the philosophy of Du Bois, the Libraries' collects original materials documenting the histories and experiences of social change in America and the organizational, intellectual, and individual ties that unite struggles for social justice, human dignity, and equality. Additional collecting foci are regional and university materials, innovation and entrepreneurship, and the spaces where these intersect with social change.

The Libraries' focus on collecting the history of social change emerged from one of Du Bois's key insights: that the most fundamental issues in social justice are so deeply interconnected that no movement—and no solution to social ills—can succeed in isolation. Rather than focusing on individual movements, the Libraries focus on the connections between and among movements, and the flow of people, organizations, and ideas. The goal of this approach was to build a more robust framework for interpreting the history of social engagement in America and to lay the foundation for a deeper understanding of the experience of social change.

Emphasizing the cross-fertilization between social movements and centers of activist energy, SCUA collects materials from individuals and organizations involved in peace and non-violence; social and racial justice; economic justice; drug policy; agricultural reform; environmentalism; sustainability; alternative energy; organized labor; gay rights; disability rights; spiritual activism; antinuclear activism; indigenous peoples, and intentional communities.

Embedding Special Collections in Library Spaces

Library spaces present opportunities to showcase social justice collections and resources. While the main library building is named for Du Bois, and the Du Bois Center on floor 22 also bears his name, there is a lack of information and entry points to his legacy in the most-used library spaces.

New initiatives seek to better utilize public space toward JEDI goals. The main library entry floor is being transformed from a pass-through service space to an exhibition area with materials from collections on display physically and digitally. A bust of Du Bois, previously tucked away on the 25th floor reading room, will be moved to the lower level, the most-visited space on campus, and joined by a bust of B.R. Ambedkar, a visual representation of intention and synergy around social justice.

JEDI Action Plan and Task Force

In recognition of the foregoing challenges, and under new leadership, the Libraries will be creating a JEDI Framework that holistically looks at services, spaces, procedures, policies, and opportunities for learning and growth across all library units and for the variety of stakeholders and patrons who engage with the Libraries. The Framework will include how the Libraries can enhance connection and belonging, which are critical areas for the entire campus, including students, staff, and faculty. By using a JEDI lens, the Libraries will seek to better understand how inclusion and diversity of thought can be increased across the Libraries' services and engagements. The JEDI Task Force will be assembled from across the Libraries staff, including both professional and paraprofessional staff, and will convene to identify the key challenges and opportunities inherent in the Libraries' engagement with the campus, and to provide recommendations that will shape an action plan that provides strategic focus areas and milestones to gauge progress. Examples that may be integrated in the action plan include many of the threads running through this chapter, such as conscious editing, applying a JEDI lens to instruction (e.g., ensuring that examples provided as part of information fluency/literacy instruction are based on diverse audiences and experiences), curating collections that help marginalized voices and experiences be heard and made available, identifying programming that supports connection and belonging, and creating opportunities for students to co-create artistic representations that can be included in library spaces. It is likely that during the work of the Task Force there will be additional themes and opportunities that will emerge and be incorporated into the action plan. This framework will also include recommendations for JEDI funding that will enable a OneLibrary approach be taken to support JEDI work and ideas and formative assessment and evaluation approaches to our programs, services, collections, and spaces. UMass Amherst Libraries sees JEDI work as a principle in which there will be continued growth and not one that will be accomplished in a "check-box" fashion or by reaching one specific goal; this will be part and parcel of the Libraries now and into the future to enable the creation of a connective thread where the UMass Amherst Libraries are a place for all.

REFERENCES

Bennett, L., Jr. (1980, Sept. 19). Lecture on opening of W.E.B. Du Bois papers [Paper presentation]. In Dedication of the W.E.B. Du Bois Papers, University of Massachusetts, Amherst, MA, United States.

Berry, W. (1970). *The hidden wound*. Counterpoint.

Bromery, R. (1974). *The W. E. B. Du Bois Center for Intellectual Leadership*. Randolph Bromery Papers (Box 2, L-2 Folder), University of Massachusetts Amherst Libraries, Amherst, MA, United States.

Du Bois, W. E. B. (1926). The Criteria of Negro Art. *Crisis, 32*(10), 296.

Du Bois, W. E. B. (1951, June 29). *Need for social change in the United States*. W. E. B. Du Bois Papers (MS 312), Special Collections and University Archives, University of Massachusetts Amherst Libraries, Amherst, MA, United States.

Research Planning and Review Committee. (2020). 2020 top trends in academic libraries: A review of the trends and issues affecting academic libraries in higher education. *College & Research Libraries News, 81*(6), 270. doi:10.5860/crln.81.6.270

ADDITIONAL READING

University Libraries, UMass Amherst. (2018). *Collections Priorities Focus Areas*. https://www.library.umass.edu/wp-content/uploads/2022/03/Colhttp://lectionsPriorities2018-final.pdf

University of Massachusetts Amherst. (2023a, June 2). *W.E.B. Du Bois Papers*. Robert S. Cox Special Collections & University Archives Research Center. Retrieved June 2, 2023, from http://scua.library.umass.edu/?s=du+bois

University of Massachusetts Amherst. (2023b, June 2). *W.E.B. Du Bois Papers*. Robert S. Cox Special Collections & University Archives Research Center. Retrieved June 2, 2023, from http://scua.library.umass.edu/irma-mcclaurin-black-feminist-archive/

University of Massachusetts Amherst. (2023c, June 2). *W.E.B. Du Bois Papers*. Robert S. Cox Special Collections & University Archives Research Center. Retrieved June 2, 2023, from http://scua.library.umass.edu/category/social-change/disability/

University of Massachusetts Amherst. (2023d, June 2). *W.E.B. Du Bois Papers*. Robert S. Cox Special Collections & University Archives Research Center. Retrieved June 2, 2023, from http://scua.library.umass.edu/quakers-of-color/

Zelanzo, M. (2022, December 2). *A place for ALL: The Libraries' critical role in supporting student success*. Retrieved from https://www.library.umass.edu/news/a-place-for-all-the-libraries-critical-role-in-supporting-student-success/

KEY TERMS AND DEFINITIONS

JEDI: The acronym stands for Justice, Equity, Diversity, and Inclusion and refers to incorporating these values into discussions and actions about belonging, community, ethics, and inclusive spaces.

OneLibrary: Being part of and functioning as OneLibrary entails embracing a holistic approach that takes into account the collective requirements. It involves nurturing our shared objectives, fostering an inclusive perspective, and acknowledging that each individual's contributions are crucial to achieving our mission. Moreover, it necessitates recognizing and valuing the distinctiveness of individuals, units, and departments that form an integral part of the entirety of our endeavors and aspirations. By adopting a OneLibrary philosophy and lens by which we connect with each other and our work, we actively demonstrate our appreciation for the diverse skills, experiences, and perspectives of all, thereby enriching the collective entity as a whole.

RECESS: A place to Recharge, Engage, Connect, Energize, Support, and Succeed—is located on the second floor of the W. E. B. Du Bois Library. This friendly space is dedicated to student wellbeing, relaxation, recharging, and connecting. In addition to being a place for students to gather, take breaks, and enjoy non-academic activities, RECESS is home to the Libraries Outreach Series.

Chapter 10

Assessment of Justice, Equity, Diversity, and Inclusion (JEDI) Initiatives in Public Libraries:
Perspectives From a Public Library in a Developing Country

Ismail Olatunji Adeyemi
https://orcid.org/0000-0001-9822-5950
Kwara State University, Nigeria

ABSTRACT

This chapter focuses on the assessment of justice, equity, diversity, and inclusion (JEDI) initiatives in a public library in a developing country; a focus on Kwara State Library Board (KSLB) in Ilorin, Nigeria. This study is case-study research designed, adopting a qualitative research approach. The findings of the study showed that there is no form of diversity in the staffing at Kwara State Library Board, which will hinder its globalization. It was revealed in the study that there is no JEDI initiative in the workforce of the library. Moreover, it was found that there is no form of book censorship in Kwara State Library Board and there is diversity in the provision of information resources for the visually impaired users. It was, however, shown that there is no form of JEDI initiative as to the information services provided at Kwara State Library Board. It was concluded that Kwara State Library Board has JEDI initiatives in information resources available in the library, but it is lacking in JEDI initiatives for information services and workforce.

INTRODUCTION

Justice, equity, diversity, and inclusion (JEDI) initiatives are ideas, strategies, and/or techniques that are adopted to ensure that all people of social strata in a society get their required recognition and acceptance in the provision of service. In this context, this means the inclusion of all members of the society

DOI: 10.4018/978-1-6684-7255-2.ch010

Copyright © 2023, IGI Global. Copying or distributing in print or electronic forms without written permission of IGI Global is prohibited.

regardless of their socioeconomic standings, gender, age, ethnicities, religions, level of education, and other factors in the provision of library and information services. Public libraries are established to ensure that all members of the society are adequately provided with relevant information services that will help combat the different challenges faced by a community (Forsyth, 2005). These information services require meeting the diverse and varying information needs of the community and have been entrenched with the advent of the Internet (Bertot *et al.*, 2009).

With the diversity in the information needs of the community of patrons, public libraries are saddled with the responsibilities of implementing initiatives that will enhance or propagate justice, equity, diversity, and inclusion (JEDI). With the paradigm shift over time in information service provision, it becomes markedly important to ensure that marginalized communities are catered for by the contemporary library systems, structures, and staff (Brimhall-Vargas, 2015). For instance, it is assumed that the increasing shift from paper to electronic resources may leave out the less educated strata of the society since they cannot make use of the computer systems to access e-resources available. Moreover, the physically challenged society may have challenges in accessing such resources when there is no provision of assistive technologies or access tools that will facilitate their information use.

Recently, Yusuf et al. (2022) made an effort to provide a possible solution in pedagogical approaches and library utilization in the Nigerian society, but there was no evidence provided on the status quo with respect to JEDI initiatives in Nigerian libraries. The authors discussed the challenges of the vulnerable library users without evidence on the nature of inequality in the library workforce, information resources, and information services. Having knowledge of these would entrench JEDI in Nigerian public libraries. In a study on excluding the visually impaired in Nigerian academic libraries' webpages, Zaid (2017) concluded that none of the ten (10) Nigerian academic libraries that were studied provided core services for persons with visual impairment. The author recommended that libraries should work with the full intent of integrating library users that are visually impaired into the mainstream library services. This call motivates this chapter to explore the reality of JEDI initiatives in Nigerian public library, using the Kwara State Library Board as a case study.

There have been several studies conducted on the information services provision in public libraries in developing countries, particularly Nigeria. Since the public libraries in Nigeria are funded by state and local governments, it has been observed that the issue of funding is a major challenge to meeting the information needs of their users. This is corroborated by the findings of Iwhiwhu and Okorodudu (2012) that users are not satisfied with the information resources and services provided at Edo State public libraries and they were satisfied with the facilities. This users' unsatisfactory report indicates that the information resources are inadequate and the information services provided in the library are not all-inclusive. Naturally, leaving out a category of prospective library users in information service provision will make the users unsatisfied with the information provided.

Information services provision has been confronted for a long time with challenges of diversity and inclusion, and in engaging with numerous groups. However, the library and information professionals have also developed a number of novel strategies for addressing information needs of the diverse community and integrating concerns about justice, rights, and equity (Jaeger *et al.*, 2015). All these are in effort towards ensuring that JEDI initiatives are implemented to propagate all-inclusive information services and resources provision. Despite the relatively extensive research on public library services in Nigeria, little or no attention has been placed on the issues of justice, equity, diversity, and inclusion. Meanwhile, Nigeria is a diverse society with well over two hundred and fifty (250) ethnic groups (Adedini *et al.*, 2015). All these arguments underscore the importance of enhancing diversity and inclusiveness

Assessment of JEDI Initiatives in Public Libraries

in information service provision. Thus, this chapter seeks to analyse the initiative of justice, equity, diversity, and inclusion initiatives in Kwara State Library Board (KSLB), Ilorin, Nigeria. The specific objectives of this essay are to:

i. Examine justice, equity, diversity, and inclusion (JEDI) initiatives among workforce in Kwara State Library Board (KSLB), Ilorin;
ii. Analyse justice, equity, diversity, and inclusion (JEDI) initiatives in information resources available in KSLB; and
iii. Evaluate justice, equity, diversity, and inclusion (JEDI) initiatives in information services provided at KSLB.

The arrangement of the chapter is such that the methodology adopted in collecting the relevant information and data are discussed after the introductory section. This is to acquaint prospective readers with the approach and technique adopted in collecting the relevant information for the chapter. The justice, equity, diversity, and inclusion (JEDI) initiatives at the Kwara State Library Board are also discussed, focusing on the workforce (staffing), information resources, and information services. Conclusion was drawn from the findings that emanated from the data and/or information collected for the study. Whence, recommendations were made to enhance justice, equity, diversity, and inclusion (JEDI) initiatives in KSLB.

METHODOLOGY

The research design for this chapter is a case-study, focusing on Kwara State Library Board (KSLB), Ilorin, Kwara State, Nigeria. This chapter adopts qualitative research approach so as to collect in-depth and detailed information about the phenomenon under study. Both primary and secondary data were collected to achieve the aim of the study. Interpretivism philosophical assumption was adopted for this study since there is no objective reality of the themes under study in the context of Nigerian public libraries (Van der Walt, 2020). According to Hammersley (2013), interpretivism is a theory based on the presumption that knowledge, related to the human and social sciences, is understood differently than knowledge related to the physical sciences. This idea is predicated on the notion that those who live in a specific location are the ones who encounter and observe social processes there. Thus, they are in the best position to provide the relevant specific answers to questions emanating from that environment. It is based on this that primary data were collected adopting participant observation and interview of two staff members of the Kwara State Library Board (KSLB), Ilorin.

In-depth interviews were conducted with the participants of the study who were staff members of Kwara State Library Board, Ilorin. The names of the staff members that were interviewed for this study are redacted in this study to ensure confidentiality and anonymity. The two participants were codified with the names, "Participant 1" and "Participant 2". Collected interview data were analysed using thematic analysis. Interview were recorded into audio format, and transcribed on a Microsoft Word. The interviewees were given their copies of the transcribed interview report to ensure that their responses were not misrepresented. This would also enhance language consistency, credibility, and trustworthiness of the interview. This is known as member check to enhance the reliability and validity of the interview (Korstjens & Moser, 2018). Participant observation was carried out by the researcher being in direct contact with the staff members of the different units of the KSLB. During the course of the observation, field notes were taken and analysed to support the interview conducted on the participants. The observation was carried out during the work hour of the Library, spending a total of three hours for three days making nine hours in total. Moreover, the secondary data that was collected for this study is the replete of literature that have been conducted on justice, equity, diversity, and inclusion in library and information centers.

RESULTS AND DISCUSSION

JEDI Initiatives of Workforce at KSLB

While these justice, equity, diversity, and inclusion terms have been used interchangeably, there are marked differences among them (Cooper & Leegwater, 2018). The purpose of diversity is to "create an inclusive culture that values and uses the talents of all would-be members" (Herring, 2009, p. 209). Baldwin *et al.* (2007) showed that multiculturalism and social justice will give employees the confidence they need to face injustices, start dismantling ingrained prejudice beliefs, and develop socially fair practices. In this context, lack of maintenance of social justice and diversity among the library staff may lead to socially unfair service provision to prospective library users. With the understanding that prospective users of public libraries are more diverse than other categories of libraries, there is a need to ingrain systemic and structural JEDI initiatives that will propel information service provision. This makes it important to promote theoretical discussions and practices in the area of JEDI in public libraries.

There has been plethora of studies on diversity and equity in library and information science education (Abdullahi, 2007; Kumasi & Manlove, 2015; Poole, 2021; Poole et al., 2021), and library as a workplace (Grissom, 2018; Ocholla, 2002). This suggests that the focus has majorly been on the workforce and LIS curriculum. Inazu *et al.* (2021) showed that the results of improper management of the diverse workforce in libraries include ineffective service delivery, conflict, subpar performance, and employee turnover. More crucially, poor management of diversity can hamper the success of a library to provide timely and current information to their patrons in this era of information explosion, where adaptability, innovation and creativity are the keys to competition (Fagbe *et al.*, 2019). Geiger *et al.* (2022) found that inadequate support for DEI in a library would lead to librarians' low morale and dismayed.

In the case of KSLB, it was found from the interview conducted that there are only Kwara State indigenes working in the Library. Meanwhile, there is diversity in the staffing of the library as to the three senatorial districts in the State, namely Kwara South, Kwara Central, and Kwara North. It was shown that most of the staff members are of the Kwara Central. Thus, this may suggest marginalization of Kwara South and Kwara North. It may be overly simplistic to take this revelation in its entirety as there is a possibility that there are limited applicants from Kwara South and Kwara North who are qualified for the available positions in the Library.

Participant 1:

"Many of our staff here (KSLB) are from Kwara Central."

Meanwhile, there is no data point or empirical evidence to show the qualified individuals across the senatorial districts that are in Kwara State. Thus, conclusion on this should be made with caution and consideration for future data point or empirical studies. Regardless of that, KSLB should endeavour to

Assessment of JEDI Initiatives in Public Libraries

ensure diversity in their workforce along different States in Nigeria if they are to enhance globalization. This is because be benefits of diversity in workplace are numerous and valuable (Foma, 2014).

JEDI Initiative in Information Resources Available at KSLB

Meanwhile, there is a need for strategic planning and implementation of library services and practices in ensuring inclusion and social equity (Cruz, 2019). Kwara State Library Board (KSLB) has different kind of information resources. The study showed that the acquisition of information resources has not been hindered by factors such as book bans, but by inadequate funding which appears to be a general problem to public libraries in Nigeria. For instance, Fiske (2022) argued that book banning is a detrimental initiative to information service provision. Hicks (2022) established that library users have their rights to read and parents/caregivers have the rights to influence their children's choices at a time when book bans are becoming more prevalent across the United States (US). The authors also support the duties and rights of school administrators, librarians, and school board members to provide books that reflect the diversity present across the country.

In Nigeria, book banning or censorship are methodically done through crude force and mostly not the use of legal framework as we have in the developed countries. Meanwhile, it has been established that some of the methods adopted in ensuring book censorship in Nigeria include burning, bombing, censorship by intimidation, author strangulation, and illegal burning. There is also a state-sponsored book burning in Kano State with the argument that the books are "immoral" and "pornographic" to the customs and tradition of the State (Ifeduba, 2018). Being a State in the northern part of Nigeria as well, there has never been issue of book censorship through whatever methods or strategy. This indicates that Kwara State Library Board (KSLB) has never engaged in the act of book censorship, which may reflect badly on the Library's diversity, inclusion, equity, and social justice.

Participant 1:

"We don't have any kind of books that we keep away from our users. We acquire only books that are useful for the users. I would say in my experience working in this library, there has never been issue of book censorship or some sort."

In the interview conducted with the two participants, it was elicited that Kwara State Library Board (KSLB) has a diverse range of resources. These resources include print resources (of all types) and Braille in the Special Unit. It was however found that KSLB does not have adequate e-resources for their teeming users. This means that the Library does not promote inclusive education with the available resources (Nachimuthu & Vijayakumari, 2012). The inclusion of more e-resources would make it easy for users to access information resources anytime and anywhere without border restriction, which would ultimately enhance inclusiveness. It will enhance inclusion as prospective users that may ordinarily need to visit the Library before making use of the available print resources would access the electronic resources provided it is available.

Participant 2:

"If you go to our Special Unit, you would find Braille for our visually impaired users."

The findings from the participant observation of the Special Unit of KSLB indicate that there is Braille resources in the Special Unit of the Library. This means that the visually impaired category of users is catered for in the available resources. It is important for librarians who work with the visually impaired students to be aware of the social advantages of culturally diverse books. They do not have to wait for more study or for the Braille book market to produce more works that represent many racial and ethnic groupings. In addition to providing their users with culturally diverse Braille books, the Special Unit librarians that cater for the visually impaired children can assist in putting Braille overlays to culturally diverse print books in the library collections (Coleman *et al.*, 2022). Other library resources that should be provided for the visually impaired users include talking books, talking newspapers, large printed materials, and electronic texts (Rayin, 2017). Meanwhile, the entrance to the Library is not helpful to this category of users as they may need helping hands to guide them through the mini-stairs at the entrance of the Library to their Unit.

Participant 1:

"We have Braille resources in our unit for the visually disadvantaged."

Moreover, findings from participant observation show that information services to the children category of users are ensured so that the young populace of Kwara State can make use of KSLB like the adults. Naidoo (2014) concluded in a White paper that diverse narratives should regularly be featured in library programs year-round and represented in print and digital material collections and displays for the children users. Meanwhile, it was found in the interview the participants that there is no children-focused program that promotes cultural diversity. It was however shown that there is an initiative program that advocates good reading culture among the users and prospective users of KSLB. The Library can consider incorporating the initiative of children-focused program that will educate children on the importance of diversity and inclusion.

JEDI Initiatives in Information Resources Available at KSLB

Kwara State Library Board (KSLB) provides broad and varying information services to users of the Library. It was found that some of these services include technical services, readers' services, acquisition, serials, reference services, special services, and children. For the technical services, based on the participant observation, it was revealed that there is no standard or careful consideration for justice, equity, diversity, and inclusion in services provision. Specifically, it was shown that the librarians-in-charge do not consider marginalized or "silenced" group in the selection of books to acquire for the Library. Moreover, there is no initiative guiding the readers' services that are provided in the Library. Meanwhile, there is a practice of taking users' statistics periodically in a day to ascertain the number of users that consult the library. This kind of practice can be redesigned to capture the need to elicit the usage of library across gender, religious, ethnicities, and other backgrounds. This will afford the Library opportunity to make informed decisions as to service provision to the diverse users.

Meanwhile, there are services provided to the special category of users in Kwara State Library Board (KSLB). The participant observation and the interview conducted showed that there are Braille resources available in the library. While there is a librarian in charge of the Special Unit, there is no specific or defined service being rendered in this Unit. It was observed that the users are more or less catering for themselves. This may inform the reason why there is low visitation of the library on the three days the

Assessment of JEDI Initiatives in Public Libraries

participant observations were conducted. There is a need to provide user-friendly services for this category of users. This can start with the provision of assistive technologies to enhance, and make easy, the services that are provided in the Unit of the Library. Some of these assistive technologies include screen magnifier, screen reader, and voice recognition software. Service provision to the visually impaired has been poor in developing countries owing to the dearth of accessible information resource (Rayini, 2017).

The findings of the interview revealed that a user of Kwara State Library Board (KSLB) is required to pay a token of NGN850 (NGN – Nigerian Naira) annually in order to make use of the library resources and services. Failure to make or renew the payment annually means that the user would be stopped from using the library. This amount of money is certainly far-reaching to some percentage of the Kwara State populace. There is however no evidence on the users' perceptions of how the fee-based approach influence their accessibility of the library. It has been established that such users' fees has impact on the social distribution of library and information services in public libraries in Denmark (Egholm & Jochumsen, 2000). The takeaway from this is that the developed nature of Denmark as a country did not stop the inequitable social distribution of information services as a result of users' fees. The anti-fee perspective is founded primarily on a communitarian ethic based on a long-standing partnership between public libraries and the communities they serve (Jaeger, 1999). Therefore, if the KSLB seeks to provide information services to those at the lower echelon of socioeconomic status, the Library should ensure that

There is a Children Section in KSLB that cater for the library and information services of teens that want to make use of the Library. Based on the findings from the participant observation, the Children Section is well-equipped with relevant facilities and resources that would satisfy the information needs of the prospective teen users. Kwara State Library Board (KSLB) categorized children as teens that cannot make use of the library without absolute support of the librarian-in-charge, which is dissimilar to IFLA's categorization of children users as those in age 0-18 (Rankin, 2018). Thus, it may be inaccurate to adopt all IFLA's guidelines and recommendations. Based on the interview conducted with the librarians, it was found that there is usually a low usage of the Children Section. Based on the participant observation, it was found that the low usage of the Children Section is owing to the lack of all-inclusive information services rendered in the Library. Therefore, the librarians and library management should consider carrying out an aggressive and strategic advocacy to bring the Section to more limelight.

CONCLUSION

The study established that there is no diversity in the staffing at Kwara State Library Board, which can hinder the Library's path to globalization. None of the staff members is from another State in Nigeria, which means all the staffers are from Kwara State. Meanwhile, employability of library staff in Nigerian public libraries should factor justice, inclusion, diversity, and equity. This can be achieved by ensuring that applicants of different origins or descents are given equal chance of being employed. The study concludes that there are no issues of book censorship in Kwara State Library Board, which indicate that JEDI initiatives in entrenched in the information resource available in the Library. This is achieved by ensuring the acquisition of information resources that are within the information needs of the library users. Moreover, Braille resources for visually impaired users can entrench diversity initiative in the information resources available in Nigerian public libraries. This is because it gives the visually impaired users the feeling of being part of the library's teeming users. Similarly, improvement in the acquisition of e-resources would also demonstrate public libraries' openness to the JEDI initiative. It can however be argued that the inclusiveness of these e-resources in Nigerian public library may be hampered by the inadequacy of the ICT infrastructure and Internet required to provide electronic information services. Moreover, it was established that information services should be provided to the children with programs that acquaint the children users to diversity and inclusion. The study concludes that there are no established progressive JEDI initiatives by the public library, which would enhance information service provision to the populace. It was established that the fee-based usage of public library would not enhance information accessibility and utilization. This can preclude prospective users to be provided library and information services, and can also be a dent on the effort to alleviate digital divide in the Nigerian society.

RECOMMENDATIONS

Based on the findings of the study, the following recommendations are made:

1. The library management and the Kwara State government should liaise on the eradication of the NGN850 annual user's fee in order to enhance inclusion of people in the low cadre of socioeconomic status.
2. JEDI initiatives that would enhance the knowledge of diversity and inclusion should be encouraged in the Children Section of the Library.
3. In order to ensure globalization, the library management and the State government should enhance the diversity and inclusion in the workforce of the Library.
4. Assistive tools and technologies should be acquired to improve information resources for the visually impaired users.
5. Future studies should empirically examine if the disparity in the workforce at KSLB is as a result of equity or marginalization in order to ensure diversity.
6. Future studies should examine the users' perceptions on how the fee-based technique and lack of promotion influence accessibility of the information resources at Nigerian public libraries.

REFERENCES

Abdullahi, I. (2007). Diversity and intercultural issues in library and information science (LIS) education. *New Library World.* https://www.emerald.com/insight/content/doi/10.1108/03074800 710823980/full/html

Adedini, S. A., Odimegwu, C., Imasiku, E. N., & Ononokpono, D. N. (2015). Ethnic differentials in under-five mortality in Nigeria. *Ethnicity & Health*, *20*(2), 145–162. https://www.tandfonline.com/doi/abs/10.1080/13557858.2014.89 0599. doi:10.1080/13557858.2014.890599 PMID:24593689

Baldwin, S. C., Buchanan, A. M., & Rudisill, M. E. (2007). What teacher candidates learned about diversity, social justice, and themselves from service-learning experiences. *Journal of Teacher Education*, *58*(4), 315–327. https://journals.sagepub.com/doi/abs/10.1177/002248710730525 9. doi:10.1177/0022487107305259

Assessment of JEDI Initiatives in Public Libraries

Bertot, J. C., Jaeger, P. T., McClure, C. R., Wright, C. B., & Jensen, E. (2009). Public libraries and the Internet 2008-2009: Issues, implications, and challenges. *First Monday*, *14*(11), 1–10. doi:10.5210/fm.v14i11.2700

Brimhall-Vargas, M. (2015). Where the rubber meets the road: The role of libraries and librarians in bringing equitable access to marginalized communities. *The Library Quarterly*, *85*(2), 193–199. https://www.journals.uchicago.edu/doi/abs/10.1086/680157. doi:10.1086/680157

Coleman, M. A., & Harrison, J. (2022). Cultural diversity in children's braille books. *Journal of Visual Impairment & Blindness*, *116*(2), 1–21. https://journals.sagepub.com/doi/abs/10.1177/0145482X221090261. doi:10.1177/0145482X221090261

Cooper, M. A., & Leegwater, L. (2018). Postsecondary equity through the lens of policy change. Change. *Change*, *50*(3–4), 102–106. doi:10.1080/00091383.2018.1509630

Cruz, A. M. (2019). Intentional integration of diversity ideals in academic libraries: A literature review. *Journal of Academic Librarianship*, *45*(3), 220–227. https://www.sciencedirect.com/science/article/pii/S009913331830377X. doi:10.1016/j.acalib.2019.02.011

Egholm, C., & Jochumsen, H. (2000). Perspectives concerning user fees in public libraries. *Library Management*, *21*(6), 298–306. https://www.emerald.com/insight/content/doi/10.1108/01435120010327605/full/html. doi:10.1108/01435120010327605

Fagbe, A. O., Fagbe, T., & Folorunso-Ako, A. O. (2019). Diversity management practices in the academic libraries in the age of globalization. *European Journal of Research in Social Sciences*, *7*(3), 15–25.

Fiske, M. (2022). *Book selection and censorship: A study of school and public libraries in California*. Univ of California Press.

Foma, E. (2014). Impact of workplace diversity. *Review of Integrative Business and Economics Research*, *3*(1), 382–410. http://buscompress.com/uploads/3/4/9/8/34980536/riber_sk14-026__402-410_.pdf

Forsyth, E. (2005). Public libraries and the millennium development goals. *IFLA Journal*, *31*(4), 315–323. https://journals.sagepub.com/doi/abs/10.1177/0340035205061389. doi:10.1177/0340035205061389

Geiger, L., Mastley, C. P., Thomas, M., & Rangel, E. (2022). Academic libraries and DEI initiatives: A quantitative study of employee satisfaction. *Journal of Academic Librarianship*, *102627*. https://www.sciencedirect.com/science/article/abs/pii/S0099133322001434

Grissom, A. R. (2018). Workplace diversity and inclusion. *Reference and User Services Quarterly*, *57*(4), 242–247. https://www.jstor.org/stable/90022643. doi:10.5860/rusq.57.4.6700

Herring, C. (2009). Does diversity pay?: Race, gender, and the business case for diversity. *American Sociological Review*, *74*(2), 208–224. https://journals.sagepub.com/doi/abs/10.1177/000312240907400203. doi:10.1177/000312240907400203

Hicks, T., Gabrion, L., Lester, K., & Schoenborn, A. (2022). Standing up and pushing back: Resources from a conversation around book bans and censorship. *Michigan Reading Journal, 54*(3), 61-73. https://scholarworks.gvsu.edu/cgi/viewcontent.cgi?article=29 28&context=mrj

Ifeduba, E. (2018). Book Censorship in Nigeria: A study of Origin, Methods and Motivations, 1805-2018. *Library Philosophy and Practice*, 1. https://core.ac.uk/download/pdf/189483740.pdf

Inazu, I. Q. I., Victoria, O., Omonori, A. A. O., Owansuan, J., & Sulaiman, A. M. (2021). Managing Workforce Diversity in Nigerian Libraries. *Covenant Journal of Library and Information Science, 4*(1), 1-10. https://journals.covenantuniversity.edu.ng/index.php/cjlis/a rticle/viewFile/2651/1315

Iwhiwhu, B. E., & Okorodudu, P. O. (2012). Public library information resources, facilities, and services: User satisfaction with the Edo State Central Library, Benin-City, Nigeria. *Library Philosophy and Practice* (e-journal), 747. https://digitalcommons.unl.edu/cgi/viewcontent.cgi?article=1 821&context=libphilprac \

Jaeger, J. (1999). User fees, community goods, and the public library. *Public Library Quarterly, 17*(2), 49–62. https://www.tandfonline.com/doi/abs/10.1300/J118v17n02_07. doi:10.1300/J118v17n02_07

Jaeger, P. T., Cooke, N. A., Feltis, C., Hamiel, M., Jardine, F., & Shilton, K. (2015). The virtuous circle revisited: Injecting diversity, inclusion, rights, justice, and equity into LIS from education to advocacy. *The Library Quarterly, 85*(2), 150–171. https://www.journals.uchicago.edu/doi/abs/10.1086/680154. doi:10.1086/680154

Korstjens, I., & Moser, A. (2018). Series: Practical guidance to qualitative research. Part 4: Trustworthiness and publishing. *The European Journal of General Practice, 24*(1), 120–124. doi:10.1080/138147 88.2017.1375092 PMID:29202616

Kumasi, K. D., & Manlove, N. L. (2015). Finding "diversity levers" in the core library and information science curriculum: A social justice imperative. *Library Trends, 64*(2), 415–443. https://muse.jhu.edu/ article/610084/summary. doi:10.1353/lib.2015.0047

Nachimuthu, K., & Vijayakumari, G. (2012). E-Resources for inclusive education. *International Education Journal, 1*(03), 27–31. https://www.researchgate.net/profile/Nachimuthu-Dr/publicati on/256032083_E-Resources_for_Inclusive_Education/links/5a5f3 d1d458515c03ee1cda9/E-Resources-for-Inclusive-Education.pdf

Naidoo, J. C. (2014). The importance of diversity in library programs and material collections for children. Association for Library Service to Children, American Library Association.

Poole, A. H. (2021, March). Promoting diversity, equity, and inclusion in library and information science through community-based learning. In *International Conference on Information* (pp. 529-540). Springer, Cham. 10.1007/978-3-030-71292-1_41

Poole, A. H., Agosto, D., Greenberg, J., Lin, X., & Yan, E. (2021). Where do we stand? Diversity, equity, inclusion, and social justice in North American library and information science education. *Journal of Education for Library and Information Science, 62*(3), 258-286. https://www.utpjournals.press/doi/abs/doi:10.3138/jelis.2020-0018

Rankin, C. (2018). IFLA Guidelines for Library Services to Children aged 0-18–2nd Edition (revision of 2003 Guidelines). IFLA.

Rayini, J. (2017). Library and information services to the visually impaired persons. *Library Philosophy and Practice (e-journal), 1510*. https://digitalcommons.unl.edu/cgi/viewcontent.cgi?article=4313&context=libphilprac

Van der Walt, J. L. (2020). Interpretivism-constructivism as a research method in the humanities and social sciences-more to it than meets the eye. *International Journal of Philosophy and Theology, 8*(1), 59–68.

Yusuf, R. A., Awoyemi, O. O., & Ademodi, D. T. (2022). Diversity, inclusion and equity: making a case for the underserved and vulnerable in the Nigerian society. *Lagos Journal of Library and Information Science, 10*(1-2), 79-94. https://www.ajol.info/index.php/ljlis/article/view/236223

Zaid, Y. A. (2017). The exclusion of persons with visual impairment in Nigerian academic libraries' websites. *Library Philosophy and Practice (e-journal),* 1601. https://core.ac.uk/download/pdf/189476139.pdf

Chapter 11
Thriving in the Community:
The Creation and Sustainment of a Community–Driven Literacy Center

Nicole R. Peritore
Augusta University, USA

Elizabeth A. VanDeusen
Augusta University, USA

Kim Barker
Augusta University, USA

Juan Walker
Augusta University, USA

Jessica Simpson
Augusta University, USA

ABSTRACT

Cross-sector, interprofessional partnerships and community collaborations offer promise for identifying and addressing the web-like factors that entangle both literacy achievement and negative public health outcomes for vulnerable populations. Literacy centers can be a conduit to promote justice, equity, diversity, and inclusion as they exist to serve all community members. This is especially impactful when partnered with minority and disadvantaged populations. This university-based literacy center (LC) utilizes a community-driven design to attain and sustain their work. This chapter will illustrate the effort made by the LC to establish access, coordinated services, education of stakeholders, and support for students of all ages, and cultural engagement which are foundational to the work being done. Lastly, the chapter will describe the past, present, and future plans for improving community engagement.

DOI: 10.4018/978-1-6684-7255-2.ch011

Copyright © 2023, IGI Global. Copying or distributing in print or electronic forms without written permission of IGI Global is prohibited.

Thriving in the Community

"Imagine a place where students are motivated, intrigued, and eager to find what the teacher has planned for the day. This is not a fantasy; this place is known as a literacy center." (Ortlieb, Grandstaff-Beckers, & Cheek Jr., 2012, p. 1)

INTRODUCTION

Education is referred to metaphorically as an "upstream" influence in the lives of humans that leads to "downstream" effects on life outcomes including health and longevity (Dahlgren & Whitehead, 2021; Whitehead & Dahlgren, 2007). Educational research has demonstrated a strong connection between literacy achievement and a variety of child, family, school, and other contextual factors linked to low socioeconomic status at the individual as well as at the school level (Buckingham, Wheldall, & Beaman-Wheldall, 2013). Children from lower socioeconomic households may begin school with a deficit in developmental skills and learning gaps that delay literacy achievement beyond early childhood and attend schools where fewer teachers are adequately prepared to deliver the high-quality instruction necessary to overcome those gaps (Aikens & Barbarin, 2008; American Psychological Association, 2017). As libraries seek to deliver targeted efforts and sustained programing that address literacy learning as an issue of justice, equity, diversity, and inclusion (JEDI), the need for outreach efforts, creating a culture of belonging, and creating inclusive spaces is foundational to those efforts. This chapter will familiarize the reader with literacy centers, introduce the Augusta University Literacy Center, narrate the application of a community-driven literacy model, describe the successes and barriers for the center, and lastly, how explain this model can be utilized by others to improve JEDI initiatives.

LITERACY CENTERS

Beyond the traditional roles of a library and the services that are offered, there are opportunities to expand offerings that promote equitable access to literacy learning and engagement. For the purposes of this chapter, literacy center is used as the descriptor for these types of settings.

Laster (2013) provides a historical view of literacy centers that highlights their evolution from "medical-type clinics to instructional powerhouses for struggling readers." (p 3). In the 1920s, Dr. Grace Fernald opened the first university-based clinic at University of California – Los Angeles, focusing on remedial readers and creating a template for literacy centers that is still used today. The 1960s and 1970s saw a sharp increase in the number of literacy centers nationwide while the mid to late 1980s saw the beginning of literacy center decline, due mostly to financial constraints. The last decade has seen another resurgence with many literacy centers, or literacy improvement efforts, established on university campuses with more funding and to support a more clinical focus on teacher preparation at all levels (Council for the Accreditation of Educator Preparation, 2022). Since the 90s, literacy clinics have served as the intersection of research, theory, and praxis in literacy.

Orlieb, Grandstaff-Beckers & Cheek, Jr. (2012) argue that, at every level and in all content areas, literacy centers can serve as a critical mechanism for fostering reading excellence. To summarize, they offer seven components that must be present:

1. Assessment data serve as the basis from which instructional goals are set (McAndrew & Mssengi, 2013; Walker, 2012). This is recognition that there is the intention and ability to gather and record data to guide important choices.
2. Instructional plans are composed of research-proven teaching strategies that are modeled for, practiced with, and successfully applied by students (Milby, 2013; McAndrew & Messengi, 2013; Strieker, Coffey, Delacruz, Holbein, & Easton, 2011).
3. Teachers motivate students by elevating self-efficacy, connecting to interests inside and outside of school, offering a wide variety of text choices, and structuring collaboration (Bronzo & Flynt, 2008; Dunston, 2007; McAndrew & Mssengi, 2013).
4. Praise is given regularly for achievements (Chapman-Carr, 2003).
5. The environment is both challenging and nurturing. Instruction is varied to maximize engagement, attention, and enthusiasm (Kelly & Wenzel, 2013).
6. Relative strengths and weaknesses are recognized and considered within instruction (Prater, Carter & Munk, 2013).
7. Teachers guide and support learners through a gradual release of responsibility, assuming a greater role when students are learning new skills and concepts and, over time, slowly shifting the responsibility to the student for their own learning and application (Pearson & Gallagher, 1983; Coffey, Hubbard, Holbein & Delacruz, 2013).

During the last two decades, four major themes have and continue to influence literacy centers: assessments, mandates, teacher reflection, and new literacies. Clinics help bring clarity to issues of assessment. The use of multiple assessments to inform reading instruction has driven clinic implementation since the mid-1990s with many current and widely used assessments used today coming out of clinic work such as the *Qualitative Reading Inventory* (Leslie & Caldwell, 2010) and *Words Their Way* (Bear, Invernizzi, Templeton & Johnson, 2011). For the most part, clinics are shielded from mandated testing and curricula and allow for the focus to be on the specific strengths and needs of the child. The purpose of a literacy center education is to help teachers be aware of extreme swings in literacy education and to use research and evidence as their guide for literacy intervention.

In addition, when partnering with local districts, literacy centers can support local educators as they navigate standards and accountability structures. Teaching demonstrations are followed by extensive peer feedback that allows teachers to "unpack their practices and extend their expertise." (Laster 2013, p. 13). Teacher reflection, an essential element of the literacy center, has emerged as a key element that advances teachers, moving them beyond their comfort zone and encouraging them to self-evaluate. This reflection can be viewed as a combination of technical, practical, conceptual, and critical awareness by the teacher (Laster, 2015). And thus, aspects of praxis are ingrained in all aspects related to best practices.

Literacy centers can function as the intersection between students' every day and school-based literacies. New literacy theory and teaching applications that emerge are easier to utilize in the clinic setting because of its smaller scale and flexibility when compared with the traditional school setting. Further, research emerged from clinics that indicates that flexible, pragmatic models of assessment and instruction within the frame of natural learning and critical literacy are the norm in clinics with most of the focus on readers struggling with reading and writing (McGrath & Erwin, 2015). Laster (2013) concludes by asserting that there is a need to continue to advance research in clinical settings that examines links between teacher learning and student learning; explore social/cultural contexts of literacy learning including digital environments.

Thriving in the Community

Literacy centers can also promote justice, equity, diversity, and inclusion as they exist to serve all community members and work with individuals beyond school age. They may be especially impactful when they partner with high-need districts where academic needs may be greater and teachers and families may be less prepared to support learners. Literacy centers assist persons with professional and personal goals related to reading and writing including but not limited to: basic literacy and numeracy skills, grant-writing, workshops for personal business owners, parent education, and industrial training opportunities (Mullin, 2001). The ability of the literacy center to not only reach these other audiences but provide them with opportunity and programming that enriches the individual but also benefits the community at large. Literacy centers offer additional resources to enhance real-world abilities with which persons in a community need to not only survive, but thrive (Latta, Raica-Klotz, & Giroux, 2021).

Collaboration is necessary for many literacy centers to thrive. Although one entity may take the lead on a literacy center, the day-to-day functions are dependent on a number of relationships and collaborations. Partnerships with local schools and colleges can provide some of the volunteers needed to assist with the one-on-one education, however additional volunteers may be needed for various other tasks such as lesson preparation and outreach (Latta, Raica-Klotz, & Giroux, 2021; Mullin, 2001). This harkens back to the concept of community building. When a community invests in their collective goals, it calls upon the resources needed for success.

Finally, literacy centers are closely tied to issues of assessment and necessity of showing positive educational and social outcomes through the work done and the relationships built. Literacy centers often have the vision, space, and flexibility to navigate the changing landscape of education, especially as a place for collective knowledge about writing and thinking that can be enacted while still demonstrating their efforts and accomplishments (Latta, Raica-Klotz, & Giroux, 2021; Savini, 2016). When evaluation is considered, literacy centers often need to demonstrate that persons that are engaged with the literacy center are achieving both educational and personal learning outcomes.

Literacy centers rooted in the community have other unique prospects for engagement and they are designed to assist individuals, families, and communities in various ways of experiencing the world. Through increased literacy, individuals and communities are able to see wider social and economic benefits and are offered opportunities of growth and achievement (Workman, 2022). Further, there is urgency for successful models to share their successes with other communities through their published research and professional development online or in person so that mechanisms for engagement can be considered and implemented (face-to-face, asynchronous, and synchronous).

Pandemic Effect and Implications for a Literacy Center

Children of this generation's prospects and opportunities will be impacted by COVID-19 far into adulthood, undermining their chances of attending post-secondary training and finding fulfilling jobs that enable them to support families. In July of 2021, McKinsey and Company completed a data analysis showing that the impact of the pandemic on K–12 student learning and well-being was significant (Dorn, Hancock, Sarakatsannis & Viruleg, 2021). This report found that, unless steps are taken to address unfinished learning, today's students may earn $49,000 to $61,000 less over their lifetime owing to the impact of the pandemic on their schooling. Additionally, the impact on the US economy could amount to $128 billion to $188 billion every year as this cohort enters the workforce.

The need for places in the community, such as a literacy center, is made more crucial considering interrupted and unfinished learning due to the COVID-19 pandemic. Dorn et al. (2021) also found that

201

students, on average, were four months behind in reading by the end of the school year, and the study recognized that the national average did not mean those losses were evenly distributed. The report's data indicated widening preexisting opportunity and achievement gaps, disproportionally impacting historically disadvantaged students hardest. More broadly, high schoolers became more likely to drop out of school. The analysis further demonstrated that the crisis not only had an impact on academics but also the broader health and well-being of students, with more than 35 percent of parents very or extremely concerned about their children's mental health (Dorn, et al. 2021).

Literacy centers can play important roles in ensuring that children impacted by the pandemic are able to have the necessary reading and writing skills to not only find more success in structured learning opportunities but also to accomplish goals and dreams beyond the classroom. This can be accomplished through additional educational opportunities such as community-driven personal and professional learning opportunities. The Augusta University Literacy Center was developed and continues to serve the surrounding communities, offering underserved clients the means and the space to grow their literacy skills.

Augusta University Literacy Center (AULC)

The AULC offers opportunities for educational growth through various instructional programming and offerings for all members of the community. This section of the chapter will describe the history and current foundational information related to who the center serves.

History and Framework of the AULC

In 1990, AULC was created as a community- based center to reach adults that struggled with literacy. Organizers recognized while working with adults from the community that local children also needed assistance with reading skills. Thus, the AULC evolved to meet the needs found within the community, which included tutoring for children, youth, and adults. The original concept for the literacy center and its goal to assist directly in the community has resulted in hundreds of individuals that have either have learned to read or have learned to read better.

The AULC is located in the center of a school system where every child is considered to be economically disadvantaged by the state of Georgia. The county in which these neighborhoods reside have approximately 30,000 students enrolled in grades Pre-K – 12 and the median household income is $39,430 with 25 percent of persons living in poverty. The population is 74 percent Black, 17 percent White, 5 percent Hispanic, 3 percent multi-Racial and 1 percent Asian/Pacific Islander. Specifically examining the schools, the Governor's Office of Student Achievement (2022) shows the following:

- 22 percent of 3rd grade students read at or above grade level
- 28 percent of 5th grade students read at or above grade level

Early literacy achievement, that is reading on grade-level by 3rd grade, is a pivotal milestone for children, and as stated by the Get Georgia Reading organization, "It takes more than good schools, great teachers, and loving parents" to get all kids reading on grade level by 3rd grade (Get Georgia Reading, 2016).

Thriving in the Community

Table 1. Mission and vision of AULC

Mission	We provide children, adolescents, and adults from the Augusta Area with free, high-quality literacy-related educational experiences that promote the development of life-long readers and writers.
Vision	To be a Community Center for access to literacy resources that serve as a conduit for measurable changes in the literacy development of children, adolescents, and adults in the Augusta area.

Note. From Literacy Center (*https://www.augusta.edu/education/literacy-center/*)

The mission and vision seen in Table 1 (Augusta University Literacy Center, 2023) have been central to the growth and expansion of the program for over thirty years and are rooted in the core values of the center. The core values state:

We believe that literacy instruction must be accessible for all. We provide positive literacy experiences that support the development of individuals who not only know how to read and write and also want to improve their reading and writing skills.

The core values are bolstered through the concept and application of a community-driven literacy center in which integrates decision-making directly with communities. The AULC acknowledges the relevance of JEDI as a scaffolding for which to build the relationships within the community. The recognition is evident within the centers work towards addressing inequalities that have arisen from an historical differential in the distribution of resources and opportunities within the community (justice), the attentiveness and constant inspection for barriers and conditions that exist that prevent participation (equity), the pursuit of representation of a wide-range of people's perspectives' and experiences (diversity), and the intentional action of embracing differences and recognition of the contribution those differences make (inclusivity).

This design serves as a means of better aligning development interventions with community needs and preferences and harnessing social resources. In order to ensure that the AULC attains and sustains the community–driven design of the literacy center, there was the formation of a local committee to help inform the program, external collaboration to support decision making within the AULC and active community involvement.

Recently, AULC has further evolved to expand its access, reach, and the ways in which to serve the community. The AULC is part of the newly formed HUB Collaborative. This unique project is designed to establish revitalization in the Augusta urban core neighborhoods. The HUB was funded through grant contributions and sustained donations from major organizations and has recently become the permanent home for AULC.

The HUB was established with guiding principles of its own which included the following commitments: to listen to people in the neighborhoods by honoring their rich histories and respecting their voices; to understand local needs by fostering collaboration between literacy center stakeholders and partners in identifying family-centered solutions; and to promote belonging through respectful inclusivity that enriches literacy center development by planning with, not for, people who live, work, learn, and worship in the neighborhoods. These ideals augmented the established goals and ideals of the AULC.

Thriving in the Community

APPLYING A COMMUNITY-DRIVEN LITERACY MODEL

Engagement of the community is the foundation of the community-driven literacy model. There were several opportunities for stakeholders to provide feedback and guidance to the AULC over a period of several months. Two specific opportunities, the Community Roundtable and the open community town hall, are discussed here to highlight the direct community involvement.

The Community Roundtable assisted the AULC leadership to develop the framework and hold open conversation with various community stakeholders on the potentially broader areas of focus. Stakeholders included members from community organizations that support children and their families through education, services or outreach, outreach coordinators from libraries and YMCAs, faculty and select administration from Augusta University, high school students, select teachers and principals, and organizations that support the AULC mission. The participants were placed in various sub-groups according to skills and background in order to take advantage of different mindsets and skills that would provide well-rounded responses to the activities of the day.

The group was introduced to the AULC and its mission, vision and values. Further, the HUB was discussed in order to provide background to the community in which the literacy center was now situated. The discussion covered various aspects to achieve the goals of the literacy center and the discussion centered on the potential for partnerships and engagement to be equitable and inclusive. This roundtable-based discussion allowed for communication across sectors and disciplines.

The community town hall was an event that was designed to bring community members to the discussion. Arranged at a time that would allow members of the community to learn about and discuss the various successes and needs, the gathering contributed to further understanding of the ways in which the AULC can work with and within the community. The event was attended by various community members, including some that were not direct beneficiaries of the AULC but understood the value of the program for both individuals and the community as whole.

Results From Community Conversations

Having this community-driven literacy model allowed for the recognition that there is a myriad of ways that the literacy center can be embedded into the community and meet their needs. Based on conversations and meetings with community members and stakeholders, the AULC recognizes that the following are paramount:

1. Access
2. Coordinated services
3. Education of stakeholders
4. Support for students of all ages
5. Cultural engagement

Access

Access is focused on ensuring that people have the ability to take advantage of the full range of services needed and offered (Center for Community Health and Development, n.d.). When the relocation of a service and space like the AULC was being planned, not only were the current participants ability to

Thriving in the Community

utilize the new space at top of mind, but also the potential participants which would now have center access at the new location. With considerations for equity and the diverse population to be served, there was acknowledgement that in order to be successful, AULC would need to have involvement from all members of the community.

Access to AULC goes beyond the physical access to the building, although the ability to get to and inside the building is critical, access also includes the informational, social, and psychological aspects as well. The community will continually need to be reminded what the AULC is and the opportunities the AULC offers on a continual basis. Furthermore, the community needs to see these offerings as being important and necessary, and knowing that the AULC is available to them is just the first step - the participants have to be willing to use it. Lastly, there is recognition that there are physical, social, and psychological barriers for participants that have to reduced or eliminated, and their opportunities to use the center have to be expanded.

Coordinated Services

As a simple definition, coordinated services happen when clients receive the services needed and there is a clear and consistent communication among several providers that allow for both delivery of needed services (Bruder et al., 2005, Martinson, 1999) but also communications and information sharing as to remove time and access barriers that the clients may have (Bunger, 2010). However, there is more involved than simply passing a client from one service provider to another; any one of the coordinated organizations may make the initial contact and have to provide for the needs gathered there but also evaluate what other services may be warranted. Bunger (2010) further notes in order to serve a client in this manner, there is a clear need to recognize the crucial nature of the inter-organizational relationships.

By the very nature of the configuration at the HUB, the AULC has the opportunity to work with other organizations for coordinated services. The organizations that work alongside and in conjunction with AULC have the potential to exchange information that could result in greater comprehensiveness and quality of care, but also benefits the client by offering time that could be used in productive ways due to less paperwork and evaluation for each of the organizations independently.

Shared Information

Another way that coordinated services allows for ease of access is the ability to share information among the various providers. Not only does the sharing of information allow for the various service providers to be on the same page and understand the needs of the individual or family, it also can save time for both the recipient and the provider (Bunger, 2010: Takahashi & Smutny, 2001). Further, when services are coordinated it is assumed that person would have greater access to services and they are certain to know more about service eligibility, diminish redundant effort, and ultimately lead to improvements for participants (Bickman, Lambert, Andrade, & Penaloza, 2000; Fleiry & Mercier, 2002). By creating an environment for volunteers to learn and interact demonstrate the fluidity of a successful shared system.

By the very nature of the HUB, it is expected that the organization will organically have opportunities to share information that will assist in services beyond literacy. Underlining this work is the assurance that the diverse groups that are served through the AULC have access to basic needs and that services are inclusive for all individuals and families. The ability to provide opportunities for the diverse group of persons seen at the AULC is rooted in the core values of the center. The AULC is working closely with all of the other organizations and partnerships for which students may be referred or they may refer a participant.

Education of Stakeholders

Stakeholders are simply people or organizations that have something to gain or lose through the outcomes of a project or program. Stakeholders can be either an individual or a group of persons that have desire and put forth the effort to support the success of an organization to fulfill its mission. Stakeholders could have a hands-on approach where they are actively involved with the organization or stakeholders could be outside entities that are impacted by the work that the organization does. Stakeholders could also be described in terms of internal and external (Australian Government Department of Foreign Affairs and Trade, 2018; Sustaining Reading First, 2009).

Internal stakeholders are those who are working with the literacy center on a daily or weekly basis. These are the persons who have direct involvement with what happens at the center. For a literacy center, the stakeholders include those seek to assist students in gaining increased levels of achievement through the interaction at the center. These include the staff, volunteers, students, and administration of the center. External stakeholders are those that interact with the literacy center but not on the day-to-day functioning. These could be individuals or organizations that have an interest in in the literacy center and the effects in the community but who do not directly define and decide the operational aspect (Australian Government Department of Foreign Affairs and Trade, 2018).

Although internal stakeholders unmistakably have greater capability to produce positive change for those individuals at the literacy center, sustainment needs external support. The AULC recognized the inherent value of a diverse group of external stakeholders and will continue to work with them in order to gain continued adaptation to meet the needs of the community. Understanding the history and barriers within the community was essential as the AULC started to formulate practices and programming. Further, the AULC understands the benefits for the community at large for their involvement and interaction not only with the center, but also the HUB.

Support for Students of All Ages

Support for students may be visualized as academic assistance, however support needed extends far beyond typical classroom settings and resources. Students of all ages need more than assistance for their learning challenges, and research has shown that students are more likely to succeed when they are directed, focused, nurtured, engaged, connected, and valued (The RP Group, 2022). Students of all ages need to be:

(1) **Directed towards goals, or reasons for their visits.** Further, students need to have a path for achieving that goal. A student knowing what they want to achieve is simply not enough, they also need to know what will need to happen to get there.
(2) **Focused on the goal they set.** When students are able to imagine and focus on their goal, they are much more likely to achieve it.
(3) **Feeling nurtured.** Students need to have the feeling that they are supported on their learning journey and that the people assisting them are vested in them and want to see them succeed.

Thriving in the Community

(4) **Actively engaged.** Students who are participating and excited to be a part of the learning community and process itself are much more likely to succeed.

(5) **Connected to others.** Students that are facing challenges both in academic and potentially personal matters, are much more likely to succeed when they feel that others understand and that they have a community to support them though their challenges.

(6) **Valued for who they are**. Students of all ages have various abilities and skills that have shaped them into the persons that they are. When students are able to apply those skills and talents to their learning, they are much more likely to feel engagement and connected to others, and ultimately, able to achieve their goals.

The AULC acknowledges that they will be working with students of all ages, with diverse backgrounds and experiences and the programming must be inclusive and recognize the history of the people and community that is being served. As the center has moved into this established community, there are efforts to actively seek to support persons of all ages in accomplishing their personal and professional goals. Undoubtedly, these concepts are crucial.

Cultural Engagement

There are hundreds of definitions of culture. Kiefer (2007) shares the definition of "a complex integrated system of thought and behavior shared by members of a group — a system whose whole pattern allows us to understand the meanings that people attach to specific facts and observations" (p. 3). Undoubtedly, culture shapes characteristics and nurtures notions of community, and inspires how individuals and groups relate to each other. Further, culture encourages ideas about partnerships, trust, and negotiation. Therefore, culture shapes the development of community engagement, and working effectively within a community necessitates an understanding of their culture (McCloskey et al., 2019).

Community-based organizations in particular must recognize the cultural undercurrents of specific groups and institutions in the communities that they serve in order to construct connections and find ways to successfully collaborate (McCloskey et al., 2019; Shoultz et al., 2006). Communities are not standardized units; they are made up of various sets of people with different pasts, collective arrangements, and considerations of the world. If completed appropriately, the community-engaged approach empowers communities and their partnerships to cultivate programs that are consistent with a community's cultural context (Airhihenbuwa, 1995; Dutta, 2007; Iwelunmor, Newsome, & Airhihenbuwa, 2014).

The AULC understands that to have successful collaboration within the community, there is the need for continual dialog and insight from not only the users of the literacy center, but others in the community such as other community-based organizations and religious entities. The essential step of recognizing the diversity in the community background, experiences, income, and education but also understanding the racism and inequalities that are present within the process of community engagement. With such a method, AULC can help connections apprehend and address the origins of literacy issues and watch against replicating repressive patterns within their partnerships.

Becoming a Community-Driven Literacy Center

Transiting to a community-driven literacy center had led the AULC to focus on current learners and building a fortified foundation plan for broader influence in the HUB for Community Innovation.

Thriving in the Community

AULC currently averages about 100 learners and 25 instructors each semester. AULC trains, supports, and collaborates with instructors as they establish relationships and work with the learners and their families. Other organizations can utilize a similar input gathering technique to guide their discussions in addressing JEDI.

Collaboration inherently means the expansion of contributing persons and the sharing of power. This expansion allows for additional voices to be heard, priories to be explored, and experiences to draw from in order to make the best decision possible for the organization. Farhang and Morales (2022) offer some guiding principles in which to help create a solid foundation within the collaboration. These principles recognize the intrinsic significance of collaboration with members from the community and other internal and external stakeholders:

- **Act with Care** — With deepest consideration for the people and community that the AULC serves, there is the understanding that the literacy center will need to be attentive, intentional, and building trusting relationships. Taplin (2017) suggests that work needs to be done "at the speed of trust" and a recognition that erroneous steps could result in irreparable partnerships moving forward. Further, acting with care allows the AULC to avoid negative consequences among the community in which they seek to support.

- **Inclusivity** — As challenges are encountered, those most affected should have prominence within the AULC discussions. Critically, those most affected by inequities are in the best position to educate about the problem, should have significant roles in designing pertinent solutions, and define what success looks like from their perspective. Resolutions should reflect the community's main concerns and the environment in which they will be applied. AULC understands that local experiences and expectations should heavily inform evidence-based interventions. These experiences and lenses will help make any collaboratively designed intervention more impactful.

- **Authentic Community Collaboration** — Collaborations should build pride in the AULC and integrate all perspectives. Knowing that challenges will happen, solutions should be created with community, implemented within the community, and examined for success with the community. To ensure that the AULC has representation of the community, the literacy center seeks input from those that are actively involved in to the community and the work being done around literacy. Further, there are efforts to counterbalance obstacles that can commonly be found: compensation, transportation, child care and accessible meeting times. Further, setting the foundation of strong collaboration also allows for trust building among the community served (Farhang & Morales, 2022; Pastor, Speer, Gupta, Han, & Ito, 2022).

- **Sustainable Solutions** — Solutions should be community-driven, shaped by community capacity, seek to develop and expand relationships, build enduring infrastructure, and ensure respect for all. AULC recognizes the critical work of creating policies and practices that seek to address literacy and educational equity through the prioritization of pursuing community input and leadership; increasing community awareness about literacy and the long-lasting effects, including economic, social, and health issues. AULC works to provide programs and activities for all ages that addresses issues as perceived by the community that is being served.

- **Commitment to Transformation** — Understanding and working to improve an organizational culture and programming takes time and effort. The AULC recognizes that in order to ensure that the organization is inclusive in their approach and the continued effort to meet the community's needs, they will need to be open to changes. When the community members speak up regarding

Thriving in the Community

their needs and see themselves as having an active voice and impact on decisions being made that impact their community, they are best positioned to push for their needs. This becomes a positive feedback loop for the AULC because the center can then utilize the information in making changes that provide the community with the assistance that is desired.

Determining Best Practices to Help AULC Serve the Community

Although the AULC is situated directly within the community that is being served, there is not a supposition of ease for the sustainment of the literacy center or the greater HUB in which it is situated. The AULC believes that the continued support will happen if there is strategic planning with the communities needs and challenges at the forefront of decision making. As such, efforts have been made among community members and stakeholders to recognize areas of strength and areas that could bring challenges. Table 2 demonstrates the conversation around best practices and considerations for making sure that the AULC continues to be community-driven.

Table 2. Considerations and suggestions from AULC stakeholders

Considerations	Community Suggestions
Determining the needs of learners [and their families]	• Ensure the community, families, children are AWARE of what we do, can create the excitement for others • Generate active engagement and invitation - not passive • Think holistically about the family context - support issues that are priority for the family right now (i.e. food insecurity, abuse, mental health)
Providing Access	• Inspire individuals to WANT to be at the AULC / HUB so they drive the attendance / tell others • Create a sense of community that fosters the access, sharing informally • Ensure multiple languages are represented • Review literacy materials for inclusivity • Do a scan for ADA access - including transportation
Making appropriate referrals to collaborative agencies for support	• Leverage soft/warm-handoffs (walking persons over, calling together, supported referrals) • Provide vision, hearing services • Provide access to dental health screenings • Provide and connect with GED and Goodwill agencies for adult learners

The diverse body of engaged stakeholders offered insights into the many considerations that the AULC needed to consider in order to make decisions with complex outcomes and to ensure a successful and intentional start to the program. Although these ideals and actions cannot begin immediately, through open dialog with stakeholders on a regular basis, the AULC can take steps to set a strong foundation for which to build a strong, productive literacy center that meets the needs of the community both now and in the future.

Sampling of Successes Associated With the AULC

The AULC has taken steps to ensure that they have reliability within academia / university and the local community. These two distinct efforts demonstrate the foundation that the AULC set to achieve the vision; they are (1) the Literacy Research Group and (2) Community Research-based Partnerships.

Literacy Research Group

The Literacy Research Group (LRG) serves as the leadership foundation for the AULC's ongoing research agenda. This group is comprised of faculty and staff from other departments at the university and meets on a regular basis. Together, the LRG develops and monitors the comprehensive plan to identify broad areas of focus and to prioritize projects based on AULC implementation, needs, and timelines. This group also brings in experts in these areas to collaborate and lead projects with ongoing support in all areas. All faculty are welcome to submit ideas for research projects in their disciplines and interest areas that align with the AULC mission and to enlist the support of the LRG. In addition, the LRG supports all efforts to disseminate findings locally, regionally, nationally, and beyond – and in a wide variety of formats.

Current Research-based Projects

The following are examples of research projects supported by the AULC.

"Community Assets in Support of Teaching and Learning: Celebrating the Golden Blocks through Multi-genre Text"

This project celebrates Augusta's cultural assets by chronicling the impact of 3 noteworthy residents who influenced as all aspects of modern life. Comic books are collaboratively created and available throughout the community. The focus is on Lucy Craft Laney who founded the Haines Institute and co-founded the Lamar School of Nursing. John Tutt who was a prolific coach at the Haines Institute. Lastly, Dr. T.W. Josey. All of these individuals were part of the historic Golden Blocks in Augusta, Ga. Many individuals reference Black Wall Street as an anomaly. However, during the Jim Crow Era, there were many self-sustaining African American communities that flourished despite many external threats such as redlining, unjust policing practices, and legal segregation to just name a few institutionalized barriers to success.

Story Walks: Integrating Reading, Movement, and the Outdoors

A story walk is an outdoor reading experience that uses a deconstructed children's book and places laminated individual pages on portable signs along a walking trail. This project seeks to provide and assess local story walks and support schools, community organizations, and groups wishing to provide one to their population. The project has sought and received additional funding to place a story walk at a local school and to examine the use and impact of the experience from an administration and teacher's perspective.

Thriving in the Community

Developing a Community Partnership

The purpose of this study is to (a) explore the experiences of community members with literacy learning in Augusta, Richmond County before the development of an interprofessional partnership and (b) to examine the feasibility and process of developing an interprofessional partnership to support literacy within the same community. We may also identify facilitators and barriers to effective interprofessional collaboration.

Sensory Paths

A sensory pathway, or sensory hall, is a colorful, creative and playful way for kids to build connections in the brain that are responsible for sight, touch, sound, etc., which enable kids to complete complex, multi-stage tasks. Sensory Paths engage students via Sensory Integration (SI) thus impacting vestibular and proprioception processing in children (Keen, 2020). Yu and Smith (2016) shared evidence that the ability to socially coordinate visual attention to an object is essential to healthy developmental outcomes, including language learning. Sensory Paths are an emerging trend in schools because districts and administrators seek to increase focus and decrease off-task behavior by allowing students to engage in gross motor movements to reduce sensory need without overstimulating the student (thesensorypath. com, 2022). Future research should study Sensory Path interventions to determine how impactful they are to the reduction of off-task behaviors and increase in early literacy skills. The AULC supports these efforts and will provide a Sensory Path at the center in order to increase this type of brain connection for younger individuals.

Community-Based or Partnership Successes

The AULC values opportunities to work with community partners and organizations to bring community-based events that offer experiences beyond the traditional literacy center-based education.

Literacy is Health: Books for Shay Event

This collaboration brought together medical students, Augusta University College of Education, other organizations such as Rise Augusta, a local non-profit that seeks to aid children in poverty, the local YMCA, and other health foundations to provide students at a local elementary school and community wide access to free health screens, and free books. Additional opportunities included STEAM activities, story walks, sensory paths, and seed planting with a local Future Farmers of America chapter. Parents also were able to receive a free mental health education material. Over 40 volunteers were organized for the event and there are plans for this to be an annual event.

Back to School Event

The AULC and other educational partners hosted a back-to-school celebration at the HUB for Community Innovation. During the event, local students enjoyed activities and received free backpacks filled with school supplies. Around 160 families with nearly 400 students attended the celebration. In addition to receiving school supplies at the event, guests could listen to local celebrities read to students, enjoy the book fair and reading rooms, and visit tables to learn more about local resources — including information on a new program called "The Basics" that will support infants and toddlers. The Augusta University Police Department, Prevent Blindness Georgia, the CSRA Economic Opportunity Authority, the Augusta Public Library, Augusta Partnership for Children and the Harrisburg Family Health Center were on hand to lend resources to families looking for information.

Potential Barriers to Sustained Success

These first successes do not mean that the AULC has no expectation for challenges in the near or far future. Currently, there are three main areas of concern: evaluation, transportation, and recruitment and training of instructors/volunteers. Each of these components has implications for the sustainment and growth of the literacy center.

One of the biggest challenges faced is how to effectively evaluate all of the various aspects that the AULC works towards. Although the LRG does provide some guidance as to where these efforts may want to start and support for on-going research projects, there will be the need for long-term evidence of the impacts that the center itself is making for and with the community. The outcomes, from a micro (individual) to macro (community-wide) stance, will require different approaches including different methodologies and expected time needed to measure.

Transportation is also expected to be a concern and issue that will need to be addressed due to the location of the center. Although the AULC is situated in a neighborhood, the service area is well beyond those geographic limitations. For example, transportation issues may include how to address children's access during after-school hours when a parent may be working. The expectation is that the stakeholders will be able to offer insight and experiences that will enable for honest discussions on how to meet this challenge.

Lastly, there is understanding that having instructors available will require recruitment and training. Recruitment has traditionally been siloed through the university and word-of mouth, however, with potential expansion of offerings and hours, ensuring that people are able to be assisted will need to be continually addressed. Furthermore, those individuals that do volunteer through the university programs and classes, are still working within the center for a limited / terminal amount of time. Recruitment models may need to be revamped. Additionally, ensuing that volunteers are not only trained how to physically complete the tasks that they are given but also ensure that they are considerate of JEDI and uphold those ideals and expectations.

Application to Other Organizations

The completion and sustainment of a community–driven design can assist organizations in addressing JEDI within their community. As organizations seek to find ways to work within their community in an engaged and informed manner, the community-driven design discussed can offer a platform for which to support collaborations that already exist and construct new relationships within the community that are essential for making change. Additionally, this design incorporates the voices and actions of the community as the foundation to build sustained relationships and cooperation. Success will be evident when organizations work towards addressing JEDI through the alignment of programming and interventions offered with the community needs.

Thriving in the Community

CONCLUSION

Whether one uses the term literacy center, or a name such as reading clinic, literacy lab, or a reading and writing center, when a facility chooses to addresses educational gaps through the incorporation of literacy directed programming, there is an opportunity to work both with and within the needs of the community that is being assisted. Further, the reach of such a facility or program allows for diversity of thoughts and experiences, employs equitable practices in an inclusionary environment to assist individuals and communities to thrive. This chapter defined literacy centers and their various functions, explained the ways that a university-led literacy center was established and continues to grow within the community it serves with JEDI as foundational elements, described elements of inclusive community collaborations, and shared examples of sustainment and proliferation of programming.

In conclusion, literacy centers have the opportunity to provide communities with additional resources concerning literacy and educational opportunities. As a community-based literacy center, the AULC is bringing opportunity and educational growth to the underserved area and JEDI is at the forefront of discussions and decisions. Through carefully planned stakeholder meetings and active engagement within the community, the AULC is making continued efforts to acknowledge the diversity of the community and be inclusive for all. Moreover, there were several examples of ways that the AULC is engaged with research and community efforts. Upon reflection of the materials provided, other organizations should be able to discover or refine the various ways that literacy and literacy access could be provided in your community.

REFERENCES

Aikens, N. L., & Barbarin, O. (2008). Socioeconomic differences in reading trajectories: The contribution of family, neighborhood, and school contexts. *Journal of Educational Psychology*, *100*(2), 235–251. doi:10.1037/0022-0663.100.2.235

Airhihenbuwa, C. O. (1995). Health and culture: Beyond the western paradigm. *Sage (Atlanta, Ga.)*.

American Psychological Association. (2017, July). Education and Socioeconomic Status. APA. https://www.apa.org/pi/ses/resources/publications/education

Augusta University Literacy Center. (2023) *Literacy Center*. AULC. https://www.augusta.edu/education/literacy-center/

Australian Government Department of Foreign Affairs and Trade. (2018). Education Learning and Development Module: The role of key stakeholders in education aid effectiveness principles. DFAT. https://www.dfat.gov.au/sites/dcfault/files/foundation-role-of-key-stakeholders-aid-effectiveness-principles.pdf

Bear, D. R., Invernizzi, M., Templeton, S., & Johnson, F. (2011). *Words their way: Word study for phonics, vocabulary and spelling instruction* (7th ed.). Pearson.

Bickman, L., Lambert, E. W., Andrade, A. R., & Penaloza, R. V. (2000). The Fort Bragg continuum of care for children and adolescents: Mental health outcomes over 5 years. *Journal of Consulting and Clinical Psychology*, *68*(4), 710–716. doi:10.1037/0022-006X.68.4.710 PMID:10965645

Braveman, P., & Gottlieb, L. (2014). The social determinants of health: It's time to consider the causes. *Public Health Reports*, *129*(1_suppl2), 19–31. doi:10.1177/00333549141291S206 PMID:24385661

Bronzo, W. G., & Flynt, E. S. (2008). Motivating students to read in the content classroom: Six evidence-based principles. *The Reading Teacher*, *62*(2), 172–174. doi:10.1598/RT.62.2.9

Bruder, M. B., Harbin, G. L., Whitbread, K., Conn-Powers, M., Roberts, R., Dunst, C. J., Van Buren, M., Mazzarella, C., & Gabbard, G. (2005). Establishing outcomes for service coordination: A step toward evidence-based practice. *Topics in Early Childhood Special Education*, *25*(3), 177–188. doi:10.1177/0 2711214050250030501

Buckingham, J., Wheldall, K., & Beaman-Wheldall, R. (2013). Why poor children are more likely to become poor readers: The school years. *Australian Journal of Education*, *57*(3), 190–213. doi:10.1177/0004944113495500

Bunger, A. C. (2010). Defining Service Coordination: A Social Work Perspective. *Journal of Social Service Research*, *36*(5), 385–401. doi:10.1080/01488376.2010.510931 PMID:21116470

Center for Community Health and Development. (n.d.). *Chapter 3, Section 10: Conducting Concerns Surveys*. University of Kansas. Community Tool Box. http://ctb.ku.edu/en/table-of-contents/assessment/assessing- community-needs-and-resources/conduct-concerns-surveys/main

Chapman Carr, K. (2003). Today's literacy center: How relevant is the graduate reading practicum? *The Reading Teacher*, *57*(3), 256–268.

Coffey, D., Hubbard, D., Holbein, M., & Delacruz, S. (2013). Creating a university- based literacy center. Evan Ortlieb & Earl H. Cheek, Jr. (Eds.), Advanced Literacy Practices: From the Clinic to the Classroom, Vol. 2. (pp. 21-35). Bingley, UK: Emerald Group Publishing Limited.

Council for the Accreditation of Educator Preparation. (2013). *CAEP accreditation standards*. CAEP. https://caepnet.org/standards/2022- itp/introduction

Dahlgren, G., & Whitehead, M. (1991). *Policies and Strategies to Promote Social Equity in Health*. Institute for Futures Studies.

Dahlgren, G., & Whitehead, M. (2021). The Dahlgren-Whitehead Model of health determinants: 30 years on and still chasing rainbows. *Public Health*, *199*, 20–24. doi:10.1016/j.puhe.2021.08.009 PMID:34534885

Dorn, E., Hancock, B., Sarakatsannis, J., & Viruleg, E. (2021). *COVID-19 and education: The lingering effects of unfinished learning*. McKinsey & Co. Retrieved from: https://www.mckinsey.com/industries/education/our-insights/covid-19-and-education- the-lingering-effects-of-unfinished-learning

Dunston, P. J. (2007). Instructional practices, struggling readers, and a university-based literacy center. *Journal of Adolescent & Adult Literacy*, *50*(5), 328–336. doi:10.1598/JAAL.50.5.1

Dutta, M. J. (2014). Communicating about culture and health: Theorizing culture-centered and cultural sensitivity approaches. *Communication Theory*, *17*(3), 304–328. doi:10.1111/j.1468-2885.2007.00297.x

Thriving in the Community

Farhang, L., & Morales, X. (2022). *Building Community Power to Achieve Health and Racial Equity: Principles to Guide Transformative Partnerships with Local Communities. National Academies of Medicine, Perspectives. Commentary.* National Academy of Medicine., doi:10.31478/202206d

Fleury, M. J., & Mercier, C. (2002). Integrated local networks as a model for organizing mental health services. *Administration and Policy in Mental Health, 30*(1), 55–73. doi:10.1023/A:1021227600823 PMID:12546256

Gallagher, K. (2010). Reversing readicide. *Educational Leadership, 67*(6), 36–41.

Get Georgia Reading. (2016). *Framework Overview* Get Georgia Reading. https://getgeorgiareading.org/framework-overview/

Governor's Office of Student Achievement. (2022, 17 October). Georgia School Grades Reports Richmond County (2020-2021). GOSA. https://public.gosa.ga.gov/noauth/extensions/SchoolGrades-Georgia/SchoolGrades- Georgia.html?SchoolName=richmond-county

Hardin, L., Trumbo, S., & Wiest, D. (2020). Cross-sector collaboration for vulnerable populations reduces utilization and strengthens community partnerships. *Journal of Interprofessional Education & Practice, 18*, 1–5. doi:10.1016/j.xjep.2019.100291

Iwelunmor, J., Newsome, V., & Airhihenbuwa, C. O. (2014). Framing the impact of culture on health: A systematic review of the PEN-3 cultural model and its application in public health research and interventions. *Ethnicity & Health, 19*(1), 20–46. doi:10.1080/13557858.2013.857768 PMID:24266638

Keene, H. (2020). *An evaluation of sensory paths as an antecedent intervention for decreasing off-task behavior in children with disabilities during small group instruction.* [Master's thesis, University of Kentucky]. doi:10.13023/etd.2020.105

Kelly, M., & Wenzel, T. (2013). Coaching for success: UCF enrichment programs in literacy. In E. Ortlieb & E. H. Cheek Jr., (Eds.), *Advanced Literacy Practices: From the Clinic to the Classroom* (Vol. 2, pp. 63–86). Emerald Group Publishing Limited. doi:10.1108/S2048-0458(2013)0000002007

Kiefer, C. W. (2007). *Doing health anthropology: Research methods for community assessment and change.* Springer.

Laster, B. P. (2013). A historical view of student learning and teacher development in literacy centers. In E. Ortlieb & E. H. Cheek Jr., (Eds.), *Advanced Literacy Practices: From the Clinic to the Classroom* (Vol. 2, pp. 3–20). Emerald Group Publishing Limited. doi:10.1108/S2048-0458(2013)0000002004

Latta, M., Taica-Klotz, H., & Giroux, C. (2021). Guest editors' introduction: Community writing centers: What was, what is, and what potentially can be. *Community Literacy Journal, 15*(1), 1–6. doi:10.25148/CLJ.15.1.009361

Laugen, K. (2021). Improving engagement and literacy skills with choice literacy centers. *School of Education and Leadership Student Capstone Projects, 635.* https://digitalcommons.hamline.edu/hse_cp/635

Leslie, L., & Caldwell, J. S. (2010). *Qualitative reading inventory-5.* Allyn & Bacon.

Martinson, K. (1999). Literature review on service coordination and integration in the welfare and workforce development systems. Urban Institute. https://www.urban.org/url.cfm

McAndrew, S. L., & Msengi, S. G. (2013). Transfer and transformation of knowledge and practices from literacy clinic to community. In Ortlieb & Earl H. Cheek, Jr. (Eds.), Advanced Literacy Practices: From the Clinic to the Classroom, Vol. 2. (pp. 21- 35). Emerald Group Publishing Limited. doi:10.1108/S2048-0458(2013)0000002013

McCloskey, D. J., McDonald, M. A., Cook, J., Heurtin-Roberts, S., Updegrove, S., Sampson, D., Gutter, S., & Eder, M. (2018). Community engagement: Definition and organizing concepts from the literature. Principles of Community Engagement.

McGrath, K. & Erwin, R. (2015). University-based literacy center: Benefits for the college and the community. *AILACTE Journal*, 93– 117.

McKenna, M. C., & Walpole, S. (2007). Assistive technology in the literacy centers: It's emerging potential. *Reading Research Quarterly*, *42*(1), 140–145. doi:10.1598/RRQ.42.1.6

Milby, T. (2013). Innovative practices: Developing effective collaboration and partnerships within school-based literacy centers. In E. Ortlieb & E. H. Cheek Jr., (Eds.), *Advanced Literacy Practices: From the Clinic to the Classroom* (Vol. 2, pp. 387–406). Emerald Group Publishing Limited. doi:10.1108/S2048-0458(2013)0000002022

Mullin, J. (2001). Writing Centers in WAC. In McLeod, Susan H., Miraglia, Eric, Soven, M., & Thaiss, C. (Eds.) WAC for the New Millennium: Strategies for Continuing Writing-Across-the-Curriculum Programs. National Council of Teachers of English, Urbana, IL.

Orleib, E., Grandstaff-Beckers, G., & Cheek, E. H. Jr. (2012). Fostering reading excellence at every level of school through literacy centers. *The Clearing House: A Journal of Educational Strategies, Issues and Ideas*, *85*(1), 1–6. doi:10.1080/00098655.2011.601356

Pastor, M. P., Speer, P., Gupta, J., Han, H., & Ito, J. (2022). Community power and health equity: Closing the gap between scholarship and practice. *NAM Perspectives Discussion Paper*. National Academy of Medicine, Washington, DC. https://doi.org/ doi:10.31478/202206

Pearson, P. D., & Gallagher, M. C. (1983). The instruction of reading comprehension. *Contemporary Educational Psychology, 8*(3), 317–344. https://doi.org/ 476X(83)90019-X doi:10.1016/0361-

Petruzzi, T., & Burns, M. F. (2006). A Literacy Center Where? A Public Library Finds Space to Promote and Provide Family Learning Activities. *Public Library Quarterly, 25*(1-2), 1–2, 191–197. doi:10.1300/J118v25n01_14

Prater, M. A., Carter, N., & Munk, J. (2013). Preparing special educators to teach reading: A pre-student teaching practicum. In Ortlieb & Earl H. Cheek, Jr. (Eds.), Advanced Literacy Practices: From the Clinic to the Classroom, Vol. 2. (pp. 21-35). Emerald Group Publishing Limited.

Savini, C. (2016). A Writing Retreat at the Intersection of WAC and Civic Engagement. *Community Literacy Journal*, *11*(1), 157–163. doi:10.1353/clj.2016.0023

Thriving in the Community

Shoultz, J., Oneha, M. F., Magnussen, L., Hla, M. M., Brees-Saunders, Z., Cruz, M. D., & Douglas, M. (2006). Finding solutions to challenges faced in community-based participatory research between academic and community organizations. *Journal of Interprofessional Care, 20*(2), 133–144. doi:10.1080/13561820600577576 PMID:16608716

Strieker, T., Coffey, D., Delacruz, S., Holbein, M., & Easton, A. (2011). *Action plans. Archives of the Center for Literacy and Learning.* Kennesaw State University.

Sustaining Reading First. (2009). *Engaging stakeholders: Including parents and the community to sustain Improved Reading Outcomes.* Sustaining Reading First. https://www2.ed.gov/programs/readingfirst/support/stakeholderlores.pdf

Takahashi, L. M., & Smutny, G. (2001). Collaboration among small, community-based organizations: Strategies and challenges in turbulent environments. *Journal of Planning Education and Research, 21*(2), 141–153. doi:10.1177/0739456X0102100203

The RPgroup. (2022). *Success Factors Framework.* The RPgroup. https://rpgroup.org/Our-Projects/Student-Support-Redefined/SuccessFactorsFramework

The RPgroup. (2022). *What is student support (re)defined?* The RPgroup. https://do-prod-webteam-drupalfiles.s3-us-west-2.amazonaws.com/bcedu/s3fs- public/4HStudentSupport_0.pdf

Walker, B. (2012). *Diagnostic teaching of reading: Techniques for instruction and assessment* (7th ed.). Allyn & Bacon.

Whitehead, M., & Dahlgren, G. (2007). Concepts and principles for tackling social inequities in health: Leveling up part 1. *Studies on social and economic determinants of population health, No 2.* World Health Organization. http://www.euro.who.int/document/e89383.pdf

Workman, J. (2022). Inequality begets inequality: Income inequality and socioeconomic achievement gradients across the United States. *Social Science Research, 107*, 1–21. doi:10.1016/j.ssresearch.2022.102744 PMID:36058607

World Health Organization. (2022). *Social Determinants of Health.* WHO. https://www.who.int/health-topics/social-determinants-of-health#tab=tab_2

Yu, C., & Smith, L. B. (2016). Multiple sensory-motor pathways lead to coordinated visual attention. *Cognitive Science, 41*(S1), 5–31. doi:10.1111/cogs.12366 PMID:27016038

ADDITIONAL READING

Gorski, P. C. (2018). *Reaching and teaching students in poverty: Strategies for erasing the opportunity gap.* Teachers College Press.

Israel, B. A., Eng, E., Schultz, A., & Parker, E. A. (Eds.). (2013). *Methods for community-based participatory research for health* (2nd ed.). Jossey-Bass.

Ledwith, M., & Springett, J. (2012). *Participatory practice: Community-based action for transformative change*. The Policy Press.

Wallterstein, N., Duran, B., Oetzel, J., & Minkler, M. (Eds.). (2018). *Community-based participatory research for health: Advancing social and health equity*. Jossey-Bass.

KEY TERMS AND DEFINITIONS

Digital Environments: The combined communication environment where digital devices are used to communicate and add to content and activities within it.

Literacy Achievement: A common term used to describe the levels of reading comprehension of the school population.

Literacy Theory: Describes how literacy changes as children gain the language and cognitive skills that underpin learning.

Literacy: Having the skills to recognize and understand printed and written information

Remedial Readers: Persons that have reading skills that are below average in reading comprehension.

Social Determinants of Health: Features and resources in the places where people live, learn, work, and play that affect various health and quality-of life outcomes.

Stakeholders: A person or persons with an interest or concern in something.

Chapter 12

Addressing the History of Discrimination and Bias in Past and Current Library Systems

Kayla Reed
Grinnell College, USA

ABSTRACT

Reviewing the history of Academic and public libraries in the United States reveals the origins and progress of inclusivity within library spaces. Although libraries take pride in being active in inclusion events and ideas, there is still a long way to go. Libraries are still prone to white bias and with that comes discrimination and exclusion of non-white, striaght, able-bodied individuals. In addition, Library Science as a field has a diversity problem and needs to improve training methods based around discrimination and biases. For libraries to move forward, library professionals must acknowledge the past and work towards reconciliation versus repentance. Past mistakes cannot be made up, actions cannot be undone. But the prevention of future instances of bias and discrimination can be achieved.

INTRODUCTION

United States libraries are making the same mistakes as United States education by not addressing the full truth of their discriminatory history. Six states have passed anti-Critical Race Theory laws while twenty have plans or discussions in the works (Ray, 2021). Banning the discussion of race and racial history does not make it go away. Libraries and librarians take pride in being active in inclusion efforts and social justice, while the truth is that while libraries have worked towards inclusion, there is still a long way to go and difficult steps ahead. Displays, events, and other wonderful efforts are popular at academic and public libraries. But these events do not include the discussion of libraries' history of exclusion and tendency toward the 'White default'. Exclusionary practices of the past and present include segregated libraries, lack of LGBT+ content well through the Aids Crisis, lack of materials for the visually challenged, collection diversity issues, and so forth. Library systems, such as Dewey and the Library of Congress, have come under fire recently for outdated terminology and procedures. In this chapter, the

DOI: 10.4018/978-1-6684-7255-2.ch012

Copyright © 2023, IGI Global. Copying or distributing in print or electronic forms without written permission of IGI Global is prohibited.

author will explore how libraries can address an exclusionary history, and what practices have persisted or developed from this history that librarians must address in current times. There are many avenues and areas of discussion for this topic, but this chapter will function as an introduction to the topic and touch on some of the principal areas in libraries where this persists as a problem.

United States and Oppression

The 'White default' founded the United States. Eliza Gleason did a comprehensive look at library access for Black Americans in 1941. As the first Black woman to receive a doctorate in library science, Ms. Gleason started the work that many libraries were not yet doing. Gleason points out, "The history of the Negro in American life is very largely involved in his different status from others under the law" (1941, p. 30). Women, LGBT+ individuals, and those who are not White have all had to have amendments added to the United States Constitution to ensure rights due to identity and a default lack of protections. Kendall summarizes by stating that White privilege exists around institutional benefits for those who match the race of those in power. The primary benefits of the system are more access to resources and power in general (2006, p.63). Leong points out that being White in the United States is just being a person, while any other race is Black American, African American, Asian American, and so forth (2020). Leong (2020) goes on to point out how White sets the default in every aspect of American life, including authorship, beauty, entertainment, and more. What is important for White individuals to understand about the white default is, "The racial default of Whiteness is a component of White privilege" (Leong, 2020, p. 1431). People of privilege need to use that privilege to create change. It is not up to the oppressed to change the system, it is up to those who uphold and benefit from the system to create change. White people must know and accept the truth.

Colorblindness is the idea that "not seeing" people's skin color and thus skin color not mattering is a way to combat racism. In modern United States society, the idea of colorblindness is popular in dealing with racial issues but there are disputes about this idea. Hitchcock (2002) emphasizes, "Successful at what it (colorblindness) did, turning the tide against White supremacy, it continues to oppose all change rather than admit its methods alone cannot dismantle a structure that has been in place for 400 years" (p. 67). Thus, when libraries create or curate collections, being 'colorblind' is not beneficial. Other privileges exist outside race, including being able-bodied, being male, and so forth, what is important to remember is that these privileges limit the resources and power of other groups, creating inequalities. To create strong, diverse collections libraries need to be aware of not only whom the collection represents but also who has little to no representation, how to improve diversity within the collections and develop a deeper understanding of practices. The pursuit of restorative justice can allow libraries to see the disparities in the past and present. Espinal (2018) expands on the idea that failing to see or even acknowledge inclusion and diversity issues is an example of "White cultural practice" which perpetuates Whiteness as default (2018, p. 148). Systems and services in the United States are set up with the straight, White, able-bodied male in mind primarily, with other groups an afterthought. Feagin (2021) states, "the constant reinforcing decisions of these elite Whites and their acolytes have perpetuated and maintained the deep structure of U.S. racism through many reciprocal linkages and social feedback loops" (p. 49). Straight, White Males were the founders of the United States, and they did not initially share rights and power. Feagin (2020) states, "Today, we still live in a hierarchical society in racial, class, and gender terms, one where White men continue to make the lion's share of major decisions about our economic development, laws and important public policies" (p. 238). Unfortunately, libraries initiated with this

Addressing the History of Discrimination and Bias in Library Systems

mindset as well, as explored later in the chapter. Carmicheal gives great insight as to why libraries may not know library history, "Librarians are rarely motivated to consider the context of their own history, since history provides only a backdrop to the mundane workings of their service ethos" (2005, p. 325). But history reveals the origins of practices and ideals that founded libraries and library workers need to be aware. Because of this, library collections, systems, and services were all initially founded to serve White men. Library professionals must accept and confront the foundation built with these values or never create true justice within the library.

Libraries Need Restorative Justice

In the criminal justice system, there is an idea called restorative justice. Rather than just punishment, restorative justice seeks to repair the harm done (What is "restorative justice" and how does it impact individuals involved in crime?). This idea has merit in the world of diversity and inclusion efforts. The goal should not just be to include others but to make efforts to repair hundreds of years' worth of harm. Davis explains,

"Restorative justice provides an opportunity for those who harm and those harmed to empathize with one another, rather than foster hostility between them and their communities. It encourages the responsible person and the community, where appropriate, to take responsibility for actions resulting in harm and make amends. Restorative justice processes invite individuals and the community to take steps to prevent recurrence" (2019, p.29).

Libraries need healing and growth. Trying to add diverse elements to an inherently exclusionary system will not create something better, it will only mask what currently exists. Systematic changes that will last and create true justice are what libraries should seek, this is no easy task. "Systemic change requires more than goodwill. It necessitates specific, far-reaching, and sustained policy revisions and company-wide commitments that outlast any single political moment and persist despite inevitable hurdles and setbacks" (Tager and Shariyf, 2023). White librarians especially have work to do internally and externally. Libraries need to consider justice versus just inclusivity.

History of Exclusion in Public Libraries

Only in the past fifty of over one hundred and twenty years of history have most libraries even been considerate of race and sexuality, let alone concerned about good or accurate representation or helpful services. To pretend that libraries have always been what libraries are now is damaging and does not acknowledge the growth libraries have seen. Private and subscription libraries existed as the primary libraries in North America for the first hundred years or so. Subscription libraries required fees or donations, limiting members who could not afford memberships (Digital Public Library of America, n.d.). Later, many individuals donated private collections to academic or public libraries, but not for several generations. Carpenter (1996) provides historical insight into early library content in the United States. Calling upon quotes and poems written about the early library collections, Carpenter paints a sad picture. Early libraries in the United States did not impress European visitors who called most of the collection "lumber". Collections consisted primarily of religious texts with few respected academic works. As early as 1656 there is documentation of attempts to share collections among a town, but none ended up lasting

221

long (Harris, 2000). Benjamin Franklin founded the Library Company of Philadelphia in Philadelphia, one of the more famous subscription or social libraries. In 1833 the Peterborough Town Libraries became, arguably, the first public library in the United States (H. Davies, 2013). Public libraries grew slowly, with the Civil War slowing progress for four years. Founded In 1876, the American Library Association (ALA) ushered in growth for the northern part of the United States resumed but less so in the southern states. Gleason states, "In 1876 Arthur Mazyck, librarian of the Charleston Library Society, Charleston, South Carolina writes, 'view of the condition of public libraries in the southern states presents mostly barren prospect. Poorly supported, no fixed system, large cities only'" (1941, p. 11). Graham (2009) reviewed factors that caused more library growth in the northern parts of the country, including economic ability, more demand for education, and more value placed upon reading.

When the development of libraries did happen in the south, White nationalists often supported it. The United Daughters of the Confederacy took an active role in southern schools, especially regarding textbooks and learning materials. These actions carried over into libraries as well, using the funding of said libraries as proof of being 'progressive' (Hand, 2011). Hand goes on to examine the literature supported by such groups and found, "as local librarians developed collections, maintained segregated spaces, and cooperated with the community, they inevitably fostered the transmission of a racial ideology based on White superiority, privilege, and Black subservience" (Hand, 2011, p. 1). Hand's study goes on to show many items that back up the claim, and Whickham and Sweeney (2018) show other ways collections can transmit Whiteness:

Both the easy reader and juvenile biography collections comprise an overrepresentation of White authors, characters, and storylines that privilege White racial frames. Though there were perhaps fewer examples of overt racist tropes than Hand's study reported, these elements were nevertheless still present in the collection. (p. 98)

Hand, Whickham, and Sweeney show that influences of the past are still within libraries today, with collections being especially vulnerable.

If a Black individual did go into a public library, often the police were called, and the individual was arrested. William DuBois gave early criticism of the practice of the segregated library. Griffis states, "DuBois questioned the legality of using tax money from blacks (who represented about a third of Atlanta's population at the time) to support a whites-only public library" (n.d.). As segregation continued, getting libraries for Black Americans was an extremely arduous process. The first library to serve and be fully operated by Black residents was the Louisville Western Branch Library in Louisville, Kentucky in the year 1905 (Newman, 2017). Other libraries for Black communities slowly opened, Griffis (n.d.) created a database of Carnegie-established segregated libraries that goes into details of the establishment of each branch. Communities that could not afford or did not invest the money or materials in a separate branch might allow if at all, Black users of the library to enter through a back door and use a side room, separate from white patrons. Greenlee (2019) describes such an event where Violet Wallach of Locust, New Jersey was shocked at the bigotry in the north. Right before World War II, the data shows disparities in library access. Although Black Americans equaled 50 percent of the population of Mississippi, only 6.6 percent of Black Mississippians had access to library services, versus 28 percent of Whites in Mississippi (Bates, 2010, p. 44). Despite there being many branches available, few services were offered to Black Americans at this time. Wheeler affirms, "A 1935 survey revealed that only 83 of the 565 libraries responding from the 13 southern states provided library services on any level to African

Addressing the History of Discrimination and Bias in Library Systems

Americans" (2004, p. 43). Overall, library access for Black Americans remained disparagingly low for the majority of the 1900s.

The southern part of the United States faced one form of racism, while the north faced another. Carmichael notes, "As one southern adage had it, life for African Americans in the South was terrible from a legal point of view, but many entertained close relationships with individual Whites; in the North, no legal barriers stood in the way of African Americans, but they could pass an entire life without any but the most superficial contacts with Whites" (2005, p. 327). In 1963 a study presented at an ALA conference showed in both the north and south discrimination still existed in library systems, though less discernable than segregation. Many White neighborhoods had higher chances to have a library branch location and would contain more books than non-White neighborhoods (Wiegand, 2018). Although some exceptions, segregation in public services and academia continued well into the late 20th century. Public library segregation still occurred as late as 1963. Wiegand states, "In twenty-one southern public libraries in cities of at least fifty thousand people, only five had fully segregated systems" (2018, p. 199). Many protests took place in libraries. The Granville County Library System (2019) highlights several of the protests that took place in the early 1960s (Granville County Library System, 2019). Public libraries have a long history with race that many do not address, but by not confronting the past, collections, services, and other areas where discrimination still exists, equity will not exist in the present library.

Geographical and economic segregation still happens in 2022. Developers still discriminate against non-white neighborhoods and areas of cities to get desirable real estate. Sauders states, "Rents and home prices in gentrifying neighborhoods generally grew at a rate twice that of non-gentrifying areas" (2022). Discrimination is not always blatant and subtle actions can be just as harmful, especially if left unaddressed. Real estate development practices impact not only the community but also the public libraries that serve those communities.

Libraries have made disability services a priority, but not necessarily a passion. There are certainly long-standing attempts at services for disabled individuals but often, the attempts seem tacked on like afterthoughts and can be meager compared to services for able-bodied individuals. The American Library Association established the National Library Service for the Blind and Print Disabled in 1931 but did not have a policy for library services and people with disabilities until 2001 (Bonnici, 2015). Concern about Library Information Systems programs not training new librarians to support the disabled community (Bonnici, 2015). Over time, more concern for accessibility for the disabled community has come through, but there are limited resources. Large print collections are usually separate and smaller collections, braille is rare, and although audiobooks are on the rise, those often require technology such as a smartphone, raising concerns about income equality. In addition, many libraries are in older buildings that may be hard to make physically accessible. Of course, a new building does not guarantee accessibility. A 41-million-dollar library, built in 2019, lacked full accessibility to wheelchairs (Kim, 2019). Even when librarians consider accessibility and plan to be inclusive in library spaces, full accessibility can be lacking. With a default to able-bodied individuals, libraries struggle to make room for others. Irvall (2005) provides a checklist for basic support of disabled patrons and is a good starting point for considerations that libraries need to make. In many areas, implementing more accessible measures improves services for all patrons. Feldman (2020) goes into detail as to how making a website accessible is worth the work for all patrons and benefits are being seen by those who take the steps to include everyone.

The LGBT+ community also has a complicated relationship with libraries. Identity is intersectional. Many LGBT+ are also not White, and Trans people have suffered even more in general. Many libraries rarely carried materials related to the LGBT+ community until after the 1969 Stonewall Riots. The ALA formed the Task Force on Gay Liberation in 1970, but in 2013 Downey, J., et al. stated, "studies have shown that the vast majority of libraries lack high-quality, comprehensive LGBT collections" (p. 104). While libraries are still trying to develop better collections, several barriers can cause complications, including budgets. In the late 2010s and early 2020s Drag story time events at libraries have become popular but have also faced backlash from communities. There is also the issue of old LGBT+ resources that may be harmful, plus a limited cataloging system that struggles with intersectionality. LGBT+ is a wide spectrum that has also become a political minefield. It is not an easy area to develop collections for, but LGBT+ patrons need to have resources that represent them.

In reviewing the timeline, full integration between races in libraries has only been for one-third of their history in the United States and has served disabled patrons for a little longer though perhaps with more consistency, and the LGBT+ community for the past fifty years, with the quality varying library to library. In addition, an inquiry should be placed into how branches were desegregated. Were the branches serving the Black community combined with the regular branches? If so, this led to a large decrease in Black library professionals and collections. Public libraries have a long history in the United States and are one of the most beloved public services. Libraries continue to evolve to better serve communities, including adding social services, services for helping patrons find jobs, social events, and more. But no institution is without flaws. The difference between a strong institution and a weak one is that a strong institution can acknowledge flaws and work on them, while a weak one ignores flaws and continues in the status quo. Libraries have already proven their strength and adaptability. Libraries have grown and changed exponentially from information storage houses to community strongholds. Public libraries are up to the challenge, but the problems must be acknowledged first.

Major Public Library Issue

The Funding Issue

Developments in most areas of library work take funding of some sort. Whether building improvements, collection growth, or staffing, money is a factor. A major issue for libraries is funding. Funding is outside of the library's control. Whether decided through taxes or an institutional budget, librarians do not control the money. As community wells of information, many libraries can be at the mercy of community ideologies that are often exclusionary. Hand (2011) summarizes the strengths and weaknesses of this ideal,

"The common culture shared by public librarians and library patrons enhanced the librarian's ability to meet the ever-evolving institutional objective of providing local user-communities with the intellectual materials requisite for the public's personal enlightenment, education, and entertainment. Thus, public libraries never operated as a neutral zone free from their unique socio-political cultures. Rather, the library would be encumbered with its respective community values and social mores through the library staff, policies, and within the collections' content" (p. 2-3).

In a perfect world where every community valued inclusivity and welcomed others there would be no issue. But many librarians have faced backlash from the community for trying to be inclusive.

A famous case is that of Ms. Ruth Brown from the Bartlesville, Oklahoma library. In the late 1940s, Ms. Brown was a member of the Congress of Racial Equality and soon became a target of communist accusations in the McCarthy era. This eventually led to her termination, and even friends of Ms. Brown

Addressing the History of Discrimination and Bias in Library Systems

shared punishment for her actions (Robbins, 2001). Similar situations are still occurring in 2022. Nair (2022) reports on how two LGBT+ employees left employment at the Vinton Public Library in Vinton, Iowa after attempts by community members to censor LGBT+ materials the library had purchased. Many other cases have existed throughout the years of library workers receiving punishment or threats for being inclusive. If there is not adequate library leadership, there may not be adequate protection for these workers. Libraries need to be aware that not all community members are interested in inclusion and have a plan for how to protect workers.

Censorship of materials saw a sharp rise in 2022. Friedman (2022) shows data that indicates over 1600 books banned with 41 percent of content containing LGBT+ themes or characters and 40 percent having primary characters who are not White. Bending to the will of the community invites corruption and educates no one. The ALA has experienced such issues firsthand. Wiegand (2018) discusses how the ALA tried to keep itself out of the racial conversation, especially regarding southern libraries in the 1960s. As explored above in the history of public libraries, groups that have special interests can easily garner control over library collections and services through political influence. Academia is similar and different at the same time. Usually, the academic institution controls the budget of the academic library, thus the library is at the mercy of the campus values.

Libraries can and have lost funding trying to remain inclusive. Brown, J. (2022) describes a Michigan library that lost 85 percent of funding due to LGBT+ materials. Carslile (2022) details a Texas library facing the same issue with LGBT+ materials and book bans. Public libraries are meant to serve the entire community, but a vocal minority can make a significant impact. Mehra (2021) identifies the main group libraries are trying to appease as the middle-class, White, Christian majority. Politics play a factor in both academic and public library funding. Academic state-funded institutions will see more impact than private, but if a state leans away from educational funding for higher education, reductions in the budget are likely. The White House's 2019 budget proposal threatened the funding of the Institute of Museum and Library Services which would have had devastating effects on libraries nationwide (Proposal jeopardizes library funding, 2018). Economic crises can affect library budgets as well. During the financial crises of 2007 and 2008, libraries experienced issues across the country with budgets, staff, and more being cut to survive (Economic crisis hits libraries nationwide, 2008). The library cannot operate outside the rest of the world. The state of the country, political and economic, impacts the library.

Library workers and administration are the ones who understand the library situation best. While there is literature explaining ways to get around low funding, Moyer (2005) as a notable example, protections for library funding in both the public and academic setting could help in preventing libraries from being punished for being inclusive, publisher inflation rates, and for lack of communication. Libraries should not have free reign as libraries still serve a specific community and need to be held accountable to that community. However, budgets should not live or die due to a few individuals, and inclusion or change should never be something that a library is punished for.

History of Exclusion in Academic Libraries

Academic libraries have a similar history to public libraries, varying in geographic location and history. Inclusion did not become a mainstream academic value until the late 20th century, and even then, only in particular cases. Academic libraries are like public libraries in that the library reflects the values of a larger community. This can mean that colleges and universities that are for certain groups only, Christian colleges, Women's colleges, and so forth, automatically install biases into libraries and collections that are part of that institution. Academic institutions started for those financially well off. While books have been part of the college system in the United States from the beginning, the library as a separate entity had to develop over time.

Many colleges began development before the revolutionary war with Britain, and most had a collection of books acting as a 'library'. Some of these institutions include Harvard, Yale, the College of New Jersey (Princeton), and The University of Pennsylvania (Harris, 2000). War slowed academic growth and many colleges did not start to recover and grow until the mid-19th century. The first library buildings built, between 1840 and 1870, based themselves on British bookrooms (Kaser, 1989). Up until the late 19th century, most academic library collections came from donations or gifts from well-off or alumni donors and thus contained little current or new literature. As the academic scene in the states grew, so too did library functions and needs. By the time the 19th century ended, libraries as an institution grew fast. Kaser states, "The first completely tri-partitioned academic library in this country, and the first to make a frank separation of books from readers, was constructed at Lehigh University in 1877" (1989, p. 62). With the development of the first separate building just for an academic library, growth within the field continued. Librarians trained through apprenticeships until 1887, when Melvin Dewey established the first formal school for librarians (Martin, 1990, p. 547). While the profession itself had a decent history formal academic training and organization did not come till almost the 20th century. As the new library buildings rose, so did the popularity of libraries as a separate department and academic libraries became a staple of colleges and universities.

Through the 19th and early 20th centuries, only the elite could afford higher education (Snyder, 1993). For many years, primarily wealthy, White men got to pursue higher education while others got few opportunities from sparse academic institutions. The first higher education institution in the United States to allow women was founded in 1803, Bradford College (Campus History & Description, n.d.), while most institutions would not accept women for much longer. Oberlin College acted as one of the first co-ed colleges in the United States, also accepting Black students and providing the first Black woman to earn a bachelor's degree, Sarah Jane Woodson (Carlton, 2022). Oberlin still had heavy limitations on women's education. Women could only participate in one program and on Mondays women got dismissed from classes to do male students' laundry (Carlton, 2022). More colleges became co-ed over the 19th century, but progress stayed slow and limited. Many Ivy League colleges, Yale, Harvard, and Princeton did not allow women until the 1960s and 1970s and only did so to stay competitive with enrollment rates (Carlton, 2022). Academia lacks women faculty, especially non-White women faculty. Despite women being half or more of enrollment at most institutions, "Within academia, women make up only 31 percent of full-time faculty in the U.S. and 27 percent of tenured faculty. Women of color held an even smaller number of positions, with Black women and Hispanic women making up only 3 percent each of full-time faculty" (Carlton, 2022). With decades of history that do not even touch on affordability (which is still an issue today with millions of student loan debt-burdening United States graduates), academia has a long way to go with inclusion. This is without even addressing race, disabilities, or LGBT+ groups.

Unfortunately, academia did not just exclude non-White students many academic institutions actively participated in slavery. Even if an institution did not acquire donations from rich slave owners, the campus itself might have had slaves, such as at the University of Virginia (Smith, 2022). Slavery is not the legacy higher education institutions want to be connected to, and thus many leave it unexplored and undocumented. Smith notes, "But Wilder says most American colleges founded before the Civil War relied on money derived from slavery" (2022). This includes at least thirty-seven institutions that

Addressing the History of Discrimination and Bias in Library Systems

had been founded before the year 1800 and another thirty-one that were founded between 1800-1820 (Snyder, 1993, p. 63).

Other connections of academia to racism include faculty scholarship. Smith, for example, (2022) laments, "Scientific racism is another of Harvard's legacies. In the 19th and 20th centuries, some Harvard professors proposed scientific theories they said proved the inherent inferiority of Black people". Libraries are not the only ones that must confront the past. Academic institutions across the United States are responsible for owning their origins, whether good or bad. Owning the past will create a better future. Smith (2022) states, "The goal is to create more historically aware young people who strive for better lives and stronger bonds with each other". Race is still an issue in academia as shown by the National Center for Education Statistics (2022) which reported that in 2019, 435 of the 757 hate crimes across college campuses were connected to race. To see a better future, the past must become known. Academic libraries must accept that the history of the academic institution is the library's history as well. For the educational history of students who are not white, the data is spotty at best, but the growth of five- to nineteen-year-olds enrolled in school jumped from less than ten percent in 1860 to almost seventy percent in the 1960s (Snyder, 1993, p. 6). For the Asian American community, the population remained small through 1965, then with new legislation, the Immigration and Nationality Act of 1965, a 900 percent increase in Asian American immigration occurred over the course of 30 years (Tamura, 2001, p. 28). Looking at the previous dates, paired with the dates higher education began in the United States, only the past fifty years or so have been substantially inclusive of non-White races. Collections, services, and so forth were all created without the input or concern of Black, Asian, Native, or other representatives and now libraries and academia, in general, must play catch-up to provide equal levels of representation. More to be discussed about racial representation is below in limitations in the field itself.

The earliest efforts to include the disabled community in higher education are spotty, but in 1864 President Lincoln authorized the creation of a college division at the Columbia Institution for the Deaf and Dumb (Madaeus, 2011, p. 5). Individuals with disabilities did succeed in higher education independently, but with no overall support or services for disabled people. Wide-spread progress did not happen till post-World War I when many disabled veterans began pursuing education leading to legislation for educational assistance with disabled individuals as a focus (Madaeus, 2011, p. 6). More veterans led to more assistance and more representation of disabled students within higher education. The pattern of growth would continue for several decades until other movements caused further growth. Madaeus remarks, "The civil rights movement and legislation, as well as education legislation at the K–12 level, served as a catalyst for an era of greatly expanded services" (2011, p. 9). The United States passed legislation requiring education for disabled students in 1975, the Education of All Handicapped Children Act, which included services for transition to adult life and post-secondary education. Pairing with the Vocational Rehabilitation Act of 1973, which disallowed the exclusion of a disabled person based solely on a handicap for any program receiving federal aid, these programs increased disabled individuals' ability to get a post-secondary education. As stated in the section above, education in information sciences rarely covers disability services. Since the 2010s, libraries' focuses have shifted to accessibility on academic library websites and guides, which are often lacking. Some libraries may still struggle with other avenues, such as assistive technology or physical access, but many libraries struggle to make websites and digital collections accessible. Academia has made great strides in including disabled students in a brief time, but once again, is a separate service and not a default. Making digital collections and websites accessible can improve functionalities for all individuals. In the next ten years, it is hoped by the disabled community that such 'accommodations will become the new norm for development. Mulliken (2017) gives several suggestions and insights on how academic libraries can improve services for patrons. More to be discussed about disability services below in limitations in the field itself.

The LGBT+ community once again rarely found support until post-Stonewall, in 1969. Pre-Stonewall, underground movements at institutions did exist. Rankin (2019) describes, "A climate of fear, due to campus administrations covertly searching for 'homosexual' faculty, staff, and students, sent queer-spectrum and trans-spectrum people underground" (p. 436). UC Berkeley Alumni Bob Plantz co-founded Students for Gay Power in 1969, one of the first-ever LGBTQ+ organizations on a college campus (Gender Equity Resource Center, UC Berkeley., 2020). In the United States, challenges to anti-sodomy laws did not reach the federal level until 2001, and the right to marriage across the nation was not until 2015. Currently, LGBT+ students can still face major difficulties. Rankin (2019) divulges how some disciplines are more welcoming of LGBT+ than others, with humanities being more inviting and sciences, in general, being less. These areas create micro-environments for students and can influence a student's level of engagement and retention. In 2019 167 out of 757 hate crimes on higher education campuses were motivated by gender identity or sexual orientation (National Center for Education Statistics, 2022). LGBT+ is a fast-growing community with many diverse groups. For academia and academic libraries to properly support the LGBT+ community, ongoing communication is necessary, as well as an understanding of what the community needs.

Today, discrimination based on race, gender identity, and other identities is occurring on college campuses, but solutions are few. The focus is wrong. Cabrera points out, "when 'diversity' initiatives are created or a racist issue occurs on college campuses, the focus tends to be on racially minoritized campus populations. Implicitly, this means ignoring the cause of the racial issue" (2017, p. 16). The discrimination comes from the White, straight, able-bodied bias in colleges and libraries, yet that aspect is usually ignored. To make progress, academic libraries and institutions must work to address White default and White supremacy and the harm caused by such beliefs and systems. Academia has a long history interwoven with not only White default but White supremacy. These institutions need to address the past and work to create a more informed, educated, and empathetic future.

Major Challenge for Academic Libraries

Demonstrating Value to Institutions

Academic libraries are facing the issue of institutions not seeing the value of the academic library or believing that a library may no longer be relevant can reduce the library's budget and staff. If a library has a reduced budget and staff, it will be unable to improve systems and work toward better inclusion. Since many academic institutions do not have funding or staff for diversity centers, libraries may be the only service on campus that offers materials for all groups of students and staff. With little history of having to 'justify' existence in the past, academic libraries are struggling to adapt, but lack time. Hinchliffe (2022) notes that "An Ithaka S+R survey of US academic library deans and directors found that by September 2020, 75 percent of those libraries that did have a budget for 2020–21 had experienced a budget cut compared with what would have otherwise been expected before the pandemic". What did libraries cut? Collection cuts occurred at 62 percent of libraries, 59 percent had cuts to staffing, and 53 percent cut funds from operations (Hinchliffe, 2022). With enrollment numbers in higher education on a current decline, academic libraries are often easy targets for budgetary cuts. Academic libraries especially struggle to communicate value to campus communities, not having the traditional academic

Addressing the History of Discrimination and Bias in Library Systems

value of credits or the ability to show retention rates of library users. Hinchliffe states, "Librarians need to ensure that they are creating value for their institutions and communicating their impact" (2022). Communication of impact is an arduous task for academic libraries but is the only solution to reducing budgetary cuts in academia. Both public and academic libraries struggle to show usage and meaningful statistics that can influence budgetary decisions while dealing with the constant inflation of digital resources, reduced staffing, and new demands for services. Academic libraries may consider showing an impact on not just retention and recruitment, but also a direct impact on students with disabilities, of the LGBT+ community, and students who are not White.

Smaller library budgets make creating more efforts in inclusion difficult, especially when faced with a lack of staff. With less staff, libraries have less time to devote to inclusion growth efforts and may stay on dated systems. Hook (2022) examined The Association of Research Libraries data and found that in the past twenty-six years, the median number of library workers at academic law libraries had decreased from twenty-seven to eighteen. Law libraries are not the only ones seeing fewer workers. Library professionals in general saw a decline. Barrows indicates, "cumulative employment among librarians, library technicians, and library assistants dropped severely in 2020 to 264,270, down from 308,000 in 2019" (2021). Despite this, many Americans still use the library as data shows that, "46 percent of adults said they used a public library or bookmobile in the previous 12 months. Millennials (aged 18 to 35) had the highest usage rate of any generation, at 53 percent" (Barrows, 2021). At an understaffed library, the services that would generate usage and therefore justification for higher budgets are impossible without enough staff. Many libraries are doing more with less, but burnout among librarians is likely if the current trends persist.

Extra challenges for higher education academic librarianship exists in two areas. One is the hiring practices of the academic institution, which can affect librarian retention. Tied to the rules and practices of the academic institution, academic library administrators need to work to garner as much support as possible in institutional administration. The other is the trend of academic librarians being removed from faculty status. Horowitz (2013) looks at the University of Virginia's change of library faculty to staff status. Librarians work to support all students and faculty and being able to attend certain councils and committees can be crucial in the library having a strong voice on campus. Horowitz (2013) notes, "Librarians who are faculty can participate in the General Faculty Council, which would not be the case for library staffers. In Academic Librarian Status (2021) currently, forty-five out of 286 academic library positions are without any faculty status, with institutions like Harvard and the University of Pennsylvania on the list. In addition, removing a status from a position is bound to create negative work environments of job insecurity and dissatisfaction. Both institutional limitations and faculty status are challenges academia has created. Being unable to have control over the library means being unable to grow the library properly.

Without demonstrated value to the institution, academic libraries may lose budget, staff, and even physical space. Academic libraries are making efforts to show value in a way that academics can appreciate in the 21st century, (Malapela and De Jager, 2018), (Oakleaf, 2010), and (Yamaguchi and Richardson, 2018) but more work needs to be done.

Racism and Discrimination Within Library Science as a Field

Another avenue of exclusion is within the field of library science itself. Mehra (2021) calls out current library efforts as performative and 'safe' and calls upon libraries to step up with more accurate information and to qualify actual anti-racist statements with apologies for past neutrality and passivity. Current library actions do not challenge the public. While they bring attention and awareness, they do not challenge the white default that has been set up by society. The idea of neutrality within the library profession is flawed. Brook et al, advocates, "Presumed and oppressive "neutrality" of Whiteness, is embedded in three particular aspects of public services in academic libraries: the physical spaces of service delivery, public services staff, and service delivery methods and values" (2015, p. 248). Neutrality ties directly to the status quo. Walker states, "Neutrality is itself a political choice, Dunn argues, and is one that bolsters the status quo" (2018). As established above, the status quo of the United States is white bias and white default, leaning more every day into white supremacy (Carless, 2020), (Meltzer and Dokoupil, 2017), and (Starks, 2021). Libraries want to provide information and services to all, and at a face value, it might seem that 'neutrality' can accomplish that idea. But the truth of the matter is that neutrality is harmful. Desmond Tutu put it best, "If you are neutral in situations of injustice, you have chosen the side of the oppressor" (Desmond Tutu). It is past time that libraries become interested in justice, not just diversity and inclusion.

Reading about libraries under attack for just doing the minimum (a book display), it can understandably be scary for a library to take strong action. The first step a library can take is to review current internal actions, familiarize themselves with the history of the library, and understand why current efforts may be only performative rather than corrective. Anti-racism is ongoing work, not a Cinderella transformation. What things at the library: hiring practices, services, systems, collections, and so forth are perpetuating the white default? What can the library do? Everything cannot be accomplished at once, starting on just one area is still progress.

Examining the younger United States Generations shows changes in demographics. Fry (2020) showed that among 6- to 21-year-olds 52 percent are non-Hispanic Whites, meaning the other 48 percent have some racial diversity. In addition, more of the younger generations identify as LGBT+ and there is 21 percent of Generation Z adults identify as LGBT+ (McShane, 2022). The United States population is also seeing a growth in people with disabilities. The Institute on Disability reports that up to 13 percent of people live with a disability of some kind (2021). Yet accessibility issues are common in library buildings, and accessibility often takes a backseat to other library concerns. Library workers are not the only ones who suffer from a lack of diversity in staff. Bocko, et al (2021), found studies that showed that although African American students more frequently used the academic library, these students approached staff less, greeted with unfriendly body language and lack of diversity making the students uncomfortable and feeling less welcomed. Many librarians also continue to report racial microaggressions in the workplace (Dalton, et al., 2018). While libraries have pushed for diversity for the past few decades, other changes such as digitizing and web access, became the forefront of library progress. True change in creating better diversity and equity remained optional at best. But Generation Z shows this may not always be the case. Whiteness can no longer be the default of library systems if libraries want to remain relevant to more diverse generations.

Even the process of becoming a librarian comes with biases and obstacles. In the past, this avenue had harsh barriers for non-White individuals, and there are still hurdles and biases to overcome today. Many libraries today commit unconscious bias actions versus intentional ones as in the past. But restrictive practices still exist and can be in performance at libraries. How can libraries stand for diversity and inclusion when library professionals cannot even include coworkers as equals? Representation is different from tokenism, and many individuals are suffering under the idea of tokenism in library spaces. Tokenism is the idea of one individual representing an entire group and is performative. Real

Addressing the History of Discrimination and Bias in Library Systems

representation seeks to create change and diversity. Library science lacks diversity. Barrows shows, "In 2020, just 9.5 percent of librarians identified as Black or African American, 9.9 percent as Hispanic or Latino (of any race), and 3.5 percent as Asian-American or Pacific Islander" (2020). Many studies have been done to discover why a profession with diversity as a value lacks diversity. Espinal (2018) explores several pieces of literature that examine how White women dominate the work field of librarianship and thus, control the perception of what is 'professional' in a library setting. Professionalism, or extreme emotional regulation, is an issue of many workplaces that claim 'professionalism' in any United States terminology. Espinal explains, "Asking POC to remain emotionless is a form of cultural bias and cultural imperialism. It is one of the ways Whiteness maintains power: power structures are maintained by policing emotions and the responses of people of color to hostility in the workplace" (2018, p. 154). Being unable to express frustration, fear, upset, or other emotions in the workplace is not healthy. Many studies, including Joe (2019), Matteson (2013), and Shuler (2013) examine how emotional labor in libraries can lead to burnout and often people leaving the workplace. The current picture of professionalism in librarianship limits what emotions are allowed to be expressed and by whom, which severely limits who will participate in the field.

Recruitment and retention of library workers is a challenge that the community faces currently. Low salaries and increased cost of living can certainly make recruitment a challenge. Discrimination in the workplace is a major issue in creating a healthy work environment, and libraries are no exception. Cunningham relays, "Thornton surveyed African American female librarians and found that one-third of the respondents reported feelings of isolation. More disturbingly, seventy out of ninety-eight respondents reported experiencing racial discrimination" (2019, p. 13). Are libraries assuming that their employees cannot discriminate based on their profession? Library workers are still human beings with biases, ignoring those biases is a mistake that will create more problems. Libraries must make a better effort to create not only training but also create a way to report discrimination so that the victims feel safe and have consequences for those who discriminate. In addition, libraries must start training all staff on biases and microaggressions. Arroyo-Ramirez (2018) reported on a Library Information Science Field Microaggressions Zine, meant to engage, and challenge the LIS community. The two most reported causes of microaggressions included race and immigration status (Arroyo-Ramirez, 2018, p. 121). To gain diversity in the field of library science systemic biases and racism within the profession need to be brought to the center stage and addressed immediately. All libraries need a form of anti-racist training for all employees to be mandatory. Not just for co-workers, but also in consideration of the patrons that the library will serve.

It may be hard to attract new and more diverse individuals to a field that the media has proclaimed terminal. The idea that libraries and therefore librarians are going to become unneeded came about when the internet became widespread. USA Today published a list of careers that would not exist in 2030, with librarians being number one (Hoon, 2017). A letter to the editor opposed this article stating that, "84% of recent graduates from American Library Association accredited schools have found jobs in public libraries" (Gannett Satellite Information Network, 2017). Even so, the myth prevails that librarianship is a sinking ship, and that does not attract many.

Library education and training can vary greatly and rarely covers disability services, LGBT+ services, or other essential diversity pieces of training. The cost of education itself can be a severe financial barrier, especially for oppressed communities. Those who do find a way to afford an education may not learn about all patrons, just the default. Poole (2021) relays, "In a 2018 report on the future of Library and Information Science (LIS) education, the Institute of Museum and Library Services (IMLS) underscored the profession's lack of racial and ethnic diversity" (p. 258). Poole (2021) dives deep into student recruitment and retention in library education and found that there needs to be more research, as separate groups saw value in different methods.

In cataloging and acquisitions, there are several issues to address. A lack of author information can create many barriers to providing materials from authors of divergent backgrounds, and relying too much on publisher lists, which have also shown to have a White bias, can further contribute to this issue. The Library of Congress has had to change many subject headings in the past fifty years due to dated terminology such as "transvestites" for the LGBT+ community and "alien" for immigration and even those changes are criticized for not being enough (Jensen, 2021). Language morphs not only with time but location. Drabinski notes, "Subject headings, often cast by catalogers as a kind of pure, objective language, are not; where and when and by whom subject headings are used makes all the difference in terms of meaning" (2013, p. 95). ("Queering the Catalog: Queer Theory and the Politics of Correction - JSTOR") Because language and cataloging are so tied to society untangling White bias and default from the process feels impossible, Drabinski states, "If social categories and names are understood as embedded in contingencies of space, time, and discourse, then bias is inextricable from the process of classification and cataloging" (2013, p. 108). While the Library of Congress has a language issue, Dewey has a racism issue. Melvil Dewey, one of the best-known names in library science, was extremely antisemitic, Weigand (1995), and racism has bled into the system. Gooding-Call (2021) breaks down how the Dewey system catalogs religion by race and highly favors Judeo-Christianity. Gooding-Call acknowledges reorganizing a whole collection is almost impossible and that library workers like Dorothy Porter are trying to make it better, but can a system that came to the world broken possibly be fixed? Cataloging is by no means a straightforward process and a truly inclusive working model has yet to come forth but knowing the limitations of the system used and the flaws it presents means librarians can start to work on alternatives and continue to improve the current system until new avenues are available.

Cataloging ties directly into acquisitions which must interact with the publishing field, another predominantly white field in the United States. Tager and Shariyf disclose,

"Penguin Random House released its first-ever public, multiyear report on the subject in December 2021. Their stats revealed that white U.S. contributors (authors, illustrators, and translators) accounted for 74.9 percent of the books released by the publishing giant between 2019 and 2021" (2023).

Penguin is not the exception either, although most publishing companies are not releasing demographic data of authors. In addition, most collection development policies are cautious against self-publishing. While this is understandable as there is less quality control in self-publishing it does not consider the bias of the publishing industry itself and the dangers of relying on the industry's expertise. As mentioned above, author information is critical in creating collections that are not just primarily white, male writers.

Education, systems, workplace environment, and training, the list is long on areas where library science can make improvements for inclusion and diversity. First, acknowledgment of problems must happen, and after that discussions and planning of courses of action to create improvements. Moving forward, library professionals need to not only acknowledge the issues but listen to the voices of Black and other non-white librarians, LGBT+, and disabled voices as they speak up. White librarians have been submerged in White culture their entire lives. It can be easy for White, able-bodied people to not be able to always tell when they are being exclusionary because they are not oppressed in that way. Elevate diverse voices for solutions, but those who are not oppressed need to be helping to complete the actions.

Addressing the History of Discrimination and Bias in Library Systems

CALL TO ACTION

How can we address the past to improve the future? Ignoring a library's past does not make it go away, nor do the systems and issues that originated in the past that may prevail today. How can the librarian field improve in this area and what actions should be taken to make the field itself more inclusive? First, learning from the mistakes of the past, Espinal (2018) points out that committees and policies or written documents or statements have not worked. Quickly forgotten or challenged, these efforts do not create institutional change alone. Having documentation saying a library stands for diversity is not in itself a terrible thing. A public statement is still projecting library values, but too often policy becomes the end of the action. Committees are also not bad in themselves, but with how little diversity there is in the library world, who is at the table? More than likely most libraries do not have enough diversity to create a committee with impact. In addition, it is unfair to expect library workers of diverse groups to participate based on identity. Not all diverse workers may want to be part of a committee or group and not wanting to participate should not be judged as a negative for individuals who live in a world that projects these problems into their lives every day.

Wagner (2010), Alburo (2020), and Foy (2021) all discuss different challenges and areas of success in creating a more diverse library workforce. Wagner describes the Urban Library Program, as a program created to, "recruit, educate, hire, and retain a diverse paraprofessional workforce. Five cohorts of students, who reflected the diversity of Saint Paul, completed

the program and received a certification in Urban Library Services from SCU" (2010, p. 129). Alburo (2020) looks at efforts that have been undertaken by other workforces to create DEI and examines how these strategies might work for libraries. Foy (2021) focuses on recruitment and retention. Additional research comes out every year for library professionals to create a more diverse workforce. But the major problem within the library world is a lack of forthright action. Espinal (2018) calls for large-scale actions and the level of innovation libraries have shown in growing into technology and renovating spaces. Small actions are unlikely to fix large problems. Library science as a field has been struggling with diversity in the field for over forty years. Librarians are highly organized and good at sharing practices, services, and other practices that work well. When working practices are found librarians are likely to share easily and readily.

Reviewing collection development practices and collection diversity audits are common steps that libraries are taking. Practices like cataloging, technology purchasing, events, programming, and so forth need evaluation. Libraries and Library science as a field, need to address the exclusionary practices of the past to create a better future. Many library workers may not be aware of the library's historical practices and marginalization of groups. Libraries need to start by educating staff on the past. When did the library de-segregate? When did it start carrying LGBT+ materials? How many materials focus on disabled users? If this knowledge is lost or not easily available, the author would encourage it as a side project for someone if possible. Many things, cataloging practices, policies, etc., that libraries still use developed during times of segregation and exclusion, and taking a deeper look reflects the values of those systems.

Libraries have internal work to do. Primarily, White librarians need to work on themselves. White librarians must understand their privileges and roles in systemic racism. Davis explains, "Structural racism is not something present-day white people chose or created. They benefit from it, however, and are responsible for changing it because the status quo is racism" (2019 p.33). Shame that leads to inaction is not helpful. Action is what is needed to combat structural inequalities. Able-bodied people need to make similar considerations, as well as non-LGBT+ individuals. Training on privilege, biases, and so forth is imperative. There can be no development, no growth without staff having an education. A library should also have a system in place for reporting issues of discrimination and dealing with the aftermath. When dealing with reported issues libraries need to keep in mind where the issue is occurring. A person of color, an LGBT+ individual, or a disabled individual is not responsible just for existing. Libraries must address the discrimination at the source, head-on. In a perfect world, an entire academic institution would educate staff and faculty on these issues and have systems in place, but if nothing else the library can be the beginning. After staff education, more work at the local level can be done. On a national level, librarians need to challenge the ALA and other institutions to listen to the disabled, LGBT+, and people of color. If those organizations choose not to change, choose to not grow, and embrace true diversity and separate from White supremacy are they worth keeping?

CONCLUSION

Libraries have come a long way from past marginalization actions in the past, and a huge part of change and growth is the willingness to do so. For libraries to move forward, library professionals must acknowledge the past and work towards reconciliation versus repentance. The mistakes of the past cannot be undone, but the prevention of future instances of bias and discrimination can be achieved. United States libraries can strive for something they have never had before, true justice for all patrons. To accomplish true justice, libraries must address the past and current systems that promote or do not go against the 'White default' and other discriminatory practices. How can individuals practice restorative justice? Davis relays,

"For white practitioners particularly, this means developing and honing skills to identify and address historical and systemic harm, navigate racial differences, and facilitate restorative justice encounters involving racially diverse participants or involving racial conflict" (2019, p. 75).

There are unfortunately many hurdles in addressing these issues, not limited to lack of budgetary control, the current state of library science as a field, and lack of knowledge about such issues. But libraries have proven resilient in the past and the author believes libraries will continue to do so in the future.

REFERENCES:

Academic Librarian Status. (2021, June 6). Evanwell. https://evanwill.github.io/academic-librarian-status/about.html

Adler, M. (2017). Classification along the color line: Excavating racism in the stacks. *Journal of Critical Library and Information Studies, 1*(1). doi:10.24242/jclis.v1i1.17

Alabi, J. (2018). From hostile to inclusive: Strategies for improving the racial climate of academic libraries. *Library Trends, 67*(1), 131–146. https://muse.jhu.edu/article/706992/pdf. doi:10.1353/lib.2018.0029

Alburo, J., Bradshaw, A. K., Santiago, A. E., Smith, B., & Vinopal, J. (2020). Looking beyond libraries for inclusive recruitment and retention practices: Four successful approaches. In *Critical Librarianship*. Emerald Publishing Limited. doi:10.1108/S0732-067120200000041009

Arroyo-Ramirez, E., Chou, R. L., Freedman, J., Fujita, S., & Orozco, C. M. (2018). The reach of a long-arm stapler: Calling in microaggressions in the LIS field through zine work. *Library Trends*, *67*(1), 107–130. doi:10.1353/lib.2018.0028

Barrows, K. (2021, June 10). *Library professionals: Facts, figures, and union membership –Department for Professional Employees, AFL.* CIO. https://www.dpeaflcio.org/factsheets/library-professionals-f acts-and-figures

Bonnici, L. J., Maatta, S. L., Brodsky, J., & Steele, J. E. (2015). Second national accessibility survey: Librarians, patrons, and disabilities. *New Library World*, *116*(9/10), 503–516. doi:10.1108/NLW-03-2015-0021

Brannen, M. H., Milewski, S., & Mack, T. (2017). Providing Staff Training and Programming to Support People with Disabilities: An Academic Library Case Study. *Public Services Quarterly*, *13*(2), 61–77. doi:10.1080/15228959.2017.1298491

Brook, F., Ellenwood, D., & Lazzaro, A. E. (2015). In pursuit of antiracist social justice: Denaturalizing whiteness in the academic library. *Library Trends*, *64*(2), 246–284. https://muse.jhu.edu/article/610078/pdf. doi:10.1353/lib.2015.0048

Brown, J. (2022, August 22). *Michigan library risks closing after voters pull funding over LG-BT-themed books.* Fox News. https://www.foxnews.com/us/michigan-library-risks-closing-vo ters-pull-funding-lgbt-themed-books

Cabrera, N. L., Franklin, J. D., & Watson, J. S. (2017). *Whiteness in higher education: The invisible missing link in diversity and racial analyses.* Wiley Subscription Services, Inc.

Campus History & Description. (n.d.). Bradford alumni assoc. http://www.bradfordalumni.org/brad-fordcampushistory/history.html

Carless, W. (2021, March 17). White supremacist propaganda hit an all-time high in 2020, New Report says. *USA Today.* https://www.usatoday.com/story/news/nation/2021/03/17/white-supremacist-propaganda-hits-all-time-high/4721323001/

Carlisle, M. (2022, September 7). Public libraries face threats to funding as book bans surge. *Time.* https://time.com/6211350/public-libraries-book-bans/

Carlton, G. (2022, February 22). *A history of women in Higher Education: Best Col-leges.* BestColleges.com. https://www.bestcolleges.com/news/analysis/2021/03/21/histor y-women-higher-education/

Carmichael, J. V. (2005). Southern Librarianship and the Culture of Resentment. *Libraries & the Cultural Record*, *40*(3), 324–352. https://www.jstor.org/stable/25541934. doi:10.1353/lac.2005.0044

Carpenter, K. E. (1996). *Readers & libraries: Toward a history of libraries and culture in America.* Library of Congress.

Bocko, A. F., Guth, L., & Broadnax, M. (2021). Library response to Black Liberation Collective: A review of student calls for change and implications for anti-racist initiatives in academic libraries. *RSR. Reference Services Review.*

Crilly, J., Everitt, R., & Clarke, M. (2022). Liberate the Library: What it Means to Decolonise and Why it is Necessary. *In Narrative expansions: Interpreting decolonisation in academic libraries.* Facet Publishing. https://research.gold.ac.uk/id/eprint/30930/

Dali, K., & Caidi, N. (Eds.). (2020). *Humanizing LIS Education and Practice: Diversity by Design* (1st ed.). Routledge. https://doiorg.grinnell.idm.oclc.org/10.4324/9780429356209 doi:10.4324/9780429356209

Dalton, S. D., Mathapo, G., & Sowers-Paige, E. (2018). Diversity Dialogues: Navigating Law Librarianship While Black: A Week in the Life of a Black Female Law Librarian. *Law Library Journal, 110*, 429. https://heinonline.org/HOL/Page?handle=hein.journals/llj110& div=26&g_sent=1&casa_token=&collection=journals

Davies, H. (2013, February 26). *About ALA.* ALA. https://www.ala.org/aboutala/1833

Davis, F. E., & Handguns, E. O. (2019). *The little book of race and restorative justice: Black lives, healing, and us social transformation.* Skyhorse Publishing Company, Incorporated.

Digital Public Library of America. (n.d.). *A history of US public libraries.* DPLA. https://dp.la/exhibitions/history-us-public-libraries/beginnings

Downey, J., Antell, K., & Strothmann, M. (2013). Self-censorship in selection of LGBT themed materials. *Reference and User Services Quarterly, 53*(2), 104–107. doi:10.5860/rusq.53n2.104

Drabinski. (2013). Queering the Catalog: Queer Theory and the Politics of Correction. *The Library Quarterly (Chicago), 83*(2), 94–111. doi:10.1086/669547

American Libraries. (2008). Economic crisis hits libraries nationwide. *American Libraries, 39*(6), 26-27. https://grinnell.idm.oclc.org/login?url=https://www.proquest .com/trade-journals/economic-crisis-hits-libraries-nationwid e/docview/197186999/se-2

Espinal, I., Sutherland, T., & Roh, C. (2018). A holistic approach for inclusive librarianship: Decentering whiteness in our profession. *Library Trends, 67*(1), 147–162. doi:10.1353/lib.2018.0030

Ettarh, F. (2018, January 10). *Vocational awe and librarianship: The lies we tell ourselves.* In the Library with the Lead Pipe. http://www.inthelibrarywiththeleadpipe.org/2018/vocational-awe/

Feagin, J. R. (2020). *The white racial frame: Centuries of racial framing and counter-framing.* Routledge. doi:10.4324/9780429353246

Addressing the History of Discrimination and Bias in Library Systems

Feldman, D. (2020, March 19). Council post: Accessible websites are better for everyone (and better for business too). *Forbes*. https://www.forbes.com/sites/forbesagencycouncil/2020/03/19/accessible-websites-are-better-for-everyone-and-better-for-b usiness-too/?sh=316ccca748aa

Foy, C. M. (2021). Successful applications of diversity, equity, and inclusion programming in various professional settings: Strategies to increase DEI in libraries. *Journal of Library Administration*, *61*(6), 676–685. doi:10.1080/01930826.2021.1947057

Friedman, J., & Johnson, N. F. (2022, October 11). *Banned in the USA: The growing movement to censor books in schools*. PEN America. https://pen.org/report/banned-usa-growing-movement-to-censor -books-in-schools/

Fry, R., & Parker, K. (2020, August 14). *Early benchmarks show 'post-millennials' on track to be most diverse, best-educated generation yet*. Pew Research Center's Social &; Demographic Trends Project. https://www.pewresearch.org/social-trends/2018/11/15/early-b enchmarks-show-post-millennials-on-track-to-be-most-diverse-best-educated-generation-yet/

Gabbat, A. (2022, December 24). 'a streak of extremism': US book bans may increase in 2023. *The Guardian*. https://www.theguardian.com/us-news/2022/dec/24/us-book-bans -streak-of-extremism

Gannett Satellite Information Network. (2017, November 6). Reader: Librarians aren't going anywhere. *USA Today*. https://www.usatoday.com/story/opinion/2017/11/06/reader-lib rarians-arent-going-anywhere/837858001/

Gender Equity Resource Center. (2020). *Part II: Being gay in a 1960s fraternity*. UC Berkeley. YouTube. https://www.youtube.com/watch?v=eqC9na4oI3A

Gleason, E. A. (1941). *The southern negro and the Public Library: A Study of the government and administration of Public Library Service to Negroes in the South, by Eliza Atkins Gleason. with a foreword by Louis R. Wilson*. The University of Chicago Press.

Gooding-Call, A. (2021, September 17). Racism in the dewey decimal system. *BOOK RIOT*. https://bookriot.com/racism-in-the-dewey-decimal-system/

Graham. (2009). *A Right to Read Segregation and Civil Rights in Alabama's Public Libraries, 1900-1965*. University of Alabama Press.

Granville County Library System. (2019, February 4). *The heroes of desegregating in public libraries*. Granville County Library System. https://granville.lib.nc.us/2019/02/the-heroes-of-desegregat ing-in-public-libraries/

Greenlee, C. J. (2019, March 26). On the battle to desegregate the nation's libraries. *Literary Hub*. https://lithub.com/on-the-battle-to-desegregate-the-nations-libraries/

Griffis, M. R. (n.d.). *Library profiles and resources: The Roots of Community*. The University of Southern Mississippi. https://aquila.usm.edu/rocprofiles/#lvw

Hand, S. (2011). *Transmitting Whiteness: Librarians, Children, and Race, 1900-1930s.* USM. https://aquila.usm.edu/masters_theses/207

Harris, M. H. (2000). *History of libraries in the Western World*. Scarecrow.

Hathcock, A. (2015, April 7). White librarianship in blackface: Diversity initiatives in lis. In *the Library with the Lead Pipe*. http://www.inthelibrarywiththeleadpipe.org/2015/lis-diversity/

Hinchliffe, L. J. (2022). Commentary: The future (budget) of the academic library. *Physics Today*, *75*(8), 10–11. doi:10.1063/PT.3.5048

Hitchcock, J. (2002). *Lifting the white veil: An exploration of white American culture in a multiracial context*. Crandall, Dostie & Douglass Books.

Hook, P. (2022, February 17). *Peak Library staff size is likely in the past*. RIPS Law Librarian Blog. https://ripslawlibrarian.wordpress.com/2022/02/17/peak-library-staff-size-is-likely-in-the-past/

Hoon, M. (2017, November 1). Careers: 8 jobs that won't exist in 2030. *USA Today*. https://www.usatoday.com/story/money/careers/2017/10/13/8-jobs-that-wont-exist-in-2030/104219994/

Horowitz, J. (2013, March 7). Library employees protest changed title. *The Cavalier Daily - University of Virginia's Student Newspaper*. https://www.cavalierdaily.com/article/2013/03/library-enacts-title-changes

Hudson, D. J. (2017). On" diversity" as anti-racism in library and information studies: A critique. *Journal of Critical Library and Information Studies*, *1*(1). http://journals.litwinbooks.com/index.php/jclis/article/view/6. doi:10.24242/jclis.v1i1.6

Huffman, G. (2019, April 10). Twisted sources: How confederate propaganda ended up in the South's schoolbooks. *Facing South*. https://www.facingsouth.org/2019/04/twisted-sources-how-confederate-propaganda-ended-souths-schoolbooks

IFLA. (n.d.). *Professional Reports, No. 89*. International Federation of Library Associations and Institutions.

Institute on Disability. (2021). *2021 Annual Report. Disability Compendium*. Retrieved.

Irvall, B., & Nielsen, G. S. (2005). Access to Libraries for Persons with Disabilities. *Check List*.

Jensen, K. (2021, November 15). Library of Congress subject heading change doesn't address the real issue. *BOOK RIOT*. https://bookriot.com/library-of-congress-subject-heading-change/

Joe, J. (2019, January). A Perspective on Emotional Labor in Academic Libraries. *Journal of Academic Librarianship*, *45*(1), 66–67. doi:10.1016/j.acalib.2018.11.002

Addressing the History of Discrimination and Bias in Library Systems

Jones, E. P., Mani, N. S., Carlson, R. B., Welker, C. G., Cawley, M., & Yu, F. (2022). Analysis of anti-racism, equity, inclusion and social justice initiatives in library and information science literature. *Reference Services Review*. https://www.emerald.com/insight/content/doi/10.1108/RSR-07-2 021-0032/full/html

Kaser, D. (1986). The American Academic Library Building, 1870-1890. *The Journal of Library History (1974-1987), 21*(1), 60–71. https://www.jstor.org/stable/25541680

Kendall, F. E. (2006). *Understanding white privilege: Creating pathways to authentic relationships across race*. Routledge.

Kim, E. (2019, October 3). *The new $41 million Hunters Point Library has one major flaw*. Gothamist. https://gothamist.com/news/new-41-million-hunters-point-libr ary-has-one-major-flaw

Leong, N. (2020). Enjoyed by white citizens. *Geological Journal, 109*, 1421.

Leung, S. Y., & López-McKnight, J. R. (2021). Knowledge justice : disrupting library and information studies through critical race theory (Leung & J. R. López-McKnight, Eds.). The MIT Press.

Library of Congress. (2022, October 31). *History - national library service for the Blind and print disabled (NLS): Library of Congress*. National Library Service for the Blind and Print Disabled (NLS) | Library of Congress. https://www.loc.gov/nls/about/organization/history/

Lucas, & Silber Mohamed, H. (2021). Gender, Race, Ethnicity, and the Racialization of Attitudes Toward Descriptive Representation. *American Politics Research, 49*(5), 517–533. https://doi.org/ doi:10.1177/1532673X211022620

Madaus, J. W. (2011). Madaus. (2011). The History of Disability Services in higher education. *New Directions for Higher Education, 2011*(154), 5–15. doi:10.1002/he.429

Malapela, T., & De Jager, K. (2018). Theories of value and demonstrating their practical implementation in academic library services. *Journal of Academic Librarianship, 44*(6), 775–780. https://www.sciencedirect.com/science/article/pii/S009913331 8302659. doi:10.1016/j.acalib.2018.09.018

Martin, R. (1994). The development of professional education for librarians and archivists in the United States: A comparative essay. *The American Archivist, 57*(3), 544–558. doi:10.17723/aarc.57.3.116720kn81j25108

Matteson, M. L., & Miller, S. S. (2013). A study of emotional labor in librarianship. *Library & Information Science Research, 35*(1), 54–62. doi:10.1016/j.lisr.2012.07.005

McShane, J. (2022, February 23). A record number of U.S. adults identify as LGBTQ. gen Z is driving the increase. *The Washington Post*. https://www.washingtonpost.com/lifestyle/2022/02/17/adults-i dentifying-lgbt-gen-z/

Mehra, B. (2021). Enough crocodile tears! Libraries moving beyond performative antiracist politics. *The Library Quarterly, 91*(2), 137–149. https://www.journals.uchicago.edu/doi/full/10.1086/713046. doi:10.1086/713046

Meltzer, L., & Dokoupil, T. (2017, August 22). Hate rising: White Supremacy's rise in the U.S. *CBS News*. https://www.cbsnews.com/news/hate-rising-cbsn-on-assignment/

Moyer, L. S. (2005). Library funding in a budget-cut world. *The Bottom Line (New York, N.Y.)*, *18*(3), 112–115. doi:10.1108/08880450510613560

Mulliken, A. (2017). "There is Nothing Inherently Mysterious about Assistive Technology" A Qualitative Study about Blind User Experiences in US Academic Libraries. *Reference and User Services Quarterly*, *57*(2), 115–126. doi:10.5860/rusq.57.2.6528

Nair, A. (2022, August 4). *A cultural power struggle at an Iowa library casts a 'dark cloud' over a small town*. NBCNews.com. https://www.nbcnews.com/nbc-out/out-news/small-town-library-shut-say-culture-wars-closed-rcna39816

Nataraj, L., Hampton, H., Matlin, T. R., & Meulemans, Y. N. (2020). "Nice White Meetings": Unpacking Absurd Library Bureaucracy through a Critical Race Theory Lens. *Canadian Journal of Academic Librarianship*, *6*, 1–15. doi:10.33137/cjal-rcbu.v6.34340

National Center for Education Statistics. (2022). Hate Crime Incidents at Postsecondary Institutions. *Condition of Education*. U.S. Department of Education, Institute of Education Sciences. https://nces.ed.gov/programs/coe/indicator/a22

Newman, A. (2017, July 16). *Louisville Western Branch Library (1905-)*. Black Past. https://www.blackpast.org/african-american-history/louisville-western-branch-library-1905/

Nitecki, D. A., & Abels, E. G. (Eds.). (2008). *Influence of funding on advances in librarianship*. Emerald Publishing Limited. doi:10.1016/S0065-2830(2008)31

November 2, 2022, from https://disabilitycompendium.org/

Oakleaf, M. (2010). *The value of academic libraries: A comprehensive research review and report.*

Poole, A. H., Agosto, D., Greenberg, J., Lin, X., & Yan, E. (2021). Where do we stand? diversity, equity, inclusion, and social justice in north american library and information science education. *Journal of Education for Library and Information Science*, *62*(3), 258–286. doi:10.3138/jelis.2020-0018

Proposal jeopardizes library funding. (2018). *School Library Journal, 64*(3), 14. https://grinnell.idm.oclc.org/login?url=https://www.proquest.com/trade-journals/proposal-jeopardizes-library-funding/docview/2017029506/se-2

Rankin, S., Garvey, J. C., & Duran, A. (2019). A retrospective of LGBT issues on US college campuses: 1990–2020. *International Sociology*, *34*(4), 435–454. doi:10.1177/0268580919851429

Ray, R., & Gibbons, A. (2021). *Why are states banning critical race theory?* The Brookings Institution. https://grinnell.idm.oclc.org/login?url=https://www.proquest.com/blogs-podcasts-websites/why-are-states-banning-critical-race-theory/docview/2548183413/se-2

Robbins, L. S. (2001). *The dismissal of miss Ruth Brown: Civil rights, censorship, and the American library*. University of Oklahoma Press.

Addressing the History of Discrimination and Bias in Library Systems

Santamaria, M. R. (2020). Concealing white supremacy through fantasies of the library: Economies of affect at work. *Library Trends*, *68*(3), 431–449. doi:10.1353/lib.2020.0000

Saunders, P. D. (2022, February 10). *The changing state of gentrification*. American Planning Association. https://www.planning.org/planning/2022/winter/the-changing-state-of-gentrification/

Shuler, S., & Morgan, N. (2013). Emotional Labor in the Academic Library: When Being Friendly Feels Like Work. *The Reference Librarian*, *54*(2), 118–133. doi:10.1080/02763877.2013.756684

Smith, S., & Ellis, K. (2022, January 7). *History shows slavery helped build many U.S. colleges and Universities*. Shackled Legacy | APM Reports. https://www.apmreports.org/episode/2017/09/04/shackled-legacy

Snyder, T. (1993, January 19). *120 years of American Education: A statistical portrait*. National Center for Education Statistics (NCES) Home Page, a part of the U.S. Department of Education. https://nces.ed.gov/pubsearch/pubsinfo.asp?pubid=93442

Starks, B. (2021). The double pandemic: Covid-19 and white supremacy. *Qualitative Social Work: Research and Practice*, *20*(1-2), 222–224. https://journals.sagepub.com/doi/pdf/10.1177/1473325020986011. doi:10.1177/1473325020986011

Stewart, A. (2017). A Subject Analysis of Pentecostalism in the Dewey Decimal Classification System. *Biblioteka*, (21 (30)), 243–250. doi:10.14746/b.2017.21.12

Tager, J., & Shariyf, C. R. (2023, January 3). *Reading between the lines: Race, equity, and Book Publishing*. PEN America. https://pen.org/report/race-equity-and-book-publishing/

Tamura, E. H. (2001). Asian Americans in the History of Education: An Historiographical Essay. *History of Education Quarterly*, *41*(1), 58–71. https://www.jstor.org/stable/369479. doi:10.1111/j.1748-5959.2001.tb00074.x

University, S. C. (2018, November 30). *The hidden history of libraries and civil rights*. University Library - Santa Clara University. https://www.scu.edu/library/newsletter/2018-11/the-hidden-history-of-libraries-and-civil-rights/

Wagner, M. M., & Willms, D. (2010). The urban library program: Challenges to educating and hiring a diverse workforce. *Library Trends*, *59*(1), 128–146.

Walker, T. (2018, December 11). *'education is political': Neutrality in the classroom shortchanges students*. NEA. https://www.nea.org/advocating-for-change/new-from-nea/education-political-neutrality-classroom-shortchanges-students

Wallenstein, P. (2022, July 26). Desegregation in Higher Education. In *Encyclopedia Virginia*. https://encyclopediavirginia.org/entries/desegregation-in-higher-education

Wheeler, M., Johnson-Houston, D., & Walker, B. E. (2004). A Brief History of Library Service to African Americans. *American Libraries*, *35*(2), 42–45. https://www.jstor.org/stable/25649066

Wickham, & Sweeney, M. E. (2018). Are We Still Transmitting Whiteness? A Case Study of a Southern, Rural Library's Youth Collections. *Library Trends*, *67*(1), 89–106. https://doi.org/ doi:10.1353/lib.2018.0027

Wiegand, W. A. (1995). "Jew Attack": The Story behind Melvil Dewey's Resignation as New York State Librarian in 1905. *American Jewish History*, *83*(3), 359–379. https://www.jstor.org/stable/23885515

Wiegand, W. A. (2015). *Part of our lives: A people's history of the American public library*. Oxford University Press.

Wiegand, & Wiegand, W. A. (2018). *The Desegregation of Public Libraries in the Jim Crow South: Civil Rights and Local Activism*. LSU Press.

Wilder, C. S. (2014). *Ebony and ivy: Race, slavery, and the Troubled History of America's universities*. Bloomsbury.

Yamaguchi, M., & Richardson, J. (2018). Demonstrating academic library impact to faculty: A case study. *Digital Library Perspectives*, *34*(2), 137–150. doi:10.1108/DLP-09-2017-0034

Chapter 13
Advancing Justice Through Strategic Partnerships:
Academic Libraries and Student Affairs

DeLa Dos
Association of Research Libraries, USA

Saira Raza
Emory Libraries, USA

ABSTRACT

As academic libraries continue to investigate and invest in justice, equity, diversity, and inclusion (JEDI) efforts, there are numerous opportunities to enhance the impact of these efforts through intentional, sustainable collaborations with other administrative units of the institution—particularly student affairs. This chapter will explore the benefits and challenges of collaborating with student affairs departments for academic libraries interested in creating, maintaining, and advancing inclusive and just learning and research communities. Using a case study, the chapter highlights specific collaborative efforts to demonstrate the value of cultivating relationships across campus divisions; additionally, it offers insights into identifying opportunities to share resources and enhance the experiences of the libraries' stakeholders. While framed by the context of the situation, the chapter presents recommendations that may be effectively implemented within academic libraries at many types of institutions.

INTRODUCTION

Academic libraries often have missions and responsibilities that can be daunting. They play an essential role for colleges and universities as they are charged with supporting the entirety of the institution's community; despite the critical nature of their function, libraries often have little influence on the actual composition of the community that they serve; libraries generally have little to no involvement in decisions related to student acceptance, employee hires beyond the library, and the management of campus visitors. Still, each of these decisions directly impacts the operation of the library and requires robust

DOI: 10.4018/978-1-6684-7255-2.ch013

Copyright © 2023, IGI Global. Copying or distributing in print or electronic forms without written permission of IGI Global is prohibited.

preparation for how to support these communities and more. Attempts to center justice, equity, diversity, and inclusion (JEDI) can be at tension with cursory considerations of other institutional values and practices. Still, when undertaken with intention, JEDI related efforts can lead to positive transformation.

Framing

Faced with such a multifaceted charge and challenge, libraries are often well served by pursuing meaningful collaborations. Whether it is with student-led organizations who wish to co-curate exhibits or faculty who seek experts to help students build confidence in their research skills, collaboration between libraries and other entities is a common practice and even essential to their mission to make information accessible and advance knowledge within their community (ACRL, 2011; ALA, 2008). Still, there may be untapped opportunities by initiating or enhancing strategic partnership with other campus colleagues, particularly those working in student affairs. As higher education institutions can be regular sources of evidence in support of the validity of Parkinson's Law (1957), creating a new partnership may not be the most desired course of action given the amount of energy and resources that are required to do so effectively. One strategy to assist in overcoming such hesitation is to provide potential partners with information to increase awareness and deepen understanding of the work being done by all parties, needs to be served in the community, and potential benefits of the partnership.

A relationship between academic libraries and student affairs can easily be dismissed due to a variety of factors (e.g., management structures, resource allocations, individual and organizational assumptions, lack of institutional support). Often, academic libraries are more closely connected with the offices of institutional Chief Diversity Officers (CDO) or similar structures, as their reporting lines and organizational positionality may be closer to one another when compared to the student affairs administrative unit. While CDOs can provide invaluable services to the academic community, their ability to engage in outreach and education can be hindered by their responsibilities related to compliance and reporting as well as their broad, enterprise-wide duties. This chapter will highlight the vast potential for academic libraries to work with student affairs units in order to access and develop expanded programs and services.

Justice, Equity, Diversity, and Inclusion in Academic Libraries

Issues related to JEDI have a strong presence in scholarly and professional literature in library and information science going back many decades (Chadley, 1992). Within the evolving scholarship about JEDI, academic libraries demonstrate concerns around consistent themes: increasing the number of library professionals from underrepresented communities, improving collections to reflect a broader range of perspectives and cultural representation among authors and publishers, and exploring ways to create inclusive and accessible library spaces and services. These thematic concerns invite experimentation among practitioners with a spectrum of specialized skills, knowledge, and analytical approaches. Still, they intersect along key points of implementation including the adoption of shared vocabulary, availability and effectiveness of professional development, and adequate institutional support to sustain, evaluate, and improve initiatives across iterative life-cycles.

As organizations that reside within larger institutions to serve their diverse learning communities, academic libraries must consider how they are positioned within the wider context of administrative leadership objectives, student needs, and available resources when it comes to developing a JEDI strategy. In recent years, some academic libraries have created new JEDI-focused leadership and administrative

Advancing Justice Through Strategic Partnerships

roles to spearhead signature library initiatives that demonstrate clear alignment with wider institutional measures of success. Libraries without these designated roles may rely on staff committees, task forces, or similar groups to define their priorities, develop strategies, generate recommendations, and implement projects. While the latter may benefit from amplified potential for buy-in among colleagues with its grassroots approach, there is an equally amplified risk of overburdening staff members most impacted by systemic inequity in the workplace with the monumental task of fixing it.

The lack of adequate attention to JEDI issues within the library profession may be most clearly demonstrated by the difficulty academic institutions experience in attracting and retaining BIPOC talent. For decades, professional associations like ALA and ARL have provided scholarships, mentorship, professional development, and leadership training to strengthen the pipeline of talent from underrepresented communities into the library profession. While their programs and dedicated staff have helped to cultivate many successful academic library professionals, BIPOC library employees continue to encounter problematic workplace behaviors and policies that tax their personal wellbeing and stifle their professional growth. These challenges diminish the perception of librarianship as a viable career for people in underrepresented communities. Through alumni scholar networks and dedicated affinity organizations, current BIPOC library professionals seek support from outside their respective institutions to maintain morale, receive guidance on effective self-advocacy, and develop collective strategies for improving workplace conditions. Their ceaseless efforts and commitment lay the groundwork for safer and more inclusive workplace experiences and reduce barriers to career growth and success in libraries.

Challenging Assumptions About Libraries and Librarianship

The ongoing dialogue about these themes within academic libraries and their respective institutions surface challenges rooted in assumptions, beliefs, and ideologies about libraries and what they represent – namely resistance to critical analysis of library institutions under the guises of "library neutrality" and "vocational awe" (Chiu et al, 2021). These concepts operate as "organizational fictions" that inherently obstruct meaningful systemic change that would improve the experiences of individuals from underrepresented communities in libraries both as users and employees (Kendrick, 2017). With this in mind, the library DEI committee embraced and promoted anti-racism and critical librarianship as foundational paradigms in which to position its JEDI work (Drabinski, 2019; Kendi, 2019).

Student Affairs

In a broad sense, student affairs encompasses the support of students' growth and development that occurs beyond an institution's formal curriculum. The specific structures, departments, programs, and services can vary greatly from institution to institution. Institutional context (e.g., history, politics, resources) can inform decisions about organizational structures. Still, similar to how libraries can take on unique forms on different campuses and still share a common purpose, student affairs units play an essential role at institutions of higher education regardless of the organizational specifics.

As a profession, student affairs face a variety of challenges. For one, many people do not know that the profession even exists. To address this issue, student affairs professional organizations coordinate a month-long initiative called Careers in Student Affairs Month each October to celebrate the field and increase awareness of and connection to the profession for current and future practitioners (ACPA, 2022; NASPA, 2022). Still, there is no shortage and a long history of misunderstandings and misperceptions

245

about student affairs (Manning, 1996; Modern Campus 2021; Shay, 1984). Many other higher education professionals are among those that are unaware of the existence of the profession. Those that are familiar with the field can hold oversimplified or pejorative beliefs about the work of their colleagues—if they even consider this term to apply. Student affairs professionals are often viewed as the party planners, mess cleaners, and boo-boo kissers of a campus environment. While aspects of these perceptions can be explicit responsibilities for some roles, the work of student affairs extends far beyond these limited perspectives.

History

While the creation of student affairs came much later than the establishment of higher education in the United States, the roots of the profession still reach into the 1800s (Schwartz & Stewart, 2017). The development of student affairs is directly linked to the challenges and barriers that women faced as they attempted to enroll in colleges and universities in the 19th century. While there were a small number of exceptions, generally, colleges and universities did not admit women. As higher education as a system was slow to shift its structures and practices, some of the institutions made internal changes that began to allow women to enroll. Along with this change, these institutions would also change, expand, and add new roles and responsibilities for their employees. "The first professionals to embrace the fundamental tenets of what would later become 'student affairs' were women faculty members" (p. 65).

Eventually, the dean of women position would emerge at several institutions and, later, the dean of men position. Individuals in these roles would soon establish professional organizations and contribute to the establishment and development of student affairs as a profession (NASPA, n.d.-b; Schwartz & Stewart, 2017). The field has continued to develop responding to trends in higher education as well as solidifying its own identity. As Schwartz and Stewart outline, the history of student affairs includes a number of eras: paternalism, college life, the student personnel movement, the golden age of higher education, consumerism, student learning, and professionalism. Through all of these times, national and international events—such as court rulings, legislation, social movements, and wars—would present a multitude of challenges and opportunities that student affairs professionals would help colleges and universities navigate.

Student affairs has regularly revisited, reviewed, and refined the standards of practice for its profession as well as higher education at large (CAS, 2022). Over time, institutions of higher education have not only employed student affairs professionals but also created numerous degree programs focusing on student affairs to support current and future scholars and practitioners working in and connected to the field while honoring the rich and storied history of the profession's development (NASPA, n.d.-a; Young, 1993). These programs often include a balance of theory and practice that explicitly works to connect the two in order to effectively prepare their graduates for impactful careers. Today, the student affairs profession continues to evolve, with a growing emphasis on the use of data and evidence-based practices to support student success, being proactive in creating solutions and improving systems, remaining nimble and relevant in times of uncertainty, and creating and advancing more just, equitable, diverse, and inclusive communities.

Advancing Justice Through Strategic Partnerships

Strategic Partnership

While collaboration can carry numerous connotations in different settings—ranging from trite and superficial to valued and essential—student affairs professionals have long recognized the importance of collaboration in their institutional contexts, particularly with partners in academic affairs. (Brown, 1988; Pace et al., 2006). Despite the immense potential for meaningful impact and positive transformation, collaboration is often not the first approach considered in higher education settings. When collaboration is intentionally sought, there can be many challenges to its implementation. Some of the best intentions can be stifled by limitations of capacity or resources. Other efforts can stall due to political sensitivities, egos and pride, or misaligned expectations. For these reasons and more, collaboration can be an elusive goal; however, structural adjustments and intentional decisions can increase the likelihood of achieving successful outcomes through strategic partnerships (Kezar & Lester, 2009).

Student affairs departments are often able to provide unique perspectives and connections to other campus stakeholders, particularly students. This is not meant to imply that student affairs professionals have all the answers or are the best for every situation; rather, as students—a key stakeholder for any institution of higher education—are often engaged in programs and services offered by student affairs that encourages the creation of different relationships and communities than those that develop in classrooms, laboratories, studios, and libraries. Collaborations between these entities and student affairs would allow the valuable insights, skills, resources, and experiences of each unit to be combined in manners that enhance the experience and well-being of students while creating new opportunities, increasing efficiency, and supporting the institutional as well as individual unit missions.

As noted earlier, there are many reasons why collaboration may be avoided or falter. One significant challenge can be the existence—or perception—of competition between different areas of a campus community. Fueled by a scarcity of resources and misaligned performance metrics (collaboration is seldom explicitly used as a metric to measure individual or departmental performance via formal structures), academic affairs and student affairs can easily allow their limited understandings of one another to transform into stereotyping and excuses not to work together; this can also contribute to an aggrandized self-perception of each division's role, value, and contribution to the larger institution. Rather than allow these beliefs to dictate the development—or unwillingness to develop—relationships between these entities, professionals in both areas would be well served by intentionally examining opportunities to work together. Student affairs is not meant to replace the academic curriculum for students; instead, it is intended to support the holistic development and well-being of students in manners that directly contribute to the fulfillment of the academic missions of institutions of higher education (NASPA, 1987).

CASE STUDY

Best practices can be a misleading concept. A simple interpretation might assert that a best practice is the most logical thing to do—inherent in the "best" that starts the phrase; however, there are two key limitations to this approach. First, this simplification can be used to set and maintain unrealistic expectations. Second, it can easily cause people to respond to complicated and complex situations in a reductive, transactional manner that lacks appreciation for nuance and overlooks the needs of many groups, especially those marginalized by systems of privilege and oppression. Rather than exclusively pursuing best practices, leaders may be better served by aiming to utilize informed practices. Beyond the shift in semantics, informed practices also impact the way that decisions are made and plans are implemented. Instead of taking a practice developed in another context and attempting to force it to suit another environment, informed practices invite strategic planners and problem solvers to collect information from varied sources and engage with multiple stakeholders before, during, and after taking action. Curiosity and decisiveness create a synergy while cynicism and hopefulness ebb and flow. Additional voices are included in conversations that can shed light on ways that a best practice may have untapped potential or unintended consequences.

For lack of a better description, informed practices are informed—context, nuance, values, goals, pressures, tensions, limitations, and opportunities are all able to be taken into consideration. Best practices and informed practices are not inherently mutually exclusive; when a best practice is considered and implemented with intentionality and care, for both the process and people, it is effectively also an informed practice. However, by focusing on informed practices, people are less likely to fall into a default pattern of behavior that can invite bias and undermine the overall effort. It encourages more inclusive processes and deliberate adjustments. Publications, personal communications, anecdotes, and aphorisms can all be lifted up as best practices; similarly, they can all be integrated in processes designed to identify and utilize informed practices. It is with this intention in mind that the following case study is presented.

Institutional Framing

This chapter details a partnership between an academic library—from here referred to as "library"— and a social justice education department within a division of student affairs—from here referred to as "SJE"—at a mid-sized, private, R1 university in an urban area of the southeastern United States of America. The university's library comprises ten library organizations across various subject areas and professional schools with nearly 400 full-time employees. The university's division of student affairs comprises nearly 25 departments with around 200 employees.

Student Engagement

This partnership was initiated when one of the co-chairs of the library's Diversity, Equity, and Inclusion (DEI) Committee invited the SJE director to attend one of the committee's meetings. In addition to learning more about the relatively new department, the committee was interested in deepening their understanding of student perspectives of the library. While the director had never intentionally collected feedback from students about their perceptions of and experiences with the library, they were able to share a number of anecdotes and themes gathered from various interactions that help expand the committee members' understanding of how students engaged with and thought about their offerings, programs, spaces, and facilities.

The committee expressed their appreciation for the insights and shifted their attention to opportunities to make improvements. While they generated many ideas, one was directly aligned with the mission of SJE: increase the capacity of library employees to create, maintain, and advance JEDI in and through their roles. SJE was charged with doing this work across the campus; while their work focused on direct engagement with students—undergraduate, graduate, and professional—across all colleges and schools within the university, SJE believed that a systems approach was necessary to effect and sustain meaningful change. As such, the SJE regularly worked with faculty, staff, administrators, alums, and local community members in addition to the enrolled students. The opportunity to work together to accomplish this goal was welcomed by SJE and the library. What started as an invitation to engage in an introductory conversation resulted in a partnership with multiple formal structures.

Formal Structures

The partnership between the library and student affairs included components that served both the library and SJE. Members of the library community were able to organize multiple educational sessions for their colleagues. An initial program was scheduled that would be open to all employees of the library organization. The planning group selected two core topics: bias and the social implications of racial determination; each topic was scheduled to be presented in a 90-minute, interactive session with a lunch break in between. As it was a pilot, attendance was voluntary. On the day of the session, a fair-sized, participatory audience arrived in the space and engaged in lively conversation and thoughtful consideration of the session content.

As a single date and time were selected, many people who were interested in attending were unable to make it work for their schedule. A few months later, one of the directors of a library unit reached out to SJE to ask for sessions to be offered specifically for their team. SJE worked with the director to co-ordinate a series of sessions for this group. It was a chance for SJE to pilot some of its newly developed learning modules. While the bias module was still one of the foundational sessions, SJE also offered sessions on diversity and inclusion as well as privilege and oppression. The library team met over a series of weeks to complete the sessions and explore opportunities to integrate it into their work. SJE continued to update and enhance the sessions based on the feedback of the participants and facilitators. These three sessions would become the core of an educational framework as well as an associated recognition program developed by SJE. The development of both of these was essential to the pursuit of the departmental mission. It was also something that required input from multiple stakeholders, which is where another manifestation of the partnership emerged.

As a new department in student affairs, SJE was exploring uncharted territory. Rather than function in a silo, SJE intentionally worked to create structures and networks that engaged stakeholders from multiple units and divisions of the university. This resulted in the creation of a robust advisory structure. Instead of forming a single committee, SJE developed a three-part structure that intentionally considered stakeholders' expertise and capacity. The first committee functioned as a general advisory committee; it was tasked with reviewing and responding to ideas being considered by SJE. It included representation from a mixture of stakeholders (i.e., students, faculty, staff, and alums) that possessed varied levels of expertise and prior experience with social justice and met regularly through the fall and spring semesters. A second committee provided thought leadership and comprised faculty from multiple colleges and schools. Its membership was expected to have high expertise and experience related to social justice; as faculty often had limited availability for additional commitments, particularly those that were strong candidates for serving on this committee, this group had a low expectation of time investment. The third committee led the development of the SJE educational framework. This involved synthesizing information from multiple sources, including the other committees, as well as the content development and process planning required to build and implement a framework. It was composed of staff and administrators from across various areas of the university—including a member of the library DEI Committee; this group met every month. A summary of the advisory structure is included in Table 1.

Table 1. SJE advisory committee structure and design

Group Role	Stakeholders	Level of Expertise	Meeting Cadence
General Advisement	undergraduate students and alums; graduate and professional students and alums; staff; faculty	varied	monthly meetings during the fall and spring semesters; 60 minutes each
Thought Leaders	faculty	high	twice a year; 3 hours each
Framework Development	staff and administrators	high	monthly meetings; 60–90 minutes each

Benefits of Partnership

The inclusion of a librarian on a student affairs committee was an uncommon occurrence. Still, by creating a continued connection between the library and SJE, both sides were able to expand their awareness of broader opportunities and needs of the university. It also provided benefits to all parties by supporting their individual missions. SJE benefited from the perspectives and contributions of the library representative on the framework committee. The library representative was able to provide updates on the progress of the SJE framework to the library committee and broader organization. Collaborating with SJE provided insights about students' needs that were difficult to obtain through traditional library outreach and assessment practices like surveys and focus groups. It also opened new avenues to communicate with students from underrepresented communities about library resources, services, and spaces that support their personal and academic growth.

Supporting the Mission of the Library

The library's DEI committee formed in 2017 based on recommendations from a year-long environmental scan by a university librarian-sponsored working group. Consisting of around two dozen volunteer employees from across various departments, ranks, functional roles, and backgrounds, the working group and resulting committee shaped guiding principles and implemented a framework for how the library should approach its DEI work. The framework consists of two themes – *representation* and *access* – in conversation with the library's areas of focus – *climate and culture, human resources, collections, user services*, and *library spaces* (Raza et al, 2022). The framework offers a conceptual launchpad for individuals, functional teams, and departments to cultivate DEI initiatives relevant to their current professional work.

The principles of *non-closure* and *unique contributions* serve as guardrails to common pitfalls of organizational DEI initiatives such as virtue signaling and scope creep. *Non-closure* accepts and embraces the ongoing and never-ending work of justice and inclusion. In practice, it means more focus on behavioral and intellectual shifts that regulate unconscious bias and less focus on competing for recognition of achieving superficial DEI milestones. By focusing on *unique contributions*, the library and its varied working parts can harmonize more inclusive and equitable practices into their systems, processes, and team culture.

To effectively support employees in developing these skills, the library organization needed to adopt a shared vocabulary and provide access to a basic level of understanding of diversity, equity, and inclusion concepts. However, it was beyond the scope and capacity of the library DEI committee to develop a customized curriculum to that end. The committee researched potential solutions such as hiring consultants and investing in asynchronous courses from DEI experts and library professional organizations. However, factors such as cost, scheduling, and difficulty measuring long-term impact undermined their viability.

As the committee established more regular communication with the SJE director, for example by participating in their social justice education task force, there were more opportunities to discover existing materials and expertise from within the campus community. Library employees were able to offer input to the SJE director on what topics and skills would be most helpful in advancing their DEI practice. When the SJE director rolled out their first iteration of a social justice curriculum, they invited the library DEI committee to take the available learning modules. Although the classes were originally designed for an undergraduate student audience, the content and structure were highly effective for library professionals as well. Moreover, it provided a consistent baseline for library employees to have a working knowledge of DEI concepts to inform their professional practice in areas like student engagement, instruction, faculty outreach, and metadata creation.

Supporting the Mission of Student Affairs

As complex, layered organizations, universities often have no shortage of mission statements. The university—or university system—will generally have an overarching mission. Traveling through the organizational structures and hierarchies, different divisions, colleges, and schools will often articulate their own missions. This process continues with individual units, centers, departments, and programs. While the sheer number of words and statements can be dizzying to some, ostensibly, they should all be connected to the original larger institutional mission. As a large tree may have a tremendous root system, the network or carefully crafted sentences and deliberately wordsmithed phrases ideally allows university stakeholders across the enterprise to find connection to both their local work as well as the institutional purpose.

For student affairs divisions, this often means recognizing the value of the work performed by its teams as a direct contributor to the overall success of the students, other administrative units, and the institutional mission (NASPA, 1987). While operational silos within institutions of higher education can be a common occurrence for a number of reasons, collaboration often unlocks potential for increased and expanded success. By partnering with the library, SJE was able to build stronger connections and relationships with colleagues working in new areas and roles of the university, thereby broadening the reach and impact of the educational interventions they provided.

Up to this point, the chapter has generally used "student affairs" to refer to the profession. While this is currently the label generally used to describe the field (ACPA, 2023; NASPA, n.d.-c), there are still many alternate ways of naming student affairs divisions and departments in higher education; these include, but are not limited to, student life, student personnel, student services, and—as is the case in the case study presented—campus life. The campus life option does not include "student" in its label. By using the word "campus", it implies that the mission, and therefore work and engagement, of student affairs is part of the larger campus community. While still focused on students, the "campus life" label honors the interconnectedness of stakeholder groups and recognizes the importance of the relationships among and between different communities.

Different institutions used various labels for any number of reasons. Regardless of the actual language selected, the spirit of interpersonal and community connections is often present, explicitly and implicitly, in the approaches and work of student affairs professionals. For SJE, the collaboration with the library was highly mission aligned. Members of the library community were eager and engaged learners that benefited from and contributed to the development of educational modules and interventions that would be used across the university. Furthermore, the participation by a member of the library on the framework committee strengthened the work of the committee, the larger advisory structure, and the work of the department, all of which was essential to the advancement of the mission of SJE.

Impact

As noted above, the collaboration between the library and SJE resulted in a number of benefits for both areas of the university. Still, the work resulted in more than these area specific benefits; an amplified impact was made possible through this strategic partnership. By forging stronger connections between the administrative units as well as the employees of the library and SJE, members of the university community were better served. Library workers possessed a deeper understanding of the role and value of student affairs. As librarians receive requests in all shapes and sizes, including questions seemingly far beyond the scope of the services provided by the library, a broadened knowledge of offerings in other areas of the campus community can be a valuable resource.

Additionally, the educational sessions that SJE provided to members of the library community were intentionally developed to be interactive and responsive to the needs and contexts of various audiences. Drawing on the support of the three-part advisory system, SJE would ultimately develop an educational framework of modular learning interventions that would gain national recognition. The success of this framework was that it could accommodate the diverse needs of different university stakeholders. The curriculum used to work with an auditorium full of mandated attendees differs greatly from the one used to work with a division's executive leadership team that has mutually agreed that JEDI is an organizational priority. This framework enabled SJE to work with stakeholders across the enterprise. It also ensured that the work would not stop at compliance.

SJE developed multiple facilitator preparation experiences to support the expansion of the framework's implementation. The curriculum committee of the undergraduate college of arts and sciences approved a course for academic credit to prepare students as potential peer-facilitators. A separate experience was created to prepare faculty and staff to serve as facilitators. With additional facilitators available to lead sessions, SJE was able to reach broader audiences. Additionally, SJE developed numerous materials that could be used for self-guided or community-led explorations of introductory content within the framework. This allowed individuals to engage at their own pace and prepare community members with no-to-very-little prior exposure to the content for more meaningful exploration (e.g., the synchronous, facilitated sessions).

While establishing a baseline is an essential component of a larger educational initiative, JEDI capacity development can sometimes offer limited opportunities for continued education and application of the content to real experiences. The SJE framework intentionally crafted options that aligned with compliance goals while also building progressive learning experiences as well as a corresponding tracking and recognition program. Through the partnership with the library, SJE was able to pilot its early modules, collect feedback to make informed decisions about edits and updates, and work with professionals leading JEDI work across the institution. Additionally, similar to the benefits of library workers deepening their understanding of the work of student affairs, the inverse also produces positive outcomes. By broadening how the library was understood by student affairs professionals, they were better equipped

Advancing Justice Through Strategic Partnerships

to make recommendations and connect university stakeholders to the many essential—and at times, underutilized—offerings of the library.

Challenges

While the case study presented resulted in numerous positive results, it was not without challenges. These included navigating institutional politics and working with limited resources as well as identifying strategies and creating systems to enable sustainable impact. This chapter aims to encourage academic libraries to consider strategic partnerships and specifically invites considerations related to working with student affairs. The challenges will likely be unique to each context as there will be differences in the numerous factors that influence the situation. Similar to how the case study invites readers to pursue informed practices in lieu of best practices, the following challenges are presented as points of information rather than a prediction of what would happen should a reader choose to embark on a similar journey.

Scope, Capacity, and Engagement

As is inherent in its name, student affairs tend to focus on students. Within the broader student population, student affairs often focus further on undergraduate students. This historical and current reality has motivated many student affairs units to broaden their scope to intentionally include graduate and professional students. While these efforts can result in beautiful opportunities, they can also generate misgivings and tensions, as institutions of higher education can be political and territorial environments. When SJE shifted to serve populations beyond the "traditional undergraduate student," some on the university community bemoaned the attempt to extend the reach of student affairs. Even within student affairs, not everyone was supportive of the additional measures undertaken by SJE. These perspectives did not mean that the partnership with the library could not occur; however, it did require SJE to adjust aspects of its communications plan. The general advisory committee provided support and guidance related to navigating these concerns; this group was well equipped to serve in this role as it included representation from a wide range of stakeholders.

One of the main concerns raised by colleagues in student affairs about SJE's work with the library related to the capacity of the department, as its staff consisted of one individual—the director. Critics would argue that supporting students across all colleges and schools as a one-person department was a large enough challenge without adding non-student stakeholders into the mix. This was another opportunity for the three-part advisory structure to support the department. While the SJE director was specifically selected to lead this newly created department, they were not interested in making decisions in a vacuum—despite being a department of one. The members of the advisory committees were able to be sounding boards and accomplices as they collectively worked to effect positive change in the university. As the members of these committees understood the importance of working with all members of the university community, not just students, SJE was able to continue with its vision. This also helped SJE decide who it worked with, which included prioritizing voluntary audiences that were invested in the learning process. SJE believed that meaningful engagement with willing participants was more impactful that mandatory sessions provided to adversarial audiences, even if the former meant connecting with smaller numbers of people than the latter.

The partnership between SJE and the library was a prime example of this situation. The sessions for the library were voluntary. As such, not all employees of the library participated; however, the ones that did participate were actively engaged and committed to the process and applying their learning to their personal growth and professional development. Still, there is a significant challenge related to deciding how to approach JEDI capacity development. Breadth and depth are often in conflict with one another as they are already in competition with the countless other commitments pulling on the capacity of professionals. Compounded by the idea that JEDI is a separate topic that is not connected to many people's everyday job responsibilities, many who work in libraries may choose not to attend a voluntary session on diversity and inclusion or bias or privilege and oppression.

The recognition of this challenge contributed to the development of the tracking and recognition program to help incentivize some to participate in the framework sessions. For some, the personal recognition served as a reward and motivator; for others, it provided a point of evidence that could be used when advocating for the time to engage in the sessions with their managers. This aspect of the program did not appeal to all and still had its shortcomings; however, its existence did help motivate some community members to continue to attend sessions. Additionally, SJE was intentional in not creating a system that asserted that people had "arrived" or "completed" their learning. Rather, the program was intended to recognize the participants' commitment to learning and taking action to advance JEDI in their environments.

Sustaining Momentum Through Organizational Changes

Every adage expressing the inevitably of change is as true as the next. Academic institutions are not exempt from the constant pressure to adapt to new realities presented by significant events like leadership changes, geopolitical shifts, economic downturns, and social movements. In this case study, both the library and students' affairs experienced sudden and substantial reorganizations, the most dramatic being the dissolution of SJE to make way for an expanded administrative and programmatic department focused on JEDI. Stemming from a transition to new leadership at the highest level of the institution, the library and SJE did not have input in the decision or agency to change course. Still, because of the success of the collaboration, the SJE director and library DEI committee proactively shared materials, documented learnings, and brainstormed new directions for the library to expand its sphere of influence and participation in advancing JEDI and student success.

Timeline

The following list includes key points in the process outlined in the case study.

- Fall 2016: SJE department founded in student affairs; inaugural director named—while still serving as director of another department
- Summer 2017: SJE director is no longer filling multiple positions; library DEI committee is formed
- Fall 2017: initial SJE session pilots with university stakeholders; library DEI committee invites SJE director to introductory meeting
- Spring 2018: SJE pilots updated and additional sessions with library employees
- Summer 2018: SJE advisory structure drafted
- Fall 2018: SJE advisory structure launched, which included representation from the library
- 2018–2019 academic year: SJE sessions are regularly piloted, assessed, and updated; series of sessions for specific library unit

Advancing Justice Through Strategic Partnerships

- Spring 2019: SJE framework is developed to organize sessions and guide learners; SJE gains approval from the undergraduate college of arts and sciences curriculum committee to offer a seminar course for academic credit to students interested in serving as volunteer peer-facilitators
- Summer 2019: SJE develops a facilitator development program for professional staff and faculty interested in serving as framework facilitators
- Fall: 2019: SJE tracking and recognition program is developed
- 2019–2020 academic year: SJE framework sessions are offered to growing numbers of university stakeholders; SJE develops materials to support individual guided and community-led introductory experiences to framework content; SJE pilots the tracking and recognition program
- Spring 2021: the SJE framework receives multiple awards from an international professional association

APPLICATION

For the parties involved, the case study presented was a success. Both the library and SJE were grateful for the chance to work together in such a meaningful manner. While the challenges were real and there were many opportunities for improvement, it was still a worthwhile undertaking. When considering how this situation can apply to other institutions and settings, it can be helpful to zoom out and consider broader concepts. Not every campus will have a department charged with leading social justice education; some may have multiple departments across the university with staff much larger than a single person. Any number of contextual specifics can contribute to circumstances not neatly matching the partnership described in this chapter. Rather than expect readers to copy and paste the specifics of this example to their own institutions, the following recommendations are offered with the goal of supporting readers in considering how to implement an informed practice that might include partnerships with student affairs.

One way to frame a potential collaboration with student affairs is to seek shared language. At times, the work of academic libraries and student affairs may seem worlds apart; finding common ground can often be easier said than done. However, trends in higher education can serve as a source for inspiration. Colleges and universities of various institutional types and profiles are increasingly focused on student success. While success may mean different things to libraries and student affairs units, it is still a shared interest that can be the foundation of establishing a shared priority. For academic libraries, taking the initiative to reach out to student affairs partners can help facilitate progress, especially if these are new relationships.

Before reaching out to potential student affairs partners, libraries do not need to have all the answers. Being clear where clarity is available is more important than waiting for all circumstances to be perfect. Libraries may be well served by attempts to use language that describes student success in ways that are aligned with all parties involved. Additionally, recognizing the work and value of the work of potential partners aid in the relationship building. Librarians can use their highly developed research skills to learn about their campus colleagues. Explore departmental websites and learn about some of the longstanding and recent programs, services, and initiatives of student affairs. Finally, identify a strategic point of contact. Asking for support from others that are already known and may have established relationships that can inform any of these decisions is well-advised (e.g., academic partners; student workers; university administrators).

When developing a "pitch" to a potential partner in student affairs, libraries can consider some of the following prompts:

- What value does the partner provide to campus?
- What needs are identified in the library?
- What work has already been done related to the identified needs?
- What are options for working together that the partner can consider?
- What are the desired results or outcomes?

From there, it is a matter of building rapport. A single person does not necessarily represent the entirety of an organization; if one invitation does not result in the desired outcome, consider who else might be a potential partner. While institutional dynamics can play a significant role in building relationships, burning bridges can have unintended consequences, particularly in highly political settings. Effectively using emotional intelligence can be an essential tool for building a successful partnership (Lynn, 2004). Sometimes, the people with the titles do not have the capacity or the people with the skills do not have the freedom. Being open to unexpected events and flexible in planning is highly recommended when exploring an initial connection between campus partners.

Even within the same academic institution, different departments and units can have significantly different working cultures and strategic priorities. For library committees who wish to explore JEDI-related collaborations across organizational divisions, having a champion at the executive leadership level is a critical factor for success. Not only can they help to establish connections with the right individuals in the organization, they can help to reduce resistance to information and resource sharing and provide a system of accountability among potential partners. They can also help JEDI organizers to acquire financial resources and provide guidance for how those resources should be allocated among competing priorities.

Libraries rarely prioritize or even include student affairs and other non-academic units in their outreach and engagement efforts. But the lack of attention to non-academic department collaborators is largely based on untested assumptions that investment in these relationships will not yield meaningful outcomes. This case study underscores the importance of reframing the relevance of student affairs to library outreach and engagement by focusing on the shared goals around student wellbeing and success. Rather than characterizing collaborations with students affairs as a digression, it is an opportunity to build capacity to provide consistent and effective support to students, particularly those who are most vulnerable to the consequences of systemic bias. With this level of alignment, SJE and the library amplified each other's efforts. Student affairs helped the library reach more students through referrals and access to marketing channels, while the library helped to reinforce the outcomes of SJE's learning modules by integrating concepts and lessons from those modules into library practices.

Although this case study describes the experience at a large institution, this approach can result in universally beneficial outcomes regardless of the size of the institution. In fact, it could be especially effective in institutions where financial and human resources are limited, such as small, regional colleges. Cross-department collaborations around JEDI goals help to build awareness and trust between the library and other campus organizations, fostering improved communication and workflows in areas beyond JEDI, such as resource allocation, institutional strategic planning, and most importantly, student success.

Advancing JEDI in academic libraries is not the responsibility of a single person; rather all people play a role. Neutrality has long been identified as an illusion when it comes to JEDI work (Kendi, 2019; Tatum, 2017). Instead, a holistic commitment to building, maintaining, and advancing JEDI efforts is

Advancing Justice Through Strategic Partnerships

required throughout an institution to achieve successful results. Systemic problems require systemic solutions. These solutions must acknowledge the roots of the challenges being addressed as well as the realities of people's lived experiences. This means creating structures to support people as they make decisions about whether or not they are going to contribute to the collective efforts in each moment. Burnout is already a major issue for academic libraries based on their job responsibilities alone (Johnson & Page, 2022; Nardine, 2019). Adding in the additional labor required to advance JEDI—especially for those that carry (multiple) marginalized identities—can quickly make an unsustainable situation untenable. While not a panacea, strategically partnering with colleagues across campus can provide tremendous support and improve outcomes. Student affairs professionals have much they can contribute to and gain from working with colleagues in academic libraries and vice versa. When implemented effectively, these efforts can not only advance JEDI in the library but potentially across the entire campus community and beyond.

REFERENCES

ACPA. (2022). *Careers in Student Affairs Month*. ACPA. https://myacpa.org/csam/

ACPA. (2023). *ACPA: College Student Educators International*. ACPA. ACRL. https://myacpa.org/

ACRL. (2011, August 2). A*bout ACRL*. ACRL. https://www.ala.org/acrl/aboutacrl

ALA. (2008, June 9). *Mission & priorities*. ALA. https://www.ala.org/aboutala/missionpriorities

Brown, S. S. (1988). Approaches to Collaboration between Academic and Student Affairs. *NASPA Journal*, *26*(1), 2–7. doi:10.1080/00220973.1988.11072071

Chadley, O. A. (1992). Addressing cultural diversity in academic and research libraries. *College & Research Libraries*, *53*(3), 206–216. doi:10.5860/crl_53_03_206

Chiu, A., Ettarh, F. M., & Ferretti, J. A. (2021). Not the Shark, but the Water: How Neutrality and Vocational Awe Intertwine to Uphold White Supremacy. In S. Y. Leung & J. R. López-McKnight (Eds.), *Knowledge justice: Disrupting library and information studies through Critical Race Theory* (pp. 49–71). MIT Press. doi:10.7551/mitpress/11969.003.0005

Council for the Advancement of Standards in Higher Education (CAS). (2022) *Standards*. CAS. https://www.cas.edu/standards

Drabinski, E. (2019). What is critical about critical librarianship? *Art Libraries Journal*, *44*(2), 49–57. doi:10.1017/alj.2019.3

Johnson, M. W., & Page, S. (2022). What's in a Workload? Affect, Burnout, and Complicating Capacity in Academic Librarians. In C. Holm, A. Guimaraes, & N. Marcano (Eds.), Academic Librarian Burnout: Causes and Responses (pp. 45–58). ACRL Press.

Jones, S. R., & Stewart, D. (2016). Evolution of Student Development Theory. *New Directions for Student Services*, *2016*(154), 17–28. doi:10.1002s.20172

Kendi, I. X. (2019). *How to be an antiracist*. One World.

Kendrick, K. D. (November 20, 2017). ShoutOut: Pauline Wilson (Ret.). *The Ink on the Page*. https://theinkonthepageblog.wordpress.com/2017/11/20/shoutout-pauline -wilson-ret/

Kezar, A. J., & Lester, J. (2009). *Organizing higher education for collaboration: A guide for campus leaders*. Jossey-Bass.

Lynn, A. (2004). *The EQ difference: A powerful plan for putting emotional intelligence to work*. AMACOM.

Manning, K. (1996). Contemplating the myths of student affairs. *NASPA Journal*, *34*(1), 36–46. doi:10.2202/1949-6605.1003

Modern Campus. (2021, October 31). 11 Spooky Myths About Student Affairs & Co-Curricular Engagement. *Modern Campus*. https://moderncampus.com/blog/spooky-myths-about-student-affairs.html

Nardine, J. (2019). The State of Academic Liaison Librarian Burnout in ARL Libraries in the United States. *College & Research Libraries*, *80*(4), 508–524. doi:10.5860/crl.80.4.508

NASPA. (1987). *A perspectives on student affairs: A statement issued on the 50th anniversary of* The Student Personnel Point of View. https://www.naspa.org/files/dmfile/A_Perspective_on_Student_Affairs_1987.pdf

NASPA. (2022). *Careers in Student Affairs Month*. NASPA. https://www.naspa.org/project/careers-in-student-affairs-month

NASPA. (n.d.-a). *Graduate Program Directory*. NASPA. https://www.naspa.org/careers/graduate-program-directory

NASPA. (n.d.-b). *Our History Leads to Our Future*. NASPA. https://history.naspa.org/

NASPA. (n.d.-c). *NASPA: Student Affairs Administrators in Higher Education*. NASPA. https://naspa.org/

Pace, D., Blumreich, K. M., & Merkle, H. B. (2006). Increasing Collaboration between Student and Academic Affairs: Application of the Intergroup Dialogue Model. *NASPA Journal*, *43*(2), 301–315. doi:10.2202/1949-6605.1641

Parkinson, C. N. (1957). *Parkinson's Law: And other studies in administration*. Houghton Mifflin Harcourt.

Raza, S., Hackman, M. J., DuVernay, J., Dragovic, N., Bruchko, E. A., & Rutledge, M. H. (2022). The Making of Emory Libraries' Diversity, Equity, and Inclusion Committee: A Case Study. In B. Lym & C. Lee (Eds.), *Implementing Excellence in Diversity, Equity, and Inclusion: A Handbook for Academic Libraries*. Association of College and Research Libraries.

Schwartz, R., & Stewart, D. (2017). The History of Student Affairs. In J. H. Schuh, S. R. Jones, & V. Torres (Eds.), *Student services: A handbook for the profession* (6th ed., pp. 63–88). Jossey-Bass.

Shay, J. E. Jr. (1984). The Chief Student Affairs Officer and the President: Revisiting an Old Issue. *NASPA Journal*, *22*(2), 56–58. doi:10.1080/00220973.1984.11071917

Advancing Justice Through Strategic Partnerships

Tatum, B. D. (2017). *Why are all the Black kids sitting together in the cafeteria? And other conversations about race.* Basic Books. (Original work published 1997)

Young, R. B. (1993). Examining the History of Student Affairs through the Lens of Professional Education. *NASPA Journal, 30*(4), 243–251. doi:10.1080/00220973.1993.11072322

Chapter 14
Creating Inclusive Spaces in Different Types of Libraries

Grace Turney
University of Missouri, USA

ABSTRACT

This chapter explores five key components of building an inclusive library space: community, collection, environment/promotions, programming, and policies/staff. These components can be implemented in every type of library, including public, school, academic, special, and more. The "Community" section explains how to identify and connect with the library's community. The "Collection" portion explores building a diverse and inclusive collection of resources. The "Environments/Promotions" section discusses the library atmosphere, including signage, displays, and digital spaces. "Programming" explains how library programs can be designed and implemented to support justice, equity, and diversity. And "Staff and Policies" explores the rules and guidelines of the library for staff and patrons, as well as hiring and training staff for inclusivity and diversity.

INTRODUCTION

Justice, equity, diversity, and inclusion (JEDI) are fundamental to all types of libraries. These values are endorsed and protected by the Library Bill of Rights, the American Library Association's statement expressing the rights of library users to intellectual freedom and the expectations the association places on libraries to support those rights. Every article in the Library Bill of Rights relates to JEDI initiatives, denoting the importance of these initiatives in the library's role of serving its community.

The first article in the Library Bill of Rights states: "Books and other library resources should be provided for the interest, information, and enlightenment of all people of the community the library serves. Materials should not be excluded because of the origin, background, or views of those contributing to their creation" (American Library Association, 2006).

And Article V in the Library Bill of Rights states: "A person's right to use a library should not be denied or abridged because of origin, age, background, or views."

DOI: 10.4018/978-1-6684-7255-2.ch014

Copyright © 2023, IGI Global. Copying or distributing in print or electronic forms without written permission of IGI Global is prohibited.

Creating Inclusive Spaces in Different Types of Libraries

This first article emphasizes the importance of serving the interests of all people in the library community. It points to the inclusion aspect of JEDI and the significance of the library community, indicating the need for library managers and employees to familiarize themselves with the community they serve. And the fifth article clearly outlines some of the reasons why library patrons should never be denied equitable access to library services.

Some believe the Internet jeopardizes the existence of libraries due to the ease of sharing and accessing information online, but the Internet has only created a greater need for libraries as a safe space for the dissemination of accurate information. Libraries offer holdings far beyond printed resources in their collections. Digital resources have not displaced libraries or printed materials; instead, they have enriched and enhanced them. In a time when anyone can publish their opinions and thoughts online and call them facts, the role of libraries, and equal access to information, is more crucial than ever. The physical presence of the library is also more crucial than ever, as it is a place that freely offers the Internet and online resources to those who may not otherwise have access.

The role of libraries and library professionals is not to gatekeep information but to help their communities access information in all forms, as well as educate their communities on how to discern accurate information. It is the library's duty to help put information in people's hands, regardless of the library professionals' opinions on the information.

Creating inclusive spaces in libraries is a critical aspect of supporting JEDI initiatives, and it is of equal importance in all types of libraries, including (but not limited to): public, school, academic, and special libraries. This chapter addresses five components of creating inclusive library spaces: **community, collection, environment/promotions, programming, and policies/staff**. These components are largely based on the Library Bill of Rights and the author's personal experience and observations from working in various types of libraries, particularly John Ehret High School Library in New Orleans, Louisiana, and Daniel Boone Public Library in St. Louis, Missouri, and the experiences of other library professionals noted throughout the chapter. Library professionals and aspiring library professionals are encouraged to look at these five categories holistically, as they are equally significant to the success of maintaining justice, equity, diversity, and inclusion in library spaces.

Finally, creating inclusive spaces in libraries is not a one-time effort, as will be explored further in this chapter. Implementing JEDI initiatives in library spaces requires ongoing efforts by every library professional to support the continued success of the library, its mission, and its community in the immediate and distant future.

IDENTIFYING AND CONNECTING WITH YOUR COMMUNITY

To best serve the library's community in alignment with JEDI principles, library professionals must first identify their community. There are two ways of gathering information about the library community: observation and data. Both are necessary to provide the most needed, desired, and accessible resources to patrons.

Observation

Observation alone is not enough to determine and serve the library community, but it is an important part of figuring out the particular services and resources your library should provide and emphasize. Make

Creating Inclusive Spaces in Different Types of Libraries

a conscious effort to observe who comes into the library and uses the various services and to be aware of other institutions surrounding the library. Is there an elementary school nearby, so the library often has children ages 5-12 coming in with their guardians? Or is there a local high school, so teens come in? And are they more drawn to the young adult space, or the adult sections for resources? Is there any number of patrons that speak a foreign language, or materials frequently requested in foreign languages?

Having open and ongoing communication among all library managers and employees is crucial to acknowledging and serving the library community. As part of initial training, employees should be advised to observe patrons and pay attention to whether the community's specific needs are being served. Allow and encourage all staff members to have regular discussions - whether through a web form, monthly meetings, or some other structured format - about the community's ongoing and changing needs.

It's important to note that libraries should cater to all patrons regardless of whether they see evidence (in data or observation) of those needs. For example, in compliance with the Americans with Disabilities Act, libraries should be accessible by wheelchair even if the staff has never observed a patron in a wheelchair at the library. But not every aspect of accessibility is protected by law. For example, access to materials in different languages should be available, even if the community does not have a large demographic who speaks those languages.

Data

Besides observation, another way to determine the library's community is collecting data. The American Library Association (ALA) website has a useful guide titled "Making Diversity Count: Finding and Using Statistics, Data, and Resources on Diversity in Libraries and Librarianship." This page provides several links where library managers and employees can access data to determine their library's demographic.

One of the top resources listed is the United States Census Bureau's website (www.census.gov/data). By searching the library's zip code, one can find recent census information about the population surrounding the library. It lists data on the population's age, race, sex, household size, household income, and more. Using resources like this and other websites provides a snapshot of the community and its needs.

The library can also collect its own data about the community. This can be as simple as providing a suggestion box where patrons can request materials, share what they'd like to see or experience at the library, and provide other valuable feedback. Patrons should also have access to a similar feedback form online. Tell patrons about ways they can provide feedback at the checkout desk, in marketing emails, at the beginning/end of programs, etc.

How to Use Information From Data and Observation

Once information on the community has been gathered through data and observation, this research can be implemented to make the library space more inclusive.

For example, if research shows the library has a large percentage of young patrons, the library may need to expand the children's section, allocate more funds toward children's resources and programming, and/or hire a children's programming librarian.

If the library has a large Spanish-speaking community, it would be helpful to add Spanish translations to the library's signage and marketing materials, purchase more Spanish media, and design more programs around Latin culture.

Creating Inclusive Spaces in Different Types of Libraries

Inclusivity efforts also extend to the library's accessibility. For example, if many people in the library's community are homebound, consider providing a bookmobile or book/media delivery service.

Supporting the inclusivity of one demographic can encourage and promote the inclusivity of others. If LGBTQ+ patrons recognize an effort to provide LGBTQ+ resources, they may feel empowered to speak up on behalf of other communities. Or, if patrons who speak French see resources in another foreign language at the library, they may be encouraged to request media in their language. It's important to acknowledge and include all communities, but even showing support for one can have a greater impact toward the inclusivity of all.

Author's personal observation: The library community and patron needs vary greatly depending on the type of library and its location. The author has worked in a public library in an affluent neighborhood in St. Louis, Missouri, and in a large public high school library in a low-income area New Orleans, Louisiana. The patron demographic and needs were vastly different in each of these libraries.

In the public library, there was a high demand for programming, and the library had a generous budget. Books and other resources were rarely contested. There was a roughly equal distribution of materials in terms of age groups (a similar number of children's, young adult, and adult materials). There was a large Asian population in the community, so the library had an Asian center providing resources (including books, magazines, audiobooks, and movies) in several Asian languages, and some of the programming focused on different Asian cultures.

Working in the high school library in New Orleans was a very different experience, and the patrons' needs vastly diverged. Instead of an equal number of resources for all ages, most of the resources in the collection were designed for young adults. The library also had to account for the different reading levels and interests of high school students by integrating some adult and children's books. There was a high demand for graphic novels, so ordering these resources and staying up to date with the latest series installments was an important part of retaining student interest, making them feel like their requests mattered, and keeping them coming back to the library. This library did not have the same access to funding as the public library, so staff had to come up with creative ways to pay for programs, decorations, and giveaways, such as hosting student-led fundraisers.

CONSIDER AND CURATE THE COLLECTION

One of the most crucial aspects of creating an inclusive library space is curating the resource collection. Article I of the Library Bill of Rights states: "Books and other library resources should be provided for the interest, information, and enlightenment of all people of the community the library serves. Materials should not be excluded because of the origin, background, or views of those contributing to their creation" (American Library Association, 2006).

Notice the wording of that article - library resources are for *all* people in the community and should cater to their interests. As the very first article in the Library Bill of Rights, it's fair to say that not only is curating the collection one of the most significant components of supporting inclusivity; it's one of the most important aspects of librarianship in general.

Assess the Collection

Adding materials to the collection is not the only way to curate the collection for inclusivity. Before making new purchases or sourcing new materials, assess the current collection for gaps, outdated items, or unpopular materials.

There are several factors to consider when assessing the collection for diversity, including the topics of the resources, the backgrounds of the authors, the type and accessibility of the materials, and more. There are also many different types of diversity to look for, including (but not limited to) cultural, racial, gender, age, ability, sexual orientation, and more.

Screening for one type of diversity, while looking for the categories of the topic, author, and type of material, is a good start to assessing the collection. A continuous effort is required to work through all categories and determine if the collection supports JEDI in every way.

Weeding

Weeding the collection through the lens of justice, equity, diversity, and inclusion is not an act of censorship. In fact, the library as an institution is against all forms of censorship, as outlined in Article III of the Library Bill of Rights, which states: "Libraries should challenge censorship in the fulfillment of their responsibility to provide information and enlightenment."

In some cases, keeping certain materials in the collection may seem counterintuitive to supporting JEDI efforts. If a book contains hateful or discriminatory characters, or is written by a prejudiced author, it may seem like that resource should be removed. But these materials can still hold educational value. Keep in mind that just because a library holds a particular resource doesn't mean the library (or its staff) supports or endorses the message of that resource. At the same time, library employees must fight against censorship and see the value of materials with controversial content or content that goes against their personal beliefs.

Take, for example, the book *To Kill a Mockingbird* by Harper Lee, which frequently appears on banned books lists. Library patrons have valid concerns when questioning this item, but it holds value as an educational resource and must remain available to the public, even if it is personally objectionable to some patrons.

An exception is the removal of non-fiction materials that are factually inaccurate. If resources are factually inaccurate, they could go against JEDI efforts.

Of course, it is important to keep the type of library in mind while curating the collection. *To Kill a Mockingbird* might not be an appropriate resource for an elementary school library, for example, due to both the reading level and the subject matter. It also wouldn't belong in the children's section of a public library. But it is important to distinguish age-appropriateness and the community the library serves as the reason for keeping it out of the collection rather than censorship.

When weeding to support JEDI initiatives, focus on removing materials that are unused or out of date. What have patrons not checked out for several years that is only cluttering instead of adding value to the collection? Most libraries have established guidelines on how much time needs to lapse since the resource was purchased or last checked out to make its removal necessary. Follow these policies or, if there are none in place, suggest creating weeding guidelines.

Creating Inclusive Spaces in Different Types of Libraries

The practice of weeding the collection in itself makes the collection more accessible, as patrons and employees won't have to dig through unused, outdated, or factually inaccurate materials to find a useful or desired resource.

If materials that support JEDI initiatives fall under the category of outdated or unused resources flagged for weeding, replace them with more modern and in-demand resources that also support JEDI.

Funding, Budgeting, and Fundraising for Resources

Once the existing library materials have been assessed and any outdated, unused materials have been removed, resources that support justice, equity, diversity, and inclusion can be added to the collection.

A portion of the library budget should be used for purchasing new materials. Allocate a percentage of the budget for new resources, and perhaps a specific percentage of the budget for materials that support JEDI initiatives.

Of course, not all libraries have the funding to purchase lots of new materials. There are ways to raise money outside of the library's budget and to use the existing collection to support JEDI efforts.

One way to raise money for new materials is to hold a fundraiser. Hosting a book sale, a trivia night, or a paid or sponsored program can help raise money for new materials. These activities can also bring new patrons into the library. Fundraising activities may promote inclusivity in themselves - design a paid program about different cultures, focus questions of the trivia night around the community, etc. Other than fundraisers, most diverse and inclusive programs should be free and accessible to all.

Building the Collection

After weeding the collection and allocating or raising funds for new resources, new materials that support JEDI initiatives can be added to the collection.

A great way to determine what resources best support the library's community is seeking direct feedback from patrons. Ask patrons at the checkout desk what they're interested in and what they would like to see more of in the library. Include a poll in the library's email newsletter asking what patrons want. Consider starting a newsletter, if the library doesn't already have one, to engage with the community and get feedback.

Use the research gathered through observation and data to determine what types of resources the library needs. If there is a large Spanish-speaking community, purchase more Spanish resources. If there is a large blind community, purchase more audiobooks and braille materials.

While the collection should cater to the library community's specific needs, it should reflect and support all cultures. In the example of a Spanish-speaking community, allocate more funds to Spanish resources, but purchase materials for other languages and cultures, as well.

It may not be possible to buy everything the library needs at once, so prepare a list for the next round of purchasing. Keep the community informed of new materials and when they are expected to become available at the library. Maintain the catalog, but having a newsletter is another great way to keep patrons updated on the collection.

The ALA website has a page devoted to Selection Criteria, and it is divided into sections based on the type of library: public, school, and academic. It also offers general selection guidelines applicable to all types of libraries.

265

According to the ALA website (Pekoll, 2017), library resources should be selected based on the following:

- Currency and timeliness of material
- Accuracy, quality, and depth of material
- Relevancy of subject or title to the institution's current and potential scholarly/curriculum needs including 'standard or important works in a field"
- Represents a variety of perspectives on controversial subjects
- Scope and content (subject representation and diversity)
- Cost
- Resources in a variety of formats and accessible both virtually and physically
- Coverage appropriate to the level of study of a subject (minimal/basic, instructional support, intermediate study, advanced study, research level)

Promoting Inclusive Resources

A crucial (and inexpensive or free) way of using the collection to support JEDI initiatives is promoting diverse and inclusive materials. These do not have to be new materials; they can be books and other resources the library already holds that align with JEDI values.

Creating a display makes accessing those resources easier and shows the library honors and supports that community. For example, the library could have an LGBTQ+ display in June to acknowledge and celebrate Pride Month. Display creators should research symbolism used in the LGBTQ+ community. Display their flags, rainbows, and other representations of pride. Have a book display showcasing books by LGBTQ+ authors and/or centered around LGBTQ+ characters and themes.

It's equally necessary to promote materials and make them easily discoverable online, as some patrons may not be comfortable exploring them in the library setting.

Author's personal observation: The author worked at a high school library in New Orleans for two years. The previous librarians did not place much emphasis on displays, decorations, or other interactive components of the library. The librarian created displays centered around a different theme every month, such as Valentine's Day and LGBTQ+ pride in February (since the school was not open in the summer months to have a display in June, Pride Month) or a Martin Luther King Jr. theme in January (since MLK Day is the third Monday in January every year, and having the display up for the entire month promotes the topic of the Civil Rights Movement and racial inequality for more than just one day). Smaller displays or activities on different themes at the same time offer even more inclusion and diversity.

When setting up the LGBTQ+ display for the first time, the author saw many students' faces light up when they entered the library and saw rainbows adorning the bookshelves and hanging from the ceiling. They flocked to the eye-catching mini-display of LGBTQ+ books, temporarily organized in rainbow color order for the month. Several expressed that they'd never seen a display like that before in any part of their school. It was obvious that it made LGBTQ+ students and allies feel more comfortable, safe, and confident in the school library. It was a clear example of how important the collection and displays in the library are in supporting justice, equity, diversity, and inclusion efforts.

Creating displays and promoting inclusive materials is a consistent, ongoing effort your library can make to support JEDI initiatives. It also allows the library to celebrate many different cultures every time employees change the theme or set up a new mini-display.

Creating Inclusive Spaces in Different Types of Libraries

Opposing Censorship

Another way the library can support JEDI efforts is by fighting censorship. As previously noted in the "Weeding" section, Article III in the Library Bill of Rights explicitly states: "Libraries should challenge censorship in the fulfillment of their responsibility to provide information and enlightenment."

Further, article IV says: "Libraries should cooperate with all persons and groups concerned with resisting abridgment of free expression and free access to ideas."

This means that, as part of supporting JEDI efforts, the library must provide materials that support all sides of an issue. Library managers should not avoid purchasing new collection items based on personal beliefs or the beliefs of staff members or patrons. As outlined in the "Weeding" section, have a policy in place for patrons to question materials and bring them to the library manager for evaluation.

The ALA website provides a helpful guide in evaluating library collections. "Reasons for inclusion or removal of materials may include but are not limited to accuracy, currency, budgetary constraints, relevancy, content, usage, and community interest. The collection-development process is not to be used as a means to remove materials or deny access to resources on the grounds of personal bias or prejudice or because the materials may be viewed as controversial or objectionable. Doing so violates the principles of intellectual freedom and is in opposition to the Library Bill of Rights" (American Library Association, 2006).

The ALA also states that some resources containing views, concepts, and opinions that were once widely held or popular could now be considered harmful, outdated, or offensive. The creators of the resources must also be considered.

Library professionals are entrusted with distinguishing the difference between controversial and harmful items. A controversial material or creator is insufficient as the sole reason not to provide or to remove a resource from the collection. Doing so is a form of censorship, and librarians should instead consider methods of providing context for how the concepts and opinions of the resource or its creator have changed over time, and why they still hold value.

"The American Library Association opposes censorship from any source, including library workers, faculty, administration, trustees, and elected officials. Libraries have a profound responsibility to encourage and support intellectual freedom by making it possible for the user to choose freely from a variety of offerings" (American Library Association, 2006).

ENVIRONMENT/PROMOTIONS

Creating a welcoming, inclusive environment is key to promoting JEDI efforts in the library and community. Once the community has been identified, library professionals can build a space that supports patrons and caters to their specific needs. The library space can also be a useful tool to educate patrons about other cultures.

Having a diverse collection that showcases a variety of cultures and backgrounds, and emphasizes the culture of your community, is the first step. But promoting these materials and displaying them in the library is equally important.

Some library displays should be temporary, while others can be more permanent. For example, holiday displays are a great way to celebrate different cultures in a time-sensitive way. If the library has

Creating Inclusive Spaces in Different Types of Libraries

a Christmas display, it should also observe other winter holidays, such as Hanukkah, Kwanzaa, Winter Solstice, and more.

Holidays can inspire inclusive displays, but they aren't the only prompts. There are many temporary and permanent displays that encourage interactions with library materials and get patrons excited about reading while supporting JEDI efforts.

Here are a few resources for brainstorming inclusive displays in different types of libraries:

Teen Services Underground: Fascinating First Sentences, Banned Books, Courage and Resilience, Mental Health, Women's History, You Build the Display, Race and Civil Rights, Feast on Books: Food and Cooking, and Blind Date with a Book are all display ideas from this website focusing on displays for young adults. These could be used in a high school library, the Young Adult section of a public library, and more.

Book Riot: This website provides several examples with photos of library displays, and it suggests resources for coming up with new display ideas. For example, Book Riot recommends searching the hashtag #LibraryDisplays to see what displays other libraries are creating and to promote your own.

Library Displays: This website has an entire list of display ideas for school libraries, including photos and a blog post on how to create each one. Some of the display ideas include Going Green, Winter Holidays, Read Around the World, and more.

Inclusive library displays should not stand out as an anomaly, but rather show ongoing consideration and reflect the library's holdings. The ALA website states: "Highlight diverse materials year-round, not just as a special occasion. So you had an incredible display during February for Black History Month with intersectional perspectives and not just stories about slavery - great! Can you include stories of POC in your Pride display in June? And in your poetry display in April? And in your holiday display in December/January? Challenge yourself to expand on the work you're already doing - it's very likely the perspectives you're looking for are already out there" (Elwood, 2019).

Library displays don't have to cost a lot of money - it's often a simple matter of arranging materials from the existing collection with appropriate signage. While it's best to budget for displays, cost does not have to prevent the library from celebrating diverse and inclusive materials.

One way to keep the displays fresh, up-to-date, and always changing is to have more than one employee work on them, and to make it an ongoing task. Perhaps the first day of each month could be display changeover day, or challenge employees to come up with new ones every two weeks. Hold a contest amongst employees for who can come up with the most creative or interactive display that promotes JEDI initiatives.

Displays aren't the only ways to support JEDI initiatives in the library environment. Posters, infographs, and other permanent signage make inclusivity a consistent rather than a temporary effort.

Failing to create a welcoming and inclusive environment can render efforts to make the collection more diverse ineffective. Even with an inclusive collection of materials, patrons may never know about the available resources or how the library supports inclusivity without proper signage, promotion, and displays.

Signage, such as directions to where materials are located and the grouping of materials themselves, are a crucial part of JEDI in libraries. Providing signs in multiple languages, using large, legible print, illustrations, and braille can make the library space and collection more accessible and inclusive.

"When selecting signage or artwork (or other décor) for the library, be sure to evaluate those choices for inclusion and (good) representation. Take note of whether your clipart or other imagery represents diversity in body type, disability, race, religion, ethnicity, gender identity, and more. Ensure the imagery

Creating Inclusive Spaces in Different Types of Libraries

you select challenges traditional gender norms and other stereotypes" (Bogan, 2022). Audit all imagery in the library, including signage, posters, artwork, handouts, and bookmarks, to ensure they support JEDI initiatives. "Also consider evaluating any imagery you use in the digital realm such as in bitmoji libraries, graphic buttons, digital fliers, video thumbnails, etc." (Bogan, 2022).

Library professionals should also assess how resources are categorized, stored, and shelved. In recent years, there has been an outcry for the amendment or abolition of the Dewey Decimal System (DDS).

Library Media Specialist Kelsey Bogan described the issues with the DDS and why library professionals might consider implementing a different cataloging system: "Dewey Decimal System is inherently problematic from an equity and antiracist (and anti-homophobic, and anti-misogynic, etc etc) lens" (Bogan, 2021). For example, in a high school library, "Dewey had books about LGBTQIA+ rights and identities in the 360s. Next to pornography and criminal acts. Because Dewey categorized those topics under 'sexual deviancy.' Dewey puts the religious faith system of Wicca outside the Religions section altogether, denying it equal status with other world religions and faiths. Dewey allocates 200s through 289 for christianity topics and squeezes the rest of humanity's religions into the 290s."

The Library Media Specialist encouraged library staff to reflect on these issues and spend time exploring the nonfiction section of their library, looking for correlations from a JEDI standpoint. "Look at what books are shelved near each other. And ask yourself if any of the groupings seem off, or wrong, or harmful to you. And if they do, I encourage you to consider implementing some form of Ditching Dewey, or Adapting Dewey to remove those harmful correlations."

Decorations, signage, and displays create a welcoming environment within the library walls, but JEDI efforts must also be reflected in promotional and digital spaces. Newsletters, flyers, the library website, and more need to be created and updated with diversity and inclusivity in mind.

Failure to create a welcoming environment does not go unnoticed by library patrons. Here is an example of how a lack of effort to build an inclusive library space through displays and signage can create an uncomfortable and even hostile environment for patrons:

"Black students largely view the Duke University Libraries as inclusive spaces in the sense that they meet their diverse learning needs as underrepresented students. However, some aspects of library spaces are unwelcoming because they center white history and culture. Students have reported a general feeling that both Duke and Duke Libraries, while not actively hostile or racist, are complicit in their silence. Students have noted the lack of visible actions and signs supporting diversity and inclusion, minimal efforts to limit white western European cultural dominance, and no attempts to educate white students about minority experiences. Students have expressed doubt that the university or Duke Libraries would take meaningful action if students reported instances of prejudice or microaggression." - *Making the Library More Inclusive by Learning from Black Students* by ARL Communications (ARL Communications, 2021).

Author's personal observation: When working at the high school library in New Orleans, inclusive displays noticeably encouraged students to engage with the library and made them feel welcome and accepted. Many students said they enjoyed coming into the library at the beginning of each month to see how the decorations transformed to fit the monthly themes and holidays. For example, in February, library staff arranged a Valentine's Day display and a Black History Month display, each with interactive components. Several students checked out materials from the displays they said they likely wouldn't have discovered otherwise. The displays were designed to motivate students to interact with the selected materials (which aligned with JEDI initiatives).

The interactive component from the Black History Month display was to write on the provided notecards what Black History Month meant to them, or to pull a quote from one of the display books that resonated with them. Students had the option to tape their notecards on the library wall behind the display for others to see. Those who participated were rewarded with a small prize, such as a piece of candy or a $0.10 library fine forgiveness.

The Valentine's Day display promoted romantic resources, including LGBTQ+ stories and authors, for all reading levels. Graphic novels and poetry books were included. The interactive component was "Blind Date with a Book." Library staff covered several books in wrapping paper (along with unwrapped books on the display), so students could check out a book without seeing the cover or knowing what it was about. Students were again rewarded for checking out a blind date book and confirming they had read at least the first ten pages.

PROGRAMMING AND EVENTS

Library professionals can support JEDI efforts by designing programs around inclusivity. Diverse and inclusive programs help create a welcoming environment and encourage engagement with the community.

Programs are opportunities to celebrate the holidays, art, food, traditions, etc. of different cultures. Much like library displays, programs should be a continuous and ever-changing effort.

While library employees can and should design programs, another way to support JEDI efforts through programming is to reach out to speakers who can present on diverse topics. Authors and community members could share their stories at promoted events. The library can also host fundraisers to support anti-racism in the local community and beyond.

When designing programs that support JEDI efforts, it's imperative to keep the cultural iceberg in mind. Library employees responsible for designing programs need to do thorough research to make programs that reflect a culture's core values and underlying beliefs instead of merely surface-level appearances and practices.

Programs such as book clubs or the library's recommended reading list need to support JEDI. Recommended reading should be on diverse topics (or the library can offer multiple clubs to cater to different interests and genres), with authors from diverse backgrounds.

Programs must be accessible to all - offer a variety of times and make modifications to the program when needed to accommodate those with limited mobility, etc. While not all programs will be suitable for everyone (for example, programs at public libraries are often sorted into age groups - children's programs, teen programs, adult programs, and all ages programs), there should be options available to everyone.

Author's personal observation: Designing programs for a broad range of interests, age groups, abilities, and cultures is a wonderful opportunity to celebrate diversity and promote JEDI initiatives at the library. At the public library in Missouri, there was a wide range of programs, ranging from learning the basics of email, painting dot art in the Australian Aboriginal style, family game nights, International Folk Dance classes, LEGO building time for kids and teens, coding courses, and author presentations. There were several programs designed around learning foreign languages and sign language, and translators were available for other programs unrelated to learning foreign languages, as well. There is no limit to the ways programming can support JEDI initiatives, with some creativity, research, and effort from library professionals.

Creating Inclusive Spaces in Different Types of Libraries

POLICIES, STAFF, AND LIBRARY CULTURE

Even with a diverse and inclusive collection and environment, the library can only be a truly welcoming and inclusive space if the staff actively works to support JEDI efforts.

Policies

The library policy is the rules of the library - it is the guidebook for all employees and patrons clearly outlining expectations to work in and use the library.

Library managers, along with other employees, must examine the library's existing policies to ensure they support diversity and inclusion. Discriminatory and non-inclusive policies and practices must be abandoned, and new policies that support JEDI initiatives may need to be established.

It is helpful to have multiple perspectives when assessing old policies and devising new ones. Hold a roundtable discussion to assess the library's policies with employees at various levels. Send the current policy and list of questions to each participant in advance, so everyone can come to the table prepared. Surveys can also be useful tools to get perspectives on policies from library employees at every level.

Here are some examples of questions for evaluating the library's policies from a JEDI standpoint: "Rewriting Existing Policies - Many libraries, including my own, are looking at rewriting policies to ensure their equity and inclusiveness. For example, we have looked at individual policies and asked the following questions: Do we need this policy (or a specific piece of this policy)? Does this policy support the culture we're trying to build? How does this policy impact specific communities or individuals differently? Is this policy targeting a particular group of patrons? Is the language unwelcoming, offensive, objectionable or inaccessible to certain communities?" - Equity, Diversity, and Inclusion in Libraries, Teen Services Underground (*Equity, Diversity, and Inclusion in Libraries*, 2021).

Having thorough policies that support JEDI efforts in place helps guide staff members and assist them in their interactions with patrons.

Staff Hiring, Training, and Attitude

In order to have a diverse and inclusive library, every single staff member, from the library manager to the maintenance crew to volunteers, needs to understand and support JEDI efforts.

Building questions about anti-racism, equity, etc. into job interviews is a way to impress the library's standards upon future employees before hiring. There are legal standards for interviews, so be sure to carefully check the wording of all questions before using them and adhere to a standardized set of questions throughout the interview.

Creating a standardized list of questions can also help avoid discriminatory, prejudiced, or offensive queries. For example, instead of asking if a prospective hire has a disability, list the essential functions of the job, and ask if they are able to perform them, with reasonable accommodation.

Consider your library's community during the hiring process. It's important that the library staff represents the community it serves and is also diverse and inclusive.

Making applications for positions accessible is another way to create equity and diversity in the library. Instead of only having paper applications or recruiting employees, make applications available to all on the internet and encourage Black, Indigenous, and People of Color (BIPOC), immigrants, women, and LGBTQ+ candidates to apply.

Consider the equity of library positions. If there is a hiring barrier, see where adjustments can be made. For example, if a candidate is the best fit for the role but they cannot meet the requirement of coming in at 7:30 a.m. because they need to take their children to school, consider shifting the designated schedule by one hour to make their start time 8:30 a.m. Many issues can be identified and negotiated, with reasonable accommodation, during the hiring process.

Many states legally require annual training on diversity and inclusion, as well as initial training upon hiring. It is the library manager's role to enforce these trainings, and it is the responsibility of each library employee to participate in training. The library can also create its own training, separate from what is legally required, on library policies and JEDI in the library. These trainings should be continuously evaluated and updated as needed.

Patron interactions are crucial to supporting JEDI in the library. Having policies in place that support equity and inclusion helps uphold the library's standards of how staff and patrons should be treated. It gives employees a reference point when handling difficult interactions with patrons, such as a patron contesting a book the patron doesn't think is appropriate for the collection, or a staff member concerned about the behavior of a patron.

Managers can use the American Library Association website and the Library Bill of Rights to guide their policies. For example, Article VI of the Library Bill of Rights outlines equitable use of library spaces. From the ALA website: "Libraries which make exhibit spaces and meeting rooms available to the public they serve should make such facilities available on an equitable basis, regardless of the beliefs or affiliations of individuals or groups requesting their use" (American Library Association, 2006).

Using this tool as a guideline can help create a policy that prevents disputes among patrons or between staff and patrons. If a group belonging to a particular political affiliation holds a meeting in a reserved library room, a patron belonging to another party might notice and complain. A library staff member or manager can then point out the policy to the patron (it's useful to keep paper copies of the library policies on hand in case of these events, and highlight the relevant portions for patrons as needed) and assure the patron they have equal opportunity to hold a meeting for a political party, and would also be permitted and supported by the library.

Finally, library management and staff should not only encourage patrons to consume diverse media but should also consume diverse media themselves. Promote use of the library's vast range of resources and help library staff become familiar with different types of media.

The ALA emphasizes the importance of consuming diverse media and provides an example of a reading list that supports this effort. From the ALA website: "Consume more diverse media! It's so difficult to recommend material that we haven't read/watched/listened to. Need help diversifying your reading list? Try consulting one of your institution's librarians or use Book Riot's Read Harder Challenge as a guide" (Elwood, 2019).

Train staff members on the proper use of different materials, such as how to play an audiobook, find resources in a foreign language, and more. When patrons need these resources and ask staff members for help, the staff should be prepared to answer their questions in a way that shows they respect the patron and value their use of library resources.

Library staff should also be encouraged to step outside of their comfort zones when it comes to the types of media they are consuming. There are many creative ways to do this. Many public libraries hold reading contests for patrons, and staff members could have their own reading competition. Create a list with a variety of fiction and non-fiction stories on diverse topics written by authors from different cultures and backgrounds.

Creating Inclusive Spaces in Different Types of Libraries

Author's personal observation: When working at the public library in Missouri, training employees on how to use different types of resources made a noticeable difference in supporting JEDI initiatives. Patrons came in who either had impaired vision or on behalf of a fellow community member with impaired vision, asking for help with using the library's online audiobook resources. Staff members were able to assist patrons in accessing these materials and recommend the physical audiobooks available for checkout in the library, which could be easier for those with impaired vision to use independently.

CONCLUSION

After reading this chapter, library professionals and aspiring library professionals should have an understanding of how to create a library space that promotes justice, equity, diversity, and inclusion. They should also recognize that this is a multi-faceted project that requires continuous effort. While implementing practices from any of the five sections outlined in this chapter supports JEDI in libraries, they are only fully effective when used in conjunction with one another.

Identifying, connecting with, and seeking feedback from the **community**, assessing, weeding, and adding to the resource **collection**, creating a welcoming and inclusive **environment** (including **digital spaces** and **promotional materials**), thoughtful **programming**, creating and supporting fair **policies**, and hiring, training, and supporting **staff** in JEDI efforts are all necessary components of building a safe and inclusive library space.

REFERENCES

American Library Association. (2006, July 26). *Evaluating Library Collections: An Interpretation of the Library Bill of Rights.* ALA. https://www.ala.org/advocacy/intfreedom/librarybill/interpre tations/evaluatinglibrary

American Library Association. (2006, June 30). *Library Bill of Rights.* ALA. https://www.ala.org/advocacy/intfreedom/librarybill

American Library Association. (2006, June 30). *Library Bill of Rights.* ALA. https://www.ala.org/advocacy/intfreedom/librarybill

American Library Association. (2007, March 29). *Making Diversity Count: Finding and Using Statistics, Data, and Resources on Diversity in Libraries and Librarianship.* ALA. https://www.ala.org/aboutala/offices/diversity/diversitycoun ts/makingdiversitycount

Bogan, K. (2021, March 2). *Developing a Library That's REALLY For Everyone.* Don't You Shush Me! https://dontyoushushme.com/2021/03/02/__trashed/

Bogan, K. (2022, April 27). *Developing an Inclusive Library Space: A Holistic Approach.* Infobase. https://www.infobase.com/blog/developing-an-inclusive-librar y-space-a-holistic-approach/

Communications, A. R. L. (2021, February 16). *Making the Library More Inclusive by Learning from Black Students*. Association of Research Libraries. https://www.arl.org/blog/making-the-library-more-inclusive-by-learning-from-black-students/

100 *Display Ideas*. (2021, October 6). Teen Services Underground. https://teenservicesunderground.wordpress.com/2021/10/06/100-display-ideas/

Elwood, C. (2019, June 5). *Daily Dose of Diversity: How Patron-Facing Library Staff Further Inclusivity*. ALA. https://www.ala.org/advocacy/diversity/odlos-blog/daily-dose-of-diversity

Equity, Diversity, and Inclusion in Libraries. (2021, April 6). Teen Services Underground. https://teenservicesunderground.wordpress.com/2021/04/06/equity-diversity-and-inclusion-in-libraries/

Maxwell, L. (2021, July 23). Great Library Displays and How Effective They Are. *BOOK RIOT*. https://bookriot.com/great-library-displays/

Pekoll, K. (2017, December 19). *Selection Criteria*. ALA. https://www.ala.org/tools/challengesupport/selectionpolicyto olkit/criteria

School Library Displays. (n.d.). *School Library Displays*. School Library Displays. https://librarydisplays.org/

The Cultural Iceberg Explained. (n.d.). Lynch Law Firm, PLLC. Www.lynchlf.com. https://www.lynchlf.com/blog/the-cultural-iceberg-explained/

US Census Bureau. (2018, October 5). *Data*. Census.gov. https://www.census.gov/data.html

KEY TERMS AND DEFINITIONS

Accessibility: An object, place, or idea's ease of use, entry, and being understood.

Censorship: The suppression, restriction, destruction, or removal of resources deemed offensive or unacceptable.

Cultural iceberg: The surface-level or apparent aspects of a culture that are visible to an observer, that does not include or address the deeper foundations, such as the underlying principles and beliefs, of the culture.

Display: Anything from a selection of books arranged on a table to an elaborate, interactive wall space. Any arrangement of materials within the library walls to promote library resources is a display. They can be temporary or more permanent. This is separate from signage, flyers, or artwork.

Microaggression: Subtle, indirect, or unintentional discrimination against a marginalized group.

Policies: A set of guidelines and rules the library staff and patrons must follow in order to work in and use the library space and its resources.

Programming: The designing and implementing of planned activities, typically group activities, that encourage patrons to use library resources. They can include book clubs, crafting groups, author presentations, classes, workshops, and more.

Weeding: The process of identifying, selecting, and removing materials from the library collection.

Compilation of References

100 *Display Ideas*. (2021, October 6). Teen Services Underground. https://teenservicesunderground.wordpress.com/2021/10/06/100-display-ideas/

Abdullahi, I. (2007). Diversity and intercultural issues in library and information science (LIS) education. *New Library World*. https://www.emerald.com/insight/content/doi/10.1108/03074800710823980/full/html

Aboriginal and Torres Strait Islander Library Information Resource Network. (2015). ATSILIRN Protocols for Libraries Archives and Information Services. AIATSIS. http://atsilirn.aiatsis.gov.au/protocols.php

About Us. (n.d.). Bookshop.org. https://bookshop.org/info/about-us

Academic Librarian Status. (2021, June 6). Evanwell. https://evanwill.github.io/academic-librarian-status/about.html

ACPA. (2022). *Careers in Student Affairs Month*. ACPA. https://myacpa.org/csam/

ACPA. (2023). *ACPA: College Student Educators International*. ACPA. ACRL. https://myacpa.org/

ACRL. (2011, August 2). A*bout ACRL*. ACRL. https://www.ala.org/acrl/aboutacrl

Adedini, S. A., Odimegwu, C., Imasiku, E. N., & Ononokpono, D. N. (2015). Ethnic differentials in under-five mortality in Nigeria. *Ethnicity & Health*, *20*(2), 145–162. https://www.tandfonline.com/doi/abs/10.1080/13557858.2014.890599. doi:10.1080/13557858.2014.890599 PMID:24593689

Adler, M. (2017). Classification along the color line: Excavating racism in the stacks. *Journal of Critical Library and Information Studies*, *1*(1). doi:10.24242/jclis.v1i1.17

Aguilera, A., Carey, F., Dommermuth, E., Li, X., Koob, A. R., Swanson, J., Tingle, N., & Watkins, A. (2022, June 14). *Anti-racist library collection building*. University of Colorado Boulder Libraries research guides. https://libguides.colorado.edu/anti-racist-collections-review-acquisitions/home

Aikens, N. L., & Barbarin, O. (2008). Socioeconomic differences in reading trajectories: The contribution of family, neighborhood, and school contexts. *Journal of Educational Psychology*, *100*(2), 235–251. doi:10.1037/0022-0663.100.2.235

Airhihenbuwa, C. O. (1995). Health and culture: Beyond the western paradigm. *Sage (Atlanta, Ga.)*.

ALA. (2008, June 9). *Mission & priorities*. ALA. https://www.ala.org/aboutala/missionpriorities

Compilation of References

Alabi, J. (2018). From hostile to inclusive: Strategies for improving the racial climate of academic libraries. *Library Trends, 67*(1), 131–146. https://muse.jhu.edu/article/706992/pdf. doi:10.1353/lib.2018.0029

Alburo, J., Bradshaw, A. K., Santiago, A. E., Smith, B., & Vinopal, J. (2020). Looking beyond libraries for inclusive recruitment and retention practices: Four successful approaches. In *Critical Librarianship*. Emerald Publishing Limited. doi:10.1108/S0732-067120200000041009

Allen, J. W. (1963). *Legends & lore of southern Illinois*. Southern Illinois University.

Allen, T., & Ebay, L. T. (2007). *The Blackwell Handbook of Mentoring: A multiple Perspectives Approach*. Blackwell Publishing., doi:10.1111/b.9781405133739.2007.x

American Indian Library Association. (n.d.). *Membership Committee*. ALA. https://ailanet.org/about/committees/

American Libraries. (2008). Economic crisis hits libraries nationwide. *American Libraries, 39*(6), 26-27. https://grinnell.idm.oclc.org/login?url=https://www.proquest.com/trade-journals/economic-crisis-hits-libraries-nationwid e/docview/197186999/se-2

American Library Association (ALA). (n.d.). *Equity, Diversity, and Inclusion*. ALA. https://www.ala.org/advocacy/diversity

American Library Association. (2006, July 26). *Evaluating Library Collections: An Interpretation of the Library Bill of Rights*. ALA. https://www.ala.org/advocacy/intfreedom/librarybill/interpre tations/evaluatinglibrary

American Library Association. (2006, June 30). *Library Bill of Rights*. ALA. https://www.ala.org/advocacy/intfreedom/ librarybill

American Library Association. (2007, March 29). *Making Diversity Count: Finding and Using Statistics, Data, and Resources on Diversity in Libraries and Librarianship*. ALA. https://www.ala.org/aboutala/offices/diversity/diversitycoun ts/makingdiversitycount

American Library Association. (2012, May 4). *Diversity standards: Cultural competency for academic libraries (2012)*. Association of College & Research Libraries (ACRL). https://www.ala.org/acrl/standards/diversity

American Library Association. (2019, June 24). *Diverse collections: An interpretation of the library bill of rights*. ALA. https://www.ala.org/advocacy/intfreedom/librarybill/interpretations/diversecollections

American Library Association. (2021). *National Survey Finds Libraries Play Expanded Role In Digital Equity, Bridging Gaps In Access To Technology*. ALA. https://www.ala.org/news/press-releases/2021/08/national-sur vey-finds-libraries-play-expanded-role-digital-equity-bridgi ng

American Library Association. (2022, February 28). *Cultural proficiencies for racial equity: A framework*. Public Library Association (PLA). https://www.ala.org/pla/initiatives/edi/racialequityframewor k

American Library Association. (n.d.) *Mentoring opportunities*. ALA. https://www.ala.org/educationcareers/mentoring-opportunities

American Psychological Association. (2017, July). Education and Socioeconomic Status. APA. https://www.apa.org/pi/ses/resources/publications/education

Anaya, T., & Maxey-Harris, C. (2017). *Diversity and Inclusion, SPEC Kit 356.* Association of Research Libraries., doi:10.29242pec.356

Anderson, J. (2005). Indigenous knowledge, intellectual property, libraries and archives: Crises of access, control and future utility. *Australian Academic and Research Libraries, 36*(2), 83–94. doi:10.1080/00048623.2005.10721250

Anderson, K. D., Jackson, M., & Trogden, B. (2021). Looking back, moving forward: Intercultural communication must be part of all learning. *Liberal Education, 107*(1), 32–39.

Anti-Oppression: Anti-Oppression. (n.d.). Simmons University Library. https://simmons.libguides.com/anti-oppression

Archibald, J. A., De Santolo, J., & Lee-Morgan, J. (2019). *Decolonizing Research: Indigenous Storywork as Methodology.* ZedBooks.

Arroyo-Ramirez, E., Chou, R. L., Freedman, J., Fujita, S., & Orozco, C. M. (2018). The reach of a long-arm stapler: Calling in microaggressions in the LIS field through zine work. *Library Trends, 67*(1), 107–130. doi:10.1353/lib.2018.0028

Ashikali, T., Groeneveld, S., & Kuipers, B. (2021). The Role of Inclusive Leadership in Supporting an Inclusive Climate in Diverse Public Sector Teams. *Review of Public Personnel Administration, 41*(3), 497–519. doi:10.1177/0734371X19899722

Asian Pacific American Librarians Association. (n.d.). *Mentoring program.* APALA. https://www.apalaweb.org/about/committees/standing-committees/mentoring-committee/mentoring-program/

Association of University Presses. (2021, March 18). University press numbers from the Lee & Low Diversity Baseline Survey 2.0. *Association of University Presses.* https://aupresses.org/news/up_data_lee_and_low_dbs_2/

Augusta University Literacy Center. (2023) *Literacy Center.* AULC. https://www.augusta.edu/education/literacy-center/

Australian Bureau of Statistics. (2022, July*). Australia: Aboriginal and Torres Strait Islander population summary.* ABS. https://www.abs.gov.au/articles/australia-aboriginal-and-torres-strait-islander-population-summary

Australian Government Department of Foreign Affairs and Trade. (2018). Education Learning and Development Module: The role of key stakeholders in education aid effectiveness principles. DFAT. https://www.dfat.gov.au/sites/default/files/foundation-role-of-key- stakeholders-aid-effectiveness-principles.pdf

Australian Institute of Aboriginal and Torres Strait Islander Studies. (2020). Code of Ethics. Australian Institute. https://aiatsis.gov.au/research/ethical-research/code-ethics

Australian Library and Information Association. (2019). *Professional Pathways Project.* ALIA. https://professional-pathways.alia.org.au/

Ayala, M. J., Carter, J. K., Fachon, A. S., Flaxman, S. M., Gil, M. A., Kenny, H. V., Laubach, Z. M., Madden, S. A., McDermott, M. T., Medina-García, A., Safran, R. J., Scherner, E., Schield, D. R., Vasquez-Rey, S., & Volckens, J. (2021). Belonging in STEM: An interactive, iterative approach to create and maintain a diverse learning community *Trends in Ecology & Evolution, 36*(11), 964–967. doi:10.1016/j.tree.2021.08.004 PMID:34561090

Baildon, M., Hamlin, D., Jankowski, C., Kauffman, R., Lanigan, J., Miller, M., Venlet, J., & Willer, A. M. (2017). *Creating a social justice mindset: Diversity, inclusion, and social justice in the collections directorate of the MIT Libraries.* MIT Libraries. https://dspace.mit.edu/handle/1721.1/108771

Compilation of References

Baldwin, S. C., Buchanan, A. M., & Rudisill, M. E. (2007). What teacher candidates learned about diversity, social justice, and themselves from service-learning experiences. *Journal of Teacher Education*, *58*(4), 315–327. https://journals.sagepub.com/doi/abs/10.1177/0022487107305259. doi:10.1177/0022487107305259

Barker, A. E., & Hoffman, A. T. (2021). Student-centered design: Creating LibGuides students can actually use. *College & Research Libraries*, *82*(1), 75. doi:10.5860/crl.82.1.75

Barnett, E. (2022). Collection and vendor relationships: Diversity evaluation and communication. *Serials Review*, *48*(3–4), 253–255. doi:10.1080/00987913.2022.2119058

Barrowcliffe, R. (2021). Closing the narrative gap: Social media as a tool to reconcile institutional archival narratives with Indigenous counter-narratives. *Archives and Manuscripts*, *49*(3), 151–166. doi:10.1080/01576895.2021.1883074

Barrows, K. (2021, June 10). *Library professionals: Facts, figures, and union membership –Department for Professional Employees, AFL*. CIO. https://www.dpeaflcio.org/factsheets/library-professionals-facts-and-figures

Bastian, J. A., & Flinn, A. (Eds.). (2020). *Community archives community spaces: Heritage memory and identity*. Facet Publishing.

Bastian, J. A., Sniffin-Marinoff, M., & Webber, D. (2018). *Archives in libraries: What librarians and archivists need to know to work together*. Society of American Archivists.

Batinski, M. C. (2021). *Forgetting and the forgotten: A thousand years of contested histories in the heartland*. Southern Illinois University Press.

Bear, D. R., Invernizzi, M., Templeton, S., & Johnson, F. (2011). *Words their way: Word study for phonics, vocabulary and spelling instruction* (7th ed.). Pearson.

Behrendt, L. (2019). Indigenous Storytelling: decolonizing institutions and assertive self-determination: implications for legal practice. In J. Archibald, J. De Santolo, & J. Lee-Morgan (Eds.), *Decolonising Research. Indigenous Storywork as a Methodology* (pp. 175–186). Zedbooks.

Bergstrom-Lynch, Y. (2019). LibGuides by design: Using instructional design principles and user-centered studies to develop best practices. *Public Services Quarterly*, *15*(3), 205–223. doi:10.1080/15228959.2019.1632245

Bernhardt, B., Hinds, L., Meyer, L., & Strauch, K. (Eds.). (2021). *Charleston Conference Proceedings, 2020*. Charleston Information Group. 10.3998/mpub.12470905

Berry, W. (2010). The hidden wound. *Collections Priorities Focus Areas*. University Libraries, University of Massachusetts Amherst. https://www.library.umass.edu/wp-content/uploads/2022/03/CollectionsPriorities2018-final.pdf

Berthoud, H., & Finn, R. (2019). Bringing social justice behind the scenes: Transforming the work of technical services. *The Serials Librarian*, *76*(1–4), 162–169. doi:10.1080/0361526X.2019.1583526

BertoleroM. A.DworkinJ. D.DavidS. U.LloredaC. L.SrivastavaP.StisoJ.ZhouD.DzirasaK.FairD. A.KaczkurkinA. N.MarlinB. J.ShohamyD.UddinL. Q.ZurnP.BassettD. S. (2020). *Racial and ethnic imbalance in neuroscience reference lists and intersections with gender*. https://www.biorxiv.org/content/10.1101/2020.10.12.336230v1 doi:10.1101/2020.10.12.336230

Bertot, J. C., Jaeger, P. T., McClure, C. R., Wright, C. B., & Jensen, E. (2009). Public libraries and the Internet 2008-2009: Issues, implications, and challenges. *First Monday*, *14*(11), 1–10. doi:10.5210/fm.v14i11.2700

BetterUp. (2021). *The value of belonging: New frontiers for inclusion*. BetterUp. https://grow.betterup.com/resources/the-value-of-belonging-at-work-the-business-case-for-investing-in-workplace-inclusion

Betts, V. (2021). Imagining Futures Through the Archives. *American Studies (Lawrence, Kan.)*, *60*(2), 19–22. https://doi-org.proxy.lib.siu.edu/10.1353/ams.2021.0005

Bickman, L., Lambert, E. W., Andrade, A. R., & Penaloza, R. V. (2000). The Fort Bragg continuum of care for children and adolescents: Mental health outcomes over 5 years. *Journal of Consulting and Clinical Psychology*, *68*(4), 710–716. doi:10.1037/0022-006X.68.4.710 PMID:10965645

Black Caucus American Library Association. (2021, November 10). *Professional Development Committee*. BCALA. https://www.bcala.org/committees

Blackburn, F. (2020). Cultural Competence: Toward a More Robust Conceptualisation. *Public Library Quarterly*, *39*(3), 229–245. doi:10.1080/01616846.2019.1636750

Blas, N., Conner-Gaten, A., Masunaga, J., & Young, J. (2021). POC in LIS summit 2021 impact report. *LMU Librarian Publications & Presentations, 131*, 164–171. https://digitalcommons.lmu.edu/librarian_pubs/131

Blas, N., Conner-Gaten, A., Deras, R., & Young, J. (2019). Empowering collaborations and creating brave spaces: People of Color in Library and Information Science Summit. *College & Research Libraries News*, *80*(5), 270–273. doi:10.5860/crln.80.5.270

Bledsoe, K., Cooper, D. M., Schonfeld, R. C., & Rieger, O. Y. (2022, November 9). Leading by diversifying collections: A guide for academic library leadership. *Ithaka S+R*. doi:10.18665/sr.317833

Bocko, A. F., Guth, L., & Broadnax, M. (2021). Library response to Black Liberation Collective: A review of student calls for change and implications for anti-racist initiatives in academic libraries. *RSR. Reference Services Review*.

Bogan, K. (2021, March 2). *Developing a Library That's REALLY For Everyone*. Don't You Shush Me! https://dontyoushushme.com/2021/03/02/__trashed/

Bogan, K. (2022, April 27). *Developing an Inclusive Library Space: A Holistic Approach*. Infobase. https://www.infobase.com/blog/developing-an-inclusive-library-space-a-holistic-approach/

Bolton, A., de Figueiredo, J. M., & Lewis, D. E. (2021). Elections, Ideology, and Turnover in the US Federal Government. *Journal of Public Administration: Research and Theory*, *31*(2), 451–466. doi:10.1093/jopart/muaa051

Bonnici, L. J., Maatta, S. L., Brodsky, J., & Steele, J. E. (2015). Second national accessibility survey: Librarians, patrons, and disabilities. *New Library World*, *116*(9/10), 503–516. doi:10.1108/NLW-03-2015-0021

Booker, L. (2020). 'Indigenous Recordkeeping and Archives Course' goes Live. *Indigenous Archives Collective*. https://indigenousarchives.net/2020/09/30/indigenous-recordkeeping-and-archives-course-goes-live/

Boon, J., Wynen, J., & Kleizen, B. (2021). What happens when the going gets tough? Linking change scepticism, organizational identification, and turnover intentions. *Public Management Review*, *23*(7), 1056–1080. doi:10.1080/14719037.2020.1722208

Bosch, E. K., Ramachandran, H., Luévano, S., & Wakiji, E. (2010). The Resource Team Model: An Innovative Mentoring Program for Academic Librarians. *New Review of Academic Librarianship*, *16*(1), 57–74. doi:10.1080/13614530903584305

Compilation of References

Brannen, M. H., Milewski, S., & Mack, T. (2017). Providing Staff Training and Programming to Support People with Disabilities: An Academic Library Case Study. *Public Services Quarterly, 13*(2), 61–77. doi:10.1080/15228959.2017.1298491

Braveman, P., & Gottlieb, L. (2014). The social determinants of health: It's time to consider the causes. *Public Health Reports, 129*(1_suppl2), 19–31. doi:10.1177/00333549141291S206 PMID:24385661

Bresnahan, M. (2022). Library diversity and inclusion statements in action. *Journal of Library Administration, 62*(4), 419–437. doi:10.1080/01930826.2022.2057125

Brimhall-Vargas, M. (2015). Where the rubber meets the road: The role of libraries and librarians in bringing equitable access to marginalized communities. *The Library Quarterly, 85*(2), 193–199. https://www.journals.uchicago.edu/doi/abs/10.1086/680157. doi:10.1086/680157

Bronzo, W. G., & Flynt, E. S. (2008). Motivating students to read in the content classroom: Six evidence-based principles. *The Reading Teacher, 62*(2), 172–174. doi:10.1598/RT.62.2.9

Brook, F., Ellenwood, D., & Lazzaro, A. E. (2015). In pursuit of antiracist social justice: Denaturalizing whiteness in the academic library. *Library Trends, 64*(2), 246–284. https://muse.jhu.edu/article/610078/pdf. doi:10.1353/lib.2015.0048

Brown, J. (2022, August 22). *Michigan library risks closing after voters pull funding over LGBT-themed books*. Fox News. https://www.foxnews.com/us/michigan-library-risks-closing-voters-pull-lgbt-themed-books

Brown, J., Cline, N., & Méndez-Brady, M. (2021). Leaning on our labor: Whiteness and hierarchies of power in LIS work. In S. Y. Leung & J. R. López-McKnight (Eds.), *Knowledge justice: Disrupting library and information studies through critical race theory* (pp. 95–110). The MIT Press. https://direct.mit.edu/books/oa-edited-volume/5114/chapter/3075317/Leaning-on-Our-Labor-Whiteness-and-Hierarchies-of doi:10.7551/mitpress/11969.003.0007

Brown, J., Ferretti, J. A., Leung, S., & Méndez-Brady, M. (2018). We here: Speaking our truth. *Library Trends, 67*(1), 163–181. doi:10.1353/lib.2018.0031

Brown, M. K. (1991). Documents and archaeology in French Illinois. In J. A. Walthall (Ed.), *French colonial archaeology: the Illinois country and the western great lakes*. University of Illinois Press.

Brown, S. S. (1988). Approaches to Collaboration between Academic and Student Affairs. *NASPA Journal, 26*(1), 2–7. doi:10.1080/00220973.1988.11072071

Bruder, M. B., Harbin, G. L., Whitbread, K., Conn-Powers, M., Roberts, R., Dunst, C. J., Van Buren, M., Mazzarella, C., & Gabbard, G. (2005). Establishing outcomes for service coordination: A step toward evidence-based practice. *Topics in Early Childhood Special Education, 25*(3), 177–188. doi:10.1177/02711214050250030501

Buckingham, J., Wheldall, K., & Beaman-Wheldall, R. (2013). Why poor children are more likely to become poor readers: The school years. *Australian Journal of Education, 57*(3), 190–213. doi:10.1177/0004944113495500

Bunger, A. C. (2010). Defining Service Coordination: A Social Work Perspective. *Journal of Social Service Research, 36*(5), 385–401. doi:10.1080/01488376.2010.510931 PMID:21116470

Burrell, D. N., & Rahim, E. (2018). Developing inclusive leaders with religious literacy in the workplace. *Leadership, 14*(5), 567–584. doi:10.1177/1742715018793745

Cabrera, N. L., Franklin, J. D., & Watson, J. S. (2017). *Whiteness in higher education: The invisible missing link in diversity and racial analyses*. Wiley Subscription Services, Inc.

CALA. (n.d.) *CALA Committees*. CALA. https://cala-web.org/about/committee/2022-2023

Campus History & Description. (n.d.). Bradford alumni assoc. http://www.bradfordalumni.org/bradfordcampushistory/history.html

Caplar, N., Tacchella, S., & Birrer, S. (2017). Quantitative evaluation of gender bias in astronomical publications from citation counts. *Nature Astronomy, 1*(6), 0141. doi:10.103841550-017-0141

Carless, W. (2021, March 17). White supremacist propaganda hit an all-time high in 2020, New Report says. *USA Today*. https://www.usatoday.com/story/news/nation/2021/03/17/white-supremacist-propaganda-hits-all-time-high/4721323001/

Carlisle, M. (2022, September 7). Public libraries face threats to funding as book bans surge. *Time*. https://time.com/6211350/public-libraries-book-bans/

Carlton, G. (2022, February 22). *A history of women in Higher Education: Best Colleges*. BestColleges.com. https://www.bestcolleges.com/news/analysis/2021/03/21/history-women-higher-education/

Carmichael, J. V. (2005). Southern Librarianship and the Culture of Resentment. *Libraries & the Cultural Record, 40*(3), 324–352. https://www.jstor.org/stable/25541934. doi:10.1353/lac.2005.0044

Carpenter, K. E. (1996). *Readers & libraries: Toward a history of libraries and culture in America*. Library of Congress.

Caruso, M., Christenberry, F., Davis, A., Gascon, L., Henchy, J. A. N., Kenny, C., Schroeder, S., Shen, Z., & Sullivan, M. (2022). *UW Libraries Task Force on diversity, equity, inclusion, and anti-racism in collections final report*. UW Libraries https://digital.lib.washington.edu:443/researchworks/handle/1773/49181

Caswell, M., Cifor, M., & Ramirez, M. (2016). "To suddenly discover yourself existing": Uncovering the impact of community archives. *The American Archivist, 79*(1), 56–81. doi:10.17723/0360-9081.79.1.56

Caswell, M., Migoni, A. A., Geraci, N., & Cifor, M. (2017). 'To be able to imagine otherwise': Community archives and the importance of representation. *Archives and Records (Abingdon, England), 38*(1), 5–26. https://doi-org.proxy.lib.siu.edu/10.1080/23257962.2016.1260445. doi:10.1080/23257962.2016.1260445

Center for Community Health and Development. (n.d.). *Chapter 3, Section 10: Conducting Concerns Surveys*. University of Kansas. Community Tool Box. http://ctb.ku.edu/en/table-of-contents/assessment/assessing-community-needs-and-resources/conduct-concerns-surveys/main

Chadley, O. A. (1992). Addressing cultural diversity in academic and research libraries. *College & Research Libraries, 53*(3), 206–216. doi:10.5860/crl_53_03_206

Chakravartty, P., Kuo, R., Grubbs, V., & McIlwain, C. (2018). #CommunicationSoWhite. *Jo urnal of Communication, 68*(2), 254–266. doi:10.1093/joc/jqy003

Chamberlain, A. W., Dunlap, J., & Russell, P. G. (2021, July). *Moving from words to action: The Influence Of Racial Justice Statements On Campus Equity Efforts*. National Association of Student Personnel Administrators (NASPA): Student Affair Administrators in Higher Education. https://www.naspa.org/report/moving-from-words-to-action-the-influence-of-racial-justice-statements-on-campus-equity-efforts

Compilation of References

Chamberlain, C. (2015). *Illinois Indians made a bid for power in early America, based on bison and slavery*. Illinois News Bureau. https://news.illinois.edu/view/6367/298688#:~:text=blog%20po sts-,Illinois%20Indians%20made%20a%20bid%20for%20power%20in% 20early,based%20on%20bison%20and%20slavery

Chan, L. (2020, November 9). *Decentering the White gaze of academic knowledge production: A paper presented at the Critical Knowledge Forum* [Presentation slides]. Zenodo. 10.5281/zenodo.4289243

Chapman Carr, K. (2003). Today's literacy center: How relevant is the graduate reading practicum? *The Reading Teacher*, *57*(3), 256–268.

Chatterjee, L. (2020). *BU Libraries aim to advance anti-racist practices by creating resources for students*. Pipe Dream. https://www.bupipedream.com/news/117857/auto-draft-380/

Chen, J., Kim, M., & Liu, Q. (2016). Do Female Professors Survive the 19th-Century Tenure System?: Evidence from the Economics Ph.D. Class of 2008. SSRN *Electronic Journal*. https://doi.org/ doi:10.2139/ssrn.2885951

Chiu, A., Ettarh, F. M., & Ferretti, J. A. (2021). Not the Shark, but the Water: How Neutrality and Vocational Awe Intertwine to Uphold White Supremacy. In S. Y. Leung & J. R. López-McKnight (Eds.), *Knowledge justice: Disrupting library and information studies through Critical Race Theory* (pp. 49–71). MIT Press. doi:10.7551/mitpress/11969.003.0005

Christen, K. (2018). Relationships, Not Records. Digital Heritage and the Ethics of Sharing Indigenous Knowledge Online. Pp. 403-412. (Ed) Sayers, J. The Routledge Companion to Media Studies and Digital Humanities. New York. Routledge.

Cifor, M., Caswell, M., Migoni, A. A., & Geraci, N. (2018). "What we do crosses over to activism": The politics and practice of community archives. *The Public Historian*, *40*(2), 69–95. https://doi-org.proxy.lib.siu.edu/10.1525/ tph.2018.40.2.69. doi:10.1525/tph.2018.40.2.69

Citation diversity statement in BMES journals. (2021). *Journal of Biomedical Engineering, 49*(3), 947-949. https://doi. org/https://doi.org/10.1007/s10439-021-02739-6

Cite Black Authors – A database for academic research by Black authors. (n.d.). Cite Black Authors. https://citeblack-authors.com/

Coalter, J., Durden, D., & Dunewood, L. A. (2022). Equitable from the Beginning: Incorporating Critical Data Perspectives into Your Research Design. In K. Getz & M. Brodsky (Eds.), *The Data Literacy Cookbook* (pp. 140–144). Association of College and Research Libraries.

Coffey, D., Hubbard, D., Holbein, M., & Delacruz, S. (2013). Creating a university- based literacy center. Evan Ortlieb & Earl H. Cheek, Jr. (Eds.), Advanced Literacy Practices: From the Clinic to the Classroom, Vol. 2. (pp. 21-35). Bingley, UK: Emerald Group Publishing Limited.

Coleman, M. A., & Harrison, J. (2022). Cultural diversity in children's braille books. *Journal of Visual Impairment & Blindness*, *116*(2), 1–21. https://journals.sagepub.com/doi/abs/10.1177/0145482X2210902 61. doi:10.1177/0145482X221090261

Columbia University Libraries. (2019, April). *Collection development policies & strategies: Diversity in and of collections*. Columbia University Libraries. https://library.columbia.edu/about/policies/collection-devel opment-policies-strategies.html

Communications, A. R. L. (2021, February 16). *Making the Library More Inclusive by Learning from Black Students*. Association of Research Libraries. https://www.arl.org/blog/making-the-library-more-inclusive-b y-learning-from-black-students/

Conerton, K., & Goldenstein, C. (2017). Making LibGuides work: Student interviews and usability tests. *Internet Reference Services Quarterly*, *22*(1), 43–54. doi:10.1080/10875301.2017.1290002

Consortium of Academic and Research Libraries in Illinois (CARLI). (2022, April). *Sample DEI language used in collection development policies*. Consortium of Academic and Research Libraries in Illinois. https://www.carli.illinois.edu/products-services/collections -management/Sample_DEI_Language_Used_in_Collection_Developme nt_Policies

Cooke, N. A. (2020). Critical library instruction as a pedagogical tool. *Communications in Information Literacy*, *14*(1), 7. doi:10.15760/comminfolit.2020.14.1.7

Cooper, M. A., & Leegwater, L. (2018). Postsecondary equity through the lens of policy change. Change. *Change*, *50*(3–4), 102–106. doi:10.1080/00091383.2018.1509630

Council for the Accreditation of Educator Preparation. (2013). *CAEP accreditation standards*. CAEP. https://caepnet. org/standards/2022- itp/introduction

Council for the Advancement of Standards in Higher Education (CAS). (2022) *Standards*. CAS. https://www.cas.edu/ standards

Craft, A. R. (2018). Creating connections, building community: The role of oral history collections in documenting and sharing campus diversity. *Serials Review*, *44*(3), 232–237. https://doi-org.proxy.lib.siu.edu/10.1080/00987913.2018.1513 750. doi:10.1080/00987913.2018.1513750

Crilly, J., Everitt, R., & Clarke, M. (2022). Liberate the Library: What it Means to Decolonise and Why it is Necessary. *In Narrative expansions: Interpreting decolonisation in academic libraries*. Facet Publishing. https://research.gold. ac.uk/id/eprint/30930/

Cruz, A. M. (2019). Intentional integration of diversity ideals in academic libraries: A literature review. *Journal of Academic Librarianship*, *45*(3), 220–227. https://www.sciencedirect.com/science/article/pii/S009913331 830377X. doi:10.1016/j.acalib.2019.02.011

D'Ignazio, C., & Klein, L. F. (2020). Our Values and Our Metrics for Holding Ourselves Accountable. In *Data Feminism*. MIT Press. doi:10.7551/mitpress/11805.003.0011

Dahlgren, G., & Whitehead, M. (1991). *Policies and Strategies to Promote Social Equity in Health*. Institute for Futures Studies.

Dahlgren, G., & Whitehead, M. (2021). The Dahlgren-Whitehead Model of health determinants: 30 years on and still chasing rainbows. *Public Health*, *199*, 20–24. doi:10.1016/j.puhe.2021.08.009 PMID:34534885

Dali, K., & Caidi, N. (Eds.). (2020). *Humanizing LIS Education and Practice: Diversity by Design* (1st ed.). Routledge. https://doiorg.grinnell.idm.oclc.org/10.4324/9780429356209 doi:10.4324/9780429356209

Dalton, S. D., Mathapo, G., & Sowers-Paige, E. (2018). Diversity Dialogues: Navigating Law Librarianship While Black: A Week in the Life of a Black Female Law Librarian. *Law Library Journal*, *110*, 429. https://heinonline.org/HOL/Page?handle=hein.journals/llj110& div=26&g_sent=1&casa_token=&collection=journals

Davenport, E., & Snyder, H. (1995). Who cites women? Whom do women cite? An exploration of gender and scholarly citation in sociology. *The Journal of Documentation*, *51*(4), 404–410. doi:10.1108/eb026958

Davies, H. (2013, February 26). *About ALA*. ALA. https://www.ala.org/aboutala/1833

Compilation of References

Davis, F. E., & Handguns, E. O. (2019). *The little book of race and restorative justice: Black lives, healing, and us social transformation*. Skyhorse Publishing Company, Incorporated.

Davis, J. E. (1998). *Frontier Illinois*. Indiana University Press.

de Jesus, N. (2014). Locating the library in institutional oppression. *In The Library With The Lead Pipe*. https://www.inthelibrarywiththeleadpipe.org/2014/locating-the-library-in-institutional-oppression/

Deards, K. D., & Springs, G. R. (Eds.). (2014). *Succession Planning and Implementation in Libraries: Practices and Resources*. IGI Global. doi:10.4018/978-1-4666-5812-7

Deci, E. L., & Ryan, R. M. (2012). Self-Determination Theory. In P. Van Lange, A. Kruglanski, & E. Higgins, Handbook of Theories of Social Psychology: Volume 1 (pp. 416–437). SAGE Publications Ltd. doi:10.4135/9781446249215.n21

Desimone, L. M., Hochberg, E. D., Porter, A. C., Polikoff, M. S., Schwartz, R., & Johnson, L. J. (2014). Formal and informal mentoring: Complementary, compensatory, or consistent? *Journal of Teacher Education*, *65*(2), 88–110. doi:10.1177/0022487113511643

Dexter, D. (2011). *Bondage in Egypt: Slavery in southern Illinois*. Center for Regional History, Southeast Missouri State University.

Digital Public Library of America. (n.d.). *A history of US public libraries*. DPLA. https://dp.la/exhibitions/history-us-public-libraries/beginnings

Dorn, E., Hancock, B., Sarakatsannis, J., & Viruleg, E. (2021). *COVID-19 and education: The lingering effects of unfinished learning*. McKinsey & Co. Retrieved from: https://www.mckinsey.com/industries/education/our-insights/covid-19-and-education- the-lingering-effects-of-unfinished-learning

Downey, J., Antell, K., & Strothmann, M. (2013). Self-censorship in selection of LGBT themed materials. *Reference and User Services Quarterly*, *53*(2), 104–107. doi:10.5860/rusq.53n2.104

Drabinski. (2013). Queering the Catalog: Queer Theory and the Politics of Correction. *The Library Quarterly (Chicago)*, *83*(2), 94–111. doi:10.1086/669547

Drabinski, E. (2019). What is critical about critical librarianship? *Art Libraries Journal*, *44*(2), 49–57. doi:10.1017/alj.2019.3

Driskill, G. W., & Brenton, A. L. (2019). *Organizational culture in action: A cultural analysis workbook* (3rd ed.). Routledge.

Duarte, M. L., & Belarde-Lewis, M. (2015). Imagining: Creating Spaces for Indigenous Ontologies. *Cataloging & Classification Quarterly*, *53*(5-6), 677–702. doi:10.1080/01639374.2015.1018396

Dunston, P. J. (2007). Instructional practices, struggling readers, and a university-based literacy center. *Journal of Adolescent & Adult Literacy*, *50*(5), 328–336. doi:10.1598/JAAL.50.5.1

Dutta, M. J. (2014). Communicating about culture and health: Theorizing culture-centered and cultural sensitivity approaches. *Communication Theory*, *17*(3), 304–328. doi:10.1111/j.1468-2885.2007.00297.x

Dworkin, J. D., Linn, K. A., Teich, E. G., Zurn, P., Shinohara, R. T., & Bassett, D. S. (2020). The extent and drivers of gender imbalance in neuroscience reference lists. *Nature Neuroscience*, *23*(8), 918–926. doi:10.103841593-020-0658-y PMID:32561883

Echavarria, T., & Wertheimer, A. B. (1997). Surveying the role of ethnic-American library associations. *Library Trends, 46*(2), 373–391.

Edmondson, A. C. (2019). *The fearless organization: Creating psychological safety in the workplace for learning, innovation, and growth*. John Wiley & Sons, Inc.

Educating with Evidence. (2017). *Using artifacts as evidence: Blacks and the Miller Grove, Illinois settlement*. Southern Illinois University. https://educatingwithevidence.siu.edu/_common/documents/the-underground-railroad-pdfs/ewe-miller-grove-artifacts.pdf

Edwards, J. B. (2015). Developing and implementing a diversity plan at your academic library. *Library Leadership & Management, 30*(2), 1–11. doi:10.5860/llm.v30i2.7129

Efron, L. (2022, July 26). What Drives a Culture of Belonging? *Gallup.Com*. https://www.gallup.com/workplace/395102/drives-culture-belonging.aspx

Egholm, C., & Jochumsen, H. (2000). Perspectives concerning user fees in public libraries. *Library Management, 21*(6), 298–306. https://www.emerald.com/insight/content/doi/10.1108/01435120010327605/full/html. doi:10.1108/01435120010327605

Else, H., & Perkel, J. M. (2022). The giant plan to track diversity in research journals. *Nature, 602*(7898), 566–570. doi:10.1038/d41586-022-00426-7 PMID:35197624

Elwood, C. (2019, June 5). *Daily Dose of Diversity: How Patron-Facing Library Staff Further Inclusivity*. ALA. https://www.ala.org/advocacy/diversity/odlos-blog/daily-dose-of-diversity

Equity, Diversity, and Inclusion in Libraries. (2021, April 6). Teen Services Underground. https://teenservicesunderground.wordpress.com/2021/04/06/equity-diversity-and-inclusion-in-libraries/

Espinal, I. R. (2020). *Microaffections & microaffirmations in library learning*. Five Colleges Innovative Learning Symposium. https://works.bepress.com/isabel_espinal/11/

Espinal, I. (2022). Microaffections and microaffirmations: Refusing to reproduce whiteness via microaffirmative actions. In T. Y. Neely & M. Montañez (Eds.), *Dismantling constructs of whiteness in higher education: Narratives of resistance from the academy* (pp. 65–76). Routledge. doi:10.4324/9781003029564-7

Espinal, I., Hathcock, A., & Rios, M. (2021). Dewhitening librarianship: A policy proposal for libraries. In S. Y. Leung & J. R. López-McKnight (Eds.), *Knowledge justice: Disrupting library and information studies through critical race theory* (pp. 223–240). The MIT Press., doi:10.7551/mitpress/11969.003.0017

Espinal, I., Sutherland, T., & Roh, C. (2018). A holistic approach for inclusive librarianship: Decentering whiteness in our profession. *Library Trends, 67*(1), 147–162. doi:10.1353/lib.2018.0030

Ettarh, F. (2018, January 10). *Vocational awe and librarianship: The lies we tell ourselves*. In the Library with the Lead Pipe. http://www.inthelibrarywiththeleadpipe.org/2018/vocational-awe/

Evans, J., Faulkhead, S., Thorpe, K., Adams, K., Booker, L., & Timbery, N. M. (2020). Indigenous archiving and wellbeing: surviving, thriving, reconciling. *Community archives, community spaces: Heritage, memory and identity*, 129-164.

Compilation of References

Fagbe, A. O., Fagbe, T., & Folorunso-Ako, A. O. (2019). Diversity management practices in the academic libraries in the age of globalization. *European Journal of Research in Social Sciences*, *7*(3), 15–25.

Farhang, L., & Morales, X. (2022). *Building Community Power to Achieve Health and Racial Equity: Principles to Guide Transformative Partnerships with Local Communities. National Academies of Medicine, Perspectives. Commentary.* National Academy of Medicine., doi:10.31478/202206d

Farmer, D., Stockham, M., & Trussell, A. (2009). Revitalizing a Mentoring Program for Academic Librarians. *College & Research Libraries*, *70*(1), 8–25. doi:10.5860/0700008

Farrell, B., Alabi, J., Whaley, P., & Jenda, C. (2017). Addressing Psychosocial Factors with Library Mentoring. *portal. Portal (Baltimore, Md.)*, *17*(1), 51–69. doi:10.1353/pla.2017.0004

Faulkhead, S. (2009). Connecting through records: Narratives of Koorie Victoria. *Archives & Manuscripts*, *37*(2), 60–88.

Feagin, J. R. (2020). *The white racial frame: Centuries of racial framing and counter-framing.* Routledge. doi:10.4324/9780429353246

Feldman, D. (2020, March 19). Council post: Accessible websites are better for everyone (and better for business too). *Forbes.* https://www.forbes.com/sites/forbesagencycouncil/2020/03/19/accessible-websites-are-better-for-everyone-and-better-for-b
usiness-too/?sh=316ccca748aa

Ferdman, B. M., Avigdor, A., Braun, D., Konkin, J., & Kuzmycz, D. (2010). Collective experience of inclusion, diversity, and performance in work groups. *RAM. Revista de Administração Mackenzie*, *11*(3), 6–26. doi:10.1590/S1678-69712010000300003

Fiedler, B. P., & Sterling, B. (2021). Conference critique: An analysis of equity, diversity, and inclusion programming. In: *Ascending into an Open Future: Proceedings from ACRL 2021 Virtual Conference*, (pp. 82–91). ACRL. https://digitalscholarship.unlv.edu/libfacpresentation/209

Figueroa, M., & Shawgo, K. (2021). "You can't read your way out of racism": Creating anti-racist action out of education in an academic library. *RSR. Reference Services Review*, *50*(1), 25–39. doi:10.1108/RSR-06-2021-0025

Finnie, E., & Arthur, M. A. (2016). Being earnest with collections—voting with our dollars: Making a new home for the collections budget in the MIT Libraries. *Against the Grain (Charleston, S.C.)*, *28*(4), 90–92. doi:10.7771/2380-176X.7496

Fiske, M. (2022). *Book selection and censorship: A study of school and public libraries in California.* Univ of California Press.

Fleming, L., & Bermas-Dawes, S. (2021). Digitized funeral programs document Black history. *GPB News.* https://www.gpb.org/news/2020/10/29/digitized-funeral-programs-document-black-history

Fleury, M. J., & Mercier, C. (2002). Integrated local networks as a model for organizing mental health services. *Administration and Policy in Mental Health*, *30*(1), 55–73. doi:10.1023/A:1021227600823 PMID:12546256

Flinn, A., Stevens, M., & Shepherd, E. (2009). Whose memories, whose archives? Independent community archives, autonomy and the mainstream. *Archival Science*, *9*(1-2), 71–86. doi:10.100710502-009-9105-2

Foma, E. (2014). Impact of workplace diversity. *Review of Integrative Business and Economics Research*, *3*(1), 382–410. http://buscompress.com/uploads/3/4/9/8/34980536/riber_sk14-026__402-410_.pdf

Food Justice. (n.d.). FoodPrint. Retrieved December 15, 2022, from https://foodprint.org/issues/food-justice/

Forsyth, E. (2005). Public libraries and the millennium development goals. *IFLA Journal, 31*(4), 315–323. https://journals.sagepub.com/doi/abs/10.1177/0340035205061389. doi:10.1177/0340035205061389

Fourmile, H. (2020). Who owns the past? Aborigines as captives of the archives. In *Terrible Hard Biscuits* (pp. 16–27). Routledge. doi:10.4324/9781003137160-2

Foy, C. M. (2021). Successful applications of diversity, equity, and inclusion programming in various professional settings: Strategies to increase DEI in libraries. *Journal of Library Administration, 61*(6), 676–685. doi:10.1080/01930826.2021.1947057

Frederick, J. K., & Wolff-Eisenberg, C. (2020). Ithaka S+R U.S. Library Survey 2019. *Ithaka SR*. https://sr.ithaka.org/publications/ithaka-sr-us-library-survey-2019/

Frederick, J. K., & Wolff-Eisenberg, C. (2021, March 17). National Movements for Racial Justice and Academic Library Leadership: Results from the Ithaka S+R US Library Survey 2020. *Ithaka SR*. doi:10.18665/sr.314931

Freedman, K. K. (2018). *A tangled web: Quakers and the Atlantic slave system 1625–1770* [Doctoral dissertation, University of Massachusetts, Amherst]. doi:10.7275/12597546

Friedman, J., & Johnson, N. F. (2022, October 11). *Banned in the USA: The growing movement to censor books in schools*. PEN America. https://pen.org/report/banned-usa-growing-movement-to-censor-books-in-schools/

Fry, R., & Parker, K. (2020, August 14). *Early benchmarks show 'post-millennials' on track to be most diverse, best-educated generation yet*. Pew Research Center's Social &; Demographic Trends Project. https://www.pewresearch.org/social-trends/2018/11/15/early-benchmarks-show-post-millennials-on-track-to-be-most-diverse-best-educated-generation-yet/

Gabbat, A. (2022, December 24). 'a streak of extremism': US book bans may increase in 2023. *The Guardian*. https://www.theguardian.com/us-news/2022/dec/24/us-book-bans-streak-of-extremism

Gabiola, J. (2018, July 13). *"Mesearching" the network of whitenessharmdiversity* [Paper presentation]. People of Color in Library & Information Science (POCinLIS) Summit, Loyola Marymount University, Los Angeles, CA, United States. https://digitalcommons.lmu.edu/pocinlis/2018/schedule/6

Galassi, M. (2019). My Cultural Competency Journey. An Italian perspective of working with Aboriginal and Torres Strait Islander Collections and Services in GLAM. *Indigenous Archives Collective*. https://indigenousarchives.net/2019/06/27/my-cultural-competency-journey-an-italian-perspective-of-working-with-aboriginal-and-torres-strait-islander-collections-and-services-in-glam/

Galassi, M. (2022). Reflections on shaping leadership across LIS. *Civica Journal*. https://www.civica.com/en-au/thought-leadership-library/reflections-on-shaping-leadership-across-lis/

Compilation of References

Gale, N. (2018). In Illinois, the Underground Railroad began in Cairo (at the confluence of the Mississippi and Ohio Rivers), Illinois' southernmost point. *Digital Research Library of Illinois History Journal.* https://drloihjournal.blogspot.com/2018/02/illinois-underground-railroad-began-in-cairo-at-illinois-southern-most-point.html

Gallagher, K. (2010). Reversing readicide. *Educational Leadership, 67*(6), 36–41.

GandhiS. (2019). How Reverse Mentoring Can Lead to More Equitable Workplaces. *Stanford Social Innovation Review.* doi:10.48558/NQJ8-H958

Gannett Satellite Information Network. (2017, November 6). Reader: Librarians aren't going anywhere. *USA Today.* https://www.usatoday.com/story/opinion/2017/11/06/reader-librarians-arent-going-anywhere/837858001/

García Peña, L. (2022). *Community as rebellion: A syllabus for surviving academia as a woman of color.* Haymarket Books.

Garcia, S. E. (2020, June 17). Where did BIPOC come from? *The New York Times.* https://www.nytimes.com/article/what-is-bipoc.html

Garnar, M. L. (2021). *Understanding the experiences of academic librarians of color* [Doctoral dissertation, University of Colorado, Colorado Springs]. ProQuest Dissertations and Theses database. https://www.proquest.com/docview/2618560641/abstract/59B5D3A66C8643F4PQ/1

Garwood-Houng, A., & Blackburn, F. (2014). The ATSILIRN Protocols: A twenty-first century guide to appropriate library services for and about Aboriginal and Torres Strait Islander peoples. *The Australian Library Journal, 63*(1), 4–15. doi:10.1080/00049670.2014.890018

Gaston, J., & Lewis, J. (2022, January 14). Contaminated wood treatment site still hurting Carbondale community 100 years later. *The Daily Egyptian.* https://dailyegyptian.com/111347/news/contaminated-wood-treatment-site-still-hurting-carbondale-community-100-years-later/

Geiger, L., Mastley, C. P., Thomas, M., & Rangel, E. (2023). Academic libraries and DEI initiatives: A quantitative study of employee satisfaction. *Journal of Academic Librarianship, 49*(1), 102627. doi:10.1016/j.acalib.2022.102627

Gender Equity Resource Center. (2020). *Part II: Being gay in a 1960s fraternity.* UC Berkeley. YouTube. https://www.youtube.com/watch?v=eqC9na4oI3A

General Assembly of the United Nations. (2007). *United Nations Declaration on the Rights of Indigenous Peoples.* UN. http://declaration.humanrights.gov.au/

Georgeac, O. A. M., & Rattan, A. (2023). The business case for diversity backfires: Detrimental effects of organizations' instrumental diversity rhetoric for underrepresented group members' sense of belonging. *Journal of Personality and Social Psychology, 124*(1), 69–108. doi:10.1037/pspi0000394 PMID:35679195

Georgia Institute of Technology. (2020). *Georgia Tech Strategic Plan.* Georgia Institute of Technology. https://strategicplan.gatech.edu/sites/default/files/georgia-tech-strategic-plan-2020-2030.pdf

Georgia Tech Library All Staff Meeting in Atlanta, GA. (2019, March 6). [Personal communication].

Get Georgia Reading. (2016). *Framework Overview* Get Georgia Reading. https://getgeorgiareading.org/framework-overview/

Ghosh, R., Reio, T. G. Jr, & Bang, H. (2013). Reducing turnover intent: Supervisor and co-worker incivility and socialization-related learning. *Human Resource Development International, 16*(2), 169–185. doi:10.1080/13678868.2012.756199

Gibson, A. N., Chancellor, R. L., Cooke, N. A., Dahlen, S. P., Patin, B., & Shorish, Y. L. (2021). Struggling to breathe: COVID-19, protest and the LIS response. *Equality, Diversity and Inclusion, 40*(1), 74–82. doi:10.1108/EDI-07-2020-0178

Gleason, E. A. (1941). *The southern negro and the Public Library: A Study of the government and administration of Public Library Service to Negroes in the South, by Eliza Atkins Gleason. with a foreword by Louis R. Wilson.* The University of Chicago Press.

Golian-Lui, L. M. (2003). Fostering Librarian Leadership Through Mentoring. *Adult Learning, 14*(1), 26–28. doi:10.1177/104515950301400107

Gooding-Call, A. (2021, September 17). Racism in the dewey decimal system. *BOOK RIOT.* https://bookriot.com/racism-in-the-dewey-decimal-system/

Goodman, A. (2017). Dick Gregory in his own words: Remembering the pioneering comedian and Civil Rights activist. *Democracy Now.* https://www.democracynow.org/2017/8/21/dick_gregory_in_his_own_words

Goodsett, M., Miles, M., & Nawalaniec, T. (2020). Reimagining research guidance: Using a comprehensive literature review to establish best practices for developing LibGuides. *Evidence Based Library and Information Practice, 15*(1), 218–225. doi:10.18438/eblip29679

Gosart, U. (2021). Indigenous librarianship: Theory, practices, and means of social action. In IFLA Journal, Special Issue: Indigenous Librarianship, 3(47), pp. 293-304

Governor's Office of Student Achievement. (2022, 17 October). Georgia School Grades Reports Richmond County (2020-2021). GOSA. https://public.gosa.ga.gov/noauth/extensions/SchoolGrades-Georgia/SchoolGrades- Georgia.html?SchoolName=richmond-county

Graham. (2009). *A Right to Read Segregation and Civil Rights in Alabama's Public Libraries, 1900-1965.* University of Alabama Press.

Granville County Library System. (2019, February 4). *The heroes of desegregating in public libraries.* Granville County Library System. https://granville.lib.nc.us/2019/02/the-heroes-of-desegregating-in-public-libraries/

Greenlee, C. J. (2019, March 26). On the battle to desegregate the nation's libraries. *Literary Hub.* https://lithub.com/on-the-battle-to-desegregate-the-nations-libraries/

Griffis, M. R. (n.d.). *Library profiles and resources: The Roots of Community.* The University of Southern Mississippi, https://aquila.usm.edu/rocprofiles/#lvw

Grissom, A. R. (2018). Workplace diversity and inclusion. *Reference and User Services Quarterly, 57*(4), 242–247. https://www.jstor.org/stable/90022643. doi:10.5860/rusq.57.4.6700

Guzmán, R. L., & Amrute, S. (2020). How to Cite Like a Badass Tech Feminist Scholar of Color. *Medium.* https://points.datasociety.net/how-to-cite-like-a-badass-tech-feminist-scholar-of-color-ebc839a3619c

Compilation of References

Hand, S. (2011). *Transmitting Whiteness: Librarians, Children, and Race, 1900-1930s.* USM. https://aquila.usm.edu/masters_theses/207

Hansman, C. A. (2002). Diversity and Power in Mentoring Relationships. In C. A. Hansman (Ed.), *Critical Perspectives on Mentoring: Trends and Issues* (pp. 39–48). Center on Education and Training for Employment, Center Publications.

Hardin, L., Trumbo, S., & Wiest, D. (2020). Cross-sector collaboration for vulnerable populations reduces utilization and strengthens community partnerships. *Journal of Interprofessional Education & Practice, 18,* 1–5. doi:10.1016/j.xjep.2019.100291

Harris, M. H. (2000). *History of libraries in the Western World.* Scarecrow.

Harris, R. B., Harris, K. J., & Harvey, P. (2008). An Examination of the Impact of Supervisor on the Relationship Between Job Strains and Turnover Intention for Computer Workers. *Journal of Applied Social Psychology, 38*(8), 2108–2131. doi:10.1111/j.1559-1816.2008.00383.x

Hathcock, A. (2015, April 7). White librarianship in blackface: Diversity initiatives in lis. In *the Library with the Lead Pipe.* http://www.inthelibrarywiththeleadpipe.org/2015/lis-diversity/

Herring, C. (2009). Does diversity pay?: Race, gender, and the business case for diversity. *American Sociological Review, 74*(2), 208–224. https://journals.sagepub.com/doi/abs/10.1177/000312240907400203. doi:10.1177/000312240907400203

Hetland, P., Pierroux, P., & Esborg, L. (Eds.). (2020). *A history of participation in museums and archives: Traversing citizen science and citizen humanities.* Routledge. doi:10.4324/9780429197536

Hicks, T., Gabrion, L., Lester, K., & Schoenborn, A. (2022). Standing up and pushing back: Resources from a conversation around book bans and censorship. *Michigan Reading Journal, 54*(3), 61-73. https://scholarworks.gvsu.edu/cgi/viewcontent.cgi?article=2928&context=mrj

Hill, J. (2011). *The future of archives and recordkeeping: a reader.* Facet Publishing. http://public.eblib.com/choice/publicfullrecord.aspx?p=1167408

Hinchliffe, L. J. (2022). Commentary: The future (budget) of the academic library. *Physics Today, 75*(8), 10–11. doi:10.1063/PT.3.5048

Hitchcock, J. (2002). *Lifting the white veil: An exploration of white American culture in a multiracial context.* Crandall, Dostie & Douglass Books.

Hodge, T. (2020). Using LibGuides to support racial justice & create inclusive communities. *SpringyNews.* https://buzz.springshare.com/springynews/news-49/libguides-tricks

Hodge, T., & Williams, J. (2021). Call to action: Envisioning a future that centers BIPOC voices. *American Libraries, 52*(1/2), 54–54. https://americanlibrariesmagazine.org/magazine/issues/january-february-2021/

Hoeve, C. D., & Macaulay, D. (2022, June 10). *Bringing DEI to the Forefront in University of Nebraska-Lincoln Libraries' Collections* [Poster presentation]. Joint Spring Meeting of the College & University Section and the Technical Services Round Table of the Nebraska Library Association, online. https://digitalcommons.unl.edu/libraryscience/431

Holland, D. C. (1998). *Identity and agency in cultural worlds*. Harvard University Press.

Hook, P. (2022, February 17). *Peak Library staff size is likely in the past*. RIPS Law Librarian Blog. https://ripslawlibrarian.wordpress.com/2022/02/17/peak-library-staff-size-is-likely-in-the-past/

Hoon, M. (2017, November 1). Careers: 8 jobs that won't exist in 2030. *USA Today*. https://www.usatoday.com/story/money/careers/2017/10/13/8-jobs-that-wont-exist-in-2030/104219994/

Hopkins, E. (2022, March 18). *Zotero Groups: DEI Assessment*. Zotero. https://www.zotero.org/groups/4633903/dei_assessment/

Hopkins, P. D. (2022). Finding place in the archive: A case study of St. John [Colored] Missionary Baptist Church, 1866–1900. *History (London)*, *107*(375), 337–355. https://doi-org.proxy.lib.siu.edu/10.1111/1468-229X.13270. doi:10.1111/1468-229X.13270

Horowitz, J. (2013, March 7). Library employees protest changed title. *The Cavalier Daily - University of Virginia's Student Newspaper*. https://www.cavalierdaily.com/article/2013/03/library-enacts-title-changes

Hudson, D. J. (2017). On" diversity" as anti-racism in library and information studies: A critique. *Journal of Critical Library and Information Studies*, *1*(1). http://journals.litwinbooks.com/index.php/jclis/article/view/6. doi:10.24242/jclis.v1i1.6

Huffman, G. (2019, April 10). Twisted sources: How confederate propaganda ended up in the South's schoolbooks. *Facing South*. https://www.facingsouth.org/2019/04/twisted-sources-how-confederate-propaganda-ended-souths-schoolbooks

Human Rights and Equal Opportunity Commission. (1997). *Bringing Them Home. Report of the National Inquiry into the Separation of Aboriginal and Torres Strait Islander Children from Their Families*. HREOC. https://humanrights.gov.au/our-work/bringing-them-home-report-1997

Hussey, L. K., & Campbell-Meier, J. (2017). Is There a Mentoring Culture Within the LIS Profession? *Journal of Library Administration*, *57*(5), 500–516. doi:10.1080/01930826.2017.1326723

Ifeduba, E. (2018). Book Censorship in Nigeria: A study of Origin, Methods and Motivations, 1805-2018. *Library Philosophy and Practice*, 1. https://core.ac.uk/download/pdf/189483740.pdf

IFLA. (n.d.). *Professional Reports, No. 89*. International Federation of Library Associations and Institutions.

Inazu, I. Q. I., Victoria, O., Omonori, A. A. O., Owansuan, J., & Sulaiman, A. M. (2021). Managing Workforce Diversity in Nigerian Libraries. *Covenant Journal of Library and Information Science, 4*(1), 1-10. https://journals.covenantuniversity.edu.ng/index.php/cjlis/article/viewFile/2651/1315

Indigenous Archives Collective. (2021). The Indigenous Archives Collective position statement on the right of reply to Indigenous knowledges and information held in archives. *Archives and Manuscripts*, *49*(3), 244–252. doi:10.1080/01576895.2021.1997609

Institute on Disability. (2021). *2021 Annual Report. Disability Compendium*. Retrieved.

Irvall, B., & Nielsen, G. S. (2005). Access to Libraries for Persons with Disabilities. *Check List*.

Compilation of References

Iwelunmor, J., Newsome, V., & Airhihenbuwa, C. O. (2014). Framing the impact of culture on health: A systematic review of the PEN-3 cultural model and its application in public health research and interventions. *Ethnicity & Health*, *19*(1), 20–46. doi:10.1080/13557858.2013.857768 PMID:24266638

Iwhiwhu, B. E., & Okorodudu, P. O. (2012). Public library information resources, facilities, and services: User satisfaction with the Edo State Central Library, Benin-City, Nigeria. *Library Philosophy and Practice* (e-journal), 747. https://digitalcommons.unl.edu/cgi/viewcontent.cgi?article=1 821&context=libphilprac \

Jaeger, J. (1999). User fees, community goods, and the public library. *Public Library Quarterly*, *17*(2), 49–62. https://www.tandfonline.com/doi/abs/10.1300/J118v17n02_07. doi:10.1300/J118v17n02_07

Jaeger, P. T., Cooke, N. A., Feltis, C., Hamiel, M., Jardine, F., & Shilton, K. (2015). The virtuous circle revisited: Injecting diversity, inclusion, rights, justice, and equity into LIS from education to advocacy. *The Library Quarterly*, *85*(2), 150–171. https://www.journals.uchicago.edu/doi/abs/10.1086/680154. doi:10.1086/680154

Jahnke, L. M., Tanaka, K., & Palazzolo, C. A. (2022). Ideology, policy, and practice: Structural barriers to collections diversity in research and college libraries. *College & Research Libraries*, *83*(2), 166–183. doi:10.5860/crl.83.2.166

James, J. M., Rayner, A., & Bruno, J. (2015). Are You My Mentor? New Perspectives and Research on Informal Mentorship. *Journal of Academic Librarianship*, *41*(5), 532–539. https://doi.org/10.1016/j.acalib.2015.07.009. doi:10.1016/j.acalib.2015.07.009

Janke, T. (1998). *Our Culture, our Future: Report on Australian Indigenous Cultural and Intellectual Property Rights*. Aboriginal Studies Press.

Janke, T. (2021). *True Tracks. Respecting Indigenous Knowledge and Culture*. UNSW Press.

Jansen, W. S., Otten, S., van der Zee, K. I., & Jans, L. (2014). Inclusion: Conceptualization and measurement. *European Journal of Social Psychology*, *44*(4), 370–385. doi:10.1002/ejsp.2011

Jaschik, S., & Lederman, D. (2021). *Survey of College and University Presidents*. Inside Higher Education.

Jensen, K. (2021, November 15). Library of Congress subject heading change doesn't address the real issue. *BOOK RIOT*. https://bookriot.com/library-of-congress-subject-heading-cha nge/

Joe, J. (2019, January). A Perspective on Emotional Labor in Academic Libraries. *Journal of Academic Librarianship*, *45*(1), 66–67. doi:10.1016/j.acalib.2018.11.002

Johnson, M. W., & Page, S. (2022). What's in a Workload? Affect, Burnout, and Complicating Capacity in Academic Librarians. In C. Holm, A. Guimaraes, & N. Marcano (Eds.), Academic Librarian Burnout: Causes and Responses (pp. 45–58). ACRL Press.

Jones, E. P., Mani, N. S., Carlson, R. B., Welker, C. G., Cawley, M., & Yu, F. (2022). Analysis of anti-racism, equity, inclusion and social justice initiatives in library and information science literature. *Reference Services Review*. https://www.emerald.com/insight/content/doi/10.1108/RSR-07-2 021-0032/full/html

Jones, E. P., Mani, N. S., Carlson, R. B., Welker, C. G., Cawley, M., & Yu, F. (2022). Analysis of anti-racism, equity, inclusion and social justice initiatives in library and information science literature. *RSR. Reference Services Review*, *50*(1), 81–101. doi:10.1108/RSR-07-2021-0032

Jones, P. M. (2017). *Forgotten soldiers: Jackson County's African American Civil War veterans* [Exhibit]. General John A. Logan Museum.

Jones, S. R., & Stewart, D. (2016). Evolution of Student Development Theory. *New Directions for Student Services, 2016*(154), 17–28. doi:10.1002s.20172

Joyce, J. (1922). *Ulysses*. https://www.gutenberg.org/cache/epub/4300/pg4300-images.html

Kandiuk, M. (Ed.). (2020). *Archives and special collections as sites of contestation*. Library Juice Press.

Kaser, D. (1986). The American Academic Library Building, 1870-1890. *The Journal of Library History (1974-1987), 21*(1), 60–71. https://www.jstor.org/stable/25541680

Kauffman, R. Y., & Anderson, M. S. (2020). Diversity, inclusion, and social justice in library technical services. In S. Marien (Ed.), *Library technical services: adapting to a changing environment* (pp. 213–236). Purdue University Press., doi:10.2307/j.ctvs1g8h5.17

Keels, M. (2019). *Campus counterspaces: Black and Latinx students' search for community at historically white universities*. Cornell University Press. https://www.jstor.org/stable/10.7591/j.ctvq2w2c6

Keene, H. (2020). *An evaluation of sensory paths as an antecedent intervention for decreasing off-task behavior in children with disabilities during small group instruction*. [Master's thesis, University of Kentucky]. doi:10.13023/etd.2020.105

Kelly, M., & Wenzel, T. (2013). Coaching for success: UCF enrichment programs in literacy. In E. Ortlieb & E. H. Cheek Jr., (Eds.), *Advanced Literacy Practices: From the Clinic to the Classroom* (Vol. 2, pp. 63–86). Emerald Group Publishing Limited. doi:10.1108/S2048-0458(2013)0000002007

Kendall, F. E. (2006). *Understanding white privilege: Creating pathways to authentic relationships across race*. Routledge.

Kendi, I. X. (2019). *How to be an antiracist*. One World.

Kendrick, K. D. (November 20, 2017). ShoutOut: Pauline Wilson (Ret.). *The Ink on the Page*. https://theinkonthepageblog.wordpress.com/2017/11/20/shoutout-pauline -wilson-ret/

Kennedy, J. T. (2020). *Key findings: The power of belonging: What it is and why it matters in today's workplace* (Belonging Series). Coqual. https://www.google.com/url?sa=t&rct=j&q=&esrc=s&source=web&c d=&cad=rja&uact=8&ved=2ahUKEwj_56bnofH5AhU9mmoFHfKcBxQQFnoEC AsQAQ&url=https%3A%2F%2Fcoqual.org%2Fwp-content%2Fuploads%2F 2020%2F09%2FCoqualPowerOfBelongingKeyFindings090720.pdf&usg= AOvVaw3Irq-XOpMB5pEP-PvKtu15

Kennedy, J. T., & Jain-Link, P. (2021, June 21). What Does It Take to Build a Culture of Belonging? *Harvard Business Review*. https://hbr.org/2021/06/what-does-it-take-to-build-a-culture -of-belonging

Kezar, A. J., & Lester, J. (2009). *Organizing higher education for collaboration: A guide for campus leaders*. Jossey-Bass.

Kiefer, C. W. (2007). *Doing health anthropology: Research methods for community assessment and change*. Springer.

Kim, E. (2019, October 3). *The new $41 million Hunters Point Library has one major flaw*. Gothamist. https://gothamist.com/news/new-41-million-hunters-point-libr ary-has-one-major-flaw

Compilation of References

King, M. M., Bergstrom, C. T., Correll, S. J., Jacquet, J., & West, J. D. (2017). Men Set Their Own Cites High: Gender and Self-citation across Fields and over Time. *Socius: Sociological Research for a Dynamic World, 3*, 2378023117738903. doi:10.1177/2378023117738903

Klimm, K., & Robertson, D. (2021). *How an old book created a commitment to better represent First Nations Australians*. Schools Catalogue Information Service. https://www.scisdata.com/connections/issue-117/how-an-old-book-created-a-commitment-to-better-represent-first-nations-au
stralians/

Knapp, J. A., Snavely, L., & Klimczyk, L. (2012). Speaking Up: Empowering Individuals to Promote Tolerance in the Academic Library. *Library Leadership & Management, 26*(1). Advance online publication. doi:10.5860/llm.v26i1.5508

Knott, E., Rao, A. H., Summers, K., & Teeger, C. (2022). Interviews in the social sciences. *Nature Reviews. Methods Primers, 2*(73), 73. doi:10.103843586-022-00150-6

Kohn, K. (2022, August 10). *Assessing Diversity in Collections*. Box. https://app.box.com/s/i8kqp7lacv1uuvolktqrx-16vcy8izjho

Komeiji, K., Long, K., Matsuda, S., & Paikai, A. (2021). Indigenous resource management systems as models for librarianship: I waiwai ka 'aina. In IFLA Journal. Special Issue: Indigenous Librarianship. 3(47), pp. 293-304

Korstjens, I., & Moser, A. (2018). Series: Practical guidance to qualitative research. Part 4: Trustworthiness and publishing. *The European Journal of General Practice, 24*(1), 120–124. doi:10.1080/13814788.2017.1375092 PMID:29202616

Kovach, M. (2021). *Indigenous Methodologies. Characteristics. Conversations and Contexts* (2nd ed.). University of Toronto Press.

Kozlowski, D., Sugimoto, C. R., Larivière, V., & Monroe-White, T. (2022). *Intersectional Inequalities in Science*. https://sciencebias.uni.lu/app/

Kozlowski, D., Larivière, V., Sugimoto, C. R., & Monroe-White, T. (2022). Intersectional inequalities in science. *Proceedings of the National Academy of Sciences of the United States of America, 119*(2), e2113067119. doi:10.1073/pnas.2113067119 PMID:34983876

Kristick, L. (2020). Diversity literary awards: A tool for assessing an academic library's collection. *Collection Management, 45*(2), 151–161. doi:10.1080/01462679.2019.1675209

Kukutai, T., & Taylor, J. (2016). *Indigenous data sovereignty: Toward an agenda*. ANU press. doi:10.22459/CAEPR38.11.2016

Kumasi, K. D., & Manlove, N. L. (2015). Finding "diversity levers" in the core library and information science curriculum: A social justice imperative. *Library Trends, 64*(2), 415–443. https://muse.jhu.edu/article/610084/summary. doi:10.1353/lib.2015.0047

Kwon, D. (2022). The rise of citational justice: How scholars are making references fairer. *Nature, 603*(7902), 568–571. doi:10.1038/d41586-022-00793-1 PMID:35318470

LaRoche, C. J. (2013). *Free black communities and the underground railroad: The geography of resistance*. University of Illinois Press. doi:10.5406/illinois/9780252038044.001.0001

Laster, B. P. (2013). A historical view of student learning and teacher development in literacy centers. In E. Ortlieb & E. H. Cheek Jr., (Eds.), *Advanced Literacy Practices: From the Clinic to the Classroom* (Vol. 2, pp. 3–20). Emerald Group Publishing Limited. doi:10.1108/S2048-0458(2013)0000002004

Latta, M., Taica-Klotz, H., & Giroux, C. (2021). Guest editors' introduction: Community writing centers: What was, what is, and what potentially can be. *Community Literacy Journal, 15*(1), 1–6. doi:10.25148/CLJ.15.1.009361

Laugen, K. (2021). Improving engagement and literacy skills with choice literacy centers. *School of Education and Leadership Student Capstone Projects*, 635. https://digitalcommons.hamline.edu/hse_cp/635

Lee, Y. (2020, January 6). Mentorship as a tool for growth, inclusion, and equity. *Idealist.* https://www.idealist.org/en/careers/mentorship-diversity-inclusion

Lee, M. (2009). Growing librarians: Mentorship In An Academic Library. *Library Leadership & Management, 23*(1), 31–37.

Lee, Y. Y., & Lowe, M. S. (2018). Building positive learning experiences through pedagogical research guide design. *Journal of Web Librarianship, 12*(4), 205–231. doi:10.1080/19322909.2018.1499453

Leong, N. (2020). Enjoyed by white citizens. *Geological Journal, 109*, 1421.

Leslie, L., & Caldwell, J. S. (2010). *Qualitative reading inventory-5.* Allyn & Bacon.

Leung, S. (2022). The Futility of Information Literacy & EDI: Toward What? *C&RL, 8*(5), 751. https://doi.org/https://doi.org/10.5860/crl.83.5.751

Leung, S. Y., & López-McKnight, J. R. (2021). Knowledge justice : disrupting library and information studies through critical race theory (Leung & J. R. López-McKnight, Eds.). The MIT Press.

Leung, S. Y., Jorge, R., & López-McKnight, J. R. (2021). *Knowledge Justice: Disrupting Library and Information Studies through Critical Race Theory.* The MIT Press. doi:10.7551/mitpress/11969.001.0001

Libguides. (n.d.). Springshare. https://springshare.com/libguides/

Library of Congress. (2022, October 31). *History - national library service for the Blind and print disabled (NLS): Library of Congress.* National Library Service for the Blind and Print Disabled (NLS) | Library of Congress. https://www.loc.gov/nls/about/organization/history/

Lilley, S. (2021). Transformation of library and information management: Decolonization or Indigenization? In IFLA Journal. Special Issue: Indigenous Librarianship, 3(47), 305-312

Lucas, & Silber Mohamed, H. (2021). Gender, Race, Ethnicity, and the Racialization of Attitudes Toward Descriptive Representation. *American Politics Research, 49*(5), 517–533. https://doi.org/ doi:10.1177/1532673X211022620

Lutz, C. (1990). the erasure of women's writing in sociocultural anthropology. *American Ethnologist, 17*(4), 611–627. doi:10.1525/ae.1990.17.4.02a00010

Lynn, A. (2004). *The EQ difference: A powerful plan for putting emotional intelligence to work.* AMACOM.

Madaus, J. W. (2011). Madaus. (2011). The History of Disability Services in higher education. *New Directions for Higher Education, 2011*(154), 5–15. doi:10.1002/he.429

Malapela, T., & De Jager, K. (2018). Theories of value and demonstrating their practical implementation in academic library services. *Journal of Academic Librarianship, 44*(6), 775–780. https://www.sciencedirect.com/science/article/pii/S0099133318302659. doi:10.1016/j.acalib.2018.09.018

Malecki, A. L., & Bonanni, M. (2020). Mentorship programs in academic libraries. *Public Services Quarterly, 16*(1), 35–40. doi:10.1080/15228959.2019.1701613

Compilation of References

Manning, K. (1996). Contemplating the myths of student affairs. *NASPA Journal, 34*(1), 36–46. doi:10.2202/1949-6605.1003

Martinez, K., & Truong, K. A. (2021, April 9). From DEI to JEDI. *Diverse: Issues in Higher Education.* https://www.diverseeducation.com/opinion/article/15109001/from-dei-to-jedi

Martin, R. (1994). The development of professional education for librarians and archivists in the United States: A comparative essay. *The American Archivist, 57*(3), 544–558. doi:10.17723/aarc.57.3.116720kn81j25108

Martinson, K. (1999). Literature review on service coordination and integration in the welfare and workforce development systems. Urban Institute. https://www.urban.org/url.cfm

Masterson, M., Stableford, C., & Tait, A. (2019). Re-imagining Classification Systems in Remote Libraries. *Journal of the Australian Library and Information Association, 3*(68), 278–289. doi:10.1080/24750158.2019.1653611

Matteson, M. L., & Miller, S. S. (2013). A study of emotional labor in librarianship. *Library & Information Science Research, 35*(1), 54–62. doi:10.1016/j.lisr.2012.07.005

Maxey-Harris, C., & Anaya, T. (2010). *Diversity Plans and Programs, SPEC Kit 319.* Association of Research Libraries. https://publications.arl.org/Diversity-Plans-and-Programs-SPEC-Kit-319/1

Maxwell, L. (2021, July 23). Great Library Displays and How Effective They Are. *BOOK RIOT.* https://bookriot.com/great-library-displays/

McAndrew, S. L., & Msengi, S. G. (2013). Transfer and transformation of knowledge and practices from literacy clinic to community. In Ortlieb & Earl H. Cheek, Jr. (Eds.), Advanced Literacy Practices: From the Clinic to the Classroom, Vol. 2. (pp. 21- 35). Emerald Group Publishing Limited. doi:10.1108/S2048-0458(2013)0000002013

McCloskey, D. J., McDonald, M. A., Cook, J., Heurtin-Roberts, S., Updegrove, S., Sampson, D., Gutter, S., & Eder, M. (2018). Community engagement: Definition and organizing concepts from the literature. Principles of Community Engagement.

McCorvie, M. R. (2002). *Women of color in southern Illinois: Free African American women in rural ante-bellum communities in southern Illinois.* Paper presented at the Annual Conference on Historical Archaeology, Mobile, Alabama.

McCorvie, M. R. (2009). *Archaeology and abolitionists: Ardent spirits, riotous mobocrats, Wide Awakes, Egypt and the presidential election of 1860.* Illinois Archaeological Awareness Month presentation, July 15, 2009.

McCorvie, M. R., & Devenport, V. (2004). *Miller Grove: An introduction.* Paper presented at the 2004 Conference on Historical and Underwater Archaeology, St. Louis, Missouri.

McDaniel, K. R. (2011). A Survey of the African American Records in UK's Special Collections. *Kentucky Libraries, 75*(4), 8–12.

McGrath, K. & Erwin, R. (2015). University-based literacy center: Benefits for the college and the community. *AILACTE Journal,* 93– 117.

McKenna, M. C., & Walpole, S. (2007). Assistive technology in the literacy centers: It's emerging potential. *Reading Research Quarterly, 42*(1), 140–145. doi:10.1598/RRQ.42.1.6

McShane, J. (2022, February 23). A record number of U.S. adults identify as LGBTQ. gen Z is driving the increase. *The Washington Post.* https://www.washingtonpost.com/lifestyle/2022/02/17/adults-identifying-lgbt-gen-z/

Mehra, B. (2021). Enough crocodile tears! Libraries moving beyond performative antiracist politics. *The Library Quarterly*, *91*(2), 137–149. doi:10.1086/713046

Meikle, G. (2018). *The Routledge companion to media and activism*. Routledge. https://search.ebscohost.com/login.aspx?direct=true&scope=site&db=nlebk&db=nlabk&AN=1729145

Mellon Foundation. (2019). *Community archives empower through access and inclusion*. Mellon Foundation News. https://mellon.org/shared-experiences-blog/community-archives-empower-through-access-and-inclusion/

Meltzer, L., & Dokoupil, T. (2017, August 22). Hate rising: White Supremacy's rise in the U.S. *CBS News*. https://www.cbsnews.com/news/hate-rising-cbsn-on-assignment/

Milby, T. (2013). Innovative practices: Developing effective collaboration and partnerships within school-based literacy centers. In E. Ortlieb & E. H. Cheek Jr., (Eds.), *Advanced Literacy Practices: From the Clinic to the Classroom* (Vol. 2, pp. 387–406). Emerald Group Publishing Limited. doi:10.1108/S2048-0458(2013)0000002022

Milner, H. R. IV. (2007). Race, culture, and researcher positionality: Working through dangers seen, unseen, and unforeseen. *Educational Researcher*, *36*(7), 388–400. doi:10.3102/0013189X07309471

Modern Campus. (2021, October 31). 11 Spooky Myths About Student Affairs & Co-Curricular Engagement. *Modern Campus*. https://moderncampus.com/blog/spooky-myths-about-student-affairs.html

Mondésir, O., Tummino, A., & Wong, J. (2021). Uplifting diverse and marginalized voices through community archives and public programming. *Urban Library Journal*, *27*(2), 1–9.

Montenegro, M. (2019). Subverting the universality of metadata standards: The TK labels as a tool to promote Indigenous data sovereignty. *The Journal of Documentation*, *75*(4), 731–749. doi:10.1108/JD-08-2018-0124

Mor Barak, M. E. (2019). Erecting Walls Versus Tearing Them Down: Inclusion and the (False) Paradox of Diversity in Times of Economic Upheaval. *European Management Review*, *16*(4), 937–955. doi:10.1111/emre.12302

Morales, M., Knowles, E. C., & Bourg, C. (2014). Diversity, social justice, and the future of libraries. *portal. Portal (Baltimore, Md.)*, *14*(3), 439–451. doi:10.1353/pla.2014.0017

Mott, C., & Cockayne, D. (2017). Citation matters: Mobilizing the politics of citation toward a practice of 'conscientious engagement'. *Gender, Place and Culture*, *24*(7), 954–973. doi:10.1080/0966369X.2017.1339022

Mott, C., & Cockayne, D. (2018). Conscientious disengagement and whiteness as a condition of dialogue. *Dialogues in Human Geography*, *8*(2), 143–147. doi:10.1177/2043820618780575

Moyer, L. S. (2005). Library funding in a budget-cut world. *The Bottom Line (New York, N.Y.)*, *18*(3), 112–115. doi:10.1108/08880450510613560

Muir, B., Qayyum, A., & Thompson, K. (2021). Jumping hurdles: 'Hurdle wording' and hiring for diversity and inclusion. *Incite*, *42*(4), 10–11.

Mulliken, A. (2017). "There is Nothing Inherently Mysterious about Assistive Technology" A Qualitative Study about Blind User Experiences in US Academic Libraries. *Reference and User Services Quarterly*, *57*(2), 115–126. doi:10.5860/rusq.57.2.6528

Compilation of References

Mullin, J. (2001). Writing Centers in WAC. In McLeod, Susan H., Miraglia, Eric, Soven, M., & Thaiss, C. (Eds.) WAC for the New Millennium: Strategies for Continuing Writing-Across-the-Curriculum Programs. National Council of Teachers of English, Urbana, IL.

Murphy, F. (2017). Engineering a gender bias. *Nature, 543*(7646), S31–S31. doi:10.1038/543S31a PMID:28328907

Myers, J. W. (1922). History of the Gallatin salines. *Journal of the Illinois State Historical Society, 14*(3-4), 337–349.

N'Diaye, D. B. (2021). Telling our own stories: Reciprocal autoethnography at the intersections of race, class, and gender. *Journal of American Folklore, 134*(533), 252–257. https://www.muse.jhu.edu/article/800148. doi:10.5406/jamerfolk.134.533.0252

Nachimuthu, K., & Vijayakumari, G. (2012). E-Resources for inclusive education. *International Education Journal, 1*(03), 27–31. https://www.researchgate.net/profile/Nachimuthu-Dr/publication/256032083_E-Resources_for_Inclusive_Education/links/5a5f3 d1d458515c03ee1cda9/E-Resources-for-Inclusive-Education.pdf

Naidoo, J. C. (2014). The importance of diversity in library programs and material collections for children. Association for Library Service to Children, American Library Association.

Nair, A. (2022, August 4). *A cultural power struggle at an Iowa library casts a 'dark cloud' over a small town.* NBCNews.com. https://www.nbcnews.com/nbc-out/out-news/small-town-library-shut-say-culture-wars-closed-rcna39816

Nakata, M. (2007). *Disciplining the Savages Savaging the Disciplines.* Aboriginal Studies Press.

Nakata, M., Nakata, V., Gardiner, G., McKeough, J., Byrne, A., & Gibson, J. (2008). Indigenous digital collections: An early look at the organisation and culture interface. *Australian Academic and Research Libraries, 39*(4), 223–236. doi: 10.1080/00048623.2008.10721360

Nardine, J. (2019). The State of Academic Liaison Librarian Burnout in ARL Libraries in the United States. *College & Research Libraries, 80*(4), 508–524. doi:10.5860/crl.80.4.508

NASPA. (1987). *A perspectives on student affairs: A statement issued on the 50th anniversary of The Student Personnel Point of View.* https://www.naspa.org/files/dmfile/A_Perspective_on_Student_Affairs_1987.pdf

NASPA. (2022). *Careers in Student Affairs Month.* NASPA. https://www.naspa.org/project/careers-in-student-affairs-month

NASPA. (n.d.-a). *Graduate Program Directory.* NASPA. https://www.naspa.org/careers/graduate-program-directory

NASPA. (n.d.-b). *Our History Leads to Our Future.* NASPA. https://history.naspa.org/

NASPA. (n.d.-c). *NASPA: Student Affairs Administrators in Higher Education.* NASPA. https://naspa.org/

Nataraj, L., Hampton, H., Matlin, T. R., & Meulemans, Y. N. (2020). "Nice White Meetings": Unpacking Absurd Library Bureaucracy through a Critical Race Theory Lens. *Canadian Journal of Academic Librarianship, 6*, 1–15. doi:10.33137/cjal-rcbu.v6.34340

National and State Libraries of Australasia. (2022). *Strategic Plan 2020-2023.* NSLA. https://www.nsla.org.au/index.php/about-nsla/strategic-plan

National and State Libraries of Australasia. (n.d.). *Culturally Safe Libraries.* NSLA. https://www.nsla.org.au/our-work/culturally-safe-libraries

National Center for Education Statistics. (2022). Hate Crime Incidents at Postsecondary Institutions. *Condition of Education*. U.S. Department of Education, Institute of Education Sciences. https://nces.ed.gov/programs/coe/indicator/a22

Neely, T. Y. (2018). I AM My Hair, and My Hair is Me: #BlackGirlMagic in LIS. In R. L. Chou & A. Pho (Eds.), *Pushing the Margins: Women of Color and Intersectionality in LIS* (pp. 121–146). Library Juice Press. https://digitalrepository.unm.edu/ulls_fsp/122

Neuhaus, C., Cox, A., Gruber, A. M., Kelly, J., Koh, H., Bowling, C., & Bunz, G. (2021). Ubiquitous LibGuides: Variations in presence, production, application, and convention. *Journal of Web Librarianship*, *15*(3), 107–127. doi:10.1080/19322909.2021.1946457

Newman, A. (2017, July 16). *Louisville Western Branch Library (1905-)*. Black Past. https://www.blackpast.org/african-american-history/louisville-western-branch-library-1905/

Neyer, L., & Yelinek, K. (2011). Beyond Boomer meets NextGen: Examining mentoring practices among Pennsylvania academic librarians. *Journal of Academic Librarianship*, *37*(3), 215–221. doi:10.1016/j.acalib.2011.02.013

Nicholson, K., & Seale, M. (2018). The Politics of Theory and the Practice of Critical Librarianship, 1-18. Litwin Books.

Nitecki, D. A., & Abels, E. G. (Eds.). (2008). *Influence of funding on advances in librarianship*. Emerald Publishing Limited. doi:10.1016/S0065-2830(2008)31

November 2, 2022, from https://disabilitycompendium.org/

Nunkoo, R., Hall, C. M., Rughoobur-Seetah, S., & Teeroovengadum, V. (2019). Citation practices in tourism research: Toward a gender conscientious engagement. *Annals of Tourism Research*, *79*, 102755. doi:10.1016/j.annals.2019.102755

Oakleaf, M. (2010). *The value of academic libraries: A comprehensive research review and report.*

Oates, E. Q. (2022). They took my hair—Racial battle fatigue in academe: Accounts from the plantation. In *Dismantling constructs of whiteness in higher education* (pp. 171–186). Routledge. doi:10.4324/9781003029564-17

Office of Academic Planning and Assessment. (2022). *UMass Amherst campus climate survey 2021: Sense of belonging matters in important ways.* Office of Equity and Inclusion. https://www.umass.edu/diversity/campus-climate-2021-belonging

Okun, T. (n.d.). *White supremacy culture*. Dismantling Racism. https://www.whitesupremacyculture.info/uploads/4/3/5/7/43579015/okun_-_white_sup_culture_2020.pdf

Orleib, E., Grandstaff-Beckers, G., & Cheek, E. H. Jr. (2012). Fostering reading excellence at every level of school through literacy centers. *The Clearing House: A Journal of Educational Strategies, Issues and Ideas*, *85*(1), 1–6. doi:10.1080/00098655.2011.601356

Ortega, A. C. (2017). *Academic libraries and toxic leadership*. Chandos Publishing, an imprint of Elsevier.

Ouellette, D. (2011). Subject guides in academic libraries: A user-centred study of uses and perceptions. *Canadian Journal of Information and Library Science*, *35*(4), 436–451. doi:10.1353/ils.2011.0024

Pace, D., Blumreich, K. M., & Merkle, H. B. (2006). Increasing Collaboration between Student and Academic Affairs: Application of the Intergroup Dialogue Model. *NASPA Journal*, *43*(2), 301–315. doi:10.2202/1949-6605.1641

Compilation of References

Paradkar, S. (2021, December 11). Why I'm saying bye-bye to 'BIPOC' this year. *Toronto Star*. https://www.thestar.com/opinion/star-columnists/2021/12/11/why-im-saying-bye-bye-to-bipoc-this-year.html

Parkinson, C. N. (1957). *Parkinson's Law: And other studies in administration*. Houghton Mifflin Harcourt.

Pastor, M. P., Speer, P., Gupta, J., Han, H., & Ito, J. (2022). Community power and health equity: Closing the gap between scholarship and practice. *NAM Perspectives Discussion Paper*. National Academy of Medicine, Washington, DC. https://doi.org/ doi:10.31478/202206

Pearson, P. D., & Gallagher, M. C. (1983). The instruction of reading comprehension. *Contemporary Educational Psychology, 8*(3), 317–344. https://doi.org/ 476X(83)90019-X doi:10.1016/0361-

Pekoll, K. (2017, December 19). *Selection Criteria*. ALA. https://www.ala.org/tools/challengesupport/selectionpolicytoolkit/criteria

Petruzzi, T., & Burns, M. F. (2006). A Literacy Center Where? A Public Library Finds Space to Promote and Provide Family Learning Activities. *Public Library Quarterly, 25*(1-2), 1–2, 191–197. doi:10.1300/J118v25n01_14

Piper, G., Ameen, M., & Lowe, M. S. (2021). An Investigation of Anti-Black Racism LibGuides at ARL Member Institutions. *Communications in Information Literacy, 15*(2), 188–207. doi:10.15760/comminfolit.2021.15.2.3

Pitts, D., Marvel, J., & Fernandez, S. (2011). So Hard to Say Goodbye? Turnover Intention among U.S. Federal Employees. *Public Administration Review, 71*(5), 751–760. doi:10.1111/j.1540-6210.2011.02414.x

Plett, C. (April 11, 2016). Zucker's "Therapy" Mourned Almost Exclusively By Cis People. *Harlot*. https://web.archive.org/web/20160607175210/http://harlot.media/articles/2582/zuckers-therapy-mourned-almost-exclusively-by-cis-people

Poole, A. H., Agosto, D., Greenberg, J., Lin, X., & Yan, E. (2021). Where do we stand? Diversity, equity, inclusion, and social justice in North American library and information science education. *Journal of Education for Library and Information Science, 62*(3), 258-286. https://www.utpjournals.press/doi/abs/ doi:10.3138/jelis.2020-0018

Poole, A. H. (2021, March). Promoting diversity, equity, and inclusion in library and information science through community-based learning. In *International Conference on Information* (pp. 529-540). Springer, Cham. 10.1007/978-3-030-71292-1_41

Porter, G. (2020). Freed faces, our past Americans: Collaborations to create, digitize and describe the "Former Slaves in Freedom" collection. *Collaborative Librarianship, 12*(1), 20–51.

Prater, M. A., Carter, N., & Munk, J. (2013). Preparing special educators to teach reading: A pre-student teaching practicum. In Ortlieb & Earl H. Cheek, Jr. (Eds.), Advanced Literacy Practices: From the Clinic to the Classroom, Vol. 2. (pp. 21-35). Emerald Group Publishing Limited.

Price, G. (2020, July 1). Statements from libraries and library organizations re: racism, Black Lives Matter, and increased violence. *InfoDocket*. https://www.infodocket.com/2020/06/01/statements-from-library-organizations-re-racism-and-increased-violence/

Price, A. C. (2021). Barriers to an inclusive academic library collection. *Collection and Curation, 41*(3), 97–100. doi:10.1108/CC-05-2021-0018

Proposal jeopardizes library funding. (2018). *School Library Journal, 64*(3), 14. https://grinnell.idm.oclc.org/login?url=https://www.proquest.com/trade-journals/proposal-jeopardizes-library-funding/docview/2017029506/se-2

Rankin, C. (2018). IFLA Guidelines for Library Services to Children aged 0-18–2nd Edition (revision of 2003 Guidelines). IFLA.

Rankin, S., Garvey, J. C., & Duran, A. (2019). A retrospective of LGBT issues on US college campuses: 1990–2020. *International Sociology, 34*(4), 435–454. doi:10.1177/0268580919851429

Rau, T. J., & Koch-Gonzalez, J. (2018). *Many voices one song: Shared power with sociocracy*. Institute for Peaceable Communities, Inc.

Ray, W. (2022). *Resources for the study of African American history in southern Illinois: Overview of Special Collections*. LibGuide. https://libguides.lib.siu.edu/c.php?g=936792&p=6751751

Rayini, J. (2017). Library and information services to the visually impaired persons. *Library Philosophy and Practice (e-journal), 1510*. https://digitalcommons.unl.edu/cgi/viewcontent.cgi?article=4313&context=libphilprac

Ray, R., & Gibbons, A. (2021). *Why are states banning critical race theory?* The Brookings Institution. https://grinnell.idm.oclc.org/login?url=https://www.proquest.com/blogs-podcasts-websites/why-are-states-banning-critical-race-theory/docview/2548183413/se-2

Raza, S., Hackman, M. J., DuVernay, J., Dragovic, N., Bruchko, E. A., & Rutledge, M. H. (2022). The Making of Emory Libraries' Diversity, Equity, and Inclusion Committee: A Case Study. In B. Lym & C. Lee (Eds.), *Implementing Excellence in Diversity, Equity, and Inclusion: A Handbook for Academic Libraries*. Association of College and Research Libraries.

Re, G. work Project. (2018). *Re:Work*. https://rework.withgoogle.com/print/guides/5721312655835136/

REFORMA. (n.d.). *Mentoring Program*. Reforma. https://www.reforma.org/content.asp?contentid=34

Research Planning and Review Committee. (2020). 2020 top trends in academic libraries: A review of the trends and issues affecting academic libraries in higher education. *College & Research Libraries News, 81*(6), 270. doi:10.5860/crln.81.6.270

Rigney, L. I. (1999). Internationalisation of an Indigenous anticolonial cultural critique of research methodologies: A guide to Indigenist research methodology and its principles. *Wicazo Sa Review, 14*(2), 109–121. doi:10.2307/1409555

Robbeloth, H., Eng, A., & Weise, S. (2013). Disconnect between literature and libraries: The availability of mentoring programs for academic librarians. *Endnotes, 4*(1), 1–19.

Robbins, L. S. (2001). *The dismissal of miss Ruth Brown: Civil rights, censorship, and the American library*. University of Oklahoma Press.

Rodriguez, M. (2020). Negotiating accessibility for electronic resources. *Serials Review, 46*(2), 150–156. doi:10.1080/00987913.2020.1760706

Roh, C. (2017). Library publishing and diversity values: Changing scholarly publishing through policy and scholarly communication education. *College & Research Libraries News, 77*(2), 82–85. doi:10.5860/crln.77.2.9446

Compilation of References

Rosa, K., & Henke, K. (2017). 2017 *ALA member demographics study*. American Library Association Office of Research and Statistics. https://www.ala.org/tools/research/initiatives/membershipsurveys

Royal Commission into Aboriginal Deaths in Custody. (1991). *National Report*. UTS Library. http://www.austlii.edu.au.ezproxy.lib.uts.edu.au/au/other/IndigLRes/rciadic/

Royal Society of Chemistry. (n.d.). *Minimum standards for inclusion and diversity for scholarly publishing*. Royal Society of Chemistry. https://www.rsc.org/new-perspectives/talent/minimum-standards-for-inclusion-and-diversity-for-scholarly-publishing/

RuPaul [@rupaul]. (2014, October 4). *Know who you are and deliver it at all times* https://t.co/3wO0iohWcv [Tweet]. Twitter. https://twitter.com/rupaul/status/518235173159456769

Russell, H. K. (2012). *The state of southern Illinois: An illustrated history*. Southern Illinois University Press.

Russell, L. (2005). Indigenous Knowledge and Archives: Accessing Hidden History and Understandings. *Australian Academic and Research Libraries*, *36*(2), 161–171. doi:10.1080/00048623.2005.10721256

Santamaria, M. R. (2020). Concealing white supremacy through fantasies of the library: Economies of affect at work. *Library Trends*, *68*(3), 431–449. doi:10.1353/lib.2020.0000

Sappington, J., De León, E., Schumacher, S., Vardeman, K., Callender, D., Oliver, M., Veeder, H., & Heinz, L. (2022). *Library impact research report: Educating and empowering a diverse student body: Supporting diversity, equity, and inclusion research through library collections*. Association of Research Libraries., doi:10.29242/report.texastech2022

Saunders, P. D. (2022, February 10). *The changing state of gentrification*. American Planning Association. https://www.planning.org/planning/2022/winter/the-changing-state-of-gentrification/

Savini, C. (2016). A Writing Retreat at the Intersection of WAC and Civic Engagement. *Community Literacy Journal*, *11*(1), 157–163. doi:10.1353/clj.2016.0023

Schein, E. H. (2017). *Organizational culture and leadership* (5th ed.). Wiley.

Schonfeld, R. C., & Sweeney, L. (2017, August 30). Inclusion, Diversity, and Equity: Members of the Association of Research Libraries: Employee Demographics and Director Perspectives. *Ithaka S+R*. doi:10.18665/sr.304524

School Library Displays. (n.d.). *School Library Displays*. School Library Displays. https://librarydisplays.org/

Schwartz, R., & Stewart, D. (2017). The History of Student Affairs. In J. H. Schuh, S. R. Jones, & V. Torres (Eds.), *Student services: A handbook for the profession* (6th ed., pp. 63–88). Jossey-Bass.

Sentance, N. (2018, November 28) Diversity means disruption. *Archival Decolonialist*. https://archivaldecolonist.com/2018/11/28/diversity-means-disruption/

Seung-Ho, A. (2019). Employee Voluntary and Involuntary Turnover and Organizational Performance: Revisiting the Hypothesis from Classical Public Administration. *International Public Management Journal*, *22*(3), 444–469. doi:10.1080/10967494.2018.1549629

Shay, J. E. Jr. (1984). The Chief Student Affairs Officer and the President: Revisiting an Old Issue. *NASPA Journal*, *22*(2), 56–58. doi:10.1080/00220973.1984.11071917

Shearer, J. J., & Chiewphasa, B. B. (2021). Radical re-imagination: Centering a BIPOC library workforce in an asset-based autoethnography. *RSR. Reference Services Review*, *50*(1), 113–126. doi:10.1108/RSR-07-2021-0029

Shore, L. M., Randel, A. E., Chung, B. G., Dean, M. A., Holcombe Ehrhart, K., & Singh, G. (2011). Inclusion and Diversity in Work Groups: A Review and Model for Future Research. *Journal of Management*, *37*(4), 1262–1289. doi:10.1177/0149206310385943

Shoultz, J., Oneha, M. F., Magnussen, L., Hla, M. M., Brees-Saunders, Z., Cruz, M. D., & Douglas, M. (2006). Finding solutions to challenges faced in community-based participatory research between academic and community organizations. *Journal of Interprofessional Care*, *20*(2), 133–144. doi:10.1080/13561820600577576 PMID:16608716

Shuler, S., & Morgan, N. (2013). Emotional Labor in the Academic Library: When Being Friendly Feels Like Work. *The Reference Librarian*, *54*(2), 118–133. doi:10.1080/02763877.2013.756684

Singh, M., & Major, J. (2017). Conducting Indigenous research in Western knowledge spaces: Aligning theory and methodology. *Australian Educational Researcher*, *44*(1), 5–19. doi:10.100713384-017-0233-z

Smith, C. (n.d.). *Cite Black Women*. Cite Black Women Collective. https://www.citeblackwomencollective.org/

Smith, S., & Ellis, K. (2022, January 7). *History shows slavery helped build many U.S. colleges and Universities*. Shackled Legacy | APM Reports. https://www.apmreports.org/episode/2017/09/04/shackled-legacy

Smith, L. T. (2012). *Decolonizing Methodologies: Research and Indigenous Peoples* (2nd ed.). ZedBooks.

Smoot, P. (2012). Alexander Lane: From slavery to freedom: The life of Alexander Lane, educator, physician and Illinois state legislator, 1860-1911. *The Simon Review (Occasional Papers of the Paul Simon Public Policy Institute)*. https://opensiuc.lib.siu.edu/ppi_papers/29

Snyder, T. (1993, January 19). *120 years of American Education: A statistical portrait*. National Center for Education Statistics (NCES) Home Page, a part of the U.S. Department of Education. https://nces.ed.gov/pubsearch/pubsinfo.asp?pubid=93442

So, R. J., & Wezerek, G. (2020, December 11). Just how white is the book industry? *The New York Times*. https://www.nytimes.com/interactive/2020/12/11/opinion/culture/diversity-publishing-industry.html

Sociocracy For All. (2023). *Learn and Share Sociocracy with the World*. Sociocracy For All. https://www.sociocracyforall.org/

Sonsteby, A., & DeJonghe, J. (2013). Usability testing, user-centered design, and LibGuides subject guides: A case study. *Journal of Web Librarianship*, *7*(1), 83–94. doi:10.1080/19322909.2013.747366

Speer, E. (2022). Communicating with vendors in support of DEI collection evaluations. *Online Searcher*, *46*(1). https://www.infotoday.com/OnlineSearcher/Articles/Features/Communicating-With-Vendors-in-Support-of-DEI-Collection-Evaluations-150915.shtml

Springs, G. R. (2014). Mentoring for Retention, Promotion, and Advancement: An Examination of Mentoring Programs at ARL Institutions. In K. Deards & G. Springs (Eds.), *Succession Planning and Implementation in Libraries: Practices and Resources* (pp. 45–63). IGI Global., doi:10.4018/978-1-4666-5812-7.ch003

Stanley, D. J., Meyer, J. P., & Topolnytsky, L. (2005). Employee Cynicism and Resistance to Organizational Change. *Journal of Business and Psychology*, *19*(4), 429–459. doi:10.100710869-005-4518-2

Compilation of References

Starks, B. (2021). The double pandemic: Covid-19 and white supremacy. *Qualitative Social Work: Research and Practice*, *20*(1-2), 222–224. https://journals.sagepub.com/doi/pdf/10.1177/1473325020986011. doi:10.1177/1473325020986011

Sterling, B. (2022). Can't we all just cathect along? *Up//Root*. https://www.uproot.space/features/bell-series-sterling

Stewart, A. (2017). A Subject Analysis of Pentecostalism in the Dewey Decimal Classification System. *Biblioteka*, (21 (30)), 243–250. doi:10.14746/b.2017.21.12

Strieker, T., Coffey, D., Delacruz, S., Holbein, M., & Easton, A. (2011). *Action plans. Archives of the Center for Literacy and Learning*. Kennesaw State University.

Sustaining Reading First. (2009). *Engaging stakeholders: Including parents and the community to sustain Improved Reading Outcomes*. Sustaining Reading First. https://www2.ed.gov/programs/readingfirst/support/stakeholderlores.pdf

Swanson, J., Tanaka, A., & Gonzalez-Smith, I. (2018). Lived experience of academic librarians of color. *College & Research Libraries*, *79*(7), 876–894. doi:10.5860/crl.79.7.876

Swist, T., Hendery, R., Magee, L., Ensor, J., Sherman, J., Budge, K., & Humphry, J. (2022). Co-creating public library futures: An emergent manifesto and participatory research agenda. *Journal of the Australian Library and Information Association*, *71*(1), 71–88. doi:10.1080/24750158.2021.2016358

Tager, J., & Shariyf, C. R. (2023, January 3). *Reading between the lines: Race, equity, and Book Publishing*. PEN America. https://pen.org/report/race-equity-and-book-publishing/

Takahashi, L. M., & Smutny, G. (2001). Collaboration among small, community-based organizations: Strategies and challenges in turbulent environments. *Journal of Planning Education and Research*, *21*(2), 141–153. doi:10.1177/0739456X0102100203

Tamura, E. H. (2001). Asian Americans in the History of Education: An Historiographical Essay. *History of Education Quarterly*, *41*(1), 58–71. https://www.jstor.org/stable/369479. doi:10.1111/j.1748-5959.2001.tb00074.x

Tatum, B. D. (2017). *Why are all the Black kids sitting together in the cafeteria? And other conversations about race*. Basic Books. (Original work published 1997)

Teich, E. G., Kim, J. Z., Lynn, C. W., Simon, S. C., Klishin, A. A., Szymula, K. P., Srivastava, P., Bassett, L. C., Zurn, P., Dworkin, J. D., & Bassett, D. S. (2022). Citation inequity and gendered citation practices in contemporary physics. *Nature Physics*, *18*(10), 1161–1170. doi:10.103841567-022-01770-1

The Cultural Iceberg Explained. (n.d.). Lynch Law Firm, PLLC. Www.lynchlf.com. https://www.lynchlf.com/blog/the-cultural-iceberg-explained/

The RPgroup. (2022). *Success Factors Framework*. The RPgroup. https://rpgroup.org/Our-Projects/Student-Support-Redefined/SuccessFactorsFramework

The RPgroup. (2022). *What is student support (re)defined?* The RPgroup. https://do-prod-webteam-drupalfiles.s3-us-west-2.amazonaws.com/bcedu/s3fs-public/4HStudentSupport_0.pdf

Thieme, K., & Saunders, M. A. S. (2018). How do you wish to be cited? Citation practices and a scholarly community of care in trans studies research articles. *Journal of English for Academic Purposes*, *32*, 80–90. doi:10.1016/j.jeap.2018.03.010

Thorngate, S., & Hoden, A. (2017). Exploratory usability testing of user interface options in LibGuides 2. *College & Research Libraries*, *78*(6), 844–861. doi:10.5860/crl.78.6.844

Thorpe, K., & Galassi, M. (2014). Rediscovering Indigenous Languages: The Role and Impact of Libraries and Archives in Cultural Revitalisation. *Australian Academic and Research Libraries*, *45*(2), 81–100. doi:10.1080/00048623.2014.910858

Trimble, V. (1993). Patterns in citations of papers by American astronomers. *Quarterly Journal of the Royal Astronomical Society, 34*(2), 235-250. <Go to ISI>://WOS:A1993LF43800007

University of Minnesota Libraries' Diversity, Equity, and Inclusion Leadership Committee. (2021, February 1). *Our approach to inclusion, diversity, equity, and accessibility.* University of Minnesota Libraries. https://www.lib.umn.edu/about/inclusion

University of Toledo Libraries. (2022, September 27). *Diversity equity, inclusion & accessibility @ UToledo Libraries: DEIA bookshelf.* LibGuides at University of Toledo Libraries. https://libguides.utoledo.edu/diversity-equity-inclusion-accessibility/DEIA-bookshelf

University, S. C. (2018, November 30). *The hidden history of libraries and civil rights.* University Library - Santa Clara University. https://www.scu.edu/library/newsletter/2018-11/the-hidden-history-of-libraries-and-civil-rights/

US Census Bureau. (2018, October 5). *Data.* Census.gov. https://www.census.gov/data.html

Van der Walt, J. L. (2020). Interpretivism-constructivism as a research method in the humanities and social sciences-more to it than meets the eye. *International Journal of Philosophy and Theology, 8*(1), 59–68.

Voigt, J. (2021). *Site of the first memorial service in Illinois.* The Historical Marker Database. https://www.hmdb.org/m.asp?m=163493

Wagner, M. J. (2019). *"The place where no one ever goes": A landscape study of the Miller Grove community.* Paper presented at the Society for Historical Archaeology Annual Meeting, St. Charles, Missouri.

Wagner, M. M., & Willms, D. (2010). The urban library program: Challenges to educating and hiring a diverse workforce. *Library Trends, 59*(1), 128–146.

Wagner, T. L., & Bischoff, B. (2017). Defining community archives within rural South Carolina. *Advances in Librarianship, 43*, 155–180. doi:10.1108/S0065-283020170000043007

Walker, T. (2018, December 11). *'education is political': Neutrality in the classroom shortchanges students.* NEA. https://www.nea.org/advocating-for-change/new-from-nea/education-political-neutrality-classroom-shortchanges-students

Walker, B. (2012). *Diagnostic teaching of reading: Techniques for instruction and assessment* (7th ed.). Allyn & Bacon.

Wallenstein, P. (2022, July 26). Desegregation in Higher Education. In *Encyclopedia Virginia.* https://encyclopediavirginia.org/entries/desegregation-in-higher-education

Wells, V. A., Gibney, M., & Paris, M. (2022). Student learning and engagement in a DEI collection audit: Applying the ACRL Framework for Information Literacy. *College & Research Libraries News, 83*(8), 335–340. doi:10.5860/crln.83.8.335

Wheeler, M., Johnson-Houston, D., & Walker, B. E. (2004). A Brief History of Library Service to African Americans. *American Libraries, 35*(2), 42–45. https://www.jstor.org/stable/25649066

Compilation of References

Whitehead, M., & Dahlgren, G. (2007). Concepts and principles for tackling social inequities in health: Leveling up part 1. *Studies on social and economic determinants of population health, No 2*. World Health Organization. http://www.euro.who.int/document/e89383.pdf

Whorton, J. W., & Worthley, J. A. (1981). A Perspective on the Challenge of Public Management: Environmental Paradox and Organizational Culture. *Academy of Management Review*, *6*(3), 357–361. doi:10.2307/257371

Wickham, & Sweeney, M. E. (2018). Are We Still Transmitting Whiteness? A Case Study of a Southern, Rural Library's Youth Collections. *Library Trends*, *67*(1), 89–106. https://doi.org/ doi:10.1353/lib.2018.0027

Wiegand, & Wiegand, W. A. (2018). *The Desegregation of Public Libraries in the Jim Crow South: Civil Rights and Local Activism*. LSU Press.

Wiegand, W. A. (1995). "Jew Attack": The Story behind Melvil Dewey's Resignation as New York State Librarian in 1905. *American Jewish History*, *83*(3), 359–379. https://www.jstor.org/stable/23885515

Wiegand, W. A. (2015). *Part of our lives: A people's history of the American public library*. Oxford University Press.

Wilder, C. S. (2014). *Ebony and ivy: Race, slavery, and the Troubled History of America's universities*. Bloomsbury.

Williams, C. (2020). The Bridgwater family: A history of an African American family in the American west from slavery to the Civil Rights era. *The Western Historical Quarterly*, *51*(4), 349–380. https://doi-org.proxy.lib.siu.edu/10.1093/whq/whaa115. doi:10.1093/whq/whaa115

Wilson Special Collections Library. (2019). *Creating and growing community-based memory projects*. The University of North Carolina at Chapel Hill. https://library.unc.edu/preservation/creating-and-growing/

Wilson, M. C., Gaunt, M. I., & Tehrani, F. (2009). Mentoring Programs In U.S. Academic Libraries – A Literature Review. In V. Jana, L. Liz, & W. Graham (Eds.), *Strategies for Regenerating the Library and Information Profession* (pp. 84-95). K. G. Saur. https://doi.org/doi:10.1515/9783598441776.2. 84

Wingfield, A. H., & Alston, R. S. (2014). Maintaining hierarchies in predominantly white organizations: A theory of racial tasks. *The American Behavioral Scientist*, *58*(2), 274–287. doi:10.1177/0002764213503329

Winters, M. F. (2013). From Diversity to Inclusion: An Inclusion Equation. In B. M. Ferdman & B. R. Deane (Eds.), *Diversity at Work: The practice of inclusion*. Jossey-Bass., https://learning.oreilly.com/library/view/diversity-at-work/9781118415153/c07.xhtml doi:10.1002/9781118764282.ch7

Witwer, R. F. (2021). *DEI and Belonging: Changing the Narrative and Creating a Culture of Belonging in Non-profit Organization* [University of San Francisco]. https://usfblogs.usfca.edu/nonprofit/files/2021/05/witwerrakiya_6199833_68188178_Rakiya-Witwer-622-Capstone-Report.pdf

Workman, J. (2022). Inequality begets inequality: Income inequality and socioeconomic achievement gradients across the United States. *Social Science Research*, *107*, 1–21. doi:10.1016/j.ssresearch.2022.102744 PMID:36058607

World Health Organization. (2022). *Social Determinants of Health*. WHO. https://www.who.int/health-topics/social-determinants-of-health#tab=tab_2

Yamaguchi, M., & Richardson, J. (2018). Demonstrating academic library impact to faculty: A case study. *Digital Library Perspectives*, *34*(2), 137–150. doi:10.1108/DLP-09-2017-0034

Young, R. B. (1993). Examining the History of Student Affairs through the Lens of Professional Education. *NASPA Journal*, *30*(4), 243–251. doi:10.1080/00220973.1993.11072322

Yu, C., & Smith, L. B. (2016). Multiple sensory-motor pathways lead to coordinated visual attention. *Cognitive Science*, *41*(S1), 5–31. doi:10.1111/cogs.12366 PMID:27016038

Yusuf, R. A., Awoyemi, O. O., & Ademodi, D. T. (2022). Diversity, inclusion and equity: making a case for the underserved and vulnerable in the Nigerian society. *Lagos Journal of Library and Information Science, 10*(1-2), 79-94. https://www.ajol.info/index.php/ljlis/article/view/236223

Zaid, Y. A. (2017). The exclusion of persons with visual impairment in Nigerian academic libraries' websites. *Library Philosophy and Practice (e-journal), 1601.* https://core.ac.uk/download/pdf/189476139.pdf

Zurn, P., Bassett, D. S., & Rust, N. C. (2020). The Citation Diversity Statement: A Practice of Transparency, A Way of Life. *Trends in Cognitive Sciences*, *24*(9), 669–672. doi:10.1016/j.tics.2020.06.009 PMID:32762966

About the Contributors

Nandita S. Mani, PhD, MLIS, is the Dean of University Libraries at the University of Massachusetts Amherst, where she provides strategic, administrative, and financial leadership of the largest publicly supported research library in New England. Oversight of the Libraries includes vast physical and digital items and the Robert S. Cox Special Collections and University Archives Research Center, which contains the papers and memoirs of W. E. B. Du Bois, Horace Mann Bond, Daniel Ellsberg, and Kenneth R. Feinberg, the Irma McClaurin Black Feminist Archive, and hundreds of other collections documenting the lives and work of activists, innovators, political figures, spiritual leaders, writers, and more. Dean Mani oversees the UMass Libraries in its role as a strategic partner supporting the academic and research enterprise of UMass Amherst, a flagship land grant institution, and represents the UMass Libraries with service as a member of the Association of Research Libraries, the Five College Library Consortium's leadership committee, and the Board of the Boston Library Consortium. Mani had transformational roles at the University of North Carolina at Chapel Hill, where she served as Associate University Librarian for health sciences and Director of the Health Sciences Library. In her role at UNC, Mani led the development of the University Libraries' data science framework, which articulated how the libraries can contribute to campus-wide data-science initiatives. She was also part of the UNC Libraries' Reckoning Initiative to build antiracism into the Libraries' policies, systems, structures, and approaches and is an Advisory Board Member of ARiA: Anti-Racism in Academia Mani's publishing experience has been in areas including information science, diversity, equity, inclusion, health literacy, and instructional design and technology. She held the role of Managing Editor for Advances in Chronic Kidney Disease from 2009-2019. A recognized expert on data science in libraries, Dean Mani is co-editor and author of Academic Libraries as Partners in Data Science Ecosystems, published in 2022. Dean Mani received her bachelor's degree from Concordia University of Edmonton, Alberta, and subsequently earned a master's in library and information science and a Ph.D. in instructional technology, both from Wayne State University in Detroit.

Michelle Cawley, MLS, MA is the Head of Clinical, Academic, and Research Engagement (CARE) unit in the Health Sciences Library (HSL) at the University of North Carolina Chapel Hill. In this role, she leads a team of liaison librarians who engage and partner with the University's schools of dentistry, medicine, nursing, pharmacy, and public health as well as multiple clinical departments within UNC Medical Center. She supports innovation, outreach, and curriculum engagement with the five Health Affairs schools and the hospital and has deep experience in the application of machine learning solutions to improve the efficiency of completing scoping reviews, systematic reviews, and other large-scale literature reviews. CARE staff also partner with health affairs researchers around visualizing their research impact through bibliometric and other analyses. Ms. Cawley also partners with the Clinical and Statewide Engagement (CaSE) unit at HSL that includes health literacy and community outreach librarians committed to engagement with communities across North Carolina. Further, Ms. Cawley is interested in how libraries can effectively support data science curricula and research on campus. In 2019, she lead a committee tasked by the University Librarian to develop a framework and recommendations around services to begin or grow, increasing data-related skills among librarians, and how to address infrastructure needs. Previously, Ms. Cawley was on the development team for a machine learning application for reducing manual burden of reviewing literature search results. She has lead or consulted on multiple projects that have successfully applied this technology and is the co-author of several publications on the topic. Finally, she has presented on applications of machine learning technology at the annual meetings for the Society of Toxicology, American Public Health Association, Society for Risk Analysis, and Medical Libraries Association.

Emily P. Jones, MLIS, AHIP is a Health Sciences Librarian at the University of North Carolina at Chapel Hill. In her current role, she serves as the team lead for systematic reviews and Liaison Librarian to the Adams School of Dentistry. She holds a Master's Degree in Library and Information Studies from the University of North Carolina at Greensboro. Previously, she served as a Research and Education Informationist and Liaison Librarian to the College of Pharmacy at the Medical University of South Carolina. In her free time, she loves to travel, spend time outdoors, and try new things.

***

Ismail Adeyemi is currently an Assistant Lecturer at the Department of Library and Information Science, Kwara State University, Malete, Kwara State, Nigeria. He holds a bachelor's and master's degrees in Library and Information Science from the Department of Library and Information Science, University of Ilorin, Ilorin, Nigeria. He was the General Secretary of National Association of Library and Information Science Students (University of Ilorin) in the 2012/2013 session. He interned at Kwara State Public Library and was part of the team that developed Roemichs International School Library in Ilorin, Nigeria. He has worked with Pinheiro LP (Law Librarian), Olusegun Obasanjo Presidential Library (Library Officer/Admin Assistant) and Lamp Bearer Islamic School (School Librarian).

Tracy Barber has extensive experience and expertise as an educator, researcher and evaluator. She has successfully initiated and led numerous research and evaluation projects including with Indigenous organisations, non-government organisations and the schools, vocational and higher education sectors. She specialises in applied research projects that can inform practice and policy development, with an emphasis on cross-disciplinary and cross-organisational collaboration. Tracy's current role at UTS Jumbunna Institute focuses on Indigenous education projects that critique and challenge mainstream practices, advocate for Indigenous voice and leadership in education, and contribute to advancing the education outcomes and experiences of Indigenous students at school and university.

Megan Benson is the Assistant Head of Instruction and Outreach at Binghamton University where she works to engage and inform the Binghamton community about information literacy and library services. She liaisons to First Year Experience and Writing courses, and the English Language Institute. She also teaches a two credit research skills class, where she incorporates yogic philosophies to her

About the Contributors

teaching. Prior to becoming a librarian, Megan earned a Master's Degree in history from the University of Nebraska - Lincoln and taught Western Civilizations I at Valencia College in Orlando, Florida before earning MLIS from Syracuse University.

Lauren Booker (Garigal) is a Research Fellow and PhD student in the Indigenous Archives and Data Stewardship Hub at Jumbunna Institute for Indigenous Education & Research, University of Technology Sydney (UTS). Lauren has worked across the museums and archives sector on projects supporting First Nations communities and organisations to access their cultural and intellectual property held in collecting institutions. This includes working in consultation with the public library network regarding language documentation identification and the use of manuscripts in language revitalisation. Lauren's work also supports Aboriginal and Torres Strait Islander peoples reclaiming archives, personal information and ICIP through focusing on digitisation, the organisation of community archives and advocating for increased Indigenous rights in records. She is a strong supporter of community archives, repatriation, Indigenous Cultural and Intellectual Property rights and Indigenous Data Sovereignty. Lauren is also a member of the Indigenous Archives Collective.

Sharon Bunch-Nunez is an unwavering advocate for student-centered services within academic libraries, in student staff supervision, and across the university. With an educational background in Human Development and Student Affairs Administration, Sharon's professional endeavors within the University are chiefly focused on supporting students to align their values with their academic and professional pursuits.

Jodi Coalter, MLIS, MPAE, is the Life Sciences Librarian at Michigan State University. She liaises with the Integrative Biology, Entomology, Evolution, Ecology, and Behavior, and Fisheries & Wildlife departments. Her research focuses on science communication and justice. Prior to her position at MSU, she worked as the Life Sciences & Outreach Librarian at the University of Maryland, where she also obtained her Masters in Applied Entomology.

DeLa Dos (they, them) serves as the senior director, Learning + Diversity, Equity, and Inclusion for the Association of Research Libraries. In this role, DeLa is responsible for leading the Association's Learning Network and Diversity, Equity & Inclusion (DEI) initiatives. The joint-coordination of these efforts provides cohesion across ARL learning-program curricula and reinforces the Association's commitment to diversity, equity, and inclusion in all its programs. DeLa has over 15 years of experience working in higher education and nonprofit settings. DeLa holds a PhD in counselor education and supervision with a cognate in educational leadership as well as an MS in community counseling from Mercer University. They earned their BA from Emory University with majors in dance & movement studies and religion with a minor in sociology.

Jennifer K. Embree is the Subject Librarian for Biology, Psychology, Comparative Literature, Latin American and Caribbean Area Studies, and Translation Research and the Sustainability Hub Coordinator at Binghamton University. She earned her MSLS from the University of North Carolina-Chapel Hill and BAs in English and Psychology from the University of Connecticut. In her free time, she loves to garden, hike, and binge-watch British comedy shows.

About the Contributors

Isabel Espinal is a Research Services Librarian for Afro American Studies, Latin American, Caribbean and Latinx Studies, Spanish & Portuguese, Native American & Indigenous Studies, and Women, Gender, Sexuality Studies at the University of Massachusetts Amherst. She is a past president of REFORMA, the National Association to Promote Library and Information Services to Latinos and the Spanish Speaking, and has written and given presentations on whiteness and diversity in librarianship, information literacy, the climate crisis and libraries, Dominican women writers in the United States, and Latinx literature, among other topics.

Elise Ferer is an Instruction and Outreach Librarian at Binghamton University Libraries and manages graduate students who staff Bartle Library's Research Help Desk.

Katherine Freedman is the librarian for History and Graduate Student Services at the W.E.B. Du Bois Library, University of Massachusetts Amherst. They hold an MLIS, University of Rhode Island, and PhD in History, University of Massachusetts Amherst.

John Mack Freeman (he/him) is the Head of Public Services Librarian at the Georgia Tech Library where he leads the 21-person, 24/7 team in all aspects of public and access services. Prior to this, he worked for nine years as a public librarian. He has a MLIS from Valdosta State University and a BA in English and a BA in Theatre from Shorter College. He is a member of the Library Freedom Project and an advocate for both open government and personal privacy. His research interests include library services to marginalized groups, privacy and surveillance in library spaces, professional development for new and mid-career professionals, and the influence of space on workplace culture.

Monica Galassi is a researcher at the Jumbunna Institute for Indigenous Education and Research (JIIER) and a PhD student at the School of International Studies, Faculty of Arts and Social Sciences (FAAS), University of Technology Sydney (UTS). With a background in cultural anthropology, Monica has worked in the Australian cultural sector on several projects and initiatives to support Aboriginal self-determination and sovereignty in libraries and archives. Her practice and research interests focus on the importance of people having the right to access and manage their cultural heritage materials, recognizing that this is a key driver for social justice. Her current work focuses on supporting Aboriginal data sovereignty on Country and across collecting institutions. In 2020, Monica was awarded a Research Excellence Scholarship to undertake doctoral studies in the field of Aboriginal and Torres Strait Islander archival records that have been displaced in Italy.

Amy Gay is the Assistant Head of Digital Initiatives at Binghamton University Libraries, where she oversees programming and services for the areas of digital scholarship and scholarly communications. Amy earned a MLIS from Syracuse University, focusing her research on cultural heritage preservation during wartime conflict, and a MAT in Education from SUNY Cortland, focusing her research on culturally relevant pedagogy. Her current research interests involve equity of open pedagogy, digital literacy education, and human-centered design.

Neyda V. Gilman is the Assistant Head of Sustainability & STEM Engagement and the librarian for the Decker College of Nursing & Health Sciences, the School of Pharmacy & Pharmaceutical Sciences, and the Environmental Studies Department at Binghamton University in Binghamton, New York. She is

312

About the Contributors

also a co-founder of the Binghamton University Libraries' Sustainability Hub and Seed Library. She has a BS in medical laboratory science from the University of Utah and worked as a medical technologist in a variety of laboratories before earning her MLS from the University at Buffalo.

Anne Graham is a Science & Engineering Librarian working within the Science & Engineering Branch Library at the University of Massachusetts Amherst.

Pam Hackbart-Dean, CA, is Associate University Librarian/head of the Special Collections and University Archives at the University of Illinois Chicago. Previously, she held positions at Southern Illinois University Carbondale, Georgia State University and the University of Georgia. She holds a BA in history from Hendrix College and an MA in history from the University of Connecticut. She is a Fellow of the Society of American Archivists and the Society of Georgia Archivists.

Anne Marie Hamilton-Brehm, PhD, CA, is Associate Dean of Southern Illinois University's Morris Library, directing the Special Collections Research Center and overseeing Records Management and the University Museum. After earning her doctorate in Linguistics from the University of Georgia in 2003, she earned her MLIS from the University of Alabama in 2008. Over the past two decades, she has developed digital and archival collections and exhibits for universities and public libraries in Georgia, Tennessee, Nevada, and Illinois. An active member of ALA, SAA, and MAC, she serves on the editorial board of MAC's Archival Issues.

Laura Haynes is a former academic librarian who now works in public libraries. She possesses a BFA in Painting from the University of South Carolina. She obtained her Master's of Science in Library and Information Science and a Master's of Science in the History of Art and Design from Pratt Institute.

Melvin "Pepper" Holder was born in St. Louis but grew up and spent most of his life in Carbondale, Illinois. He worked in the trucking and construction industries, owning his own companies. Hosting a long-running show on a local public interest radio station, he interviewed people ranging from Howard Zinn to David Horowitz, including Bobby Seale, Bernice Johnson Reagon, Robert Moses, and many more. He looks back fondly on the people in the community who inspired him, including his father, James Holder, teachers at Thomas and Attucks Schools, and pastors at Bethel AME and Rock Hill Baptist Churches, especially Rev. Lenus Turley, as well as progressive whites like Dr. Delyte Morris, president of Southern Illinois University, who reached out to the community with support. He prides himself on his public activism and pursuit of justice.

Adam Holmes has been at the W. E. B. Du Bois Center since 2018. He is responsible for the Center's programming, outreach, and events, and manages the fellowship program which supports original scholarship on Du Bois's life and work. Before arriving at the Center, Adam worked at the National Literacy Trust in the United Kingdom and received his Master's Degree in American Studies from King's College London.

Aaron Lisec, MA, is Research Specialist in Morris Library's Special Collections Research Center. He provides virtual and in-person reference services to scholars from around the world and promotes the Center's collections through exhibits and social media. He has master's degrees in English and His-

About the Contributors

tory from Southern Illinois University Carbondale and previously served as assistant editor on Volumes 21-31 of the Papers of Ulysses S. Grant. He currently serves as book reviews editor for the Journal of the Illinois State Historical Society.

Lauren Loewen was exposed to a wide variety of opinions and experience as a student. This inspired her to go to graduate school, where she expanded on her education and practical experience. As she enters a career in clinical research, she will use her experience working at the library to facilitate important conversations and learning opportunities

Michael Mercurio lives and writes in the Pioneer Valley of Western Massachusetts. His poems, critical essays, and interviews have appeared in Palette Poetry, Sierra (the magazine of the Sierra Club), Lily Poetry Review, Thrush Poetry Journal, The Common, Bear Review, Sugar House Review, The Inflectionist Review, Rust + Moth, Hare's Paw Literary Journal, and elsewhere. Michael curates What The Universe Is: A Reading Series, which happens monthly on Zoom. He is the Director of Community Engagement for the Faraday Publishing Company, a nonprofit organization dedicated to fostering discourse of enduring value rooted in the work and experiences of the global majority, and he also serves as a member of the steering committee for the Tell It Slant Poetry Festival, held each September at Emily Dickinson's house.

Alanna Aiko Moore is the Head of Community Engagement and Inclusion and Librarian for Ethnic Studies at the University of California, San Diego. She is the Executive Director of the Asian/Pacific American Librarians Association, a Past President, and a representative to the Joint Conference of Librarians of Color II Steering Committee. Within ALA, she serves on Council, is a Spectrum Scholar, and has past appointments on the Steering Committee for Organizational Effectiveness, the Task Force for Equity, Diversity, and Inclusion, and has chaired the Committee on Diversity. Her work with the Association of Research Libraries included a year long role as the Visiting Program Officer for Diversity, Equity, and Inclusion. Alanna presents and trains widely on microaggressions, intersectionality, LGBTQ identity, invisible labor, mentoring, activism in the profession, self-care, and issues affecting women of color librarians. Prior to librarianship, she worked at social justice-centered non-profits and community organizations.

Colleen Mullally is the Associate University Librarian for Collections, Technical Services, and Scholarly Communication at Pepperdine University.

Walter Ray, PhD, is Political Papers Archivist of the Special Collections Research Center at Southern Illinois University's Morris Library. He acquires, arranges, describes, promotes and provides reference for the records of politicians, civic and grass roots organizations, and labor unions from Southern Illinois and the surrounding region. A graduate of St. Vladimir's Seminary, he earned his PhD in Liturgical Studies from the University of Notre Dame. He taught five years at the University of St. Thomas before working at SIUC and is the author of Tasting Heaven on Earth: Worship in Sixth-Century Constantinople.

Saira Raza (she/her or they/them) is a business librarian at Emory University's Goizueta Business Library. She holds an MSLS from University of North Texas, an MPS in Africana Studies from Cornell University, and a BA in International Studies from Wells College. She has led Emory Libraries DEI

314

About the Contributors

Committee since its start as a working group in 2016, witnessing the committee's sustained growth and impact across over the years to nearly 30 highly engaged volunteer members. Prior to working at Emory, Saira worked as a business librarian at Lehman Brothers (now Barclays) and King & Spalding. Saira's interests are in decolonizing libraries and educating future leaders to harness the power of good research skills to make informed, ethical, and equitable decisions.

Kayla Reed obtained her master's from Kent State University in 2017, then worked at Missouri Southern State University Library for fourteen years in a variety of roles. From Cataloging clerk to Systems Librarian, Kayla has explored many departments of the library. In 2021, Kayla accepted the position of Discovery, Systems, and Digital Strategy Librarian at Grinnell College.

Maria Rios is a Humanities Research Services Librarian at the University of Massachusetts Amherst who is committed to dismantling all forms of oppression while centering and amplifying historically marginalized voices. She earned her MLIS from the University of South Carolina, and is recognized as an Association of Research Libraries Kaleidoscope Scholar 2016–2018 cohort, she is also a member of the fourth class of Library Freedom Institute, a Library Freedom Project initiative. She has co-authored two book chapters, "Vision, Voices, and Self-care in academic library residencies" (Residencies Revisited Reflections on Library Residency Programs from the Past and Present, 2022) and "Dewhitening Librarianship: A Policy Proposal for Libraries (Knowledge Justice: Disrupting Library and Information Studies through Critical Race Theory, 2021).

Rennae (Ren) Robinson is a doctoral candidate in the English department at Binghamton University (SUNY). Her major research and teaching interests include Black women's literature (as it relates to identity formation and resistance), African and Caribbean Diaspora/Transnationalism, and Creative Writing; minor research interests, which she has also taught on, concern the study and practice of embodied living, agency under duress, as well as the (re)conceptualizations of "home", "family", and "community."

Leslie N. Sharp (she/her) is Dean of Libraries at Georgia Tech. Previously, she served as the associate vice provost for Graduate Education and Faculty Development at Tech, where she managed operations, including communications, human resources, finance, and general administration. Sharp oversaw an expanding organizational mission and operations, including growing personnel and services that offered enhanced graduate student and postdoctoral support, and more intentional faculty development. Sharp has worked to improve the recruitment and retention of faculty and staff through systemic changes based on equitable practices and building a positive culture in all her roles. Sharp teaches historic preservation in the College of Design, where she formerly served as the assistant dean. Sharp holds a Ph.D. and a master's in history of technology from Tech. Her research explores the impact of technology on people and places within the framework of historic preservation, gender, and race.

Jessica Simpson is Assistant Professor & Program Coordinator for Special Education at Augusta University.

Kirsten Thorpe (Worimi, Port Stephens) is a Senior Researcher at Jumbunna Institute for Indigenous Education & Research, University of Technology Sydney (UTS). Kirsten leads the Indigenous Archives and Data Stewardship Hub, which advocates for Indigenous rights in archives and data and develops

About the Contributors

research and engagement in relation to refiguring libraries and archives to support the culturally appropriate ownership, management and ongoing preservation of Indigenous knowledges. Kirsten has broad interests in research and engagement with Indigenous protocols and decolonising practices in the library and archive fields, and the broader GLAM sector. Kirsten advocates for the 'right of reply' to records and capacity building and support for the development of Living Indigenous Archives on Country.

Rachel Berman Turner is the Senior Metadata Strategy Librarian at VCU Libraries. Prior to this position she worked at Binghamton University. In addition to an MSIS, Rachel also has an M.A. in East Asian Art, and worked in museums before going back to school for her library degree. Besides information organization, Rachel enjoys reading, drawing, and spending time with friends and family.

Grace Turney is a writer, artist, and former librarian living in St. Louis, MO. She earned her Master's degree in Library Science and Information Technology from the University of Missouri. Grace has worked in various types of libraries, including public, school, and university libraries. She currently works as an entertainment writer and looks forward to publishing her first novel.

Kayla Valdivieso is the Resource Acquisitions Specialist at Wellesley College.

Elizabeth A. VanDeusen is the Director of the Augusta University Literacy Center whose mission is to make literacy accessible for all children, adolescents, and adults in the Metro-Augusta area; she also holds the Cree-Walker Endowed Chair. She received her Ph.D. from Oakland University in Reading Education and spent 11 years at Central Michigan University as a Professor in Reading and Literacy and the Director of the Literacy Center. She has also served as the Marie Berrell Endowed Chair (in support of literacy development and community outreach in early childhood and elementary education) as well as Assessment Coordinator and Department Chairperson. Prior to that, she served as a Grant Administrator and Facilitator for the Michigan Department of Education. Dr. VanDeusen has 12 years of K-12 teaching experience.

Juan Walker served at Augusta University as the Secondary Program Coordinator for close to 9 years. From a research perspective, Walker has over 11 publications and a strong track record in regards to addressing aspects associated with addressing social justice in a social studies classroom setting. Based on primary source usage, Walker has started working the Richmond County, the Literacy Center, and the Lucy Craft Laney Museum. Walker's research requires collective community action and participation. When the opportunity presents itself, Walker introduced people in the community that have similar interest or referred faculty to individuals that would benefit from their research expertise.

Jeremy Whitt is Head of Licensing & E-resources Acquisitions at UCLA Library.

Index

A

Abolitionists 152-153, 164, 176

Aboriginal and Torres Strait Islander Peoples 125-127, 129, 132, 141, 143, 145

Aboriginal peoples 145

Academic Library 1-2, 5, 38, 41, 58, 79, 87, 104, 106, 108, 118-121, 179, 225-230, 235, 238-239, 241-242, 245, 248

Academics 67-68, 71-72, 202, 229

Accessibility 50, 56, 105, 114-115, 121-122, 172, 179, 193-194, 223, 227, 230, 235, 262-264, 274

Acquisitions 84, 105-108, 112-118, 122, 183, 232

American Library Association 23-24, 37, 110, 119, 121, 129, 142, 196, 219, 222-223, 231, 260, 262-263, 267, 272-273

Anti-Racism 1-2, 7, 9, 11, 13, 17, 78-93, 95-97, 106, 119, 129, 143, 230, 238-239, 245, 270-271

Archives 21, 25-26, 31, 124-128, 130-131, 134, 141-149, 160, 162-165, 167, 169, 171-174, 182-183, 185, 217

Assignments 62-63, 67, 69, 73, 79

Association of Research Libraries 20-21, 39, 106, 110, 119-121, 219, 229, 243, 274

Authenticity 28, 36, 40, 42, 53

B

Best Practices 21, 47, 92-93, 200, 209, 243, 247-248, 253

Bibliodiversity 114, 122

Binghamton University 78-81, 85, 87, 90, 92

BIPOC 1-5, 7-15, 17-18, 20-24, 31, 33-35, 66, 73, 87, 105, 108, 111, 245, 271

BIPOC Support 1, 9-11, 13-14

Black history 44, 116, 146, 148, 156, 160-161, 163, 175, 268-270

Black settlement 146, 152-153

C

Case Study 1-2, 20-21, 24, 35-36, 40-41, 78-80, 92-93, 106, 146, 149, 163, 188, 235, 242-243, 247-248, 251, 253-256, 258

Censorship 187, 191, 193, 195-196, 225, 240, 264, 267, 274

Challenging Assumptions 20, 245

Citation 62-77, 180

Citation Gaps 62-65, 69, 73, 75

Citation Justice 62-64, 66-69, 71-75

Class Assignments 62

Collaboration 41, 59-60, 72, 78, 113, 147-148, 152, 182, 200-201, 203, 207-208, 211, 215-217, 243-244, 247, 251-252, 254-255, 257-258

Collection 5, 44, 84, 86, 88, 96, 104-122, 127, 134-135, 138, 149, 156, 158-160, 164, 168-169, 173, 175-177, 183, 219-222, 224, 226, 228, 232-233, 236, 260-261, 263-268, 271-273, 275

Collection Assessment 104, 107, 176

Collection Building 104-109, 111, 113, 116, 118

Collection Development 86, 104-105, 107-110, 113-114, 116-117, 119-120, 122, 138, 175, 183, 232-233

Collections 3, 11, 13, 47, 73, 80-81, 84, 104-114, 116-122, 124-135, 137, 139-141, 143-144, 146, 148-149, 160-161, 163-167, 169, 172, 175-176, 182-185, 192, 196, 220-227, 230, 232, 242, 244, 250, 261, 267, 273

Colonial Project 126, 145

Colonialisation and Libraries 124

Community activism 146-147

Community-Driven 198-199, 202-204, 207-209, 212

Conscious Editing 166, 184

Country 44, 81, 136, 145, 159, 162, 169, 187, 191, 193, 222, 225-226

Cultural iceberg 270, 274

Culture 2, 6-7, 13, 17-18, 21-22, 26, 35-36, 38, 41-44, 46-59, 77, 82, 86, 93, 126-130, 134, 143-144,

147, 160-161, 190, 192, 199, 207-208, 213-215, 224, 232, 235-236, 238, 250, 260, 262, 267, 269-271, 274

Culture Change 40, 57

Curriculum Building 78

D

Decolonization 93, 126, 138-139, 144, 168

Decolonizing Libraries 124

Dewey Decimal System 237, 260, 269

Digital Environments 200, 218

Disabilities 87, 111, 114, 122, 215, 219, 223, 226-227, 229-230, 235, 238, 262

Disadvantaged Populations 198

Discrimination 3-4, 8, 46, 135, 157, 219, 223, 228-229, 231, 234, 260, 274

Display 116, 140, 170, 176, 184, 230, 266, 268-270, 274

Diversity 1-3, 7-18, 20, 23-26, 36, 38-41, 43-44, 46-47, 51, 54, 58-60, 64, 74-77, 81, 84-86, 88, 92, 104-108, 110, 112, 114-122, 129, 131, 135, 139, 142, 144-145, 147-148, 156, 163, 166-167, 169, 175-176, 182-184, 186-189, 191-199, 201, 203, 207, 213, 219-221, 228, 230-238, 240, 243-244, 248-250, 254, 257-258, 260-262, 264-266, 268-274

Du Bois 166-178, 182-185

E

Enslaved people 146, 150-151, 153-154

Equity 1-3, 7-9, 11, 13-18, 20, 23, 25-26, 36-39, 43-44, 47, 54, 74-75, 84, 104-105, 108-110, 114, 116, 118-119, 121-122, 129, 135, 137, 142-143, 147, 166-167, 169, 176, 181-183, 186-199, 201, 203, 205, 208, 214-216, 218, 223, 228, 230, 237, 239-241, 243-244, 248, 250, 258, 260-261, 264-266, 269, 271-274

Events 7, 13, 24, 31-32, 36, 92, 105, 159-161, 166, 169, 172, 174-179, 211, 219, 224, 233, 246, 254, 256, 270, 272

F

Funding 1-4, 9-12, 14-15, 30-32, 46, 86, 115-116, 118, 141, 147, 161, 169, 182, 184, 188, 191, 199, 210, 222, 224-225, 228, 235, 240, 263, 265

G

Georgia Institute Of Technology 40-41, 49, 58-59

I

Impact 16, 19, 24-26, 29-32, 35-37, 43-44, 47-48, 58-59, 66, 71, 74, 87, 105, 108, 112-113, 115-118, 121, 126, 131-132, 135, 140-141, 145, 147, 161-162, 169, 176, 178, 182, 193, 195, 201-202, 209-210, 215, 221, 223, 225, 229, 233, 242-243, 247-248, 251-253, 263, 271

Inclusion 1-3, 7-13, 15-18, 20, 23, 25-26, 30, 36, 38-39, 42-43, 47, 53-54, 56-59, 74, 84, 87, 104-106, 108, 110-112, 115, 118-122, 129, 131, 137-140, 142-144, 147, 149, 156, 164, 166-167, 169, 176, 181-184, 186-199, 201, 220-221, 225-226, 228-230, 232, 237, 239-240, 243-244, 248-250, 254, 258, 260-261, 264-269, 271-274

Inclusivity 21, 40, 47, 114, 203, 208, 219, 221, 224, 260, 263-265, 268-270, 274

Indentured servitude 146, 151-152

Indigenizing Libraries 124, 128

Indigenous peoples 124-132, 135, 140, 143, 145, 168, 175, 183

Indigenous Research 125, 130, 145

Indigenous Sovereignty 127, 139-140

Information Literacy 62, 74, 76, 93, 122, 125, 142, 180

Informed Practices 243, 247-248, 253

Innovation 38, 42-43, 58-59, 179, 183, 190, 207, 211, 233, 243

Instruction 62-63, 66-67, 69, 73-75, 81, 87, 108, 122, 142, 155, 161, 180, 184, 199-200, 203, 213, 215-217, 251

Integration 21, 195, 211, 216, 224

Isolation 1, 7, 27, 44, 183, 231

J

JEDI 1-2, 11, 13-15, 17, 20-21, 31, 36, 104-118, 122, 129, 166-167, 174-177, 181-184, 186-194, 199, 203, 208, 212-213, 243-245, 248, 252, 254, 256-257, 260-261, 264-273

Jumbunna 125, 129, 131, 134, 141

Justice 2, 7-8, 11, 13, 15-17, 19-21, 23-24, 36-38, 62-64, 66-69, 71-76, 79-82, 86, 91-93, 104-106, 108, 110, 118-122, 125-126, 129, 143-144, 147-149, 153, 166-167, 169, 173, 175-176, 182-184, 186-194, 196-199, 201, 203, 219-221, 230, 234-236, 239-240, 243-244, 248-251, 255, 257, 260-261, 264-266, 273

L

LGBT+ 220, 223-226, 228-234

Index

Liaison 66, 108, 111, 122, 181, 258
Libguides 78-80, 88-89, 92-94, 99, 118, 121, 164
Librarianship 1-2, 5-6, 11-13, 15-16, 19, 21, 37-38, 64, 79, 81, 93, 120, 129, 143-144, 164-165, 195, 229, 231, 235-236, 238-240, 245, 257, 262-263, 273
Libraries 1-21, 23, 25-26, 31, 34, 37-39, 41, 43, 47, 58, 73, 76, 78-81, 84-88, 90, 92-94, 104-110, 112, 114-122, 125-142, 144-145, 147, 149, 162, 164, 166-167, 172, 174-177, 179-185, 187-191, 193-197, 199, 204, 219-231, 233-245, 247, 253-258, 260-265, 267-274
Library 1-9, 11-18, 21-26, 32, 34-60, 63-64, 69-70, 75, 78-81, 83-84, 87-89, 92-94, 104-122, 124-131, 133-135, 137-146, 148, 156, 158, 160-161, 163-165, 167, 170-171, 173-181, 184-185, 187-197, 199, 212, 216, 219-245, 248-257, 260-275
Library Acquisitions 104
Library Culture 40, 54, 271
Library Studies 125
Literacy 12, 57, 62, 74, 76, 93, 122, 125, 142, 155, 180, 184, 199-218
Literacy Achievement 198-199, 202, 218
Literacy Center 199-204, 206-209, 212-214, 216
Literacy Theory 200, 218

M

Massachusetts 1-3, 5, 17, 166-169, 174, 176, 182, 185
Mentoring Programs 20-24, 35, 38-39
Microaggression 269, 274

N

Nigeria 187-189, 191, 193-194, 196

O

OneLibrary 184-185
One-Shot 63, 74
Outreach 10-12, 81, 87, 106, 112, 122, 147, 149, 160-161, 169, 177-179, 185, 199, 201, 204, 244, 250-251, 256

P

Partnership 13, 22, 25, 174-176, 193, 211-212, 244, 247-250, 252-253, 255-256
Policies 3, 13, 21, 25-27, 31, 35, 37, 41, 110, 112, 114, 119-120, 138, 147, 152, 184, 208, 214, 220, 224, 232-233, 245, 260-261, 264, 271-274
Positionality 1, 4-5, 17, 244

Preservation 127, 146, 148-149, 159-160, 165, 171
Program Design 20-21
Program Review 20
Programming 3, 16, 112, 148, 161, 164, 166, 174-179, 184, 201-202, 206-208, 212-213, 233, 235, 237, 260-263, 270, 273, 275
Programs 3, 6, 12, 20-24, 26-27, 34-36, 38-39, 109-110, 116, 120, 129-132, 134, 140, 147-148, 159-160, 163, 169, 176, 179, 181, 184, 192, 194, 196, 207-208, 212, 215-217, 223, 227, 240, 244-248, 251, 255, 260, 262-263, 265, 270
Public Library 6, 78, 119, 126, 142, 145, 175, 187-188, 194, 196, 212, 216, 221-225, 229, 236-237, 242, 261, 263-264, 268, 270, 273

R

Race 12, 14, 16-17, 19, 22-24, 33, 56, 63-64, 66, 68-69, 71, 75, 90, 144, 155-156, 164, 173, 182, 195, 219-221, 223, 226-228, 231-232, 236, 238-242, 257, 259, 262, 268
Racial Equity 1-2, 11, 14, 109-110, 119, 215
Racial Healing 1-2, 15
Racism 14, 18, 21, 23, 80-81, 86, 90, 92-93, 105, 109, 120-121, 125-126, 129, 134, 140, 145, 151, 156, 167, 207, 220, 223, 227, 229, 231-234, 237
RECESS 177-179, 185
Remedial Readers 199, 218
Representation 12, 26, 29, 47, 77, 106, 117, 124-125, 127-128, 133-135, 140, 148, 162, 184, 203, 208, 220-221, 227, 231, 239, 244, 249-250, 253-254, 266, 268
Research Guide 73, 78, 93
Resource Guide 78-83, 85-89, 91-92, 95-97

S

Selector 108, 122
Slavery 6, 148, 150-153, 159, 162-165, 226, 241-242, 268
Social Determinants of Health 214, 217-218
Spaces 1-10, 15-16, 19, 26, 33, 36, 105, 126, 130, 142, 145, 147-149, 162, 173, 175-176, 178-179, 181, 183-184, 186, 199, 219, 222-223, 230, 233, 244, 248, 250, 260-261, 269, 272-273
Special Collections 146, 148, 161, 163-167, 169, 172, 176, 182-185
Stakeholders 25, 31-32, 35-36, 84-85, 105, 108-109, 111-112, 118, 177, 184, 198, 203-204, 206, 208-209, 212-213, 217-218, 243, 247-249, 251-255
Student Engagement 181, 248, 251

319

Index

Student Success 87, 177-178, 180-181, 185, 246, 254-256

Student Workers 10, 88, 255

Students 3-4, 8, 11-12, 17, 21, 25, 31, 59, 62-64, 66-73, 75, 79, 81, 85-86, 88-89, 92-93, 111-114, 122, 156-157, 161, 169-171, 173-175, 177-185, 192, 198-200, 202, 204, 206-207, 211, 214, 217, 226-230, 233, 241, 244-245, 247-256, 263, 266, 269-270, 274

Subject Bibliographer 108, 122

Sustainable Impact 253

Systemic Change 20, 23, 27, 36, 221, 245

T

Technical Services 44, 48, 106-107, 117, 119-120, 122, 192

U

Underground Railroad 147, 150, 152-155, 163-164

W

Weeding 117, 264-265, 267, 273, 275

White Supremacy 1, 6-7, 13, 18, 21, 74, 134, 220, 228, 230, 234, 240-241, 257

Workshops 63, 66, 69-73, 75, 92, 137, 146, 169, 179-180, 201, 275

Recommended Reference Books

IGI Global's reference books are available in three unique pricing formats:
Print Only, E-Book Only, or Print + E-Book.

Order direct through IGI Global's Online Bookstore at
www.igi-global.com or through your preferred provider.

Autoethnographic Perspectives on Multilingual Life Stories

ISBN: 9781668437384
EISBN: 9781668437407
© 2022; 343 pp.
List Price: US$ 215

Innovative Technologies for Enhancing Knowledge Access in Academic Libraries

ISBN: 9781668433645
EISBN: 9781668433669
© 2022; 317 pp.
List Price: US$ 215

Social Justice Research Methods for Doctoral Research

ISBN: 9781799884798
EISBN: 9781799884804
© 2022; 397 pp.
List Price: US$ 215

Opportunities and Challenges for Computational Social Science Methods

ISBN: 9781799885535
EISBN: 9781799885559
© 2022; 277 pp.
List Price: US$ 215

Global Perspectives on Sustainable Library Practices

ISBN: 9781668459645
EISBN: 9781668459652
© 2023; 376 pp.
List Price: US$ 240

Research Anthology on Innovative Research Methodologies and Utilization Across Multiple Disciplines

ISBN: 9781668438817
EISBN: 9781668438824
© 2022; 663 pp.
List Price: US$ 415

Do you want to stay current on the latest research trends, product announcements, news, and special offers?
Join IGI Global's mailing list to receive customized recommendations, exclusive discounts, and more.
Sign up at: **www.igi-global.com/newsletters.**

Publisher of Timely, Peer-Reviewed Inclusive Research Since 1988

www.igi-global.com   Sign up at www.igi-global.com/newsletters   facebook.com/igiglobal   twitter.com/igiglobal   linkedin.com/igiglobal

Ensure Quality Research is Introduced to the Academic Community

Become an Evaluator for IGI Global Authored Book Projects

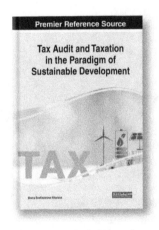   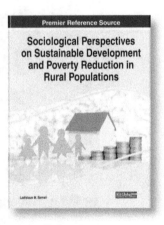

The overall success of an authored book project is dependent on quality and timely manuscript evaluations.

Applications and Inquiries may be sent to:
development@igi-global.com

Applicants must have a doctorate (or equivalent degree) as well as publishing, research, and reviewing experience. Authored Book Evaluators are appointed for one-year terms and are expected to complete at least three evaluations per term. Upon successful completion of this term, evaluators can be considered for an additional term.

If you have a colleague that may be interested in this opportunity, we encourage you to share this information with them.

Easily Identify, Acquire, and Utilize Published Peer-Reviewed Findings in Support of Your Current Research

IGI Global OnDemand

Purchase Individual IGI Global OnDemand Book Chapters and Journal Articles

For More Information:
www.igi-global.com/e-resources/ondemand/

Browse through 150,000+ Articles and Chapters!

Find specific research related to your current studies and projects that have been contributed by international researchers from prestigious institutions, including:

- Accurate and Advanced Search
- Affordably Acquire Research
- Instantly Access Your Content
- Benefit from the InfoSci Platform Features

"*It really provides* an excellent entry into the research literature of the field. *It presents a manageable number of* highly relevant sources *on topics of interest to a wide range of researchers. The sources are* scholarly, but also accessible *to 'practitioners'.*"

- Ms. Lisa Stimatz, MLS, University of North Carolina at Chapel Hill, USA

Interested in Additional Savings?

Subscribe to
IGI Global OnDemand *Plus*

Learn More

Acquire content from over 128,000+ research-focused book chapters and 33,000+ scholarly journal articles for as low as US$ 5 per article/chapter (original retail price for an article/chapter: US$ 37.50).

7,300+ E-BOOKS.
ADVANCED RESEARCH.
INCLUSIVE & AFFORDABLE.

IGI Global e-Book Collection

- **Flexible Purchasing Options** (Perpetual, Subscription, EBA, etc.)
- Multi-Year Agreements with **No Price Increases** Guaranteed
- **No Additional Charge** for Multi-User Licensing
- No Maintenance, Hosting, or Archiving Fees
- Continually Enhanced & Innovated **Accessibility Compliance Features** (WCAG)

Handbook of Research on Digital Transformation, Industry Use Cases, and the Impact of Disruptive Technologies
ISBN: 9781799877127
EISBN: 9781799877141

Handbook of Research on New Investigations in Artificial Life, AI, and Machine Learning
ISBN: 9781799886860
EISBN: 9781799886877

Handbook of Research on Future of Work and Education
ISBN: 9781799882756
EISBN: 9781799882770

Research Anthology on Physical and Intellectual Disabilities in an Inclusive Society (4 Vols.)
ISBN: 9781668435427
EISBN: 9781668435434

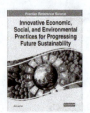

Innovative Economic, Social, and Environmental Practices for Progressing Future Sustainability
ISBN: 9781799895909
EISBN: 9781799895923

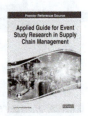

Applied Guide for Event Study Research in Supply Chain Management
ISBN: 9781799889694
EISBN: 9781799889717

Mental Health and Wellness in Healthcare Workers
ISBN: 9781799888130
EISBN: 9781799888147

Clean Technologies and Sustainable Development in Civil Engineering
ISBN: 9781799898108
EISBN: 9781799898122

Request More Information, or Recommend the IGI Global e-Book Collection to Your Institution's Librarian

For More Information or to Request a Free Trial, Contact IGI Global's e-Collections Team: eresources@igi-global.com | 1-866-342-6657 ext. 100 | 717-533-8845 ext. 100

Are You Ready to Publish Your Research?

IGI Global offers book authorship and editorship opportunities across 11 subject areas, including business, computer science, education, science and engineering, social sciences, and more!

Benefits of Publishing with IGI Global:

- Free one-on-one editorial and promotional support.
- Expedited publishing timelines that can take your book from start to finish in less than one (1) year.
- Choose from a variety of formats, including Edited and Authored References, Handbooks of Research, Encyclopedias, and Research Insights.
- Utilize IGI Global's eEditorial Discovery® submission system in support of conducting the submission and double-blind peer review process.
- IGI Global maintains a strict adherence to ethical practices due in part to our full membership with the Committee on Publication Ethics (COPE).
- Indexing potential in prestigious indices such as Scopus®, Web of Science™, PsycINFO®, and ERIC – Education Resources Information Center.
- Ability to connect your ORCID iD to your IGI Global publications.
- Earn honorariums and royalties on your full book publications as well as complimentary content and exclusive discounts.

Join Your Colleagues from Prestigious Institutions, Including:

Learn More at: www.igi-global.com/publish
or Contact IGI Global's Aquisitions Team at: acquisition@igi-global.com

Individual Article & Chapter Downloads
US$ 29.50/each

 Easily Identify, Acquire, and Utilize Published Peer-Reviewed Findings in Support of Your Current Research

- Browse Over **170,000+ Articles & Chapters**
- **Accurate & Advanced** Search
- Affordably Acquire **International Research**
- **Instantly Access** Your Content
- Benefit from the **InfoSci® Platform Features**

" *It really provides* an excellent entry into the research literature of the field. *It presents a manageable number of* highly relevant sources *on topics of interest to a wide range of researchers. The sources are* scholarly, but also accessible *to 'practitioners'.* "

- Ms. Lisa Stimatz, MLS, University of North Carolina at Chapel Hill, USA

Interested in Additional Savings?

Subscribe to
IGI Global OnDemand *Plus*

Learn More

Acquire content from over 137,000+ research-focused book chapters and 33,000+ scholarly journal articles for as low as US$ 5 per article/chapter (original retail price for an article/chapter: US$ 29.50).

Printed in the USA
CPSIA information can be obtained
at www.ICGtesting.com
LVHW080002051224
798213LV00006B/727